Mr. Richar[...]

With Comp[...]

[illegible handwriting]

28 January 2019

# BOUNDARIES AND SECESSION IN AFRICA AND INTERNATIONAL LAW

This book challenges a central assumption of the international law of territory. The author argues that, contrary to the finding in the *Frontier Dispute* case, *uti possidetis* is not a general principle of law enjoining states to preserve pre-existing boundaries on state succession.

It demonstrates that African state practice and *opinio juris* gave rise to customary rules that govern sovereign territory transfer in Africa. It explains that those rules changed international law as it relates to Africa in many respects, leading chiefly to creating norms of African *jus cogens* prohibiting secession and the redrawing of boundaries.

The book examines in-depth the singularity of secession in Africa exploring extensive state practice and case law. Finally, it advances a daring argument for a right to egalitarian self-determination, addressing people-to-people domination in multi-ethnic African states, to serve as an exception to the fast special customary rule against secession.

DIRDEIRY M. AHMED LLB honours (Khartoum), LLM (London), MSt (Oxford), PhD (Leicester), was the delegate of Sudan to the Sudan/South Sudan peace talks in Kenya, 1999–2005. He was also a member of the joint team that followed implementation of the peace agreement until the South Sudan self-determination referendum, January 2011, was conducted. Currently he practices law in Khartoum.

# BOUNDARIES AND SECESSION IN AFRICA AND INTERNATIONAL LAW

## Challenging *Uti Possidetis*

DIRDEIRY M. AHMED

CAMBRIDGE
UNIVERSITY PRESS

# CAMBRIDGE
## UNIVERSITY PRESS

University Printing House, Cambridge CB2 8BS, United Kingdom

Cambridge University Press is part of the University of Cambridge.

It furthers the University's mission by disseminating knowledge in the pursuit of
education, learning and research at the highest international levels of excellence.

www.cambridge.org
Information on this title: www.cambridge.org/9781107117983

© Dirdeiry M. Ahmed 2015

First published 2015

*A catalogue record for this publication is available from the British Library*

*Library of Congress Cataloguing in Publication Data*
Ahmed, Dirdeiry M., 1957– author.
Boundaries and secession in Africa and international law : challenging
*uti possidetis* / Dirdeiry M. Ahmed.
pages   cm
Based on author's thesis (Doctoral – University of Leicesester, 2013) under title:
The African territorial regime : establishing its customary existence and arguing
for its augmentation by a right to egalitarian secession
Includes bibliographical references and index.
ISBN 978-1-107-11798-3 (hardback)
1. Africa–Boundaries.   2. Customary law, International–Africa.   3. Uti possidetis
(International law)   4. Boundaries.   5. State succession.   I. Title.
KZ3684.5.A37A36   2015
341.4′2–dc23        2015022571

ISBN 978-1-107-11798-3 Hardback

To Mohamed *Telfa* and Ghalia *Samah-ratab*

# CONTENTS

# FIGURES

# MAPS

ACKNOWLEDGEMENTS

This study has been long in gestation. Throughout the protracted years of the South Sudan peace talks in Kenya and the subsequent uneasy transitional period in Sudan, the profound question of the durability of the inherited African boundaries was persistent. While secession was stridently debated and seriously considered, being perceived as the pragmatic solution for ending the longest civil war of Africa, the principled abhorrence of the 's' word by the entire continent became palpable and encountered first hand.

My thanks go to the teams dedicated by the Government of Sudan and the Sudan Peoples' Liberation Movement (SPLM) to the talks throughout the period 1999–2005. Their passionate negotiation of the puzzling issues of unity and secession greatly inspired this study. I am also indebted to the group that shouldered the responsibility for the implementation of the Comprehensive Peace Agreement (CPA) 2005–11, across their divide. They helped by their successes, and exhorted by their failures, to anchor this inquiry in the toughest issues of conflict and state in Africa. That decade of intense working experience within those two exclusive groups had indeed privileged this study.

When the long-anticipated referendum of South Sudan was all set, and in a bid to help demystify the unmistakeable African enigma, I ventured on a much-dreaded foray into the grandeur of academia. I am very much obliged to Andrew Shacknove, Director of the Masters' Programme of International Human Rights Law at the University of Oxford, for welcoming me warmly to that unparalleled course. This study was advantaged immensely, even if indirectly, by the informed tutoring of my distinguished lecturers, Margaret Bedggood, Dapo Akande, Christof Heyns, Patricia Sellers, Patrick Thornberry and Nazila Ghanea, as well as by stimulating long discussions with my learned classmates.

At the University of Leicester, I benefited from the notable supervision of Malcolm Shaw, who guided my initial steps in the law of territory, read my early drafts, and made encouraging remarks. The painstaking scrutiny of Eki Omorogbe, all-supportive and insisting on perfection, is much appreciated. Katja Zeigler went meticulously time and again through the final drafts and made significant, and at times challenging, suggestions at that critical stage of the research. My thanks also go to Joshua Castellino, Middlesex University, and Loveday Hudson, Leicester University, for reading thoroughly Part I and Part II, respectively, and making reassuring observations.

The benefit drawn from the tremendous research facilities provided by the University of Leicester, particularly the David Wilson Library, is immeasurable. Additionally, during my background study of the law and making of African boundaries I drew on the resources of the Bodleian Law Library, Oxford; the Durham University Sudan Archive, Durham; the Radcliffe Camera Library, Oxford; and the British National Archives, London. I am grateful to all those who made my job easier and my visits rewarding. In particular, my thanks go to Sandra Meredith of the Bodleian Law Library. I am also thankful to Jane Sowler, Postgraduate Research Administrator, University of Leicester and to Anne Yule of John Foster Hall, Oadby.

At the publishing stage, I express gratitude to Finola O'Sullivan of Cambridge University Press. I also recognise Gillian Dadd, Deborah Renshaw, and Louise Morgan. I am grateful to the family of the late Ali Mazrui, the BBC and Little, Brown & Co for the permission to use as an epigraph a quote from Ali Mazrui, *The Africans: A Triple Heritage*.

Back at home, and throughout the long years of the CPA and the subsequent period of study in England, I left responsibility of my children, along with the demanding tasks of an expanded family, to be shouldered fully and ably by my dear wife Saneya Mustafa Ibrahim. This project would not have been pursued to fruition if it were not for her sacrifice and exemplary support. The professionalism and dedication of my colleagues at Dirdeiry & Associates, Khartoum, relieved me for months on end from the individual tasks of a small law firm.

This all being said, the responsibility for all ideas and arguments in this book, and any failings that might appear, rests on me alone.

31 March 2015.

# CASES

## International Courts and Tribunals

Award in regard to the Validity of the Treaty of Limits between Costa Rica and
Nicaragua of 15 July (1858) XXVIII RIAA 89, 27–28
The Guiana Boundary Case (Brazil/Great Britain) (1904) XI RIAA 11, 166
The Border Dispute between Honduras and Nicaragua (1906) XI RIAA 101, 30, 167
Bolivia-Peru: Arbitral Award in Boundary Dispute Rendered by the President of
the Argentine Republic AJIL (1909) 1029, 25
The Grisbadarna Case (Norway v Sweden) (1909) Hague Court Reports 121, 212
Aaland Islands Case LNOJ (1920) Sp Supp 3, 38–39, 258
Case of the Colombian-Venezuelan Frontier (Colombia v Venezuela) (1922) IV
RIAA 223, 21, 56, 259
Case of the SS 'Lotus' [1927] PCIJ Rep Series A No 10, 108, 119, 120
Island of Palmas (Netherlands/USA) (1928) II RIAA 829, 136, 265
Free City of Danzig and International Labour Organization, Advisory Opinion
PCIJ Rep Series B No 18, 68, 259
Case concerning the Border between Guatemala and Honduras (Guatemala/
Honduras) (1933) II RIAA 1307, 25, 26, 32, 33, 165, 166, 257
Legal Status of Eastern Greenland (Denmark/Norway) [1933] PCIJ Rep Series
A/B No 53, 95, 96, 158
International Status of South-West Africa (Advisory Opinion) ICJ Rep [1950] 128,
156, 157
Colombian-Peruvian Asylum Case (Judgment) [1950] ICJ Rep 266, 65, 117, 119
The Fisheries Case (United Kingdom v Norway) Judgment, [1951] ICJ Rep 116, 118
Reservations to the Convention of Genocide (Advisory Opinion) [1951]
ICJ Rep 15, 127
The Minquiers and Ecrehos Case (United Kingdom/France) (Pleadings VII)
[1953] ICJ Rep 47, 136, 137, 140, 141
Case concerning Sovereignty over Certain Frontier Land (Belgium/Netherlands)
(Judgment) [1959] ICJ Rep 209, 33, 34, 257
Case concerning Right of Passage over Indian Territory (Merits) [1960] ICJ Rep 4,
60, 65, 136
Temple of Preah Vihear Case (Merits) [1962] ICJ Rep 6, 36, 37, 88, 258
Case concerning the Northern Cameroons (Cameroon/United Kingdom)
(Preliminary Objections) [1963] ICJ Rep 15, 42, 146, 175, 176, 178
The Indo-Pakistan Western Boundary (Rann of Kutch) between India and
Pakistan (1968) XVII RIAA 1, 34, 36–37, 60, 61, 148, 257, 258

# Decisions of the African Commission of Human and Peoples' Rights

# National and Regional Cases

# Reports

## UN Resolutions

## OAU/AU Resolutions and Decisions

# ABBREVIATIONS

| | |
|---|---|
| AHRLJ | African Human Rights Law Journal |
| ACHPR | African Commission on Human and Peoples' Rights |
| AJIL | American Journal of International Law |
| AJICL | African Journal of International Comparative law |
| AU | African Union |
| AUCISS | AU Commission of Inquiry on South Sudan |
| AUPSC | African Union Peace and Security Council |
| Boston | College ICLR Boston College International and Comparative Law Review |
| CAA | Contemporary Arab Affairs |
| Canadian | JAS Canadian Journal of African Studies |
| Columbia HRLR | Columbia Human Rights Law Review |
| Cornell ILJ | Cornell International Law Journal |
| CPA | Comprehensive Peace Agreement |
| EJIL | European Journal of International Law |
| EPLF | Eritrean People's Liberation Front |
| EPRDF | Ethiopian People's Revolutionary Democratic Front |
| HRQ | Human Rights Quarterly |
| ICG | International Crisis Group |
| ICJ | International Court of Justice |
| ICJ Rep | International Court of Justice Reports |
| ICLQ | International Comparative Law Quarterly |
| IGAD | Inter-Governmental Authority for Development |
| ILC | International Law Commission |
| ILR | International Law Reports |
| Indiana LJ | Indiana Law Journal |
| Indian JIL | Indian Journal of International Law |
| JAH | Journal of African History |
| JMAS | Journal of Modern African Studies |
| LNOJ | League of Nations Official Journal |
| Leiden JIL | Leiden Journal of International Law |
| Mich JIL | Michigan Journal of International Law |
| MNLA | National Movement for the Liberation of Azawad |

| | |
|---|---|
| NCP | National Congress Party |
| NDA | National Democratic Alliance |
| NFD | Northern Frontier District |
| OAU | Organization of African Unity |
| Oklahoma CULR | Oklahoma City University Law Review |
| PASIL | Proceedings of the American Society of International Law |
| Review APE | Review of African Political Economy |
| RIAA | Reports of International Arbitration Awards |
| SADR | Sahrawi Arab Democratic Republic |
| SPLM | Sudan Peoples' Liberation Movement |
| SRF | Sudan Revolutionary Front |
| SSLM | South Sudan Liberation Movement |
| UN | United Nations |
| UN YBK | Yearbook of the United Nations |
| Washington LR | Washington Law Review |
| Wisconsin ILJ | Wisconsin International Law Journal |
| Yale JIL | Yale Journal of International Law |
| Yale LJ | Yale Law Journal, the |
| YBK Int'l LC | Yearbook of the International Law Commission |

**Map 1** African boundaries of independence

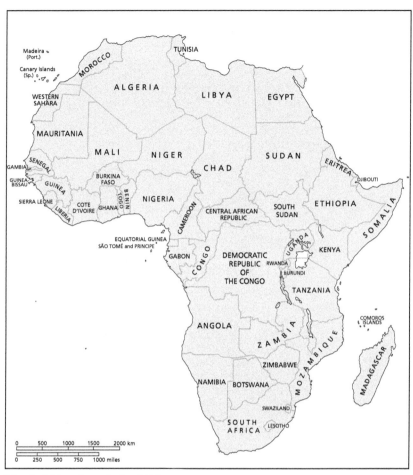

**Map 2** African boundaries, 2014

**Map 3** Spanish America, 1821

**Map 4** Spanish America, 1871

**Map 5** European boundaries, 1945

**Map 6** European boundaries, 1995

# Introduction

In May 2013, African states celebrated the fiftieth anniversary of the formation of the Organization of African Unity/African Union (OAU/ AU). On 21 July 2014, fifty years had passed since the renowned Cairo Resolution on African borders was adopted. Colonialism is long gone and Africa has been independent for half a century. The African state is a fully fledged subject of international law. Yet, it is not an ordinary subject. An inventory of the successes and failures of the African state in five decades immediately reveals the following.

First, the boundary alignments inherited by African states on independence are maintained all over the continent. Except for the alterations that resulted from the separation of Eritrea and South Sudan the political map of Africa has remained the same for the last fifty years. This turn of events is unexpected and rather surprising. When it is remembered that African boundaries are notoriously arbitrary, derided for paying little attention to the cohesiveness of peoples randomly fenced or divided by them, their survival becomes baffling. In contrast, boundaries of other continents that are not as disreputable underwent substantial change. Within an equivalent period, 90 per cent of the old boundary lines left in Spanish America had been redrawn. In Europe and Asia, twenty-odd states have been created in the last quarter of a century following the end of the Cold War.

Second, the only two African states created since the Cairo Resolution, Eritrea and South Sudan, had to wrest their statehood through fighting long civil wars. The processes that led to their recognition were disorderly, marred by bitter boundary disputes leading to acrimonious arbitrations, and impaired by military confrontation. Poignantly, the entire course of events was engulfed by hatred and ethnic tension. The possibility of new states peacefully springing out of old states is unthinkable in Africa. The likes of the remarkable Quebec referendum or the democratic 'yes' and 'no' campaigns of Scotland might recur anywhere on the globe but not in Africa.

Third, it was clear right from the beginning that secession was the only and inexorable outcome of the protracted civil wars of Eritrea and South Sudan. Nonetheless, secession of those two countries was opposed by the entire African continent. An early concession that would have minimized the senseless squandering of life and resources and guaranteed a soft landing for the splinter states eluded Africa until the bitter end. Other similar and dissimilar boundary-related conflicts are still raging unabated.

Fourth, in addition to the wars of secession, Africa witnessed the pitting of entire communities against one another in situations that did not necessarily involve claims to statehood. While in secession struggles the dominated group wages a war against the state, in ethnic strife it is mostly the dominating ethnicity that targets the subjugated in a bid to purge the state from its ilk. The pandemic of uneasy ethnic relations, accompanied by monopolizing of the government apparatus by one group, led to despotism, widespread human rights violations, and genocide.

Fifth, despite those tragic episodes the OAU/AU considers the territorial definition of each and every African state sacrosanct, unquestionable, and belonging first and foremost to Africa as a whole. Throughout those fifty years, the preservation of the African boundaries formed the primary responsibility of the African organization. The United Nations (UN) endorses in full this state of affairs.

Those realities question profoundly the way Africa relates to international law. While the entry of Spanish America into the international community is hailed as having radically modified the character of international law, the advent of Africa is considered to have simply widened its geographical outreach. This author cannot disagree more. Africa joined the community of nations very late and did not have an opportunity, equal to that of Spanish America 150 years before, to contribute to the moulding of international law. Inversely, the African state was itself the creation of international law. Yet, it was not too late for Africa to have an impact. To be sure, Africa managed to set the rules that govern its own territorial affairs. As soon as the rights available under the decolonization law were extinguished by setting Africa free, Africa discovered that international law has nothing more in stock. A law system predicated on the assumption that the state predates the law has no rules for a state fully dependent for its creation and bare existence on the international law regime itself. The African community of nations had to develop its own rules if it had to take account of the nonconforming circumstances of the creation of the African state, its endurance and future viability. The exclusive and robust edifice of African customary rules that was soon generated made it possible for the OAU/AU to oversee the prescribing of inherited boundaries and the proscription of secession with the cooperation of the UN.

Part I of this book explains why and how the African territorial regime was created and articulates what makes this regime distinct. It clarifies that by accepting to respect the pre-existing frontiers without being obligated by any law principle to do so African states created new customary rules. Additionally, the Cairo Resolution generated state practice and discrete *opinio juris* enjoining African states to respect indefinitely the territorial status quo that was obtained on the achieving of independence. As a result, a special customary territorial regime that changes in many respects the way international law applies to Africa was created. Notably, the prohibition of redrawing African boundaries and the African rule against secession are of African *jus cogens*.

Part II shows that the African rule against secession mirrors the infatuated concern over hallowing the boundaries of independence concomitant with the rule of respecting the status quo. Because of this rule it is not officially permitted to advance secession claims in Africa. An ethnic group that seeks to break away is viewed to offend the central African customary rule, provoking the entire continent to side with the parent state. In order to spare this inordinate cost, African secessionists put up a pretence of abiding by the African rule by contriving arguments to excuse or disguise their real cause. It is clarified that while secession as a simple claim to territory should continue to be proscribed in accordance with the African regime, a right to egalitarian secession should be available when one ethnicity is subjected to the domination of another.

Even as it is hale and hearty and enthusiastically treasured by African states, the African territorial regime was denied recognition at judicial level because of the fateful ruling in the *Frontier Dispute (Burkina Faso/ Mali)*. The International Court of Justice (ICJ) missed the opportunity to establish the African territorial regime and specifically denied any possibility of 'the gradual emergence of [an African] principle of customary international law'.[1] Even worse, the ICJ Chamber posited that Africa had on independence applied *uti possidetis*. The norm-creating OAU Cairo Resolution 1964 was reduced by the Court to a declaratory instrument that merely 'defined and stressed the principle of *uti possidetis*'.[2] The ruling in the *Frontier Dispute* was accepted uncritically leading to a pervasive failure to understand how the African territorial regime functions.

---

[1] *Frontier Dispute (Burkina Faso/Mali)* (Judgment) [1986] ICJ Rep 554, 565.
[2] *Ibid.* 566.

African states referring their boundary disputes to the ICJ and international tribunals normally designate 'the principle of intangibility of inherited frontiers' as the applicable law rule. Yet, after the ruling in the *Frontier Dispute,* the Court and arbitration tribunals have invariably applied instead the principle of *uti possidetis.*

Part I of this book comprises five chapters. Chapter 1 argues that the ruling of the ICJ Chamber in the *Frontier Dispute* is erroneous. *Uti possidetis* is not a general principle of law applicable to Africa on independence. Nor did it, in its Spanish-American cradle, generate the concept of intangibility of frontiers. Chapter 2 examines the consistent practice of respecting the pre-existing boundaries by all African states that attained independence. It contends that this practice evinces the *opinio juris* required to give rise to the rule of intangibility of inherited frontiers as an African customary rule. Chapter 3 studies the implicit commitment made in the OAU Charter to respect the territorial status quo. It establishes that the principle of respecting the territorial integrity of states and the concept of recognizing mediation as a peaceful means of dispute settlement were put to special use by the OAU to give priority to the status quo over conflicting territorial claims. Chapter 4 demonstrates how the customary rule of respecting the territorial status quo was created. It studies the Cairo Resolution 1964, attests its immediate legal force and establishes its norm-creating character. It surveys the *usus* and *opinio juris* generated by the Cairo Resolution to give rise to the central African rule of respecting the territorial status quo. Chapter 5 shows the changes made by the African customary rules in international law. It clarifies that the prohibition of redrawing boundaries and the rule against secession, introduced by the African territorial regime, are peremptory African norms. Additionally, it examines how the African territorial regime reformulates cardinal concepts of the international law of territory with respect to Africa.

Part II, composed of three Chapters, is focused on studying the prohibition of secession in Africa. It makes a proposal for addressing the problem of secession in a post-colonial context in order to enable the African regime to survive and thrive. Chapter 6 inspects the arguments for reviving colonial self-determination, constitutional self-determination, remedial secession, and national self-determination currently advanced to justify secession in Africa. It is explained that in addition to being flawed, none of those arguments could serve as a viable exception to the African rule against secession. Chapter 7 argues normatively that domination forms a viable instance of external self-determination under Paragraph 2 of the Declaration on Friendly Relations among States. Chapter 8 explains that Articles 19 and 20(2) of the African Charter on Human and Peoples' Rights provide for *sui generis* egalitarian rights to guarantee equality between different ethnic groups in African multi-ethnic states. It argues that Articles 19 and 20(2) of the African Charter, read together with Paragraph 2 of the Declaration on Friendly Relations, could potentially give rise to a right to secession in the event of denying one ethnicity its egalitarian rights. The egalitarian rights and the right to secession accruing on their denial constitute the right to egalitarian self-determination. This external form of the right to self-determination augments the African territorial regime and serves as an exemption to the African rule against secession.

To explain the concepts of the customary African territorial regime introduced in this study, particular terminology is used.

The simple term '*uti possidetis*' is preferred to the unnecessarily complex '*uti possidetis juris*'. The qualifier '*juris*' is of no more than vestigial content relevant to the eighteenth- and nineteenth-century concepts of occupation and possession. The accuracy of its usage was contested even in the Spanish-American context.[3] Obviously, this shibboleth is of no value in modern international law where it no longer tells '*uti possidetis*' apart from any other current law doctrine.

The author agrees with Schachter that the two terms 'rule' and 'principle' are not synonymous.[4] Legal rules dictate specific results whereas legal principles, even as they have the dimension of weight when they are found relevant, are open-textured and of potential vagueness. Because *uti possidetis* is characterized by a laissez-faire approach, while the 'intangibility of inherited frontiers' is a strict edict that offers itself to rigorous implementation, in this book '*uti possidetis*' is referred to as a principle, while the 'intangibility of inherited frontiers' is referred to, as far as

---

[3] Moore states: 'Apart from the usual and reasonable interpretation above defined, the phrase "*uti possidetis juris*" is meaningless and self-contradictory. To say that the word "juris" excludes altogether the consideration of possession de facto, is to make the words self-destructive. The judgment of "*uti possidetis*" cannot be predicated of a situation from which the thought of continued physical possession is wholly excluded. Such a use of terms would be purely fanciful.' John Bassett Moore, *Costa Rica-Panama Arbitration 1911: Memorandum on Uti Possidetis* (The Commonwealth Company 1913) 35; G. Pope Atkins, *Encyclopaedia of the Inter-American System* (Greenwood 1997) 41.

[4] Oscar Schachter, *International Law in Theory and Practice* (Kluwer 1991) 20–1; R. Dworkin, *Taking Rights Seriously* (Duckworth 1977) 22–45; also see R. Dworkin, *The Philosophy of Law* (Oxford University Press 1977) 47.

possible, as a rule.[5] For the same reasons, 'the territorial status quo rule' and 'the rule against secession' are styled as such.

Even as the terms 'intangibility of inherited frontiers' and 'territorial status quo' are commonplace, they are used in this book in reference to specific customary rules with the particular normative content recognized for them in this study. The term 'African territorial regime' denotes the legal construction of customary international law obtained as the result of the interplay between those two customary rules.

The term 'vertical territory transfer' is used to indicate the sovereign territory transfer that took place on the day of decolonization. A vertical claim is a claim aiming to establish the boundary line left by an outgoing colonial power on the critical date. Disputes over where the inherited boundary line runs are typical vertical disputes. Vertical territory transfers, claims or disputes are governed by the rule of intangibility of inherited frontiers.

Conversely, the term 'horizontal territory transfer' refers to a territorial claim incongruent with the inherited boundary, denying the existence of such boundary, or challenging it substantially. A claim to revive a pre-colonial boundary is a typical horizontal claim. Secession claims, by virtue of their vying to create a boundary of no colonial origin or to confer international status on a frontier that was not of such status on decolonization, are horizontal claims. Horizontal claims offend the territorial status quo rule and are as such proscribed in Africa.[6]

The rights that accrue to sub-national groups in multi-ethnic states under Article 19 of the African Charter are referred to as 'egalitarian rights'. The term 'egalitarian secession' denotes a right of external self-determination argued to be normatively feasible under Article 20(2)

---

[5] However, this does not apply to some instances, particularly in Chapter 1, in which reference was made to 'the *principle* of intangibility of inherited frontiers', which is the term used in the Special Agreement in the *Frontier Dispute*. Sometimes it is also referred to as the *concept* of intangibility of inherited frontiers in general terms rather than to the African customary rule.

[6] This distinction between vertical and horizontal transfers does not replicate the division made in the 1920s between 'delimitation disputes' and 'disputes as to attribution of territory', which has since largely fallen into disfavour. The conventional categorization is based on whether the land in dispute forms a geographically autonomous portion or not. When this point is determined no particular conclusion applies, because in either case a line would fall to eventually be drawn, see *Frontier Dispute* 563–4, Memorial of Burkina Faso 65–6. Conversely, the applied significance of the categorization made in this study is that whereas a vertical claim is allowed, a claim betraying horizontal inklings should be thrown out by a court of law applying the customary rule of respecting the territorial status quo.

of the African Charter read together with Paragraph 2 of the Declaration on Friendly Relations among States.

Due care has been taken to make sure that this study reflects the law and African state practice as at 31 March 2015.

# PART I

## The African territorial regime

[W]hile the pre-colonial African states have indulged in ... land worship in relation to both agriculture and the burial of ancestors, the post-colonial state indulged in the worship of territory in relation to power and sovereignty. The dichotomy between the land worship of old and territorial worship in post-colonial states has not yet been resolved. All we know is that the last legacy of the colonial order to be decolonised is likely to be the territorial boundary between one African country and another ... The ghosts of ancestors and land worship have been overshadowed by the imperative of sovereignty and territorial possessiveness, inherited from the Treaties of Westphalia.

Ali Mazrui*

* Ali Mazrui, *The Africans: A Triple Heritage* (Little, Brown & Co 1986) 272. The author expresses his profound gratitude and appreciation to the family of the late Professor Ali Mazrui, notably his widow, Pauline Uti Mazrui, and the Co-Executors of the Mazrui Estate, Professor Alamin Muhammad Mazrui and Professor Kim Abubakar Ali Forde-Mazrui, for their approval to use the above quote as an epigraph. My thanks also go to the BBC and Little, Brown & Co for granting their respective copyright permissions.

# The *Frontier Dispute* case and applying *uti possidetis* to Africa

## 1.1.  The significance of the *Frontier Dispute* case

### 1.1.1.   *The finding in the* Frontier Dispute

The *Frontier Dispute (Burkina Faso/Mali)* is a determination of a disputed band of territory between Burkina Faso, formerly Upper Volta, and Mali.[1] The question posed in Article I of the Special Agreement was 'What is the line of the frontier between the Republic of the Upper Volta and the Republic of Mali in the disputed area?'.[2] This question needed to be determined in accordance with 'the principle of the intangibility of frontiers inherited from colonization'.[3] The ICJ Chamber constituted under the Special Agreement found that:

> Since the two Parties have, as noted above, expressly requested the Chamber to resolve their dispute on the basis, in particular, of the 'principle of the intangibility of frontiers inherited from colonization', the Chamber cannot disregard the principle of *uti possidetis juris*, the application of which gives rise to this respect for intangibility of frontiers.[4]

Pursuant to this finding, the concept of intangibility of inherited frontiers is a consequence of the principle of *uti possidetis*. The two principles, according to the ICJ Chamber, are coextensive to the extent that if a court of law is requested to apply the principle of intangibility of frontiers *uti possidetis* is automatically elicited and falls to be applied.

The Chamber added that *uti possidetis* is a firmly established general principle of international law logically connected to decolonization with

---

[1] *Frontier Dispute (Burkina Faso/Mali)* (Judgment) [1986] ICJ Rep 554, 562.
[2] *Ibid.* 557.   [3] *Ibid.*    [4] *Ibid.* 565.

the obvious purpose of preventing the challenging of frontiers on independence.[5] In an elaborate *obiter dictum* the ICJ Chamber found:

> In this connection it should be noted that the principle of *uti possidetis* seems to have been first invoked and applied in Spanish America, inasmuch as this was the continent which first witnessed the phenomenon of decolonization involving the formation of a number of sovereign States on territory formerly belonging to a single metropolitan State. Nevertheless the principle is not a special rule which pertains solely to one specific system of international law. It is a general principle, which is logically connected with the phenomenon of the obtaining of independence, wherever it occurs. Its obvious purpose is to prevent the independence and stability of new States being endangered by fratricidal struggles provoked by the challenging of frontiers following the withdrawal of the administering power. It was for this reason that, as soon as the phenomenon of decolonization characteristic of the situation in Spanish America in the 19th century subsequently appeared in Africa in the 20th century, the principle of *uti possidetis*, in the sense described above, fell to be applied.[6]

According to this dictum even if *uti possidetis* was first invoked in Spanish America, because it is a general principle of law aimed at preventing boundary struggles on independence, it applies wherever decolonization occurs. Consequently, when African independence occurred and boundary struggles were feared, *uti possidetis* fell to be applied to Africa. The reasoning of the ICJ Chamber takes the simple form of a syllogism:

a) The major premise: *uti possidetis* is a general principle of law preordained to address boundary struggles on independence.
b) The minor premise: independence occurred in Africa and boundary struggles were impending.
c) The conclusion: therefore *uti possidetis* applies to Africa.

The minor premise of this syllogism is fully attested. Historically, it is established that independence took place in Africa and the African continent was on the verge of profuse boundary struggles. Consequently, the truthfulness of the conclusion hinges critically on verifying the major premise. Despite this weighty prerequisite, the Chamber did not care to validate the status of 'general principle of law' it attributed to *uti possidetis*. Nor did it demonstrate that the objective of this principle was the prevention of boundary struggles. Nonetheless, this dictum was accepted uncritically to precipitate far-reaching effects.

[5] *Ibid.*   [6] *Ibid.*

### 1.1.2.   *The implications of the ruling in the* Frontier Dispute

The *Frontier Dispute* was hailed as the definitive statement on the application of *uti possidetis* to Africa. This unwitting endorsement had two momentous consequences.

First, after the ruling in the *Frontier Dispute* the Court and arbitration tribunals had invariably applied *uti possidetis* to African disputes notwithstanding that African states normally designate 'the principle of intangibility of inherited frontiers' as the applicable law, and in no instance did they refer to *uti possidetis* in their Special Agreements.[7] Examples of this uniform reception are abundant.

In *Guinea-Bissau/Senegal* the arbitration tribunal found that:

> The Organization of African Unity (OAU) has admitted the principle of *uti possidetis*, endorsed indirectly in its Charter of May 1963 and more directly in its Cairo Resolution of 1964. As stated in the Judgment of the Chamber of the International Court of Justice in the case concerning *the Frontier Dispute (Burkina Faso/Republic of Mali)*: 'The elements of *uti possidetis* were latent in the many declarations made by African leaders in the dawn of independence'.[8]

In *Eritrea/Ethiopia* Article 4.2 of the Special Agreement provides that 'the parties reaffirm the principle of respect for the borders existing at independence as stated in resolution AHG/Res 16(1) adopted by the OAU Summit in Cairo in 1964'. Although the Commission did not refer to *uti possidetis* specifically, it acted on its basis and attached little importance to establishing or applying the designated law principle. The Commission

---

[7] See: the preamble of the Special Agreement between Upper Volta (Burkina Faso) and Mali, *Frontier Dispute* (n 1) 557; the Arbitration Agreement of 18 February 1983 signed by Guinea-Bissau and Guinea, *Arbitral Award of 31 July 1989 (Guinea-Bissau/Senegal)* [1995] ICJ Rep 1, 54; Article 4 of the Agreement of 12 December between Eritrea and Ethiopia signed in Algiers on 12 December 2000, *Decision Regarding delimitation of the Border between Eritrea and Ethiopia* (2002) XXV RIAA 83 1, 21; Article 6 of the Special Agreement between the Republic of Benin and the Republic of Niger, *Frontier Dispute (Benin/Niger)* (Judgment) [2005] ICJ Rep 90, 96; Article 6 of the Special Agreement Seizing the ICJ of the Boundary Dispute between Burkina Faso and the Republic of Niger, *Frontier Dispute (Burkina Faso/Niger)* (Judgment) [2013] ICJ Rep 1, 9. Reference to general principles of law was made in Paragraph 2(a) of the Accord Cadre of 31 August 1989, *Territorial Dispute (Libyan Arab Jamahiriya/Chad)* (Judgment) [1994] ICJ Rep 6, 10–11 and Article 1 of the Agreement between Botswana and Namibia, signed at Gaborone on 15 February 1996, *Kasikili/Sedudu Island (Botswana/Namibia)* (Judgment) [1999] ICJ Rep 1045,1049.The issue was determined judicially in *Land and Maritime Boundary between Cameroon and Nigeria (Cameroon/Nigeria)* (Preliminary Objections) [1998] ICJ Rep 275.
[8] *Guinea-Bissau/Senegal* (n 7) 89.

concluded that this provision is having 'one particular consequence', which is that 'the Parties have thereby accepted that the date as at which the borders between them are to be determined is that of the independence of Eritrea, that is to say, on 27 April 1993'.[9] In *Benin/Niger* the ICJ Chamber determined the dispute explicitly on the basis of the principle of *uti possidetis*. Article 6 of the Special Agreement provides that the rules applicable to the dispute include 'the principle of State succession to the boundaries inherited from colonization, that is to say, the intangibility of those boundaries'. Referring to this Article, the ICJ Chamber held:

> It follows from the wording of this provision and from the arguments of the Parties that they are in agreement on the relevance of the principle of *uti possidetis juris* for the purposes of determining their common border. As the Chamber formed in the case concerning the *Frontier Dispute (Burkina Faso/Republic of Mali)* had occasion to state, the existence of this principle has been recognized on several occasions in the African context.[10]

In *Burkina Faso/Niger*, the Court cited Article 6 of the Special Agreement, which provided for 'the principle of the intangibility of boundaries inherited from colonization'. Then the Court recalled with approval that:

> A reference to the principle of intangibility of boundaries inherited from colonization also appeared in the preamble of the Special Agreement on the basis of which the case concerning the *Frontier Dispute (Burkina Faso/Republic of Mali)* was brought before the Court. The Chamber of the Court which dealt with the case concluded that it could not 'disregard the principle of *uti possidetis juris*, the application of which gives rise to this respect for intangibility of frontiers.[11]

Second, before this finding, scholars commenting on the practice of African states on independence were more intrepid in arguing that an African customary rule was in the making. Brownlie stated in his encyclopaedia on African boundaries, published in 1979, in reference to the Cairo Resolution, that: 'In any case the resolution and the conduct of governments based upon it, provides the basis for a rule of regional customary international law binding those states which have unilaterally declared their acceptance of the rule of the status quo as at the time of independence'.[12] Malcolm Shaw observed, shortly before the ICJ judgment, also in reference to the Cairo Resolution, that 'The border resolution

[9] *Eritrea/Ethiopia* (n 7) 118.
[10] *Benin/Niger* (n 7) 108.
[11] *Burkina Faso/Niger* (n 7) 73.
[12] Ian Brownlie, *African Boundaries: A Legal and Dipolmatic Encyclopedia* (1st edn, University of California 1979) 11.

can be said to have marked the acceptance by Africa as a whole of a new territorial regime, one based on the legal validity of the colonial frontiers of independent States. It is no longer possible to deny the impact of this rule as a binding practice of African States'.[13] However, this trend was dramatically reversed after the ruling, which patently denied the emergence of an African customary rule in a categorical passage that reads:

> The fact that the new African States have respected the administrative boundaries and frontiers established by the colonial powers must be seen not as a mere practice contributing to the gradual emergence of a principle of customary international law, limited in its impact to the African continent as it had previously been to Spanish America, but as the application in Africa of a rule of general scope.[14]

Swayed by this emphatic repudiation, lawyers acquiesced into the idea that the Cairo Resolution was a mere reinstatement of the principle of *uti possidetis* and failed to detect the emergent African customary rule. Naldi stated in a commentary on *the Frontier Dispute* that:

> The principle has been given implied recognition in the OAU Charter. According to Article 3, paragraph 3, member States solemnly affirm the principle of respect for the sovereignty and territorial integrity of every State. It was felt necessary to emphasise this principle further and the following year the OAU Assembly of Heads of State and Government adopted the Resolution on the Intangibility of Frontiers where the principle of *uti possidetis* was expressly affirmed.[15]

Shaw, changing his former position, opined: 'The numerous affirmations of the intangibility of colonial borders made by African statesmen and by the OAU itself thus recognized and confirmed an existing principle and neither created a new rule nor extended to Africa a rule previously applied only in another continent.'[16] Radan asserted that: 'With the decolonisation of Africa after World War II, the principle of *uti possidetis juris* was effectively adopted by a resolution of the Organisation of African Unity at its Cairo Conference in 1964.'[17] Commenting on 'the approach that the ICJ took in its judgement on the *Frontier Dispute*' Tomuschat stated: '*Uti*

[13] Malcolm Shaw, *Title to Territory in Africa: International Legal Issues* (Clarendon 1986) 186.

[14] *Frontier Dispute* (n 1) 565.

[15] G. Naldi, 'The Case Concerning the Frontier Dispute (Burkina Faso/Republic of Mali): Uti Possidetis in an African Perspective' (1987) 36 *ICLQ* 893, 898–9.

[16] Malcolm Shaw, 'The Heritage of States: The Principle of Uti Possidetis Juris Today' (1996) 67 *British YBK Intl L* 75, 103–4.

[17] P. Radan, 'Post-Succession International Orders: A Critical Analysis of the Workings of the Badinter Commission' (2000) 24 *MULR* 50, 59.

*possidetis* has thus become the leading maxim for the territorial delimitation of Africa, relegating self-determination in that respect to an insignificant, inferior place.'[18]

The *obiter dictum* on *uti possidetis* was also of worldwide consequences. Ever since the *Frontier Dispute*, *uti possidetis* does not require an explicit treaty provision to apply to a border dispute.[19] After Opinion No 3 of the Badinter Commission *uti possidetis* was found applicable outside the context of decolonization.[20]

To refute this misconceived finding, no less real for being widely held, this chapter advances two arguments:

First, in theory, *uti possidetis* was not initially perceived with the prevention of boundary struggles as its primary objective. In practice, it did not give rise to the concept of intangibility of inherited frontiers.

Second, *uti possidetis* is a special Spanish-American custom. There exists no state practice or *opinio juris* to elevate it to the status of a general principle of law.

When the major premise of the ICJ Chamber is refuted the ensuing conclusion, that *uti possidetis* applies to Africa, falls apart. Likewise, the associated consequences of negating the possibility of an African customary territorial regime, applying *uti possidetis* without treaty provisions to border disputes anywhere in the world, and asserting that it applies even outside the context of decolonization, simply crumble.

---

[18] Christian Tomuschat, 'Secession and Self-determination' in Marcelo G. Kohen (ed.), *Secession: International Law Perspectives* (Cambridge University Press 2006) 27. See also J. Klabbers and R. Lefeber, 'Africa: Lost between Self-determination and Uti Possidetis' in C. Brolmann (ed.), *Peoples and Minorities in International Law* (Martinus Nijhoff 1993) 58;T. M. Franck, 'Postmodern Tribalism and the Right to Secession' in Catherine Brolmann, Rene Lefeber and Marjoleine Zieck (eds.), *Peoples and Minorities in International Law* (Martinus Nijhoff 1993) 9–10; Rosalyn Higgins, *Problems & Process: International Law and How We Use It* (Clarendon 1994) 122.

[19] Radan, 'Post-succession International Orders' 60.

[20] For the viewpoint defending the interpretation in Opinion No 3 see A. Pellet, 'The Opinions of the Badinter Arbitration Committee a Second Breath for the Self-Determination of Peoples' (1992) 3 *EJIL* 178; Malcolm Shaw, 'Peoples, Territorialism and Boundaries' (1997) 8 *EJIL* 478, 496–8. Against: Radan, 'Post-succession International Orders' 61–3; Steven R. Ratner, 'Drawing a Better Line: Uti Possidetis and the Border of New States' (1996) 90 *AJIL* 590, 613–14; Suzanne Lalonde, *Determining Boundaries in a Conflicted World: The Role of Uti Possidetis* (McGill-Queen's University Press 2002) 188–92; Joshua Castellino and Steve Allen, *Title to Territory in International Law: A Temporal Analysis* (Ashgate 2003) 180–1; Matthew Craven, 'The European Community Arbitration Commission on Yugoslavia' (1995) 66 *British YBK Int'l L* 333.

## 1.2.   Incompatibility of *uti possidetis* with the concept of intangibility of frontiers

### 1.2.1.   *The purpose of* uti possidetis

It is well established that *uti possidetis* had its *fons et origo* in the undertaking to prevent the renewal of Spanish colonization under the pretext that parts of the Spanish-American continent were *terrae nullius*.[21] Although in modern international law the nonexistence of *terra nullius* is presumed everywhere on the globe this had not been the case all along. At the time when occupying new territory was one of the means of acquiring sovereignty, *terra nullius* was a precondition for valid occupation.[22]

At the beginning of the nineteenth century the Spanish-American republics found in the principle of *terra nullius* a Eurocentric and self-serving vestige of the past incompatible with their new independent status. Unless it was recognized that the vast uninhabited parts of those republics were not *nullius*, i.e. not new, Spain would have had the right to return and legally annex Spanish-American territory by occupation.[23] In view of this, the new republics concluded among themselves confederation treaties in which they provided for the rejection of the *terra nullius* principle along with other 'principles of European public law which did not harmonize with the special character of' Spanish America.[24] In this regard, the Confederation Treaty of 1848, 'which established international norms of such great importance',[25] is of particular significance.

In 1846–7, the independent existence of many Spanish-American republics was endangered when it was announced that General Flores was

[21] A. Alvarez, 'Latin America and International Law' (1909) 3 *AJIL* 269, 321; Castellino and Allen, Title to Territory in International Law 66–89; E. J. De Arechaga, 'Boundaries in Latin America: Uti possidetis Doctrine' in R Bernhardt (ed.), *Encyclopedia of Public International Law*, vol. 6 (Oxford University Press 1984) 46; Lalonde, Determining Boundaries in a Conflicted World 28–9; Joshua Castellino, 'Territorial Integrity and the Right to Self-Determination: An Examination of the Conceptual Tools' (2007) 33 *Brook J Int'l L* 503, 529–34; Separate Opinion of Judge Abdulqawi A. Yusuf *Frontier Dispute (Burkina Faso/Niger)* (n 7) 4.
[22] *Western Sahara* (Advisory Opinion) [1975] ICJ Rep12, 39; Ian Brownlie, *Principles of Public International Law* (6th edn, Oxford University Press 2003) 133; Malcolm Shaw, *International Law* (6th edn, Cambridge University Press 2008) 503.
[23] Alvarez, 'Latin America and International Law' 321.
[24] *Ibid.* 269.
[25] *Ibid.* 282. The Confederation Treaty, like most of the Spanish-American treaties, was not ratified.

preparing an expedition in Spain to occupy the entire coast of Western South America including Ecuador, New Granada, Venezuela, Peru, Bolivia and Chile.[26] Alvarez described as follows the reaction in Spanish America to the disquieting news:

> The Spanish-American states had well-grounded motives for the belief that the real object of the expedition was to create in America a monarchy over which a Spanish prince would be placed ... Public opinion in the Spanish-American countries was aroused and the governments echoing the general indignation, discussed the affair and made arrangements to resist the expedition at whatever point it might arrive. At the same time it was believed that the most opportune measure was the convening of an American Assembly to consider the matter.[27]

The alarmed states met in Lima between December 1847 and March 1848. The instructions of the Peruvian Government to its plenipotentiary included this paragraph: 'There will be a stipulation made between the allied nations to preserve their territorial integrity: consequently, they will not permit any foreign power, under any pretext whatever, to occupy any part whatever, no matter how small it may be, of the territory of any of the allied State.'[28] The other plenipotentiaries, apparently equipped with similar instructions, agreed to include the principle of territorial integrity invoked by Peru in the Treaty of Confederation 1848. The first Article of this Treaty reads:

> The High Contracting Parties confederate, league and unite themselves to sustain the independence and sovereignty of each and every one of them; to maintain the integrity of their respective territories; to assure their power and dominion in them; and to prevent that ... any of them be unduly outraged or offended.[29]

Alvarez observed that this article, along with Article 2 of the same Treaty, 'have closely followed, and completed the declarations contained in the Monroe Doctrine on the same point'.[30] The Monroe Doctrine, declared by US President James Monroe in 1823, had at its core the idea that 'no one of the two continents (America and Europe) may intermeddle in the affairs

---

[26] *Ibid.* 280; John Bassett Moore, *Memorandum on Uti Possidetis* (The Commonwealth Company 1913) 35; G. Pope Atkins, *Encyclopaedia of the Inter-American System* (Greenwood 1997) 302.

[27] Alvarez, 'Latin America and International Law' 280.

[28] Moore, Memorandum on Uti Possidetis 35.

[29] Martin Sticker, *The Geopolitics of Security in the Americas: Hemispheric Denial from Monroe to Clinton* (Greenwood 2002) 38.

[30] Alvarez, 'Latin America and International Law' 281.

of the other'.[31] However, while the Monroe Doctrine was intended to forestall intentions to occupy *terrae nullius* in Spanish America through policy guidelines, the Treaty of Confederation was aimed at creating a legal principle that denies the possibility of occupation in Spanish America *ipso jure*.

In the *Beagle Channel* case the tribunal affirmed that the commitments to respect territorial integrity made in Spanish-American treaties had the effect of excluding *terra nullius* status from the whole of Spanish America. In that case, it was found that as a result of those undertakings: 'all territory in Spanish America, however remote or inhospitable, is deemed to have been part of one of the former administrative divisions of Spanish colonial rule (vice-royalties, captaincies general, etc.). Hence there is no territory in Spanish America that has the status of *res nullius* open to an acquisition of title by occupation'.[32]

The existential threat that faced the new republics did not start with the notorious expedition of General Flores, but had been looming large since the early days of Spanish emancipation. For that reason, the principle against *terra nullius* had started to develop in Spanish America well before the Treaty of Confederation 1848. The agenda of the conferences that preceded the Lima Congress 1847–8 typically included as their first point: 'the solemn renovation between the confederated States of the pacts of union and offensive and defensive alliance'.[33] The exclusion of *terra nullius*, normally stated in the treaties in the form of a pledge of maintaining the independence and territorial integrity of all contracting parties, was usually considered under this agenda item. A typical example of the provisions included in the pre-1848 Treaties is Article I of the Pact of Union, Alliance and Perpetual Confederation 1823 concluded by Mexico, Central America, Colombia and Peru. That article provides that the objective of the Treaty was 'to maintain defensively and offensively, if necessary, the sovereignty, independence and territorial integrity of all and each of the Confederated Republics of America against all foreign domination'.[34] Likewise, the Colombian Congress of 1826 that brought together Colombia, Central America, Peru and Mexico provided

---

[31] *Ibid.* 311. See generally D. Perkins, *A History of the Monroe Doctrine* (Brown Little 1955).

[32] *Case concerning a Dispute between Argentina and Chile concerning the Beagle Channel* (1977) XXI RIAA 1, 81–2.

[33] The agenda of the Congress of Panama 1826, see G. A. De la Reza, 'The Formative Platform of the Congress of Panama (1810–1826): the Pan-American Conjecture Revisited' (2013) 56 *Revista Brasileira de Politica Internacional* 5, 14.

[34] Alvarez, 'Latin America and International Law' 277.

in Article 21 that: 'The contracting parties solemnly obligate and bind themselves to uphold and defend the integrity of their respective territories, earnestly opposing any attempt of colonial settlement in them without authority of and dependence upon the Governments under whose jurisdiction they are, and to employ to this end, in common, their forces and resources if necessary.'[35]

The denial of *terra nullius* that was eventually achieved indirectly by asserting the principle of territorial integrity was not styled in the treaties concluded by the Spanish republics as *uti possidetis*. The time-honoured term was reserved to the treaties concluded during the same period between the Spanish republics and Brazil, the successor of Portugal. In the treaties with Brazil, the contracting parties typically recognize that the boundary between them should be 'regulated on the principle of *uti possidetis*'.[36] This was a reference to the old Spanish–Portuguese boundary agreed in the Treaty of Madrid signed in 1750 and later reinforced by the First Treaty of San Ildefonso signed in 1777. In the Treaty of Madrid the two imperial powers resolved their age-long boundary dispute, which went back to the Bull issued by Pope Alexander VI in 1493, by agreeing that 'each party should remain in possession of what it then held'.[37] This provision reiterates the private Roman law interdict *uti possidetis, ita possideatis*, or 'as you possess, so may you possess', which 'was briefly designated in Latin America as *uti possidetis*'.[38] Because of this historical background, the term *uti possidetis* was familiar in Spanish America. In due course the idiom associated in the past only with the exclusion of Portugal from the Spanish territories became synonymous with eliminating Spain itself from its old empire. However, among the Spanish-American republics the term acquired the genitive 'juris' on the

---

[35] Moore, *Memorandum on Uti Possidetis* 34.

[36] The Treaty between Brazil and Peru 1851. See also: the Treaty of Limits between Brazil and Uruguay 1851, which provides 'as the basis which is to regulate their limits the *uti possidetis*'; the Treaty of Limits between Brazil and Venezuela 1852 which states that the contracting parties agreed upon and recognized 'as a basis for the determination of the frontier between their respective territories the *uti possidetis*'; the Convention between Brazil and Paraguay 1856 in which the contracting parties agreed that they would 'respect and reciprocally cause the present *uti possidetis* to be respected'; the same provision also appears in the Treaty of Limits and the accompanying Protocol between Brazil and the Argentine Confederation 1857; the Treaty between Brazil and Bolivia 1867 in which the contracting parties agreed 'In recognizing as a basis on which to determine the boundaries between their respective territories, the *uti possidetis*', Moore, *Memorandum on Uti Possidetis* 17–19.

[37] Moore, *Memorandum on Uti Possidetis* 17.

[38] *Ibid.* 8.

basis of a disputed assumption that this suffix reflects that only legal title, as opposed to *de facto* title, counts.[39]

Against this backdrop, it is unsurprising that judicial precedents before and after the *Frontier Dispute* are unanimous in establishing *terra nullius* as the paramount purpose of the principle of *uti possidetis*. The leading case in this regard is the *Colombian-Venezuelan Frontier*.[40] In this case it was found that because of *uti possidetis* 'Encroachments and ill-timed efforts at colonization beyond the frontiers, as well as occupations in fact, became invalid and ineffectual in law.'[41] It was also clarified that the principle had finally 'put an end to the designs of the colonizing states of Europe against lands which otherwise they could have sought to proclaim as *res nullius*'.[42] In the *Beagle Channel* case, and in the same vein, the tribunal asserted that as a result of the treaty arrangements undertaken in Spanish America 'there is no territory in Spanish America that has the status of *res nullius* open to an acquisition of title by occupation'.[43] Likewise, in *El Salvador/Honduras* the Court found that 'certainly a key aspect of the principle [of *uti possidetis*] is the denial of the possibility of *terra nullius*'.[44] In *Nicaragua/Honduras* the Court asserted its former finding in *El Salvador/Honduras* and reiterated that 'It is well established that "a key aspect of the principle is the denial of the possibility of *terra nullius*".'[45] Recently in *Nicaragua/Colombia*, Nicaragua asserted its rights of sovereignty on the Mosquito Coast and its appurtenant maritime features on the basis that as a result of adopting the principle of *uti possidetis* there was no *terra nullius* in Spanish America.[46]

In addition to the purpose of uniting to exclude Spain, the new Spanish-American republics hoped, by asserting the *uti possidetis*, to avoid boundary disputes among themselves. Some of the treaties concluded provide that in the absence of any agreement to the contrary the contracting parties must observe the *uti possidetis* of 1810.[47] Used with

---

[39] *Ibid.* 35; Atkins, Encyclopaedia of the Inter-American System 41.

[40] RIAA, VI 1922, 223.

[41] *Ibid.* 228.    [42] *Ibid.*

[43] *The Beagle Channel* (n 32) 81–2.

[44] *Case concerning the Land, Island and Maritime Frontier Dispute (El Salvador/ Honduras: Nicaragua intervening)* (Judgment) [1992] ICJ Rep 315, 387.

[45] *Territorial and Maritime Dispute between Nicaragua and Honduras in the Caribbean Sea (Nicaragua/Honduras)* (Judgment) [2007] ICJ Rep 659, 707.

[46] *Territorial and Maritime Dispute (Nicaragua/Colombia)* [2012] ICJ Rep 1, 27.

[47] While 1810 is accepted to be the year of independence of the republics of South America, for Central America the corresponding year was 1821. Hence the principle is expressed

the qualifier 1810 (or 1821 in the case of Central American republics) the term *uti possidetis* refers to 'the territory which the respective countries had the right to possess according to the Spanish administrative divisions obtaining at that date, the date of the beginning of the movement for emancipation'.[48] Obviously, this qualified usage refers to the internal administrative boundaries left on independence by Spain in the year indicated, not to the international boundary of Spain and Portugal created by the Treaty of Madrid 1750. Alvarez and Moore agree that *uti possidetis* of 1810 is 'of purely American origin ... and at the same time is influenced by the general principle of long continued pacific possession of disputed territory'.[49]

The Treaty of Confederation 1848 is widely accredited for proclaiming the principle of the *uti possidetis* of 1810. Moore contends that this finding 'appears not to be altogether accurate'.[50] Alvarez, however, is of the opinion that the *uti possidetis* of 1810 was 'recognized in fact by all the states, and proclaimed at The Congress at Lima in 1848'.[51] The debate triggered by the proposal of the Peruvian plenipotentiary to the Congress of Lima 1847–8 attests that the *uti possidetis* of 1810 was not agreed upon earlier, and was eventually endorsed by the Treaty of Confederation even if it was not specifically mentioned in it by name. The background to this is the Peruvian proposal that the new republics 'shall adhere to the rule of the *uti possidetis* of 1824, when the war of independence ended with the battle of Ayacucho'.[52] Bolivia opposed setting the date as that of the Ayacucho battle and made a counterproposal that the republics should 'recognize as a principle founded in perfect right, for the fixing of their respective limits, the *uti possidetis* of 1810'.[53] New Granada also made a similar proposal.[54] Finally:

> A majority of the Plenipotentiaries expressed the view that the battle of Ayacucho had nothing to do with the discussion, and had created no new right as to limits; that the Spanish-American Republics could found their territorial rights only on the dispositions of the Spanish Government, in

with regard to Central America as *uti possidetis* of 1821, see Moore, *Memorandum on Uti Possidetis* 47–8; *El Salvador/Honduras* (n 44) 380.

[48] Alvarez, 'Latin America and International Law' 290.

[49] Moore, *Memorandum on Uti Possidetis* 33, quoting with approval A. Alvarez, *American Problems of International Law* (Baker, Voorhis 1909) 96.

[50] Moore, *Memorandum on Uti Possidetis* 35–6.

[51] Alvarez, 'Latin America and International Law' 290, fn 13.

[52] Moore, *Memorandum on Uti Possidetis* 35.

[53] Moore, *Memorandum on Uti Possidetis* 36.

[54] *Ibid.* 37.

force at the time of the declaration of independence, and on the treaties and conventions celebrated since that date.[55]

Eventually, the principle that the limits should be those obtained at the time of independence was enshrined in Article 7 of the Treaty of Confederation. The Article reads in part that: 'The Confederated republics declare their right is perfect to keep the boundaries of their territories as they existed at the time of the independence from Spain of the respective Viceroyalties, Captaincies-general, or Presidencies, into which Spanish America was divided'.[56]

Yet, this objective, of setting a standard to avoid boundary disputes, was subordinate to the main goal of denying *terra nullius*. The instructions of the Peruvian envoy indicate that for the Government of Peru the priority was to make sure that no foreign government would be allowed to occupy parts of the Spanish-American territories. Peru would not have found satisfactory anything less than concrete agreement on this point. Second to that objective was the hope to agree on a yardstick for fixing the boundaries of the new republics. For this secondary purpose even if Peru proposed at one stage the boundaries that resulted from the battle of Ayacucho, it later conceded that standard and agreed to another suitable date.[57] The same prioritization was stated in the Memoir on Foreign Relations, presented at the Congress of Gran Colombia in 1823. The Memoir reads in part:

> first, that the American States be allied and confederated perpetually, in peace and in war, to consolidate their liberty and independence, mutually guaranteeing the integrity of their respective territories; and second, to make that guarantee effective, they would abide by the *uti possidetis juris* of 1810, according to the demarcation of each General Captaincy or Viceroy established as a Sovereign State.[58]

When an objective of a treaty is always considered inferior to another, it can by no means be its primary purpose.

Shaw commented on this ancillary status of the goal of eliminating boundary disputes stating: 'It is particularly interesting to note that the intention of preventing boundary disputes as between the successor States of the former Spanish Empire was referred to almost in passing.'[59]

---

[55] *Ibid.*    [56] *Ibid.*
[57] Moore, *Memorandum on Uti Possidetis* 35.
[58] De la Reza, 'The Formative Platform of the Congress of Panama' 13.
[59] Shaw, 'The Heritage of States' 99.

He further asserted that 'Only in passing did [*uti possidetis*] appear to concern itself with avoidance of boundary disputes as such.'[60] In *Colombia/Venezuela* the Court found that the principle 'also had the advantage, it was hoped, of doing away with boundary disputes between the new states'.[61] Indeed, doing away with boundary disputes was a mere 'hope'.

Consequently, the finding in the *Frontier Dispute* that the *obvious* purpose of the principle of *uti possidetis* was to prevent endangering independence of new states by fratricidal struggles is not entirely accurate. The preeminent purpose of denying *terra nullius* gave the Spanish-American principle distinct external orientation that makes it implausible to argue that *uti possidetis* was originally intended to prevent internal boundary struggles. The ICJ Chamber in the *Frontier Dispute* could by no means ordain a concern that had been a mere 'hope' as the 'obvious purpose' of *uti possidetis*. In particular, it was not justifiable of the Chamber to make this finding while a different objective for the principle was consistently identified in a number of previous rulings.

The ICJ Chamber would have been accurate if it had stated that while the primary objective of the principle of *uti possidetis* was the prevention of *terra nullius* the principle had another purpose of preventing boundary struggles; and that the Chamber needed to bring forth this subsidiary purpose. Such finding was avoided because it would not have helped the ICJ reasoning. It was only the assumption that preventing boundary disputes was the main fixation of *uti possidetis* that would make it possible for the Chamber to formulate its major premise the way it did and henceforth arrive at that conclusion. In other words, it would not have been feasible for the Chamber to apply the principle of *uti possidetis* to a case the parties of which designate 'the principle of the intangibility of frontiers' as the applicable law doctrine if the prevention of boundary struggles were not the preeminent purpose of *uti possidetis*.

Nonetheless, the turn of events suggests that the meagre hope of avoiding boundary disputes soon evaporated. The Spanish-American practice of *uti possidetis* witnessed a flurry of boundary changes and was marred by myriad disputes incongruent with the concept of intangibility of inherited frontiers. We now turn to this point.

---

[60] *Ibid.*
[61] *Colombia/Venezuela* (n 40) 223.

## 1.2.2. *Readjustment of frontiers under* uti possidetis

Four reasons militate against the ICJ finding that the application of *uti possidetis* gave rise to the concept of intangibility of inherited frontiers.

First, the Spanish-American boundaries were not definite and were as such incapable of consecration as intangible:

Moore observed that when the Spanish-American emancipation was complete, 'not a single boundary line had been actually agreed upon and defined, much less marked'.[62] The want of precise geographical data and the insufficiency of the Spanish law were the reasons behind that unsatisfactory state of affairs.[63] Finding it impossible to do anything with such unclear alignments, the Spanish-American republics tended, particularly during the early decades of the emancipation, to postpone the process of border delimitation in its entirety.[64] When border disputes were eventually referred to arbitration, arbitrators had to escape the gaps in data and law in the *uti possidetis* of 1810 and determine a new boundary. In the *Bolivia-Peru Arbitration,* the sole arbitrator, 'Having studied with the greatest attention the titles of both parties', did not find 'sufficient grounds for considering as the boundary between the Audiencia of Charcas and the Viceroyalty of Lima in 1810, either of the demarcations supported by the respective advocates of the interested state'.[65] This is because the boundaries 'had not been fully determined' by Spain.

Delivering the Award in *Guatemala/Honduras,* in which the task of the arbitrator was to determine the 'juridical line' of the *uti possidetis* of 1821, Chief Justice Hughes stated:

---

[62] Moore, *Memorandum on Uti Possidetis* 22.
[63] *Ibid.*
[64] For examples of agreements to postpone boundary making see: Article 2 of the Fundamental Law of the Sovereign Congress of Venezuela for the Union of the Republics of New Granada and Venezuela, under the Title of Colombia (1819) *ibid.* 21; Article IX of the Treaty of Perpetual Union, League and Confederation between Colombia and Peru (1822), *ibid.* 22; Article 7 of the Constitution of the Federal Republic of Central America (1824); Article 9 of the Treaty of Perpetual Union, League and Confederation between Colombia and Mexico (1823); Article 7 of the Treaty of Perpetual Union, League and Confederation between Colombia and the United Provinces of Central America, both in Lalonde, *Determining Boundaries in a Conflicted World* 29–30 and fn 20, 260–1. See also Ecuador agreement with Peru in 1832, Moore, *Memorandum on Uti Possidetis* 23; Lalonde, *Determining Boundaries in a Conflicted World* 30–1; Castellino and Allen, *Title to Territory* 83.
[65] *Bolivia/Peru: Arbitral Award in Boundary Dispute Rendered by the President of the Argentine Republic* AJIL (1909) 1029, 1032.

It must be noted that particular difficulties are encountered in drawing the line of 'uti possidetis of 1821', by reason of the lack of trustworthy information during colonial times with respect to a large part of the territory in dispute. Much of this territory was unexplored. Other parts which had occasionally been visited were but vaguely known. In consequence, not only had boundaries of jurisdiction not been fixed with precision by the Crown, but there were great areas in which there had been no effort to assert any semblance of administrative authority.[66]

In *El Salvador/Honduras,* the Court found:

While it was from the outset accepted that the new international boundaries should be determined by the application of the principle generally accepted in Spanish America of the *uti possidetis juris*, whereby the boundaries were to follow the colonial administrative boundaries, the problem, as in the case of many other boundaries in the region, was to determine where those boundaries actually lay.[67]

In the same case, the ICJ clarified that: 'it is perfectly possible that that [Spanish] law itself gave no clear and definite answer to the appurtenance of marginal areas, or sparsely populated areas of minimal economic significance'.[68] The same conclusion was confirmed in the recent case of *Territorial and Maritime Dispute (Nicaragua/Colombia)*: 'In the present case the principle of *uti possidetis juris* affords inadequate assistance in determining sovereignty over the maritime features in dispute between Nicaragua and Colombia because nothing clearly indicates whether these features were attributed to the colonial provinces of Nicaragua or of Colombia prior to or upon independence.'[69]

Because of this notorious vagueness, the Spanish-American boundaries were the reason for dispute rather than harmony. The Spanish-American republics had witnessed numerous boundary disputes that were caused by the undesirable condition of the boundaries left by Spain. Alvarez noted that the vague and sometimes conflicting boundaries, 'often led to three countries claiming the same territory'. [70] He asserted, 'all the states of America have had boundary disputes with all of their neighbours'.[71]

---

[66] *Case concerning the Border between Guatemala and Honduras (Guatemala/Honduras)* (1933) II RIAA 1307, 1325.
[67] *El Salvador/Honduras* (n 44) 380.
[68] *Ibid.* 559.
[69] *Nicaragua/Colombia* (n 46) 28.
[70] Alvarez, American Problems of International Law 94, quoted in Moore, *Memorandum on Uti Possidetis* 32.
[71] Alvarez, 'Latin America and International Law' 290.

Second, Spanish-American states considered the *uti possidetis* 1810 line to form a default boundary that applies temporarily until the final boundary is agreed:

The treaties concluded by different republics state clearly that while the contracting parties adhere, for the time being, to the *uti possidetis* of 1810, they reserve for themselves the right to determine their final boundaries by agreement.

In the Confederation Treaty 1848, the concluding paragraph of Article 7 provides:

> The Republics which, having been parts of the same State at the proclamation of independence, were separated after 1810, shall be kept within the boundaries which they recognized for themselves, without prejudice to the Treaties they may have celebrated or shall celebrate in order to vary or perfect them in conformity with the present article. What is provided in this article shall in no way alter the Treaties or Conventions concerning boundaries celebrated between any of the Confederated Republics, nor constrain the liberty which these Republics may have to arrange among themselves their respective boundaries.[72]

In the Treaty of Limits of 1852, the Argentine and Paraguay undertook to fix their boundaries by direct negotiation taking account of the bases on which commerce and navigation should be arranged.[73] The Argentine and Chile, by their Treaty of Peace, Commerce and Navigation 1855, agreed to respect the limits of the year 1810 and 'to adjourn the questions which have been or may be raised on this matter, in order to discuss them later in a pacific and friendly manner'.[74] When the time came for addressing the adjourned issues 'adjustment proceeded with negotiation, mediation, and arbitrations, till at length the divisional line was established, claims of right giving way'.[75] In 1858, Costa Rica and Nicaragua adjusted their *uti possidetis* 1810 boundary by direct negotiation.[76] The award of the President of the United States rendered in 1888 declared valid the 1858 agreement that determined the boundaries between the two states, which

---

[72] Moore, *Memorandum on Uti Possidetis* 38.

[73] *Ibid.* 27–8.     [74] *Ibid.* 28–9.

[75] *Ibid.* 29. Also see S. E. Baldwin, 'The International Congresses and Conferences of the Last Century as Forces Working Towards the Solidarity of the World' (1907) 1 *AJIL* 808, 808; Alvarez, 'Latin America and International Law' 277–90; Moore, *Memorandum on Uti Possidetis* 21–45; generally C. G. Fenwick, 'The Third Meeting of Ministers of Foreign Affairs at Rio de Janeiro' (1942) 36 *AJIL* 169; Castellino and Allen, *Title to Territory* 66–74; Lalonde, *Determining Boundaries in a Conflicted World* 32–60.

[76] Moore, *Memorandum on Uti Possidetis* 30.

did not take account of the *uti possidetis* line.[77] In a preliminary agreement signed in 1882 by Guatemala and Mexico, it was stated that:

> In the demarcation of the boundary line actual possession shall, as a general rule, serve as the basis by which to be guided; but this shall not prevent said basis from being laid aside by both parties, by mutual consent, for the purpose of following natural lines, or for any other reason, and in such case the system of mutual compensations shall be adopted. Until the boundary line of demarcation be determined, each of the contracting parties shall respect the actual possession of the other.[78]

Therefore, even as the Spanish republics temporarily accepted the old Spanish alignments, new territorial arrangements acknowledged to be at variance with the *uti possidetis* line were commonplace.[79] The numerous boundary treaties concluded by the Spanish-American republics made significant adjustments to the inherited boundaries. For instance, Chiapas was annexed to Mexico despite the acknowledgement that Chiapas had been part of the Audiencia of Guatemala.[80] Nicoya was left in the possession of Costa Rica after the breakup of the Central American Republic although under Spanish rule it belonged to the Province of Nicaragua.[81] On studying those treaties, Castellino and Allen doubted whether 'the notion that the boundaries inherited from the Spanish Empire were as sacrosanct as the literature surrounding the doctrine of *uti possidetis* seems to suggest'.[82] Alvarez considered that Article 7 of the Treaty of Confederation 1848 laid a principle for dispute prevention that the contracting parties accept the *uti possidetis* of 1810 'in default of special stipulations' and the territories possessed by each republic on independence should be the subject of demarcation. He explained that Article 7:

> further proposed to prevent conflicts between the confederates, especially those arising out of boundary disputes, establishing for this purpose that, in default of special stipulations between the interested parties, the boundaries should be those possessed by the respective countries in the epoch of the conquest of independence from Spain, and further providing rules for their demarcation.[83]

---

[77] *Award in regard to the Validity of the Treaty of Limits between Costa Rica and Nicaragua of 15 July* (1858) XXVIII RIAA 89.
[78] Moore, *Memorandum on Uti Possidetis* 30–1.
[79] C. C. Hyde, *International Law Chiefly as Interpreted and Applied by the United States*, vol. 1 (Brown Little 1922) 504–5; Lalonde, *Determining Boundaries in a Conflicted World* 36.
[80] Lalonde, *Determining Boundaries in a Conflicted World* 37–8.
[81] *Ibid.*
[82] Castellino and Allen, *Title to Territory* 68.
[83] Alvarez, 'Latin America and International Law' 281.

The demarcation mentioned by Alvarez was an extensive exercise in which boundaries were sometimes changed altogether as we see next.

Third, the boundary demarcation commissions treated the line of the *uti possidetis* of 1810 as a general basis of settlement, not as a definite alignment to be adhered to precisely:

In the practice of demarcation commissions of Spanish America, the *uti possidetis* of 1810 was merely the starting point for demarcation and not necessarily its final outcome. The aspirations of the local communities and considerations of equity and convenience were taken into account and considered to warrant exchanges of territory. The reason behind this free-hand style of the Spanish-American commissions is that the *uti possidetis* 1810 treaties displayed an overriding concern to make natural boundaries, preferring them to the artificial lines inherited from Spain. Commissions are typically instructed not to defy the geographic features or offend the population along the boundary line.

In the treaty concluded between New Granada and Peru in 1829 the parties 'engage to cede to each other, reciprocally, such small portions of territory as may be necessary to fix the boundary line in a more natural and precise manner' and to avoid offending the inhabitants on the frontiers.[84] The Definitive Treaty of Peace and Friendship, signed at Arequipa in 1831 between Bolivia and Peru, provided for a Commission to draw up a topographical map so that cessions could be made reciprocally and rivers, lakes, or mountains would form the boundaries.[85] The Commission was also ordered to draw a map 'on the statistics of the population located upon' the frontiers.[86] The parties to the Confederation Treaty 1848 agreed that the dividing line of the republics would be determined 'taking the summits that separate the waters and *thalweg* of the rivers, or other natural lines, provided the localities permit it; to which end they shall be able to make the necessary and compensatory exchanges of land, in such manner as may best suit the reciprocal convenience of the Republics'.[87] The Continental Treaty signed in 1856 by the Ministers of Peru, Chile, and Ecuador, prohibits cession of territory to foreign establishment, i.e. to Spain. It clarified that 'This stipulation shall not prevent the cessions which the said States may make one to the other to regulate their geographical demarcations or to fix natural limits to their territories, or to

---

[84] Moore, *Memorandum on Uti Possidetis* 24.
[85] *Ibid.* 25.    [86] *Ibid.*    [87] *Ibid.* 37–8.

determine with mutual advantage their boundaries'.[88] The Bonilla-Gamez Treaty of 1894 signed between Honduras and Nicaragua provides that the Mixed Commission shall work 'in order to establish in so far as possible a well-defined, natural, boundary line'.[89] The award rendered by the King of Spain in 1906 explained that on the basis of this provision it was worked to bring about well-defined natural boundaries where possible.[90]

In addition to considerations of geography and demography, the demarcation commissions of Spanish America were also authorised to consider equity. In the boundary convention between Guatemala and Honduras in 1895, the contracting parties stipulated that 'Possession shall only be considered valid so far as it is just, legal, and well founded, in conformity with general principles of equity, and with the rules of justice sanctioned by the law of nations.'[91]

Nineteenth-century demarcations, wherever undertaken, were mostly based on inadequate mapping. This made it necessary to give demarcators of that time latitude in 'adjusting the delimited boundary in order to take account of differences between reality and a delimitation based on inadequate information'.[92] Because of advancements in mapping, consequent to scientific progress, this exceptional authority was soon revoked. Yet, the scope of that liberty in its heyday did not exceed filling data gaps. Certainly, it did not include empowering the demarcators to consult local communities or exchange territory. When substantial changes in the agreed line were found necessary because of encounters with geographical realities that were not reflected on maps the demarcators referred the matter to their principals and required alteration in the boundary treaty itself.

During the first decade of the twentieth century, Sir Thomas Holdich, a leading demarcator of his generation, was instructed to demarcate a boundary for Afghanistan and India on the basis of an agreement that defined the boundary as 'running parallel to the Chitral River at an even distance of 4 miles from the river bank'.[93] It was discovered that this line 'fell on the spurs of a flanking range, about halfway between the summit and the foot'.[94] On finding that demarcation of such a line was 'an utter

[88]  *Ibid.* 39.
[89]  *The Border Dispute between Honduras and Nicaragua* (1906) XI RIAA 101,107.
[90]  *Ibid.* 117.
[91]  Moore, *Memorandum on Uti Possidetis* 30
[92]  Dennis Rushworth, 'Mapping in Support of Frontier Arbitration: Delimitation and Demarcation' (1996, summer) IBRU Boundary and Security Bulletin 60, 63.
[93]  *Ibid.*    [94]  *Ibid.*

impossibility' an alternative was suggested, which was 'the well-marked crest, or divide of the range, instead of being halfway down its ragged side'.[95] This alternative involved concession of 'utterly unimportant' territory to Afghanistan. Yet, the alteration was considered to fall beyond the latitude accorded to demarcators. Sir Thomas Holdich found that 'effecting an alteration in the text of the agreement' was required, and the matter was eventually referred to the parties.[96]

This shows that the autonomy accorded to Spanish-American demarcators was way beyond the leeway available to their counterparts elsewhere. A Spanish-American demarcation commission was typically empowered to 'fix the boundary line in a more natural and precise manner', to take account of 'the summits that separate the waters', or to 'make the necessary and compensatory exchanges of land'. Consequently, if the situation encountered by Sir Thomas Holdich were to be faced by a Spanish-American commission, the commission would have mostly found it possible to act without seeking fresh mandate. With this extensive authority of the Spanish-American demarcation commissions, it would be surprising if executing the precise *uti possidetis* of 1810 were anything other than a rarity.

Fourth, when agreements to change the inherited boundary line were not forthcoming Spanish-American republics did not always respect the *uti possidetis* of 1810 and often resorted to war for determining the disputed borderline.[97]

For instance, Brazil and the Provinces of the River Plate fought the Cisplatine wars in 1825 over Montevideo. Peru and Colombia battled over the Maranon River Basin in 1829 and again more recently in 1941. Paraguay lost 55,000 square miles of territory to Brazil because of its military defeat in 1869. War raged between Chile and Bolivia in 1879–83 over Antofagasta and the Bolivian Pacific coastline.[98] Spanish-American republics accepted the consequences brought about by those wars as *jus post bellum* arrangements and did not consider them unjust gains from aggression. Radan opines that border disputes in Spanish America were resolved by these wars, rather than by *uti possidetis*.[99]

[95] *Ibid.* 64.    [96] *Ibid.*
[97] For Spanish-American wars see Lalonde, *Determining Boundaries in a Conflicted World* 38–41.
[98] *Ibid.*
[99] Radan, 'Post-succession International Orders' 68.

Because of those four factors, *uti possidetis* led in Spanish America to a series of horizontal territory transfers. Fifty years after emancipation, the map of Spanish America was changed beyond recognition. Alvarez described as follows the net result of those incessant adjustments:

> At the time of struggle for emancipation, there were four vice royalties in Spanish America (Mexico, New Granada, Peru and Buenos Aires) and seven Capitanis Generales (Yucutan, Cuba, Puerto Rico, Santo Domingo, Guatemala, Venezuela and Chile). Bolivar formed of New Granada, Venezuela and northern Peru, the United States of Colombia, which fell away in 1830 into three States: New Granada, Venezuela and Ecuador. The old vice royalty of Buenos Aires became sub-divided into four States: Bolivia (which was separated from the vice-royalty by Bolivar in 1825), Uruguay, Paraguay, and the United Provinces of the River Plate. The United States of Central America, founded in 1823 split up into five separate States in 1839.[100]

On comparing the map of Spanish America under Spanish rule with its map at the turn of the twentieth century, Lalonde found that the colonial lines accounted for only 10 per cent of the new international boundaries in that continent.[101]

In view of the foregoing, the application of the principle of *uti possidetis* in Spanish America could by no means be considered to have given rise to the notion of intangibility of inherited frontiers or the prevention of fratricidal boundary struggles. Far from being 'intangible', the *uti possidetis* 1810 boundary line was merely a general basis. It was set aside more often than not and at each and every stage of the boundary-making process.

## 1.3.    Whether *uti possidetis* is a general principle of law

### 1.3.1.    Juridical pronouncements before the Frontier Dispute

It is agreed that *uti possidetis* '*juris*' was a special custom, within Latin America itself, limited to the territories under the Spanish Crown.[102] Even within Spanish America, universal applicability of the principle was questioned. Commenting in 1933 on *the Guatemala and Honduras*

---

[100]  Alvarez, 'Latin America and International Law' 289.
[101]  Lalonde, *Determining Boundaries in a Conflicted World* 56.
[102]  Shaw, 'The Heritage of States' 100. See also Shaw, 'Peoples, Territorialism and Boundaries' 493; Lalonde, *Determining Boundaries in a Conflicted World* 31–2; Castellino and Allen, *Title to Territory* 11.

*Boundary Dispute* Fisher spoke of *uti possidetis* as 'indefinite and illusory' and talked of efforts 'to elevate it to the dignity of a principle of American international law'.[103] The status of the principle in Spanish America did not improve and those misgivings still persist. In the *Beagle Channel* case it was found that 'the scope and applicability of the doctrine were somewhat uncertain, particularly in such far-distant regions of the continent'.[104]

Additionally, the principle was found not to apply where one of the parties is non-Spanish-American. Chief Justice Hughes concluded in *Guatemala/Honduras* that the system of *uti possidetis* operated on the basis that both states involved in the boundary dispute were part of the Spanish colonial regime and that the only source of authority was the Spanish Crown.[105] In 1948, while debating the disputed sovereignty over the Falkland Islands, Waldock argued that the principle of *uti possidetis* could not be regarded as available to Argentina and Chile in their dispute with the United Kingdom. He stated:

> Consequently, in the absence of express agreement as to its meaning, there is some difficulty in applying the doctrine even between Latin-American states which subscribe generally to the *uti possidetis* theory of succession from Spain. The difficulty is obviously much greater when one of the disputants is a non-American state which does not subscribe to the doctrine at all.[106]

The first judicial reference to the principle of *uti possidetis* outside Spanish America was in the case of *Belgium/Netherlands*.[107] In this case, Judges Armand-Ugon and Moreno Quintana stated in their dissenting opinions, in no dissimilar terms, that Article 14 of the Convention of Maastricht 1842 forms the basis for applying the principle of *uti possidetis* to the dispute in question because it provides for the status quo.[108] A few years

---

[103]  F. C. Fisher, 'The Arbitration of the Guatemalan-Honduran Boundary Dispute' (1933) 27 *AJIL* 403, 415.

[104]  *The Beagle Channel* (n 32) 81; see Lalonde, *Determining Boundaries in a Conflicted World* 59.

[105]  *Guatemala/Honduras* (n 66) 1324.

[106]  Humphrey Waldock, 'Disputed Sovereignty in the Falkland Islands Dependencies' (1948) 25 *British YBK Int'l L* 311, 326. For a recent confirmation of this viewpoint see Elihu Lauterpacht *et al.*, *Legal Opinion on Guatemala's Territorial Claim to Belize* (2001), 60–1 at https://amandala411.files.wordpress.com/2013/03/bz-legal-opinion.pdf (accessed 9 March 2015).

[107]  *Case concerning Sovereignty over Certain Frontier Land (Belgium/Netherlands)* (Judgment) [1959] ICJ Rep 209.

[108]  *Ibid.*, Dissenting Opinion of Judge Armand-Ugon 240; Dissenting Opinion of Judge Moreno Quintana 255.

later, in the *Rann of Kutch Arbitration* it was found that the Agreement of 30 June 1965, unlike the Convention of Maastricht 1842, 'does not include a rule analogous to the principle known as *uti possidetis juris*'. Accordingly, the tribunal concluded that it could not apply the principle for the purpose of ascertaining or giving effect to administrative or other boundaries existing on a postulated historical date.[109] Evidently, at the time of the decisions in the *Belgium/Netherlands* and the *Rann of Kutch Arbitration* it was accepted as sound law that *uti possidetis* applies only by agreement.

Furthermore, in *the Dubai-Sharjah Border Arbitration*, determined a few years before the *Frontier Dispute*, it was found that African states were not bound by *uti possidetis* to abide by the inherited colonial boundaries. The tribunal acknowledged that the doctrine was at the root of the respect afforded to boundaries in South America, and seems to have been revived in Africa. Yet, it added that the African and South-American states on achieving independence, 'could of course, have adopted quite a different attitude and have rejected such boundaries'.[110] If African states were free not to follow *uti possidetis* and to reject the pre-existing boundaries, this means that *uti possidetis* was not a general principle of law at the time of African decolonization.

Against this background, it is not surprising that the ICJ Chamber in the *Frontier Dispute* found no support in judicial literature for its newfangled conclusion that *uti possidetis* is a general principle of law. Before the *Frontier Dispute* Judge Bedjaoui, the Chairman of the ICJ Chamber in the case, made the only contention to this effect. In his capacity as counsel for Algeria in the *Western Sahara* Advisory Opinion, Bedjaoui stated during the oral pleadings that *uti possidetis*

> is not a special rule, inherent only to a certain continental type of international law. It is a general principle logically linked to the phenomenon of decolonization wherever it occurs. Its obvious purpose is to prevent the decolonization itself and all its fruits be endangered by fratricidal struggles provoked by setting discussion of borders at the time when the former colonial power disappears.[111]

This statement was copied almost word for word in the judgment in the *Frontier Dispute*.[112] When Burkina Faso argued that *uti possidetis* was a

---

[109] *The Indo-Pakistan Western Boundary (Rann of Kutch) between India and Pakistan* (1968) XVII RIAA 1, Opinion of the Chairman 526; see also the Dissenting Opinion of Ales Bebler 448–9.

[110] (1981) 91 ILR 543, 578.

[111] *Western Sahara, Pleadings* (Advisory Opinion) [1975] ICJ Rep vol. V, 315, translation from the French original.

[112] *Ibid.* 314–18.

general principle of law, it found no support anywhere other than in this solitary statement of Bedjaoui.[113] The failure of Burkina Faso to provide any concrete authority in support of its position, given the utmost care normally accorded to preparation of written pleadings, shows that such authority is lacking.[114]

In addition to a lack of authoritative findings or scholarly statements indicating that *uti possidetis* lays some claim to universality, state practice in support of the ICJ ruling is also missing.

### 1.3.2.   *The lack of* uti possidetis *state practice*

After the completion of the Spanish-American emancipation, the principle of *uti possidetis* featured nowhere in state practice. In the aftermath of the two World Wars, the principle of self-determination, the antithesis of *uti possidetis,* emerged in relation to the *en masse* sovereign territorial transfers that took place and the great legal debates that ensued. *Uti possidetis* was well-nigh dropped from the international agenda.[115] During those defining times, the principle of self-determination was generally considered the basis for determining territorial limits and was never deemed irrelevant unless 'the people's will was certain to run counter to the victor's geopolitical, economic and strategic interest'.[116]

---

[113] *Frontier Dispute* (n 1) Memorial of Burkina Faso 74.

[114] In addition to citing Bedjaoui's statement Burkina Faso referred in a footnote in its Memorial to the intervention of Mr Ago during the works of the International Law Commission, *Frontier Dispute* (n 1) Memorial of Burkina Faso 74. On examining that reference, it is found that although Mr Ago discussed decolonization in Latin America, Asia and Africa he did not conclude that *uti possidetis* was connected with the phenomenon of independence wherever it occurs. See YBK Int'l LC, *Summary Records of the Twentieth Session 27 May–2 August 1968*, vol. I (1968) 120.

[115] For the debate of the principles included in the League Covenant see D. H. Miller, *The Drafting of the Covenant*, vol. I (Johnson Reprint Corp 1969). For the absence of *uti possidetis* from the records of the Paris Conference 1919 see Lalonde, *Determining Boundaries in a Conflicted World* 62. For the debates on including self-determination in the UN Charter which did not consider *uti possidetis,* see generally Library of Congress, *Documents of the United Nations Conference on International Organization, San Francisco, 1945,* vol. III (United Nations Information Organizations 1945); L. M. Goodrich, E. I. Hambro and World Peace Foundation, *Charter of the United Nations: Commentary and Documents* (World Peace Foundation 1949); Antonio Cassese, *Self-determination of Peoples: A Legal Appraisal* (Cambridge University Press 1995) 37–43; Shaw, *Title to Territory in Africa* 59–91. For the debate related to the inclusion of self-determination in the Atlantic Charter 1941, in which also no reference was made to *uti possidetis,* see United States Congress, Senate Committee on Foreign Relations and Dept of State, *A Decade of American Foreign Policy: Basic Documents, 1941–49* (US Govt Print Off 1950).

[116] Cassese, Self-determination of Peoples 25.

Nonetheless, Naldi argued in his commentary on the *Frontier Dispute* that it is not unreasonable to assert that *uti possidetis* was a customary rule of international law at the time of African independence.[117] He provided as follows an account of state practice allegedly supporting his contention:

> Nevertheless, the principle has not been confined to Latin America but has become of universal application. It was adopted by the newly emancipated African States. It has been invoked in disputes between Asian States. It has also found expression in Europe, in Principle III of the Helsinki Final Act 1975. And it has been recognised by international agreements of a universal character, namely Article 62, paragraph 2(a) of the Vienna Convention on the Law of Treaties 1969 and Article 11 of the unratified Vienna Convention on Succession of States in Respect of Treaties 1978. There was therefore some justification for the Chamber stating that *uti possidetis* is a general principle.[118]

This list contains no evidence to support the above finding. First and foremost, the African practice mentioned by Naldi at the top of his list does not count as justification for the Chamber's finding that *uti possidetis* is a general principle 'at that time'; i.e. the time of the African decolonization. Practice that counts at African decolonization should have taken place before that time. Second, the other instances of state practice mentioned by Naldi did not involve *uti possidetis,* as we shall presently see.

The 'disputes between Asian States' to which Naldi refers are the *Temple Case* and the *Rann of Kutch Arbitration*.[119] Those are not cases in which *uti possidetis* was applied. Indeed, they were both cases where particular agreements were found to entirely dispose of the matter in question. It is well established that when boundary delimitation is fully governed by a treaty *uti possidetis* does not apply.[120] In the *Rann of Kutch Arbitration* it was found that:

> Pursuant to the Agreement of 30 June 1965, the Tribunal is called upon to determine the border between India and Pakistan in the light of their respective claims and of the evidence produced before it. The Agreement does not include a rule analogous to the principle known as *uti possidetis,* under which the administrative or other boundaries existing on a postulated historical date are to be ascertained and given effect by the Tribunal, nor have the Parties later agreed on such a date.[121]

[117] Naldi, 'The Case Concerning the Frontier Dispute' 898–9.
[118] *Ibid.* 898.
[119] *Ibid.* 898, fn 27.
[120] Shaw, *International Law* 528–9.
[121] *Rann of Kutch Arbitration* (n 109) Opinion of the Chairman 527–8.

In his dissenting opinion Judge Ales Bebler agrees with the tribunal that neither of the two parties 'can now repudiate the legal consequences of any express agreement or express recognition of the State whose successor it is'.[122] Notably, Judge Bebler referred to 'the readiness of African States to accept the boundaries of colonial administrative boundaries as their national boundaries' and considered it to form a *repetition* of a *Latin American* principle and not an application of a general principle of law.[123] An early commentary on the *Rann of Kutch* observed appositely that that case 'was decided exclusively on facts' and 'the Award did not enunciate or expound principles of international law other than incidentally'.[124] In the *Temple Case*, the ICJ found that the dispute had its origins in the boundary settlements of 1904–8 between France, then conducting the foreign relations of Indo-China (Cambodia), and Siam (Thailand). The Court found that the Treaty of 13 February 1904 established the general character of the frontier and considered it to form the grounds of the delimitation.[125] Additionally, it was found that the disputed map of 1808 was accepted by Thailand by conduct. The dispositif reads in part:

> Even if there were any doubt as to Siam's acceptance of the map in 1908, and hence of the frontier indicated thereon, the Court would consider, in the light of the subsequent course of events, that Thailand is now precluded by her conduct from asserting that she did not accept it. She has, for fifty years, enjoyed such benefits as the Treaty of 1904 conferred on her, if only the benefit of a stable frontier.[126]

With a view to the above, it is not possible to agree with Naldi that the *Temple Case* is an example of the cases in which *uti possidetis* was invoked. Nor is it possible to agree with the finding of Shaw that although the principle of *uti possidetis* is not in terms referred to in *the Temple Case* 'it is clear that the Court and the parties operated on the basis of it'.[127]

The Helsinki Final Act 1975 asserts the principle of the inviolability of frontiers, not *uti possidetis*. *Uti possidetis* is the principle that, historically, upgraded Spanish administrative borderlines on independence into international boundaries. Currently, it designates, in the absence of agreement to the contrary in Spanish America, or by agreement elsewhere, the

---

[122] *Ibid.*, Dissenting Opinion of Judge Ales Bebler 452.
[123] *Ibid.* 448.
[124] I. G. Wetter, 'The Rann of Kutch Arbitration' (1971) 65 *AJIL* 346, 349.
[125] *Temple of Preah Vihear Case* (Merits) [1962] ICJ Rep 6, 32.
[126] *Ibid.*
[127] Shaw, 'The Heritage of States' 105.

boundaries to be respected in the event of decolonization.[128] In contrast, the inviolability of frontiers is the law doctrine that proscribes assaulting international boundaries militarily. As such, it is a subset of the prohibition of the use of force in international law. Article III of the Helsinki Final Act, markedly entitled 'inviolability of frontiers', reads in part: 'The participating States regard as inviolable all one another's frontiers as well as the frontiers of all States in Europe and therefore they will refrain now and in the future from assaulting these frontiers.'[129] Even as such acts violating frontiers may or may not aim at disrupting the territorial integrity of states, the principle of inviolability of frontiers is occasionally confused with the principle of territorial integrity. Remarkably, Shaw finds in the Helsinki Final Act the example where the principle of inviolability of frontiers is stated distinctly without being confused with the principle of territorial integrity.[130]

Likewise, the claim that Article 62, Paragraph 2(a) of the Vienna Convention on the Law of Treaties 1969 and Article 11 of the Vienna Convention on Succession of States in Respect of Treaties 1978 are treaty provisions embodying *uti possidetis* is unsubstantiated. Both articles provide essentially for an exception to the doctrine of *rebus sic stantibus*.[131] They state that a fundamental change of circumstances may not be invoked as a reason for terminating or withdrawing from a treaty that establishes a boundary. Additionally, while *uti possidetis* applies on decolonization, those articles singularly disapply at that time. This is because Article 16 of the Vienna Convention on Succession of States in Respect of Treaties exempts newly independent states from the obligation to maintain boundary treaties in force. This brings us to the end of Naldi's list, and to the end of his contention that the finding of the ICJ Chamber that *uti possidetis* was a general principle of law at the time of African independence is justifiable.

Notably, Naldi did not include the *Aaland Islands Case* in his list. The reason for this conspicuous omission is that this landmark case is not

---

[128] Moore, *Memorandum on Uti Possidetis* 20, 40; Shaw, 'The Heritage of States' 97; Lalonde, *Determining Boundaries in a Conflicted World* 104.

[129] Article III, Conference on Security and Co-operation in Europe Final Act, Helsinki, 1 August 1975.

[130] Shaw, *Title to Territory in Africa* 181.

[131] O. Corten and P. Klein, *The Vienna Conventions on the Law of Treaties: A Commentary* (Oxford University Press, USA 2011) 1424; Mark E. Villiger, *Commentary on the 1969 Vienna Convention on the Law of Treaties* (Martinus Nijhoff 2009) 776; Malcolm Shaw, 'Boundary Treaties and their Interpretation' in Eva Rieter and Henri de Waele (eds.), *Evolving Principles of International Law: Studies in Honour of Karel C Wellens* (Martinus Nijhoff 2012) 242.

open to any interpretation to the effect that *uti possidetis* is a general principle of law. On the contrary, the *Aaland Islands Case* could be cited to show that at the time when it was determined *uti possidetis* was not recognized as a general principle of law. This argument is expanded below.

First, if *uti possidetis* were a general principle of law at the time of determining the *Aaland Islands Case* it would have been invoked, *inter alia*, by Finland. This is because the Aaland Islands fall within the borders inherited by Finland from Russia. Consequently, if *uti possidetis* applies, Finland would have argued that this principle worked on the independence of Finland to upgrade the administrative boundaries it had within Russia into international frontiers, resulting in the inclusion of the Aaland Islands within the territories of independent Finland. Additionally, the Commission of Jurists and the Rapporteurs did not refer to *uti possidetis* in their deliberations. Bearing in mind that those two bodies of jurists were free to consider any principle of law, even if it was not invoked by the parties, the Commissioners and the Rapporteurs would have exercised their exceptional latitude to draw on *uti possidetis* if it were a general principle of law at that time. It is instructive that in the entire splendid exercise of judicial reasoning that was assumed in the *Aaland Islands Case, uti possidetis* was conspicuous only by its absence.[132]

Second, the Commission of Jurists concluded that if the state is not yet fully formed, the transition from a *de facto* to a *de jure* situation tends to lead to readjustments between the members of the international community and to alterations in their territorial and legal status.[133] The Commission referred to situations when a state is 'not yet fully formed', 'not definitively constituted', 'undergoing transformation or dissolution', or at a state of formation because of war situations warranting readjustments between states. In those circumstances, the state undergoes a constitutive phase analogous to decolonization. Consequently, the finding of the Commission could be interpreted to mean that at stages comparable to decolonization international law tends to allow boundary readjustments as opposed to restricting them. In other words, the finding means that there was no general principle of law, whether expressed in terms of *uti possidetis* or not, that stabilizes boundaries at the time of sovereign transition.

---

[132] LNOJ (1920) Sp Supp 3 Report of the International Commission of Jurists 5.
[133] *Ibid.* 6.

## 1.4. Whether *uti possidetis* could otherwise be of normative value

The finding in the *Frontier Dispute* that *uti possidetis* is a general principle of law is sometimes defended unassumingly on the basis that it is viable for a court of law to arrive at that conclusion through cognitive reasoning inherent in the judicial function.

Even as Shaw did not contend specifically that state practice supports the existence of *uti possidetis* as a general principle of law,[134] he found it possible for the ICJ Chamber in the *Frontier Dispute* to arrive at that conclusion. He based his finding on three arguments. First, that it is normal for courts 'to move step by step from examining a set of facts, to inferring from them a legal principle expressed in generalizable form, to applying that principle to a set of facts deemed analogous to, but not identical with, the original scenario'.[135] Second: 'It is not unusual for legal concepts over time to alter their meaning or emphasis as new circumstances arise.'[136] Here Shaw argues that the principle 'intended in Latin America to forestall any renewal of European colonization upon the basis that parts of the continent constituted *terra nullius*' altered its emphasis 'to prevent boundary conflicts as between the successor states of the Spanish Empire'.[137] Third, 'a new norm of customary law would require a lower level of evidential support where there is in existence no prior contradictory norm than would be the case where it is sought to overturn or seriously modify an existing norm'.[138]

Ratner, although disagreeing with Shaw on the applicability of *uti possidetis* outside the context of decolonization, is of the same understanding as Shaw that *uti possidetis* is having the normative content accorded to it in the *Frontier Dispute*. He argued that *uti possidetis* draws its value form two considerations: first, the universally agreed policy of orderly decolonization that it served, and, secondly, the lack of competing norms of self-determination.[139]

Evidently, those arguments presuppose that the ICJ Chamber in the *Frontier Dispute* had in actuality applied established rules of judicial reasoning and that the finding in question was the result of the application of such rules. On examining the approach adopted by the ICJ Chamber,

---

[134] Shaw, 'The Heritage of States' 100; Shaw, 'Peoples, Territorialism and Boundaries' 493.
[135] Shaw, 'Peoples, Territorialism and Boundaries' 499.
[136] *Ibid.* 492.
[137] *Ibid.*
[138] *Ibid.* 497.
[139] Ratner, 'Drawing a Better Line' 614.

it immediately becomes clear that this assumption is unjustifiable. The course taken by the ICJ Chamber in the *Frontier Dispute* has nothing to do with recognized tenets of cognitive reasoning. Three reasons are cited in support of this conclusion:

First, when a principle of law is designated by parties to a treaty as applicable to their dispute, that principle constitutes 'the law for the parties' and the Court has only one duty, which is to apply that law principle.[140] This doctrine derives from the maxim *pacta sunt servanda*, reinstated in Article 26 of the Vienna Convention on the Law of Treaties 1969. Its implication on the judicial function is provided for in Article 38(1)(a) of the ICJ Statute, which stipulates that the Court 'shall apply international conventions, whether general or particular, establishing rules expressly recognized by the contesting states'. When the meaning of the recognized law principle is ambiguous or disputed, the Court is entitled to embark on a second task of interpreting the principle 'to determine, clarify, and define the concepts involved'.[141] Those are imperative rules that no court of law could sidestep in any circumstances. Their paramount significance was stressed as follows in the *North Sea Continental Shelf Cases*:

> [A]s between the Parties the relevant provisions of the Convention represented the applicable rules of law – that is to say constituted the law for the Parties – and its sole remaining task would be to interpret those provisions, in so far as their meaning was disputed or appeared to be uncertain, and to apply them to the particular circumstances involved.[142]

Astonishingly, the ICJ Chamber did not follow those rules. The principle of intangibility of inherited frontiers was recognized as applicable law by the disputant states in a particular convention and hence should have been applied. However, the Chamber laid the principle recognized by the parties beside another one, namely *uti possidetis*, to decide whether the latter squared with the former or not. On concluding that the two principles corresponded, the ICJ Chamber decided to apply the one it knew better. This exercise has nothing to do with the judicial technique explained above. Nor is it justified by judicial discretion. While the Court might desist from engaging its judicial function in its

---

[140] See Alain Pellet, 'Article 38' in A. Zimmermann, C. Tomuschat and K. Oellers-Frahm (eds.), *The Statute of the International Court of Justice: A Commentary* (Oxford University Press 2006) 800–9.

[141] A. G. Guest, 'Logic in the Law' in A. G. Guest (ed.), *Oxford Essays in Jurisprudence: A Collaborative Work* (Oxford University Press 1961) 193.

[142] *North Sea Continental Shelf Cases (Federal Republic of Germany/Denmark, Federal Republic of Germany/Netherlands)* (Judgment) [1969] ICJ Rep 3, 24.

entirety when the law principle specified by the parties is inapplicable or unclear,[143] it cannot avoid applying a provision in a Special Agreement, or any other convention in force, unless that provision violates *jus cogens* norms.

Second, the principle of intangibility of inherited frontiers is clear and was not disputed by the parties to the case. This means that there might not have been an imperious need for the ICJ Chamber to move substantially to the second task of interpretation and clarification. Yet, it is accepted that any law principle or treaty provision, however plain and unambiguous, might require a form of interpretation or to be related to a context. But this was not what the ICJ Chamber did. Even if it was entitled to interpret or clarify the principle of intangibility of inherited frontiers and study its evolution, the Court had instead examined the principle of *uti possidetis*. Only parenthetically did it consult the sources of the principle of intangibility of inherited frontiers and with the view to establishing that *uti possidetis* could not be disregarded.

Third, in carrying out the task of interpretation and explanation the ICJ Chamber depended largely on the rules of logic as opposed to sources of law. It has been explained earlier that the entire ruling was based on a syllogism. Additionally, the Court based its findings as to the law principles involved on assumptions of the 'obvious' and the 'logical' and did not require or examine any evidence. For establishing the existence of legal norms rules of logic are complementary tools of cognitive reasoning, but not a proper alternative to sources of law. Adjudication is not simply a matter of logical argumentation. Indeed, 'what logically may be required is not *ipso facto* legally demanded'.[144] The ICJ Chamber should have examined sources of law to verify the alleged universality of *uti possidetis*, to establish its connection with the phenomenon of independence, and to prove that it actually gave rise to the concept of intangibility of inherited frontiers. Drawing attention to the risks attendant on depending wholly on logic, Justice Robert Jackson of the US Supreme Court warned that 'if the [US Supreme] Court does not temper its doctrinaire logic with a little practical wisdom, it will convert the constitutional Bill of Rights into a suicide pact'.[145] This was what the ICJ Chamber did in the *Frontier Dispute*. The ICJ Chamber simply turned the unobvious into obvious and the illogical into logical, fatefully

---

[143] *Case concerning the Northern Cameroons (Cameroon/United Kingdom)* (Preliminary Objections) [1963] ICJ Rep 15, 38.
[144] T. Halper, 'Logic in Judicial Reasoning' (1968) 44 *Indiana LJ* 33, 36.
[145] *Terminiello v Chicago* (1948) 337 US 1, 37.

leading to the application of a law principle that was neither designated in the Special Agreement nor applicable to the disputant states.

We now turn to the arguments of Shaw and Ratner. There are four reasons why their approach could not justify the finding of the ICJ Chamber that *uti possidetis* is a general principle of law.

First, applying legal principles to facts analogous to the original scenario is indeed inherent to the cognitive judicial process. Even as this methodology of inductive reasoning is more pertinent to the common law system of *stare decisis*, it could be drawn upon for the purposes of verifying the relevance of international law principles that apply to particular situations or bar particular circumstances. The purpose of adapting this technique to international law is to show that the new factual situation in hand corresponds to an old one to which the principle was initially applied. The reliable method to follow in this regard is to cluster the facts of the two situations in opposing categories. Levi described as follows the procedure of doing this:

> [T]he circumstances before the court, are compared with a number of somewhat similar circumstances which have been classified in terms of opposing categories ... The fact cluster before the court could be included within either category ... If reliance is to be on the authority of a prior case for the scope and effectiveness of an announced rule of law now to be applied, then the similarity and difference between the present fact cluster now up for decision and the fact cluster of the prior case are decisive.[146]

The ICJ Chamber did not adopt this methodology. While it analysed in every little detail the original scenario, which is the Spanish-American case, it failed to examine the African set of facts. If the ICJ Chamber adopted this method and compared the African situation to that of Spanish America, it would have found that the two situations could not be more different.[147] However, as explained earlier in this section, the legal principle inferred from the Spanish-American practice is not 'expressed in generalizable form'. *Uti possidetis* was embedded in the special custom of a particular part of Latin America and was conceived and developed as regional custom. A special customary principle remains special and could not be exported to a situation similar to the original one occurring elsewhere. Only general custom could be found applicable to a similar new scenario.

---

[146] E. Levi, 'The Nature of Judicial Reasoning' (1965) 32 *The University of Chicago Law Review* 395, 399–400.

[147] The first four chapters of this book show the differences between the factual and legal situations of the two continents.

Second, *uti possidetis,* and indeed any other law principle, could not be argued to enjoy normative value as the *lex lata* unless its customary or conventional status is confirmed. The fact that a principle was once adopted as a policy of decolonization is of no relevance as to its legal force.[148] It is true that a court of law is entitled to conclude that an 'original *rule of law* has changed its meaning'.[149] However, for such conclusion to stand, it is vital to first establish that as a matter of the *lex lata* the principle concerned enjoys the status of a *rule of law.* In other words, it draws legal force either from a recognized customary origin or from a valid treaty. Consequently, *uti possidetis* could change its name or its compass only if it were a positive principle of law.

Third, it is not true that there exist no legal norms contradictory to *uti possidetis.* This argument is based in particular on an erroneous assumption expressed by Ratner that there is a 'lack of competing norms of self-determination'. Because the principle of *uti possidetis* applies on decolonization it competes with the right to colonial self-determination accorded to colonial peoples and the clean slate principle, both applicable within the same time frame. The right to colonial self-determination entitles the colonial people to disregard pre-existing boundaries and sub-divide the colonial unit. Equally, the clean slate principle relieves the newly independent state of the obligation to maintain boundary treaties, making it possible for such state to lawfully cede territory or claim part of the territory of a neighbouring state. Those two principles are explained in more detail in Chapter 2.[150] The ICJ Chamber assumed that *uti possidetis* was already an established general principle at the time of African decolonization and did not require even the 'lower level of evidential support', let alone the higher level needed 'to overturn or seriously modify' those established norms. The Chamber did not examine the clean slate principle and considered only in passing the relation between *uti possidetis* and self-determination. In manifest underestimation of the preponderant status of the right to colonial self-determination, the ICJ Chamber stated that only 'at first sight' *uti possidetis* conflicts with the right of self-determination and did not show how this conflict was resolved. The Chamber simply went on to posit vaguely that the requirement of stability 'has induced African States judiciously to consent to the respecting

[148] See Helen Ghebrewebet, *Identifying Units of Statehood and Determining International Boundaries* (Peter Lang GmbH 2006) 76.
[149] Levi, 'The Nature of Judicial Reasoning' 399 (emphasis added).
[150] Sections 2.1.1 and 2.1.2.

of colonial frontiers, and to take account of it in the interpretation of the principle of self-determination of peoples.'[151] The right of colonial peoples to self-determination is of *jus cogens* and could not be overturned.[152] Likewise, the clean slate principle is of established traditional status and as such unassailable. While the customary lineage of the clean slate principle was initially doubted, the overwhelming support it attracted at the time of decolonization particularly in Africa led to its inclusion in the Vienna Convention on Succession of States in respect of Treaties.[153]

Fourth, while courts could give prominence to a secondary role of a principle in a new application, this was not what the ICJ Chamber in the *Frontier Dispute* was intending. Nor was it what the Chamber actually did. In the *Frontier Dispute,* the Court acted on the assumption that prevention of boundary disputes, as opposed to *terra nullius*, was already the primary purpose of *uti possidetis*.

### 1.5.    Scholarly critique of the finding that *uti possidetis* is a general principle

Despite the gratuitous support in legal literature for the finding of the ICJ Chamber in the *Frontier Dispute*, the conclusion that *uti possidetis* is a general principle of law is not without critics.

Lalonde contended in her monograph on *uti possidetis* that the principle did not acquire customary status even in Latin America itself. She stated: 'it appears difficult to characterize *uti possidetis juris* as a rule of customary law. Indeed state practice does not reveal the necessary uniformity and consistency, nor does it indicate that the republics (of Latin America) felt in any way compelled to adhere to the principle of *uti possidetis juris* – all essential preconditions of customary law'.[154] In similar vein, Ratner opined that: 'And the mere presence of *uti possidetis* in constitutions, bilateral treaties (including arbitration *compromis*) or Resolution 1514 does not demonstrate *opinio juris*. This gap suggests a

---

[151] *Frontier Dispute* (n 1) 567.

[152] *Legal Consequences for States of the Continued Presence of South Africa in Namibia (South West Africa) notwithstanding Security Council Resolution 276 (1970)* (Advisory Opinion) [1971] ICJ Rep16, 31; Lauri Hannikainen, *Peremptory Norms (Jus Cogens) in International Law: Historical Development, Criteria, Present Status* (Lakimiesliiton Kustannus 1988) 421; Cassese, *Self-determination of Peoples* 133–40.

[153] YBKILC (1974) vol. II, I 84.

[154] Lalonde, *Determining Boundaries in a Conflicted World* 55 and 60. Moore also doubted the customary status of the principle in Spanish America and concluded that it 'has not been so constantly invoked', Moore, *Memorandum on Uti Possidetis* 32.

less than rock-solid basis for a customary norm and at least the possibility that *uti possidetis was* no more than a policy decision adopted to avoid conflicts during decolonization.'[155] Jure Vidmar stated parenthetically in a study on new international borders that 'The position of the Chamber of the ICJ that *uti possidetis* forms a part of customary international law remains controversial'.[156]

In his separate opinion in *Burkina Faso/Niger* Judge Yusuf found the statement of the ICJ Chamber in the *Frontier Dispute*, that *uti possidetis* is a general principle, 'sweeping' and without justification. However, he agrees that *uti possidetis* applies to some situations of decolonization, namely where there are administrative delimitations to be upgraded to international frontiers.[157] Yusuf did not explain how this subsidiary aspect could apply outside Spanish America if *uti possidetis* is not a general principle of law.

The ICJ Chamber had indeed shown scant concern for the conventional means of establishing the customary existence of rules of law through evidencing uniformity of practice or demonstrating the necessary *opinio juris* alluded to by Lalonde and Ratner. However, the African *compromises* referred to by Ratner did not designate *uti possidetis* as the applicable law.[158] Nor did UN General Assembly Resolution 1514 refer to *uti possidetis* as Ratner assumes. The finding in the *Frontier Dispute* is flawed because of an utter absence of state practice related to *uti possidetis* as opposed to a mere failure to demonstrate *opinio juris*.

Even though scholarly statements criticising the finding in the *Frontier Dispute* are a rarity, the scathing nature of those critiques show that after a quarter of a century the *obiter dictum* on *uti possidetis* is not home yet.

In sum, it has been shown in this chapter that *uti possidetis* is not a general principle of law, did not give rise to the concept of intangibility of inherited frontiers, and was as such inapplicable to Africa on independence. The following chapter explains that whereas there was no law principle obligating African states to respect the pre-existing boundaries, the consistent African practice of adhering to those boundaries on independence created a new customary rule *in vacuo*.

---

[155] Ratner, 'Drawing a Better Line' 598.
[156] Jure Vidmar, 'Confining New International Borders in the Practice of Post-1990 State Creations' (2010) 70 *Heidelberg JIL* 319, 324.
[157] Separate Opinion of Judge Yusuf, *Frontier Dispute (Burkina Faso/Niger)* (n 7) 8.
[158] See n 7 for African Special Agreements referring to the principle of intangibility of inherited frontiers.

# The rule of intangibility of inherited frontiers

## 2.1.   The liberty not to respect pre-existing frontiers

On independence, all African states chose to respect the frontiers left by the outgoing colonial administrations and to take them for their new international boundaries. Two reasons, one political and the other legal, make this decision unexpected.

First, at the political level, it is axiomatic that colonial boundaries were drawn without the involvement of African peoples and without having them in mind.[1] Being notorious for dividing congruent communities between different states and juxtaposing antagonistic ones in the same political unit, colonial boundaries were invariably disparaged by early pan-African congregations.[2] The Declaration of the All-African Peoples Conference, Accra, December 1958, avowed that those boundaries should be abolished or adjusted.[3] Touval depicted as follows how the political elite correlated the rejection of the pre-existing boundaries with the abolishing of the colonial legacy:

> The ideas and values prevalent among nationalist leaders at the time of independence predisposed them to view critically the international borders inherited by their states. Their anti-colonial nationalism led them to resent all the arbitrary impositions of colonial rule, borders included. For those

[1] See J. S. Keltie, *The Partition of Africa* (2nd edn, Edward Stanford 1895) 114–35, 207–39; T. Pakenham, *The Scramble for Africa* (Abacus 1991) 141–258; Ian Brownlie, *African Boundaries: A Legal and Dipolmatic Encyclopedia* (1st edn, University of California 1979) 6; Malcolm Shaw, *Title to Territory in Africa: International Legal Issues* (Clarendon 1986) 30.

[2] See the Declaration of the All-African Peoples Conference, Accra, December 1958 and the Declaration of the Pan-African Manchester Conference 1945, reproduced in Colin Legum, *Pan-Africanism: A Short Political Guide* (Praeger 1962) 231.

[3] The opening paragraph of the third part of the Accra Declaration reads 'Whereas artificial barriers and frontiers drawn by imperialists to divide African peoples operate to the detriment of Africans and should therefore be abolished or adjusted'.

who wished to abolish the colonial legacy, a logical corollary would have
been to reject the colonial borders as well.[4]

Second, African states were not legally bound to respect the pre-existing
boundaries. Chapter 1 clarified at length that *uti possidetis* is a special
Spanish-American custom not applicable to Africa on decolonization.
As such, *uti possidetis* gave rise to no obligation on the part of newly
independent African states to respect pre-existing boundaries. The law
doctrines applicable to African independence were the right to colonial
self-determination and the pertinent rules of state succession. Under
those law regimes, it was possible for African states to reject the colonial
boundaries, as we shall presently see.

### 2.1.1.   Colonial self-determination and pre-existing frontiers

The right of colonial peoples to self-determination was the principal
legal doctrine applicable to African decolonization. It is expressed in UN
General Assembly Resolution 1514 (XV) (1960), entitled Declaration on
the granting of Independence to Colonial Countries and Peoples, together
with Resolution 1541 (XV) (1960). Resolution 1514 was of special status
among all the Resolutions of the UN General Assembly and was considered to form an authentic interpretation and amplification of the UN
Charter.[5] By modelling Resolution 1514 on the French Declaration of the
Rights of Man and of the Citizen 1789, African and Asian states intended
to emulate the liberalization role of that iconic instrument.[6] Paragraph 2
of Resolution 1514 gives all peoples subjected to colonial rule the right to
'freely determine their political status and freely pursue their economic,
social and cultural development'.[7] This terse provision was understood

---

[4] Saadia Touval, *The Boundary Politics of Independent Africa* (Harvard University Press
1972) 32.

[5] Obed Asamoah *The Legal Significance of the Declarations of the General Assembly of the
United Nations* (Martinus Nijhoff 1967) 163.

[6] Edward McWhinney, 'Declaration on the Granting of Independence to Colonial
Countries and Peoples' (UN Audiovisual Library of International Law 2008) 1. According
to Rosenstock most of the African and Asian nations regarded Resolution 1514 'as a
document only slightly less sacred than the Charter and as stating the law in relation to
all colonial situations'. R. Rosenstock, 'The Declaration of Principles of International
Law concerning Friendly Relations: A Survey' (1971) 65 *AJIL* 713, 730. Crawford
opined that the Declaration on the Granting of Independence 'has achieved in practice a quasi-constitutional status. Clause 7 of the Declaration places it on a par with the
Universal Declaration of Human Rights and the Charter itself', James Crawford, *The
Creation of States in International Law* (2nd edn, Oxford University Press 1979) 604.

[7] Paragraph 2 of UNGA Res 1514 (XV) (14 December 1960).

THE RULE OF INTANGIBILITY OF INHERITED FRONTIERS    49

to encapsulate an unequivocal commitment to guarantee to all colonial peoples the right to make 'the choice of the international status of the people and the territory where it lives'.[8]

The right of colonial peoples to self-determination provided for in Resolution 1514 pertains exclusively to the respective colonial territory and does not enable the colonial people to claim neighbouring or any other territory. This is because making such a claim violates the territorial integrity of the target country. Sir Francis Vallat, the Special Rapporteur of the International Law Commission (ILC) on the Succession of States in respect of Treaties explained this point as follows: 'Indeed, in the case of a newly independent State which has acquired independence by the exercise of self-determination, it may well be said that it can only acquire the territory in respect of which self-determination has been exercised and not part of the territory of a neighbouring State'.[9] However, the colonial people were under no obligation to preserve the unity of the colony. Paragraph 6 of Resolution 1514 is the crucial paragraph in this regard.

Paragraph 6 provides that 'Any attempt aimed at the partial or total disruption of the national unity and territorial integrity of a country is incompatible with the purposes and principles of the Charter of the United Nations.' Compliance with Paragraph 6 clearly concerns exclusively states bound by the UN Charter, i.e. UN Member States. The paragraph requested those states not to divide colonial units so as not to contradict the purposes and principles of the UN Charter to which they are privy. In UN practice, Paragraph 6 was interpreted, in the light of Chapters XI and XII of the Charter, as imposing a duty on administering states not to divide non-self-governing units. In 1965, when the UK, as the administering power of Mauritius, was about to detach islands from the territory of that country to establish a military base, the UN General Assembly invoked Paragraph 6. General Assembly Resolution 2066 (XX) (1965) considered that 'any step taken by the administering Power to detach certain islands from the Territory of Mauritius for the purposes of establishing a military base would be in contravention of the Declaration, and in particular of Paragraph 6 thereof'.[10] When detaching territory from colonial units for

---

[8] Antonio Cassese, *Self-determination of Peoples: A Legal Appraisal* (Cambridge University Press 1995) 72.

[9] YBKILC (1974) vol. II, I 84; see also the Report presented by Sir Humphrey Waldock, Special Rapporteur to the ILC Session on Articles on Succession of States and Governments in Respect of Treaties, YBKILC (1968) vol. II 93.

[10] UNGA Res 2066 (XX) (16 December 1965).

military purposes became a matter of general concern, the General Assembly issued another Resolution addressed to administering powers. Resolution 2430 (XXIII) (1968) denouncing 'the policy of some of the administering Powers in establishing and maintaining military bases in some of the territories under their administration' considered that policy incompatible with the purposes and principles of the Charter of the United Nations and General Assembly Resolution 1514.[11] While administering states were members of the UN and bound to respect the UN Charter, the colonial peoples were not. Consequently, Paragraph 6 could not implore upon colonial peoples to desist from particular acts on the basis that those acts are incompatible with the purposes and principles of a Charter to which they were not yet party. In UN practice, on no occasion did the General Assembly interpret Paragraph 6 as imposing on colonial peoples a duty to preserve the colonial unit comparable to the duty imposed on administering states.

Yet, Cassese was of the opinion that Paragraph 6 obligated the colonial peoples not to divide their country. Cassese posited that the right to colonial self-determination:

> belongs to the peoples as a whole: if the population of a colonial territory is divided up into various ethnic groups or nations, they are not at liberty to choose by themselves their external status. This is because the principle of territorial integrity should here play an overriding role.[12]

Cassese argued that the letter of Paragraph 6 sustains his view. He also cited in support the preparatory works of the Resolution. Those arguments are examined below.

Paragraph 6 of the Resolution did not mention expressly the entity prevented from aiming to disrupt the territorial integrity of a country. As such, the letter of the Paragraph does not establish the opinion of Cassese, nor does it bear out the opposing stand. However, the only law principle mentioned expressly in the paragraph is the principle of territorial integrity. Indeed, the principle of territorial integrity is of 'overriding role' if the colonial people claims neighbouring territory or if the colonial power intends to divide the colony. In those two instances, the principle of territorial integrity prevails and proscribes the intended action. However, this principle is of no relevance and is not offended in the slightest if the colonial people decides, unaided, to sub-divide the colonial unit.[13] While in domestic law a warning

---

[11]  UNGA Res 2430 (XXIII) (18 December 1968).
[12]  Cassese, *Self-determination of Peoples* 72.
[13]  Malcolm Shaw, 'The Heritage of States: The Principle of Uti Possidetis Juris Today' (1996) 67 *British YBK Int'l L* 75, 143–4; see Section 5.1.3, text to footnotes 33–5.

against trespass does not restrain the proprietors, in international law a call not to disrupt the territorial integrity of a colony does not admonish the colonial people. Consequently, the caveat in Paragraph 6, that any attempt aimed at disrupting the national unity and territorial integrity of a country violates the Charter, concerns exclusively third states.

Most prominent among the preparatory works referred to by Cassese is the Guatemalan proposal. Guatemala proposed adding an addendum to read: 'the principle of self-determination of peoples may in no case impair the right of territorial integrity of any state or its right to recovery of territory'.[14] The Guatemalan proposal provides no particular support to the central idea argued by Cassese that the right of colonial self-determination pertains to the colonial unit as is. In particular, the right to recovery of territory, the only discernible addition introduced by the Guatemalan proposal, involves reshaping the colonial unit by its people as opposed to keeping it unchanged. The focus of Guatemala's proposal was the principle of territorial integrity, which was already sufficiently emphasized in the agreed text. When Indonesia highlighted this point, rightly arguing that the addendum adds no meaning, the proposal was withdrawn.[15] The support of the Socialist Bloc to the idea of adhering to colonial boundaries, referred to by Cassese in the context of citing the preparatory works, might have influenced the decision of newly independent states at political level.[16] However, bearing in mind the lack of support to this position by the Western states it is difficult to accept that the singular socialist standpoint formed an authentic interpretation of Paragraph 6.

In a nutshell, even if the right to colonial self-determination, as expressed in Resolution 1514, does not amount to a licence to claim neighbouring territory, it does not prevent the colonial people from ignoring the pre-existing boundaries if they decide to subdivide their own country.

### 2.1.2.    State succession and pre-existing frontiers

The ICJ Chamber in the *Frontier Dispute* posited that African states were bound to respect pre-existing frontiers by a general rule of international law applicable in the event of state succession. The Chamber found that:

> There is no doubt that the obligation to respect pre-existing international frontiers in the event of a State succession derives from a general rule of

[14]  UN YBK 1960, 48.
[15]  *Ibid.*
[16]  Cassese, *Self-determination of Peoples*, 72–3.

international law, whether or not the rule is expressed in the formula *uti possidetis*.[17]

Drawing only vaguely on state succession, this statement hardly identifies the rule that the ICJ Chamber found to be applicable. However, rules applicable at state succession generally stem from principles governing succession to treaties. This is because succession to treaties forms the core and most regulated area of the law of state succession. The 1978 Vienna Convention on Succession of States in Respect of Treaties, which protects treaties including boundary treaties during state succession, is the principal convention in this regard. Article 11(a) of this Convention provides that a succession of states does not as such affect a boundary established by a treaty. When read with Article 62(2)(a) of the Vienna Convention on the Law of Treaties 1969, it is concluded that state succession does not form grounds for terminating or withdrawing from a boundary-establishing treaty even if state succession is considered to amount to a fundamental change of circumstances.

However, those general rules of state succession do not apply to newly independent states. This is because the right of newly independent states to declare *tabula rasa* pursuant to the clean slate principle prevails over the obligation to respect boundary treaties on state succession. The clean slate principle entitles newly independent states to denounce treaties concluded by the metropolitan administrations in respect of the territory the subject of state succession.[18] Article 16 of the Vienna Convention on Succession of States in respect of Treaties 1978 provides that:

> A newly independent State is not bound to maintain in force, or to become a party to, any treaty by reason only of the fact that at the date of the succession of States the treaty was in force in respect of the territory to which the succession of States relates.

Even as a succession of states does not in general affect a boundary established by a treaty, this article entitles newly independent states to do as they please with boundary-establishing treaties. Consequently, and unlike what the ICJ Chamber in the *Frontier Dispute* found, there is no general rule of international law for newly independent states 'to respect pre-existing international frontiers in the event of a State succession'. While the right of colonial people to self-determination gives a newly

[17] *Frontier Dispute (Burkina Faso/Mali)* (Judgment) [1986] ICJ Rep 554, 566.
[18] See Arnold McNair, *The Law of Treaties* (Clarendon 1961) 601; Oscar Schachter, 'State Succession: The Once and Future' (1992–1993) 33 *Virginia Journal of Int'l Law* 253, 256–7.

independent state the choice to subdivide its own territory, the clean slate principle allows that state to disregard a treaty in force establishing the boundaries of that territory.

The clean slate principle is a traditional law doctrine in its own right and not a mere manifestation of the comparatively recent right to colonial self-determination. It was applied to the earlier cases of decolonization of the United States of America and the Spanish-American republics.[19] Notably, the UN Secretariat gave an opinion in 1947 relieving Pakistan, on its secession, from the obligation to abide by the UN Charter. It was found that 'The territory which breaks off, Pakistan, will be a new State; it will not have the treaty rights and obligations of the old State, and will not, of course, have membership in the United Nations'.[20] The clean slate principle was confirmed by the right to colonial self-determination when it emerged in the twentieth century to enable the newly independent states to avoid inheriting the colonial boundaries if they so wished. Sir Francis Vallat clarified this point as follows:

> the 'traditional' principle that a 'new State' begins its treaty relations with a clean slate, if properly understood and limited, was in the opinion of the Commission more consistent with the principle of self-determination as it is applicable in the case of newly independent States ... the Commission was of the opinion that the main implication of the principle of self-determination in the law concerning succession in respect of treaties was precisely to confirm the traditional clean slate principle as the underlying norm for cases of newly independent States or for cases that may be assimilated to them.[21]

Indeed Somalia exercised the right to start with a clean slate, rejected all three treaties delimiting its boundaries with Ethiopia and Kenya, and maintained this position long after independence. Entering strong reservations with regard to the part related to the boundary regime of the report of the ILC and the report of the Sixth Committee,[22] the delegation of Somalia to the 27th Session of the UN General Assembly 1972–3 stated:

---

[19] Francis Vallat, YBK Int'LLC (1974) vol. II, I, 211. The clean slate principle was also applied to earlier cases of secession of Belgium from the Netherlands, Ireland from Great Britain, Finland from Russia, and Pakistan from India. Likewise, it applied to the creation of Panama, Poland and Czechoslovakia, *ibid.*

[20] YBK Int'LLC (1962) vol. II Document A/CN 4/149 and Add. l para. 3, 101.

[21] Official Records of the General Assembly (n 21), Plenary Meetings 169.

[22] YBK Int'l LC (1972) vol. II document A/8710/Rev I 219; Official Records of the General Assembly, Twenty-seventh Session, Annexes, agenda item 85 document A/8892 sect. Ill B.

> The Somali Democratic Republic does not recognize the legal validity of treaties concluded between other parties against the interests and without the consent of its people. As far as my country is concerned, we consider these treaties devoid of any legality since they were stipulated between foreign colonial Powers without the supreme will, or even the knowledge, of our people. The treaties to which the report refers with regard to my country are probably the 1897 Anglo-Ethiopian Treaty, the 1908 Italo-Ethiopian Treaty and the 1924 Anglo-Italian Treaty, none of which the Somali Democratic Republic recognizes for the reasons I have just stated.[23]

Even as the OAU did not support the Somali position, Somalia could not be faulted for insisting on exercising her legal right. The OAU pursued a policy of persuasion to prevail on Somalia to respect the inherited boundaries, as we shall see in Chapter 3.[24]

The issue of the applicability of the clean slate principle to Africa was examined in *Guinea-Bissau/Senegal*.[25] Guinea-Bissau objected to the Agreement of 1960 signed by France and Portugal, which pertained to the boundary in dispute, on the grounds that on independence Guinea-Bissau's Peoples' Assembly declared *tabula rasa*.[26] Guinea-Bissau further contended that the disputant states could not draw rights under this Agreement unless they are acting as successors of France and Portugal. As such, it was argued by Guinea-Bissau, *uti possidetis* does not apply to the boundary created by that treaty because the boundary itself is non-existent. The tribunal upheld in principle the argument that the 1960 Agreement could not be applied to a state that declared *tabula rasa*. Nonetheless, the tribunal added, if a state accepts to adhere to the idea of automatism in the succession to boundary treaties as an exception to the *tabula rasa* principle, then boundary treaties bind that state.[27] Based on this conclusion the tribunal found that the Agreement binds Guinea-Bissau because Guinea-Bissau 'recognized the principle of the African *uti possidetis* proclaimed by the Organization of African Unity, and ... reiterated it expressly in the present arbitration'.[28] The tribunal

---

[23] *Ibid.*, Plenary Meetings, 209 1st meeting, para. 9 ff.
[24] Section 3.1.4.
[25] *Arbitral Award of 31 July 1989 (Guinea-Bissau/Senegal)* [1995] ICJ Rep 1, 49.
[26] *Ibid.* 131.   [27] *Ibid.*
[28] In his Dissenting Opinion, Judge Bedjaoui found that there was no way for the 1960 Agreement between France and Portugal to apply to Guinea-Bissau unless the agreement became part of Guinea-Bissau's domestic law by being published in Guinea-Bissau by the Portuguese authorities. This contention has no base in law. Publishing a treaty by the metropolitan administration in the colonial territory does not change the fact that that treaty was concluded by the metropolitan state. Nor does it render that treaty

had clearly recognized the right of Guinea-Bissau to avail itself of the clean slate principle and denounce the 1960 Agreement. Yet again, the tribunal had rightly pointed out Guinea-Bissau's recognition of the OAU proclamation as the source of the obligation of Guinea-Bissau. The tribunal could be faulted only in referring to the African rule as 'the principle of the African *uti possidetis*' thus equating the African custom with the Spanish-American principle.

The absence of any law principle to obligate African states to inherit the colonial frontiers was established in the *Dubai-Sharjah Arbitration*. In that case the tribunal stated *obiter* that African states 'could of course, have adopted quite a different attitude and have rejected such boundaries'.[29] While the principle of *uti possidetis* was not applicable to Africa at the time of decolonization, the right to colonial self-determination and the clean slate principle made it possible for African states to denounce the pre-existing alignments if they so wished.

## 2.2.    Why African states chose to respect pre-existing frontiers

Despite the fact that the African decision to respect the colonial frontiers was not in fulfilment of a legal obligation, lawyers hardly cared to study its motivations and consequences.[30] Bowett noted briefly the justifications given at the meetings of the OAU for accepting the inherited boundaries.[31] However, he did not explain why while all vestiges of imperialism were ruthlessly removed 'this one particular remnant of colonialism, the frontier, is zealously safeguarded' by African states.[32] Brownlie considered the African move as the way things tended to be without providing any further clarification. He stated: 'It is a fact that a high proportion of independence

---

binding on state succession. Because Guinea-Bissau was entitled to declare *tabula rasa* on boundary treaties on independence if the *tabula rasa* was not qualified by the African rule it would have rendered the 1960 Agreement unenforceable against Guinea-Bissau even if that agreement was published by the Portuguese authorities in Guinea-Bissau. Dissenting Opinion of Judge Bedjaoui, *Guinea-Bissau/Senegal* (n 25) 124–5.

[29] *Dubai-Sharjah Arbitration Award* ILR vol. 91(1981) 543, 578.
[30] Conversely, historians and political scientists did write about the African decision. See: J. D. Hargreaves, 'Towards a History of the Partition of Africa' (1960) 1 *JAH* 97, 108–9; J. D. Hargreaves, *Prelude to the Partition of West Africa* (Macmillan & Co 1963) 337–8, 347–49; Saadia Touval, 'Treaties, Borders and the Partition of Africa' (1966) VII *JAH* 279, 293.
[31] D. W. Bowett, 'Self-determination and Political Rights in the Developing Countries' (1966) 60 *PASIL* 129, 130.
[32] *Ibid.*

movements have adopted the parcels of colonial administration as the units for self-determination ... There is nothing good or bad about this: it is simply the way things tended to happen'.[33] Bedjaoui presented a superficial explanation for the African decision. In a report to the ILC he suggested that the practice 'was inspired by realism and political wisdom'. He stated: 'Colonial administrative boundaries were made international boundaries in an effort to avoid throwing the political map of Africa into dangerous confusion.'[34] However, Bedjaoui did not explain why accepting those arbitrary boundaries was a judicious decision that would lead to stability, not an ill-advised move liable to trigger struggles for unifying divided ethnic groups. In fact Bedjaoui was not sure that there was no rule of law obligating African states to accept the inherited boundaries. In this regard, he invited the ILC 'to consider whether a rule exists and, if so, how it should be stated'.[35]

Some scholars were suspicious, bordering on cynical, of the objectives of the decision. Mutua opines that the African decision to inherit the colonial boundaries was driven by the desire of African elites not to give up privileges that come with controlling the inherited state.[36] Likewise, Irele asserts that African authoritarian rulers decided to inherit the colonial state because they wanted to maintain the colonial arsenal of laws that prohibited freedoms of assembly and movement.[37]

On a closer look at the motivation behind the decision of African states to respect the inherited boundaries, the pursuit of internal legitimacy and the quest for international recognition are identified as the *raisons d'être* behind that historical action. These two reasons are studied below.

### 2.2.1.    The pursuit of internal legitimacy

African states did not encounter on independence the problem of *terra nullius* faced in Spanish America.[38] Even if anti-imperial rhetoric

[33] Brownlie, *African Boundaries*, 9.

[34] YBK Int'l LC (1968) vol. II, 112–13. This statement was echoed later in the *Frontier Dispute* when it was found that 'The essential requirement of stability ... has induced African States judiciously to consent to the respecting of colonial frontiers', *Frontier Dispute* (n 17) 567.

[35] YBK Int'l LC (1968) vol. II, 113.

[36] Makau wa Mutua, 'Why Redraw a Map of Africa: A Moral and Legal Inquiry' (1994–1995) 16 *Mich JIL* 1113, 1119.

[37] Abiola Irele, 'The Crisis of Legitimacy in Africa' [1992] *Dissent* 296, 298.

[38] See the *Case of the Colombian-Venezuelan Frontier (Colombia/Venezuela)* (1922) IV RIAA 223, 228; *Western Sahara* (Advisory Opinion) [1975] ICJ Rep12, 39. Also see C. H. Alexandrowicz, 'The Juridical Expression of the Sacred Trust of Civilization' (1971) 65

continued to define pan-Africanism long after actual decolonization, the return of colonial rulers the likes of General Flores was not feared. The new independent status of African states was fully guaranteed by international law. When Belgium intervened in the Congo after independence, in the only incident of its kind, the UN took it upon itself to face the situation. The UN Security Council (UNSC) Resolution 143 (1960) called upon the Government of Belgium 'to withdraw its troops from the territory of the Republic of Congo'.[39] The UN Secretary General was authorised by that Resolution to provide the Government of the Republic of the Congo with such military assistance until the national security forces were able to meet fully their tasks. Yet, while they faced no foreign threat on their independence comparable to that encountered by their Spanish-American counterparts, African states were challenged from within by a profound crisis of legitimacy.

The new African state needed to convince its internal populace that the artificial political unit left by the former colonial power was legitimate and should be the locus of their allegiance. While in Europe the state derives its legitimacy from either an historical ruling dynasty or a developed sense of nationhood, these two legitimizing factors were missing in Africa.[40] As a result, the new African states adhered to the pre-existing frontiers being the only 'tangible' reality it had, considered them intangible, and adopted them for a substitute principle of legitimacy.

Kapil, Touval and Shaw examined the African decision to respect the pre-existing frontiers and concluded that it was taken in pursuit of a legitimizing factor. Kapil identified the legitimizing role of colonial frontiers and considered it a pre-requisite of political modernization in independent Africa. He stated:

> The current limits of territorial authority have become, therefore, essential reference points in the definition of a nontraditional concept of political legitimacy. Thus even if the boundaries are objectively superimposed across traditional interaction systems, the goal of political modernization requires the affirmation of their permanence.[41]

---

AJIL 149, 153; Separate Opinion of Judge Yusuf, *Frontier Dispute (Burkina Faso/Niger)* (Judgment) [2013] ICJ Rep 1, 4.

[39] UNSC Res 143 (14 July 1960) UN Doc S/RES/143; see also UNSC Res 146 (1960) (9 August 1960) UN Doc S/RES/4549 and UNSC Res 161 (21 February 1961) UN Doc S/RES/4741.

[40] Touval, *The Boundary Politics of Independent Africa* 33; Shaw, *Title to Territory* 27–8; Pierre Englebert, *State Legitimacy and Development in Africa* (Lynne Rienner 2002) 71 ff.

[41] Ravi L. Kapil, 'On the Conflict Potential of Inherited Boundaries in Africa' (1966) 18 *World Politics* 656, 671.

Touval was also as positive in linking the African decision with the quest for legitimacy. For him, since most African states, unlike their European counterparts, were neither nation states nor dynastic states, they suffered from 'vulnerability' and 'fragility'. African states that could not avail themselves of those conventional legitimizing principles had, as Touval says, 'to define themselves according to colonial boundaries'.[42] Shaw agrees with this analysis. He concurs that new states in Africa and elsewhere were not founded on a genuine sense of community like their European counterparts. He opines that the state in Asia, Africa and South America, as compared to Europe,

> precedes the development of territorial nation, but is faced with powerful loyalties generated by sub-State community ties. This creates a crisis of legitimacy, since the State is founded not upon a genuine sense of community, but upon the vagaries and power-ranking of nineteenth century European colonial empires. Thus the emphasis upon the necessity of maintaining colonial frontiers clearly demonstrated by the overwhelming majority of Afro-Asian and South American States can be understood in terms of the necessity of establishing stable legitimacy factors.[43]

Kapil and Shaw, on identifying the crisis of legitimacy as the driving force behind the African move, went further to read the legal implications of inheriting the colonial boundaries. Kapil, writing relatively early on the subject, predicted that the African decision means that 'an African version of the doctrine of *uti possidetis* may, in time, come to constitute the legal basis for determining territorial questions on the continent'.[44] For his part, Shaw foresaw the possibility of the creation of an African territorial regime 'based on the legal validity of the colonial frontiers of independent States'.[45] On the other hand, Touval failed, despite his crystal-clear vision as to the reason behind the African decision, to foresee the emergence of a stable territorial regime as a consequence of that historical move. He thought of the African practice of refraining from advancing territorial claims as simply a transient 'general tendency'. He opined that African governments might soon alter this position 'and demand border rectifications or raise territorial claims'.[46]

---

[42] *Ibid.* 33.
[43] Shaw, *Title to Territory* 92–3.
[44] Kapil, 'On the Conflict Potential of Inherited Boundaries' 671.
[45] Shaw, *Title to Territory* 186. However, Shaw seems to consider 'territorial legitimation' a function of *uti possidetis*, see Shaw, 'The Heritage of States' 97–8.
[46] Touval, *The Boundary Politics of Independent Africa* 271–2.

Although the crisis of legitimacy identified by Kapil, Touval and Shaw was the most important reason behind the African decision, it was not the only reason.

### 2.2.2.  The quest for international recognition

International recognition had three implications for the African state.

First, international recognition is the means through which the African state acquires title to its territory.[47] While in Spanish America the new republics acquired title through state succession,[48] by the time of African independence new law doctrines came into play, largely restricting the operation of the traditional rules of state succession. At the time of the Spanish rule in South America three assumptions formed the basis of the colonial enterprise: a) the colony was considered to form part of the territory of the metropolitan state; b) the legitimacy of Spanish rule in South America and its title as the metropolitan state were not questioned; and c) the right of the metropolitan state to pass title to its colony was unconstrained. All three assumptions had changed by the time the scramble for Africa began and, subsequently, on African independence. As to assumption a), Paragraph 6 of the Principle of Self-determination of the Declaration on Friendly Relations among States provides that 'the territory of a colony or other Non-Self-Governing Territory has, under the Charter, a status separate and distinct from the territory of the State administering it'.[49] The separate status assumed during the colonial stage continues until the people exercise their right to colonial self-determination. Because of the right to colonial self-determination and the right to equal sovereignty a newly independent state is considered 'sufficiently detached from its predecessor'.[50] Regarding assumption b), while imperialism was not tainted with illegality during the eighteenth century, the illegitimacy of colonialism was now well established. An argument that African states derive title to their territories from colonial administrators legitimates retroactively an institution on which law had since passed its final verdict as unjust and

---

[47] Malcolm Shaw, *International Law* (Sixth edn, Cambridge University Press 2008) 448, 492; See also Quincy Wright, 'Recognition and Self-Determination' (1954) 48 *PASIL* 23, 33.

[48] *Case concerning the Land, Island and Maritime Frontier Dispute (El Salvador/ Honduras: Nicaragua intervening)* (Judgment) [1992] ICJ Rep 351, 598.

[49] Declaration on Principles of International Law concerning Friendly Relations and Co-operation among States in accordance with the Charter of the United Nations, UNGA Res 2625 (XXV) (24 October 1970).

[50] Sir Francis Vallat, YBK Int'l LC (1974) vol. II, I, 219.

illegal.[51] Some of the African states that were under a pre-colonial form of organized government could not be considered on independence to have acquired title to their territories for the first time. It has been suggested that those states were recovering independence lost long since.[52] In the cases of states under the Mandate system and some unorthodox cases of colonialism, like that of the Anglo-Egyptian condominium over Sudan, it was unclear whether the administering state, or any particular entity or state, had undivided sovereignty over the administered country in order to be able to pass title on independence.[53] Finally, with respect to assumption c), in general the colonial title acquired by the administering state was found not to be affected by Chapter XI of the UN Charter,[54] and the sovereignty of the administering state over its colony was recognized.[55] Yet, in the decolonization law the right of the metropolitan state to dispose of the territory in question was substantially limited by Article 73(b) of the UN Charter.[56] When the non-self-governing territory attained full measure of self-government, the title of the colonial power to the colonial territory terminated, as opposed to passed, through one of the three means specified in Principle VI of Resolution 1541.

Second, recognition is the unified source of the legal force of the African boundaries regardless of whether they originate in treaties or in administrative divisions. In Spanish America, all boundaries among the Spanish-American republics were administrative lines that were upgraded to international boundaries by operation of the principle of *uti possidetis* and as such they draw their legal force from that principle. In Asia, boundaries born in treaties are considered to draw their legal force from the maxim *pacta sunt servanda,* whereas recognition is considered to form the source of legal force for boundaries with no treaty base. In his dissenting opinion in the *Rann of Kutch* Judge Ales Bebler explains as follows the source of the binding force of non-treaty based boundaries:

> Why are all those boundaries, not born in treaties, binding boundaries? Where resides their legal force? It is obvious that the legal force of such

---

[51] Separate Opinion of Judge *ad hoc* Abi-Saab, *Frontier Dispute* (n 17) 659; Declaration of Judge Bennouna, *Burkina Faso/Niger* (n 38) 95.

[52] See Dissenting Opinion of Judge Moreno-Quintana, *Case concerning Right of Passage over Indian Territory* (Merits) [1960] ICJ Rep 4, 95–6.

[53] Crawford, *The Creation of States* 570–3; V. O'Rourke, *The Judicial Status of the Anglo-Egyptian Sudan* (Johns Hopkins Press 1935) 142–70.

[54] *Western Sahara Advisory Opinion* (n 38) 28.

[55] *Right of Passage Case* (n 52) 39.

[56] Crawford, *The Creation of States* 615.

boundaries is the result of an agreement of the neighbours expressed in their lasting acceptance of a given boundary alignment, be it a tacit acceptance or an outspoken one. The case of a tacit acceptance has acquired, in legal doctrine, the technical term of acquiescence, and the outspoken one the technical term of recognition.[57]

It is doubtful with regard to African states created as a result of the twentieth-century process of decolonization that there is any base in law for differentiating between the sources for the legal force of boundaries born in treaties and boundaries created otherwise. The process of setting colonial treaty-based boundaries is a matter of fact with no significance or importance in international law.[58] What matters in international law is the subsequent process of recognition of those boundaries. Oppenheim clarified that:

> It is through recognition, which is a matter of law, that such new States become a member of the Family of Nations and subject to International Law. As soon as recognition is given, the new State's territory is recognized as the territory of a subject of International Law, and it matters not how this territory is acquired before the recognition.[59]

Consequently, the argument advanced by Judge Bebler that considers recognition the source of legal force for boundaries not born in treaties holds good, at least in the African context, for boundaries established by treaties. When newly independent African states chose to accept the boundaries formerly created by the administering powers, recognition elevated those boundaries into international frontiers regardless of whether they were originally administrative or treaty-based.

Third, recognition assigns legal and moral legitimacy to African boundaries. Legally, recognition serves as the cut-off point that ends a state of affairs lacking in legitimacy and marks the beginning of a lawful situation. Morally, through recognition the colonial boundaries were converted from despised relics of the Berlin Conference to recognized international frontiers.[60] Having in mind the strong abhorrence of African peoples to colonial boundaries and that pan-Africanism was largely weaved of anti-boundary sentiments the shift achieved by recognition is huge.[61]

---

[57] Dissenting Opinion of Judge Ales Bebler, *The Indo-Pakistan Western Boundary (Rann of Kutch) between India and Pakistan* (1968) XVII RIAA 1 448–49.

[58] See Crawford, *The Creation of States* 16.

[59] Lasa Oppenheim, *International Law*, vol. I (1st edn, Longmans 1905) 264.

[60] See generally Margret Kohn, 'Colonialism', *The Stanford Encyclopedia of Philosophy* (Spring 2014).

[61] Touval, *The Boundary Politics of Independent Africa* 56 ff.

As such, it is recognition, not state succession, which endowed the African state with title to its territory. It is recognition, not *uti possidetis*, that upgraded the African colonial boundaries, be they administrative or treaty-based, into boundaries that are respected internationally. Again, it is recognition that transformed the loathed, arbitrary, and artificial political divisions of Africa into the most revered and protected boundaries on earth. To all intents and purposes, an unrecognized African state does not exist, as opposed to merely not having rights and obligations in international law.

Because of those extraordinary implications of recognition in the decolonization epoch, recognition of African states was not simply declaratory. Lauterpacht argued that rising to full international personality could not be automatic. He suggested that someone had to undertake the prior determination of difficult circumstances of fact and law before admitting new subjects to the international community.[62] He concluded that recognition is constitutive but with a legal duty to recognize.[63] During decolonization, recognition was analogous to this conception of Lauterpacht. Recognition of newly independent African states was constitutive with a duty on the UN to recognize an African state properly decolonized.

Even as the existence of a body that determines qualifications of states is not the pattern generally applicable in international law, as Crawford rightly observed,[64] the UN played this exceptional role with regard to the creation of African states. In his separate opinion in the *Advisory Opinion of Western Sahara*, Judge Dillard stated that several pronouncements of the ICJ indicate that 'a norm of international law has emerged applicable to the decolonization' giving the UN and its Resolutions special weight and supremacy.[65] The weight given to admission to the UN General Assembly, and attendant international recognition, formed occasions in which the norm identified by Dillard featured prominently.[66]

In granting the right of self-determination to colonial peoples, Shaw observed, a trend emerged in the UN 'in favour of restricting the notion of "peoples" to the inhabitants of a particular state or colony, that is, to

---

[62] Hersch Lauterpacht, *Recognition in International Law* (Cambridge University Press 1947) 55.

[63] *Ibid.*

[64] Crawford, *The Creation of States* 20.

[65] Separate Opinion of Judge Dillard, *Western Sahara* (Advisory Opinion) (n 38), 121.

[66] John Dugard, *Recognition and the United Nations* (Cambridge University Press 1987) 78; Ian Brownlie, *Principles of Public International Law* (6th edn, Oxford University Press 2003) 93–4.

clearly defined political units'.[67] To put it the other way round, for the UN the population of a colony is preferred to accept that it forms one people, regardless of any circumstances to the contrary, and be prepared to attain independence as one political unit.[68] Automatic admission to membership of the UN General Assembly was guaranteed when the new state accepted the colonially defined territory as the unit for self-determination. Consequently, in granting independence in Africa the UN developed a policy that was decidedly against dismembering the colonial unit.[69] The Ewe, for instance, were divided between British and French Togolands, and were initially aspiring to unite their community by hiving off territory from the two colonies. Soon the Ewe leaders found that it was against UN policy to demand reunification and had to change their tactic. Touval stated that 'When it became doubtful that the principle of ethnic unity could advance their case in the United Nations, the Ewe leaders in the 1950s redefined their aspirations as the reunification of the two Togolands.'[70] In addition to the considerations that related to the smooth completion of the process of decolonization, the UN also had its own concerns.

Article 4(1) of the UN Charter restricts membership in the UN to peace-loving states accepting the obligations in the UN Charter. Additionally, the article emphasizes that such states should be 'in the judgment of the Organization … able and willing to carry out these obligations'. UN Secretary General U Thant referred to this article in the Annual Report of 1967, emphasizing that:

> It is, of course, perfectly legitimate that even the smallest territories, through the exercise of their right to self-determination, should attain independence as a result of the effective application of General Assembly resolution 1514 (XV) on the granting of independence to colonial countries and peoples. However, it appears desirable that a distinction be made between the right to independence and the question of full membership in the United Nations. Such membership may, on the one hand, impose obligations which are too onerous for the 'micro-states' and, on the other hand, may lead to a weakening of the United Nations itself.[71]

---

[67] Shaw, *Title to Territory* 99; and generally 105–34.
[68] Cassese, *Self-determination of Peoples* 59.
[69] Shaw, *Title to Territory* 105–34.
[70] Touval, *The Boundary Politics of Independent Africa* 36.
[71] Introduction to the Twenty-second Annual Report, 15 September 1967, A. Cordier and M. Harrelson (eds.), *Public Papers of the Secretaries General of the United Nations: U Thant*, vol. 7: 1965–1967 (Columbia University Press 1977) 573–4.

Secretary General U Thant referred in his statement to 'micro-states' exceptionally small in area and population like Pitcairn and Nauru. However, because no line of demarcation was drawn this policy was obviously of relevance to all newly independent states aspiring to be admitted to the UN General Assembly. The Northern and Southern Cameroons were denied the alternative of independence and constrained to choose between joining either Cameroon or Nigeria mainly because it was feared they would form 'micro-states'.

As such, African leaders knew that a coveted seat at the UN General Assembly came at a price. Guaranteed membership of the UN presupposes maintaining the unity of the colonial entity and avoiding subdividing it into units that might be found, in the sole judgment of the UN, unable to perform the UN Charter obligations. In return, the UN guarantees to the African state, born in compliance with this reality, automatic admission to the UN General Assembly, recognition of its territorial definition and sovereignty over all its 'national' soil regardless of actual possession.

Jackson referred to the state created in accordance with the above paradigm as the 'juridical state'. He opined that 'The independence and survival of African states is not in jeopardy because their sovereignty is not contingent on their credibility as authoritative and capable political organizations. Instead, it is guaranteed by the international community, especially as embodied in the United Nations'.[72] While the controversial concept of 'juridical state' is predicated on an assumption that the prototype of state sovereignty protects the African state passively, the actions taken by the UN during the crisis of Katanga demonstrate the proactive role played by the UN pursuant to recognition in creating and sustaining the African state.

At the height of the Katanga crisis the UN Security Council issued Resolution 145 (1960) asserting that the Congo was recognized 'as a unit' pursuant to the recommendation to the Security Council for the admission of the Republic of the Congo to UN membership.[73] When Katanga secessionists were feared to tear the Congo apart, the UN Security Council did not stop at deprecating the secessionist activities carried out with the aid of external resources. It went on to declare in Resolution 169 (1961) that 'all secessionist activities against the Republic of the Congo are contrary to the *Loi fondamentale* and Security Council decisions'.[74]

---

[72] Robert H. Jackson, 'Juridical Statehood in Sub-Saharan Africa' (1992) 46 *Journal of Int'l Affairs* 1.

[73] UNSC Res 145 (22 July 1960) UN Doc S/RES/4405.

[74] UNSC Res 169 (24 November 1961) UN Doc S/RES/5002.

The provision 'all secessionist activities' includes secessionist activities with no foreign backing. Furthermore, Resolution 169 declared 'full and firm support for the Central Government of the Congo and the determination to assist that Government, in accordance with the decisions of the United Nations, to maintain law and order and national integrity'.

Commenting on the UN successful effort to prevent Katanga's secession, U Thant stated in a press conference on 4 January 1970 that:

> as far as the question of secession of a particular section of a Member State is concerned, the United Nations' attitude is unequivocal [sic]. As an international organization, the United Nations has never accepted and does not accept and I do not believe it will ever accept the principle of secession of a part of its Member State.[75]

Obviously, U Thant was speaking only to Africa, being the continent subject to the emergent decolonization norm that gave the UN and its Resolutions special weight and supremacy. When a year later Bangladesh seceded from Pakistan, the UN hastened to welcome Bangladesh to its fold.[76]

### 2.3.    The customary status of 'the rule of intangibility of inherited frontiers'

The African state practice of inheriting colonial frontiers on independence, in pursuit of legitimacy and recognition, gave rise to the rule of intangibility of inherited frontiers as a customary rule limited to Africa. The possibility that regional state practice leads to the emergence of special or particular custom is well established in law.[77] To create special

---

[75] UN Monthly Chronicle 36 (Feb 1970) cited in Rupert Emerson, 'Self-determination' (1971) 65 *AJIL* 459, 464.

[76] See generally T. M. Franck and N. S. Rodley, 'After Bangladesh: The Law of Humanitarian Intervention by Military Force' (1973) 67 *AJIL* 275.

[77] *Colombian-Peruvian Asylum Case* (Judgment) [1950] ICJ Rep 266, 277–8; *Right of Passage Case* (n 52) 6. See also Humphrey Waldock, 'General Course on Public International Law' (1962) II *Recueil des Cours de l'Académie de Droit International* 1, 44; Anthony A. D'Amato, 'The Concept of Special Custom in International Law' (1969) 63 *AJIL* 211; Micheal Akehurst, 'Custom as a Source of International Law' (1974–75) 47 *British YBK Int'l L* 1, 28–30; Mark E. Villiger, *Customary International Law and Treaties: A Study of their Interactions and Interrelations with Special Consideration of the 1969 Vienna Convention on the Law of Treaties* (Martinus Nijhoff 1985) 33–4; Lassa Oppenheim, *International Law* ed. by Robert Jennings and Arthur Watts (9th edn, Oxford University Press 1992) 30; Alain Pellet, 'Article 38' in A. Zimmermann, C. Tomuschat and K. Oellers-Frahm (eds.), *The Statute of the International Court of Justice: A Commentary* (Oxford University Press 2006) 762–4. Against: S. P. Sinha, 'Identifying a Principle of International Law Today' (1973) 11 *Canadian YBK Int'l L* 106, 112–16.

custom the same criteria required for general custom, provided for in Article 38(1)(b) of the Statute of the International Court of Justice, must be satisfied.[78] This means the usage in question needs to amount to a settled practice in order to satisfy the *usus* (the objective criterion), and should be accepted as law to satisfy the *opinio juris* (the subjective criterion). The African custom of intangibility of inherited frontiers satisfies both criteria, as we shall presently see.

### 2.3.1.  Satisfying the usus and opinio juris

Six African states attained independence between December 1951 and October 1958. This was the first group of African countries to achieve independence under the auspices of the UN and in accordance with the law of decolonization.[79] All six newly independent states respected the pre-existing frontiers, and were immediately recognized and admitted to the UN. By December 1961, nineteen more states attained independence and they all accepted inheriting the pre-existing frontiers.[80] This usage, consistently followed by all African states that attained independence until 1961 forms 'evidence of a general practice' satisfying the first requirement of Article 38(1)(b) of the ICJ Statute.[81] Now we move to establishing the *opinio juris* required to accompany that practice in order to give rise to customary rule.

The African practice described above is exceptionally uniform. The twenty-five African states referred to above inherited the pre-existing boundaries without exception and with no protest from any quarter. It is established that *uniform* conduct of states is presumed to evince *opinio juris*. Lauterpacht explained that 'all uniform conduct of Governments [should be taken] as evidencing the *opinio juris* except when it is shown that the conduct in question was not accompanied by any such intention'.[82] Judge Sørensen cited this passage with approval in his dissenting

---

[78]  For refuting the contention that the *opinio juris* required for special custom is of a less consensualist nature see Section 4.3.1, text to footnotes 105–7.

[79]  Those states were Libya (1951), Sudan, Morocco, and Tunisia (1956), Ghana (1957), and Guinea (1958).

[80]  See generally Legum, *Pan-Africanism*; see AU list of Member States at www.au.int/en/member_states/countryprofiles (accessed 10 March 2015).

[81]  The use of the word 'general' in this context is criticised as reflective of the failure of the drafters of Article 38(1)(b) of the ICJ Statute to cater for special practice, and as such it is not indicative that only general custom is admitted, Pellet, 'Article 38' 764.

[82]  Hersch Lauterpacht, *The Development of International Law by the International Court* (Grotius Publications 1982) 380.

opinion in *the North Sea Continental Shelf Cases*. Sørensen found that uniform conduct of states with regard to the practice of the continental shelf 'may be taken as sufficient evidence of the existence of any necessary *opinio juris*'.[83] The practice generated by the Geneva Convention on the Continental Shelf 1858, referred to by Sørensen, consisted of particular limited acts. Those were: the adoption of the Convention itself, ratification or accession to the Convention by a considerable number of states, and the fact that no state that had exercised sovereign rights over its continental shelf – in conformity with the provisions of the Convention – was met with protests by other states.[84] On comparing the African practice with the continental shelf practice, it could be easily found that the African practice of intangibility of inherited frontiers was not less uniform. Additionally, while the African practice was exercised with full consensus and harmony, the continental shelf practice was marred by controversies. Apart from Articles 1 to 3, the Convention is not considered to reflect or crystallize customary rules and was as such subject to reservation.[85] The controversy did not exempt Articles 1 to 3 either. Questions of the seaward extent of the shelf, the nature of the rights exercisable, and the kind of natural resources to which these relate, among others, attracted divergent points of view.[86]

Consequently, it is not unreasonable to argue that the African practice of respecting pre-existing frontiers was uniform to the extent required to presume that it evinces *opinio juris*. The uniformity of that practice means that it was 'accepted as law', thus satisfying the subjective criterion of Article 38(1)(b) of the ICJ Statute. However, for the *usus* and *opinio juris* to give rise to custom, they need to spread over a reasonable period of time.

### 2.3.2.    *The requirement of the reasonable period*

The length of the reasonable period considered sufficient for custom to emerge is not authoritatively determined. On surveying the different proposals made, Akehurst found that the adequate period ranges from time immemorial to ten years and even less.[87]

---

[83] Dissenting Opinion of Judge Ad Hoc Sørensen, *North Sea Continental Shelf Cases (Federal Republic of Germany/Denmark, Federal Republic of Germany/Netherlands)* (Judgment) [1969] ICJ Rep 3, 247.

[84] *Ibid.* 246.

[85] Geneva Convention on the Continental Shelf 499 UNTS 311.

[86] *North Sea Continental Shelf Cases* (n 83) 39–41.

[87] Akehurst, 'Custom as a Source of International Law' 16.

In the *Advisory Opinion on the Free City of Danzig and International Labour Organization,* a practice related to the conduct of foreign affairs of the Free City was found to have emerged in a period comparable to that of the African practice.[88] The Treaty of Versailles, 1919, stipulated that the Government of Poland should undertake the conduct of foreign relations of the Free City pursuant to a treaty to be concluded later. The Treaty of Paris, 1919, which was the treaty anticipated to regulate the matter, was not sufficiently detailed on this point. The Permanent Court of International Justice (PCIJ) had to determine the question as to who conducts the foreign relations of the Free City to find out whether the Free City had the legal status required to join the International Labour Organization (ILO). The Court concluded that 'a practice, which seems now to be well understood by both Parties, has gradually emerged', during the period 1920–9, making it 'common ground between Poland and the Free City that the rights of Poland as regards the conduct of the foreign relations of the Free City are not absolute'.[89] In the *North Sea Continental Shelf Cases,* the custom of the continental shelf was found to have been created within the period extending between 29 April 1958, the date of the adoption of the Geneva Convention on the Continental Shelf, and 20 February 1967, the day when the proceedings were brought up.[90] As such, it is not unreasonable to argue that a period of about ten years satisfies this requirement. On this ground, the African practice of respecting the inherited frontiers, which started on the independence of Libya on 24 December 1951, could be assumed to have satisfied, at the close of the height of decolonization in December 1961, the reasonable period required for custom to emerge.

Furthermore, the unanimous acceptance of the practice of respecting the pre-existing frontiers makes it possible to dispense with the requirement of passage of a reasonable period of time. The ICJ held in the *North Sea Continental Shelf Cases* that:

> With respect to the other elements usually regarded as necessary before a conventional rule can be considered to have become a general rule of international law, it might be that, even without the passage of any considerable period of time, a very widespread and representative participation in the convention might suffice of itself, provided it included that of States whose interests were specially affected.[91]

---

[88]  PCIJ Rep Series B No 18, 1.
[89]  *Ibid.* 13.
[90]  *North Sea Continental Shelf Cases* (n 83) 43.
[91]  *Ibid.* 42.

This finding was interpreted to mean that a customary rule emerges rapidly, if: first, participation in the norm concerned was widespread and representative, and, second, the states whose interests are specially affected take part in the practice in question.[92] As to the first requirement, Akehurst concluded that 'the number of States taking part in an act or acts is more important than the time over which the acts are spread'.[93] The fact that by 1961 twenty-five African states adhered to the pre-existing frontiers shows that a large number of states had taken part in the African custom. As such, the first requirement of widespread participation is undoubtedly satisfied.

To find out whether the second requirement is satisfied or not, we need to know whether Morocco and Somalia, which were special cases,[94] are 'specially affected states' and, if so, whether they, nevertheless, participated in the said practice. Morocco, which drew its legitimacy from a dynasty, and Somalia, yearning for a nation, did not need the colonial frontiers to serve any legitimizing purpose. Besides, because they were vying to create bigger states, as opposed to ethnic statelets normally aspired to in Africa, they had no reason to worry about not being admitted to the UN for not being able to satisfy the requirements of Article 4(1) of the UN Charter. In the context of the *North Sea Continental Shelf Cases,* the Court used the term 'specially affected states' to refer to landlocked states that would have no interest in becoming parties to the Convention.[95] It is clear that Morocco and Somalia had no interest in becoming parties to a custom of sanctifying pre-existing frontiers, and should have wished to gain independence within their historical/national boundaries. As such, the two states qualify as 'specially affected states'.

Nonetheless, Morocco and Somalia attained independence within the pre-existing frontiers and participated in the African practice. The fact that after independence the two states laid territorial claims on their respective neighbours did not detract from their respect of the frontiers of independence. While they exercised actual state authority within the inherited frontiers, they merely aspired to include claimed territories within their respective domains.

Although the creation of instant custom is having little support in legal literature,[96] modern international developments have witnessed the rapid

---

[92] Pellet, 'Article 38' 752; Villiger, *Customary International Law and Treaties* 24–5.

[93] Akehurst, 'Custom as a Source of International Law' 16.

[94] See Section 3.1.1, text to footnotes 1–11.

[95] *North Sea Continental Shelf Cases* (n 83) 42; Villiger, *Customary International Law and Treaties* 14.

[96] For the instant custom theory see Bin Cheng, *Custom: The Future of General State Practice in a Divided World in the Structure and Process of International Law: Essays in*

emergence of custom on special occasions of extraordinary unanimity on a new norm. The emergence of the custom pertaining to outer space is an example in hand.[97] Similarly, the African decolonization was a special occasion in the development of the international community that justifies the rapid emergence of the custom of intangibility of inherited frontiers.

## 2.4.   Intangibility of inherited frontiers in legal literature

Before the ruling in the *Frontier Dispute*, lawyers, writing mostly in French, notably Charpentier and Tredano, argued that the intangibility of inherited frontiers is a law principle of universal application.[98]

Charpentier clarified that intangibility of inherited frontiers, inviolability of frontiers, and *uti possidetis* are different doctrines. He argued:

> The only specific meaning of the intangibility principle seems to me to be ... that States must not dispute the validity of the title on the basis of which the boundary is established, even if this title appears somewhat questionable, as can be *uti possidetis*. I believe that this is its only meaning. In other words while the inviolability principle protects territorial integrity, the intangibility principle protects the territorial unit.[99]

For Charpentier the 'intangibility principle', unlike *uti possidetis*, does not allow for questioning of title. While claims to validate title could be advanced under the *uti possidetis* doctrine, and obviously in contravention of the *uti possidetis* boundary, such claims could not be made under the intangibility principle. On this basis Charpentier differentiates also between the doctrines of 'intangibility' and 'inviolability'. He is of the opinion that while the thrust of the doctrine of intangibility is

---

*Legal Philosophy Doctrine and Theory* ed. by Ronald St. J. Macdonald and Douglas M. Johnston (Martinus Nijhoff 1983) 513.

[97] See B. Cheng, 'United Nations Resolutions on Outer Space: "Instant" International Customary Law?' (1965) 5 *Indian JIL* 23. See also B. Langille, 'It's "Instant Custom": How the Bush Doctrine became Law after the Terrorist Attacks of September 11' (2001) 26 *Boston College ICLR* 145, 154–6.

[98] See J. Charpentier, 'Le Problème des Enclaves' in *Société Française pour le Droit International Colloque de Poitiers, La Frontière* (A Pedone 1980) 163; A. B. Trédano, 'Le Principe de l'intangibilité des Frontières Comme Obstacle au Dépassement des Conflits Frontaliers en Afrique' (1985) 9 *Revue Marocaine de Droit et d'Economie de Development* 117. See also A. B. Trédano, *Intangibilité des Frontières Coloniales et Espace Etatique en Afrique*, vol. 47 (Librairie Générale de Droit et de Jurisprudence 1989).

[99] Charpentier, 'Le Problème des Enclaves' 163 translated in Suzanne Lalonde, *Determining Boundaries in a Conflicted World: The Role of Uti Possidetis* (McGill-Queen's University Press 2002) 152.

the prevention of claims counter to the territorial unity, the doctrine of inviolability prohibits forceful actions aimed at disrupting the territorial integrity of a state.

Along similar lines, Tredano differentiates between the implications of *uti possidetis* and the intangibility of inherited frontiers. He stated:

> The request made to the African States to respect the colonial boundaries is acceptable even where juridical titles exist supporting the claims of the plaintiff State. For they are simply requested to accept their colonial territorial inheritance and to refrain from putting forward any claim which might compromise this inheritance and therein lies the difference between the principle of intangibility of frontiers and *uti possidetis*, at least according to Latin American practice.[100]

Obviously, for both writers there is difference between Spanish and African practice. In Spanish America when *uti possidetis* was applied, it was possible to advance claims against the territorial inheritance. For the two lawyers this is not feasible in Africa where the intangibility doctrine applies.

However, the problem with the approach of Charpentier and Tredano is that the two scholars consider the intangibility of frontiers a general principle of law. For them while both law principles are of universal application, Africa opted for the principle of intangibility of inherited frontiers.

Lalonde, influenced by Charpentier and Tredano, also perceives the doctrine of intangibility of inherited frontiers as a principle of universal applicability. For Lalonde it is 'the need to ensure stability in international relations' that gave rise to this doctrine. She gave no further clarification as to how that doctrine emerged. She opined:

> The need to ensure stability in international relations has given rise to an important rule expressed in terms of the intangibility of boundaries. From a strict legal perspective the intangibility principle implies that existing boundaries, whether established by international agreement or through effective occupation, cannot be called into question through the use of force.[101]

Unlike the other two scholars, Lalonde confuses the doctrine of intangibility of inherited frontiers with that of the inviolability of boundaries. The law doctrine that implies that boundaries cannot be called into question through the use of force is obviously the doctrine of inviolability

---

[100] Trédano, *Intangibilité des Frontières Coloniales et Espace Etatique en Afrique* 90 translated in Lalonde, Determining Boundaries in a Conflicted World 122–3.
[101] Lalonde, Determining Boundaries in a Conflicted World 152.

of boundaries, not 'the intangibility principle' referred to by Lalonde. Lalonde also agrees with Charpentier that the doctrine of intangibility of inherited frontiers is based on accepting the alignments obtained on independence without investigating title root. She states: 'In contrast to the *uti possidetis juris* principle, the intangibility principle is limited to the juridical consequences flowing from a situation already in existence and does not formulate any presuppositions as to the title at the root of the delimitation'.[102]

Lalonde suggests that the Cairo Resolution reinstates the doctrine of intangibility of frontiers rather than the principle of *uti possidetis*.[103] On the basis of this assumption, she should have concluded that African states accepted the inherited boundaries because they were bound to do so by the principle of intangibility of inherited frontiers, as a general principle of law. Yet, Lalonde presents three mismatched interpretations for the African decision: first, 'African states were not bound to accept their artificial colonial boundaries and that the eventual decision to respect the boundaries existing at the time of independence was made for practical reasons';[104] second, in the case where the boundaries were created by treaties, African states were bound by the principle of *rebus sic stantibus* to respect such boundaries;[105] and third, 'the operation of the *nemo dat* principle would itself have contributed substantially to the preservation of administrative and international boundaries in Africa'.[106]

The first interpretation of Lalonde is irreconcilable with her position that intangibility of inherited frontiers is a general principle of law. If the intangibility of inherited frontiers were a principle of law binding on African states then the adoption of the colonial frontiers would have been made for legal, as opposed to practical, reasons. However, Lalonde did not clarify the 'practical reasons' that prompted African states to take that gratuitous decision. The second interpretation of *rebus sic stantibus* is misguided. As explained earlier in this chapter, newly independent states are absolved from the rule that a change of circumstances does not as such affect a boundary established by treaty. African states were free to denounce a boundary treaty by virtue of the clean slate principle. As to the third interpretation, the principle of *nemo dat quod non habet* is of limited relevance in modern international law. Brownlie posits that it

---

[102] *Ibid.*    [103] *Ibid.*    [104] *Ibid.* 135.
[105] *Ibid.* 144–5.    [106] *Ibid.* 151.

does not go beyond construing treaties of secession.[107] With the law of decolonization taking the lead in the case of newly independent African states, little room is left for the principle of *nemo dat* in Africa.

The *nemo dat* argument was examined in the African context in *Cameroon/Nigeria* case.[108] In that case Nigeria claimed that title in the Bakassi Peninsula lay in 1911 with the Kings and Chiefs of Old Calabar, and was retained by them until the territory passed to Nigeria upon independence. Nigeria argued: 'Great Britain was therefore unable to pass title to Bakassi because it had no title to pass (*nemo dat quod non habit*); as a result, the relevant provisions of the Anglo-German Agreement of 11 March 1911 must be regarded as ineffective'.[109] The Court dismissed the *nemo dat* argument on the basis that there was no evidence that until the independence of Nigeria in 1961 the Bakassi Peninsula had remained under the sovereignty of the Kings and Chiefs of Old Calabar.[110] By dismissing the *nemo dat* argument only on the basis of lack of evidence, it sounds that if evidence had existed the ICJ would have found that the United Kingdom did not convey Bakassi Peninsula to the Cameroon along with Southern Cameroons. Such finding would have been erroneous. In the true construction, the *nemo dat* argument should have been dismissed on the following three grounds.

First, the obligations of the United Kingdom, under Chapter XI of the UN Charter and Resolution 1514 (XV), make it imperative for the UK to convey the entire colonial territory under its administration to the newly independent state. If the Treaty of Protection with the King and Chiefs of Old Calabar of 1884 were to bind the United Kingdom to do otherwise that agreement would conflict with the 'sacred trust' obligations under Article 73 of the UN Charter and UK obligation under Paragraph 6 of Resolution 1514. The right of colonial self-determination provided for in those provisions is of *jus cogens*.[111] An agreement in contravention to this peremptory norm is invalid.

---

[107] Brownlie, *Principles of Public International Law* 121.
[108] Maurice Mendelson, 'The Cameroon-Nigeria Case in the International Court of Justice: Some Territorial Sovereignty and Boundary Delimitation Issues' (2004) 75 *British YBK Int'l L* 223, 228–34.
[109] *Land and Maritime Boundary between Cameroon and Nigeria (Cameroon/Nigeria)* (Preliminary Objections) [1998] ICJ Rep 275, 400.
[110] *Ibid*. 410.
[111] H. Gros-Espiell, 'Self-Determination and Jus Cogens' in A. Cassese (ed.), *UN Law/ Fundamental Rights: Two Topics in International Law* (Martinus Nijhoff 1979) 167–71; Cassese, *Self-determination of Peoples* 171.

Second, according to Article 103 of the UN Charter, in the event of conflict between Charter obligations and any other treaty the obligations under the UN Charter prevail. Consequently, the obligations of the United Kingdom under Chapter XI of the UN Charter prevail over any obligations to the contrary in the Treaty of Protection of 1884.

Third, title to the territory of newly independent states in Africa is acquired by recognition, not through state succession from the colonial administration. Consequently, as long as it is established that Bakassi was part of the territory recognized on independence as forming the Cameroon, any defect in the title of the United Kingdom over Bakassi Peninsula is inconsequential.

In conclusion of this chapter, the unanimous practice of all African states of accepting the pre-existing frontiers on independence gave rise to the customary rule of intangibility of inherited frontiers. This is the African rule that governed the vertical territory transfers that took place on the departure of the colonial administrations and the creation of the newly independent African states. This rule, not *uti possidetis*, is the rule that falls to be applied in determining African boundary disputes, regardless of whether it is expressly named and designated as applicable by disputant states or not. The content and legal implications of the rule of intangibility of inherited frontiers, which differ greatly from those of the principle of *uti possidetis*, are explained in Chapter 5.

However, the rule of intangibility of inherited frontiers is not the only rule created by African state practice. In addition to this rule, African custom gave rise to the legal doctrine of respecting the territorial status quo. While the rule of intangibility of inherited frontiers governs vertical territory transfers, the status quo rule precludes post-independence horizontal territory transfers. Again, whereas the rule of intangibility of inherited frontiers is constrained, similar to the principle of *uti possidetis*, to the moment of independence, the status quo rule applies way beyond that moment. The following two chapters explain how the African rule of respecting the territorial status quo was created.

3

# The conventional obligation to respect the
# territorial status quo

## 3.1.  The commitment in the OAU Charter to the status quo

By 1963, African independence was largely achieved and it became obvious that reopening the boundaries issue was liable to reverse the gains
made by adhering to pre-existing frontiers. Support mounted for the
idea of freezing the territorial status quo obtained on independence. Yet
that support was not unanimous. The irredentist and radical states, even
if they accepted the pre-existing frontiers on independence, aspired to
alter or demolish the colonial boundaries further down the line. Because
a collective approach to this all-Africa matter was crucial to its success,
organizing the African home from within, by establishing an all-inclusive
African organization, became paramount. To achieve this goal, it was
incumbent on moderate African states to tread carefully in order not to
alienate the abolitionists and revisionists and to secure the consensus
required.

### 3.1.1.  The challenges that faced the agreement on the status quo

Because all African states adhered on independence to the pre-existing
frontiers, boundary claims in Africa should be typically restricted to verifying the course of colonial alignments. Nonetheless, the claims made
by Morocco and Somalia went further. While Greater Morocco evolved
around the Alaoui dynasty, which had continued in power since 1631,[1] the
Somali people form a nation in the European sense of the term, divided
into a number of colonies and trust territories.[2] Consequently, rather than

---

[1] See generally Jamil M. Abun-Nasr, *A History of the Maghrib in the Islamic Period*
(Cambridge University Press 1987).
[2] I. M. Lewis, *A Modern History of the Somali* (4th edn, East African Studies 2002) 22–39;
Malcolm Shaw, *Title to Territory in Africa: International Legal Issues* (Clarendon
1986) 197.

seeking legitimacy in preserving the pre-existing frontiers, the two states aspired to conventional legitimizing principles of dynastic and national character. As such the claims advanced by Morocco and Somalia aimed at altering the inherited boundary lines to an extent that denied neighbouring states the right to independent existence, or at least the right to territorial integrity.[3] Because of the high stakes thus involved, those claims became of concern to the entire continent.[4]

The call for a Greater Morocco, which comprises Mauritania, Western Sahara and parts of Algeria and Mali, was incompatible with the right of colonial self-determination of those countries.[5] Uneasy about the right to colonial self-determination, Morocco grounded her claim in the classical argument that within a sovereign state the right of the existing state to territorial integrity trumps the right of the units composing that state to self-determination.[6] In this regard, Morocco advanced a peculiar interpretation of the Declaration on the Granting of Independence to Colonial Countries and Peoples.[7] Morocco construed Paragraph 6 of that Declaration as prohibiting colonial France 'to partition [Greater] Morocco and disrupt its national territorial unit, by setting up an artificial state in the area of Southern Morocco which the colonialists call Mauritania'. It clarified: 'Thus the Soviet draft declaration for which we voted follows a line simillar to that of the African Asian declaration demanding the radical and complete elimination of … balkanization that is being practised in Africa, the Middle East and elsewhere'.[8] As such, Morocco understood the Declaration to apply to her pre-colonial territory.[9]

Conversely, the case for Somali reunification was based on national self-determination. One of the side effects of the Second World War was the awakening of Somali nationalism in all five countries in which

---

[3] Shaw, Title to Territory in Africa 196–214; see also Ian Brownlie, *African Boundaries: A Legal and Diplomatic Encyclopedia* (1st edn, University of California 1979) 12–15. For a list of African boundary disputes known during the 1960s see Saadia Touval, *The Boundary Politics of Independent Africa* (Harvard 1972) 279–90. See also R. Waters, 'Inter-African Boundary Disputes' in C. G. Widstrand (ed.) *African Boundary Problems* (Scandinavian Institute of African Studies 1969) 183–5.

[4] Touval, *Boundary Politics* Chapters 9 and 10.

[5] See Joshua Castellino, *International Law and Self-determination: The Interplay of the Politics of Territorial Possession with Formulations of Post-Colonial National Identity* (Martinus Nijhoff 2000) 215 ff.

[6] See *Western Sahara* (Advisory Opinion) (Pleadings) [1975] ICJ Rep vol. III 11–16.

[7] UNGA Res 1514 (XV) (14 December 1960).

[8] United Nations General Assembly, 15th Session Official Records, 947th Plenary Meeting, Wednesday 14 December 1960, at 1284 UN Doc A/PV 947 (Minutes 1960) 1284.

[9] Shaw, *Title to Territory in Africa* 187–8.

ethnic Somalis lived.[10] As a result, after the independence of Italian
Somalia and British Somaliland, and their eventual unification on 1 July
1960, the united Republic of Somalia openly called for Somali reunification. According to that call ethnic Somalis living in French Somaliland
(Djibouti), the Northern Frontier District (NFD) of Kenya and the
Ogaden of Ethiopia were to freely determine their political status with
a view to uniting in one nation state.[11] Because Djibouti was still under
French colonization and as such entitled to exercise the right to colonial
self-determination, the Republic of Somalia focused on claiming national
self-determination for the Somali regions in Kenya and Ethiopia. Even
though the Moroccan and Somali claims were the most significant in the
early 1960s, they were not the only threat to African unity and the emergent consensus on the status quo.

The 1940s and 1950s witnessed a number of calls to abolish colonial
boundaries and unite divided African communities.[12] The Pan-African
Conference, Manchester 1945, and the All-Africa Conference, Dakar
1958, formed the climax of those abolitionist calls.[13] Although those radical trends subsided gradually, leaving the scene for pragmatism, at the
turn of the 1960s they were of some appeal to highly regarded African
leaders. Notably, the Ghanaian President Kwame Nkrumah called for the
uniting of Africa by dismantling colonial boundaries.[14] This alarmed the
more reserved African heads of state, including Emperor Haile Selassie of
Ethiopia and Modibo Keita of Mali, and prompted them to adopt a cautious approach fearing an alliance of sorts between the irredentists and
the radicals. Against this background, the African leaders converged in
Addis Ababa in May 1963 to adopt the OAU Charter as the constitutive
instrument for their regional organization.

In Addis Ababa, the radical African leaders made fervent calls to abolish the inherited boundaries and unite Africa politically.[15] Yet it was
clear that the majority of African states favoured continuing their independent existence and aspired to solve the boundary problem by adopting an express provision in the OAU Charter freezing for posterity the

[10] Lewis, *A Modern History of the Somali* 116–38.
[11] Shaw, *Title to Territory in Africa* 197–201.
[12] See Touval, *Boundary Politics* 56 ff.
[13] For the Declaration of the All-African Peoples Conference, Accra, December 1958 see
Colin Legum, *Pan-Africanism: A Short Political Guide* (Praeger 1962) 231.
[14] Touval, *Boundary Politics* 56 ff.
[15] *Proceedings of the Summit Conference of Independent African States, May 1963* (1963) vol.
I, sec. 2, Document CIAS/Gen/Inf/34 the Speech of President Milton Obote of Uganda,
36 the speech of Nkrumah.

pre-existing frontiers.[16] However, such direct language was liable to disaffect Morocco and Somalia, incense the abolitionists, and eventually jeopardize the unanimity required for the birth of the African Organization. The summit found it wise to treat this matter with great circumspection and adopt a piecemeal approach.[17] Consequently, the African leaders made circumlocutory use of the OAU Charter to serve, indirectly, the goal of perpetuating the territorial status quo. The approach chosen by the OAU Charter was that of confirming respect for the principle of territorial integrity and asserting peaceful settlement as the means for resolving boundary disputes. Article III of the OAU Charter emphasized concisely seven paramount principles forming, according to Elias, 'the articles of faith of the Member States of the Organization of African Unity'.[18] The third and fourth of those principles, enshrined in Articles III(3) and (4) respectively, are the most notable in this context. Article III(3) provided for 'respect for the sovereignty and territorial integrity of each State and for its inalienable right to independent existence'. Article III(4) stressed the 'peaceful settlement of disputes by negotiation, mediation, conciliation or arbitration'. In the African context where the pre-existing frontiers were preserved, the amplification of those two principles indirectly gave priority to the status quo over conflicting territorial claims. We shall now see how this materialized.

### 3.1.2.   Territorial integrity and the status quo

We have seen in Chapter 1 that the principle of territorial integrity was included in the Spanish-American treaties, in a form of a solemn commitment to safeguard the territorial integrity of the new republics.[19] The same principle was incorporated in the OAU Charter and corroborated with a scrupulous pledge to be respected by all African states. While the commitment to protect the territorial integrity served in Spanish America the objective of excluding *terra nullius,* in Africa the pledge to respect the territorial integrity works to perpetuate the status quo of the boundaries obtained on independence.

---

[16] Touval, *Boundary Politics* 83–6; see also B. B. Ghali, 'The Addis Ababa Conference' (1963–1965) 35 *International Conciliation* 5, 29.
[17] See generally Touval, *Boundary Politics* 83–6; see also T. O. Elias, 'The Charter of the Organization of African Unity' (1965) 59 *AJIL* 243, 248.
[18] Elias, 'The Charter of the Organization of African Unity' 248.
[19] Section 1.2.1, text to footnotes 29–35.

During the decolonization era, the principle of territorial integrity was perceived by newly independent states as the doctrine consecrating the colony, territorially defined for the purposes of decolonization, as the eternal unit of self-determination. In 1960, shortly after the adoption of Resolution 1514, Emerson observed that this perception defined the African understanding of the 1960 UN Declaration. According to Emerson, African states understood the relevant paragraphs of the Declaration as 'to deny the legitimacy of any further disintegration or reshaping which impairs the integrity of the colonially defined States'.[20]

Shaw agrees that this was indeed the view of African states at that time. He commented as follows on this African outlook:

> In Africa, therefore, the notion of the nation-State has been replaced by the concept of territorial State. In so linking the principle of territorial integrity with the preservation of the inviolability of the colonial frontiers and thus establishing a legal basis for the rejection of both irredentist and secessionist demands, African States have laid down the basic thesis relating to questions regarding territory on the continent.[21]

He concluded that: 'Whichever phrase is used, the essence of the proposition remains, namely that the doctrine of territorial integrity has been adopted specifically in Africa as a rule operating as a blocking mechanism to any post-independence territorial rearrangement.'[22] Those undercurrents were in sync with the aspired after purpose of consecrating the status quo.

To bring to the fore this sense of the term, Article III of the OAU Charter was stressed by Article VI, which reads: 'The Member States *pledge* themselves to observe *scrupulously* the principles enumerated in Article III of the present Charter.'[23] The use of the word pledge in this article is suggestive of the technique followed by Article 56 of the UN Charter in corroborating Article 55. According to Quincy Wright, the word 'pledge' used in Article 56 of the UN Charter indicates that an international obligation has been accepted to which no final interpretation could be given by individual states.[24] In similar vein, by using the word pledge, Article VI of

---

[20] Rupert Emerson, *From Empire to Nation: The Rise to Self-assertion of Asian and African Peoples* (Harvard 1960) 35.

[21] Shaw, *Title to Territory in Africa* 186–7.

[22] *Ibid*. 187.

[23] Emphasis added.

[24] Quincy Wright, 'Recognition and Self-Determination' (1954) 48 *PASIL* 23, 30; cf. Shaw, *Title to Territory in Africa* 63.

the OAU Charter accentuates the inter-state nature of the commitment undertaken. It clarifies that the obligation accepted could not be curtailed because of internal considerations, and that the final word about it rests with the continent as a whole. In addition to the word 'pledge', Article VI also used the word 'scrupulous'. Elias clarified that the word 'scrupulous' was also employed to remove individual state discretion. He stated that this entrenchment was intended to 'emphasize that the Member States accept the obligation scrupulously to observe all the principles in their relations with one another'.[25] By virtue of this extraordinary commitment, the territorial status quo was tacitly given precedence over territorial claims of the Moroccan and Somali type and radical calls to abolish the colonial boundaries.

Scholars highlighted the significance of the provisions of the OAU Charter that stress the status quo. Elias commented that Article III(3) and (4) drew their importance from being the principles that were meant to prevent disruption of the unity of African states and exclude 'internecine disputes and bad relations among them'.[26] Shaw concluded that: 'Although the Charter of the Organization of African Unity does not specifically refer to the sanctity of the colonial borders its provisions are unambiguous.'[27] Even though no law principle or provision sanctifying the boundaries was explicitly included in the OAU Charter, the implicit undertaking made to respect the status quo was visible for states with territorial claims. Morocco, fearing the impact of Article III(3), immediately entered a reservation to that article, which read:

> The signing of the Charter could not in any fashion be interpreted as either an explicit or implicit acknowledgment of these facts which Morocco refuses to recognize nor as renunciation of the pursuit of our rights by the legitimate means at our disposal.[28]

---

[25] Elias, 'The Charter of the Organization of African Unity' 250.
[26] T. O. Elias, 'The Commission of Mediation, Conciliation and Arbitration of the Organization of African Unity' (1964) 40 British YBK Int'l L 336, 338.
[27] Shaw, Title to Territory in Africa 185.
[28] Gino J. Naldi, The Organization of African Unity: An Analysis of its Role (2nd edn, Mansel 1999) 57. Naldi doubted the legality of Morocco's reservation on the basis of its incompatibility with the OAU Charter. He clarified that because the Charter is a constituent instrument of an international organization a reservation to it requires the acceptance of the competent organ of the organization concerned. Nonetheless, he found the Moroccan reservation operative because the OAU did not object to it, ibid. 57–8.

### 3.1.3.   Mediation as a means of confirming the status quo

In the early years of African independence, mediation played an exceptional role in fostering respect for the territorial status quo. In addition to the principle of peaceful settlement stated in Article III(4), which is also confirmed by the entrenchment in Article VI, Article XIX provides for the establishment of a Commission of Mediation, Conciliation and Arbitration. This Commission was initially intended to be one of the principal four organs of the OAU with a Special Protocol forming an integral part of the Charter.[29] Although the Special Protocol was approved in 1964, the Commission of Mediation did not function.[30] By and large, OAU mediation on boundary matters was undertaken on an ad hoc basis at the most senior level of the Assembly of Heads of State and Government.[31]

African mediation on boundary disputes works on the assumption that the parties to the dispute: (i) recognize the *status quo ante*; (ii) take no action on the ground to change it; (iii) refer their dispute to amicable settlement; and (iv) desist from taking that dispute outside the African continent. The first two of those four features operate to accord priority to the territorial status quo over counter claims throughout the mediation process. To achieve this consequence, African mediators put to use Articles III and VI of the OAU Charter, as we will see in Section 3.1.4. The last two features are intended to eliminate the possibility of changing the status quo and to make sure that it forms the final outcome. This distinctive aspect of African mediation is expanded below.

Because it was not quite certain whether international mediation, arbitration or adjudication would take into account the overall African common interest in respecting the status quo, African states opposed decisively the idea of referring African disputes to non-Africans. In this context, the OAU put to good use the spectre of imperialism that portrayed foreign involvement as neo-colonialism in disguise. Unlike the Spanish-American republics, which found no harm in referring their disputes to non-American arbitrators including the Vatican, Switzerland,

---

[29]   T. O. Elias, *Africa and the Development of International Law* (AW Sijthoff 1972) 160–76; Elias, 'The Charter of the Organization of African Unity' 263.

[30]   Elias, *Africa and the Development of International Law* 339; see OAU CM/Res 25 (II) (29 February 1964); OAU CM/Res 42 (III) (17 July 1964).

[31]   The Commission was not established because it was feared that the ferocity of the border conflicts that ensued with Morocco and Somalia would put the nascent mechanism to too difficult a test, see P. Mweti Munya, 'The Organization of African Unity and Its Role in Regional Conflict Resolution and Dispute Settlement: A Critical Evaluation' (1999) 19 *Boston College Third World Law Journal* 537, 551–2.

and even Spain, the former imperialist power,[32] African states 'have adopted the policy that inter-African disputes should be settled in an African cadre rather than by outsiders'.[33] OAU Resolutions of the early 1960s typically and repeatedly emphasize 'the imperious necessity of settling, by peaceful means and within a strictly African framework, all disputes between African States'.[34] It is stressed that African states are 'convinced that the Unity of Africa requires the solution to all disputes between Member States be sought first within the Organization of African Unity'.[35] OAU Resolutions also underscore 'the imperative need of settling all differences between African States by peaceful means and within a strictly African framework'.[36] Having in mind this decided collective stand against foreign involvement in African disputes, and because the OAU had no mechanisms for adjudication or arbitration, mediation became the only feasible process for resolving boundary disputes in Africa.

While elsewhere in the world, when mediation fails other means could be employed, in Africa there was no substitute for mediation. Hence, African mediation was interminable. According to Elias, 'Should the parties refuse the mediator's proposal, the Commission might ask the same or different mediator(s) to try again and again until the dispute is resolved, or until the parties agree to settle it between themselves or to abandon it.'[37] Because of this unique African mechanism, the referring of disputes to international arbitration, or even to the ICJ, was largely avoided during the first two decades of independence.[38] Until 1980, only twelve African states accepted the facultative clause of the ICJ.[39] According to Elias, preclusion or at least reduction of the occasions of recourse to the ICJ was part of the policy behind mediation.[40]

---

[32] For examples of Spanish-American disputes referred to international arbitration see Suzanne Lalonde, *Determining Boundaries in a Conflicted World: The Role of Uti Possidetis* (McGill-Queen's University Press 2002) 38–47.

[33] A. J. G. M. Sanders, *International Jurisprudence in African Context* (Butterworths 1979) 128.

[34] The preamble of the Cairo Resolution, OAU AHG/Res 16 (I) (21 July 1964).

[35] OAU CM/Res 18 (II) (29 February 1964).

[36] OAU ECM/Res I (I) (18 November 1963).

[37] Elias, *Africa and the Development of International Law* 171.

[38] See Kithure Kindiki, 'The Proposed Integration of the African Court of Justice and the African Court of Human and Peoples' Rights: Legal Difficulties and Merits' (2007) 15 *AJICL* 138, 139.

[39] Cf. Article 31 of the Pact of Bogota 1948, which provides that all Spanish-American republics that are parties to the Pact recognize the jurisdiction of the ICJ as compulsory *ipso facto*.

[40] Elias, *Africa and the Development of International Law* 176. By that time, African states that accepted the compulsory jurisdiction had, all bar Uganda, entered the domestic

On the whole, in the initial years of African independence mediation had served as a means of assigning priority to the territorial status quo. Notably, mediation helped to contain the threatening Moroccan and Somali claims. Despite the proclaimed stand of Morocco and Somalia, they could not defy the provisions of the OAU Charter that tacitly gave priority to the status quo. Those provisions were considered to form the undisputable basis of African unity and the term of reference for African mediation, as we shall now see.

### 3.1.4.  Using the OAU Charter for securing respect for the status quo

Articles III and VI of the OAU Charter were used successfully by African mediators to control the Moroccan and Somali territorial claims.

When the boundary dispute between Morocco and Algeria erupted in October 1963, Algeria refused to discuss the Moroccan claims arguing that 'the OAU Charter had confirmed the territorial status quo in Africa'.[41] Certainly, the OAU Charter had confirmed, even if tacitly, the respect of the territorial alignments obtained upon independence. Consequently, the Moroccan argument for reviving its post-colonial territorial integrity was effectively discredited. Nonetheless Morocco felt morally bound not to take its claim anywhere outside the African continent and the matter was referred to African mediation.

The Ethiopian Emperor Haile Selassie and the Malian President Modibo Keita facilitated a meeting for the leaders of Morocco and Algeria, in Bamako, Mali, in October 1963. The Bamako Communiqué declared cessation of hostilities and recommended to the OAU Council of Ministers the formation of an arbitration committee 'to effect a definitive solution for the Algerian Moroccan dispute'.[42] On endorsing the Bamako Communiqué in November 1963, the OAU Council of Ministers laid special emphasis on the commitments undertaken by Article III as corroborated by Article VI. The Resolution issued in this regard states that all Member States are 'bound by Article 6 to respect scrupulously all the principles formulated in Article 3 of the Charter of the Organization of African Unity'.[43] However, when the recommended arbitration committee was formed it did not look into the merits of the dispute and functioned

---

jurisdiction reservation or exempted from the ICJ jurisdiction disputes in respect of which the parties had agreed to recourse to another means of settlement.

[41]  Touval, *Boundary Politics* 106–7, citing *Le Monde*, 8 and 16 October 1963.
[42]  Munya, 'The Organization of African Unity' 557.
[43]  See also OAU CM/Res 18 (II) (29 February 1964); OAU CM/Res 37 (III) (17 July 1964).

as a mediation body to assist the parties to conclude an agreement for cessation of hostilities.

The principles and mechanisms of the OAU Charter were used also to downscale the claims of Somalia. Before the independence of Kenya, Somalia negotiated with the British Government the future of the NFD arguing that the district should be handed over to Somalia or at least administered jointly by Kenya and Somalia until its final status was determined.[44] When that request was not heeded, and Kenya attained independence on 14 December 1963 with the NFD as part of its territory, Somalia rejected the 1924 Anglo-Italian Treaty that drew its boundary with Kenya.[45] Likewise, Somalia denounced the 1897 Anglo-Ethiopian Treaty and the 1908 Italian-Ethiopian Treaty delineating the Somali-Ethiopian boundaries.[46] Armed conflict erupted between Somalia and its two neighbours.

The OAU Council of Ministers, in February 1964, called upon the Governments of Somalia and Kenya to take the necessary steps to settle their dispute 'in the spirit of paragraph 4 of Article III of the Charter'.[47] In the same session, a similar call was made with regard to the Somali–Ethiopian dispute, which also led to border skirmishes.[48] In its following session in Lagos, Nigeria, in February 1964, the OAU Council of Ministers reminded Somalia, Ethiopia and Kenya of their commitment to observe Article III(4). The disputants were invited to open as soon as possible direct negotiations 'with a view to finding a peaceful and lasting solution to differences between them', and to refrain from all acts 'which may aggravate the situation or jeopardize the chance of peaceful and fraternal settlement'.[49] The three states were also called upon to act 'with due respect to paragraph 3 of Article III of the Charter'.[50] Obviously, the calls to observe Article III(4) and to respect Article III(3) of the OAU Charter were in effect enjoining Somalia to withdraw its troops from the disputed areas and to resign itself to recognizing the territorial status quo without any prospect for a process in which the merits of the claim would be examined.

---

[44] Lewis, *A Modern History of the Somali* 185–95.
[45] Official Records of the General Assembly, Twenty-seventh Session, Plenary Meetings, 209 1st meeting, para 9 ff.
[46] *Ibid.*
[47] OAU CM/Res 4 (II) (15 February 1964).
[48] OAU CM/Res 3 (II) (15 February 1964).
[49] OAU CM/Res 16 (II) (29 February 1964).
[50] *Ibid.*

The principles of the OAU Charter were used effectively by mediators to control the most intransigent claims of Morocco and Somalia, and to influence those two states to respect the territorial status quo. However, the tacit undertaking in the OAU Charter was feared to be open to different interpretations and calculated as short of the ambitious objective of adopting a fast rule. As a result, the Cairo Resolution 1964 was shortly adopted to augment the OAU Charter and to amplify explicitly what was undertaken implicitly in that Charter, as the following section shows.

### 3.2.    The undertaking in the Cairo Resolution to respect the status quo

#### 3.2.1.    The explicit commitment in the Cairo Resolution

Initially African states that were keen to keep Morocco and Somalia within the African fold for the purposes of inaugurating an all-encompassing OAU were content with an implicit affirmation of the territorial status quo. However, as soon as that purpose was achieved, African leaders pushed ahead with their paramount goal of affirming unequivocal respect for the territorial status quo established on independence. The OAU Second Summit, convened in Cairo from 17 to 21 July 1964, availed Africa with the first opportunity to agree on an express undertaking to perpetuate the territorial status quo. A draft resolution tabled by Tanzania was the subject of a brief discussion and was eventually adopted by acclamation as Resolution AHG/Res 16 (I), better known as the Cairo Resolution.[51]

Formatted in two parts, an evocative preamble and two concise operative paragraphs, the Cairo Resolution reads as follows:

The Assembly of Heads of State and Government meeting in its First Ordinary Session in Cairo, UAR, from 17 to 21 July 1964;

Considering that border problems constitute a grave and permanent factor of dissention;

Conscious of the existence of extra-African manoeuvres aimed at dividing African States;

Considering further that the borders of African States, on the day of their independence, constitute a tangible reality;

---

[51] For a summary of the proceedings of the adoption session, see Touval, *Boundary Politics* 86–7.

Recalling the establishment in the course of the Second Ordinary Session
of the Council of the Committee of Eleven charged with studying further measures for strengthening African Unity;

Recognising the imperious necessity of settling, by peaceful means and
within a strictly African framework, all disputes between African
States;

Recalling further that all Member States have pledged, under Article VI of
the Charter of African Unity, to respect scrupulously all principles laid
down in paragraph 3 of Article III of the Charter of the Organization
of African Unity:

1. SOLEMNLY REAFFIRMS the strict respect by all Member States of
   the Organization for the principles laid down in paragraph 3 of Article
   III of the Charter of the Organization of African Unity;

2. SOLEMNLY DECLARES that all Member States pledge themselves
   to respect the borders existing on their achievement of national
   independence.[52]

The preamble of the Resolution is loaded with meaning. It starts by allud-
ing to the acrimonious disagreement on the future of the colonial borders
that dominated the African scene immediately after independence.[53] The
warning of the 'existence of extra-African manoeuvres aimed at dividing
African States' was the assured African way for casting in a bad light any
attempt at changing the territorial status quo at that time of intense anticolonial feeling.

The assertion that the borders of African states on the day of their independence 'constitute a tangible reality' is a reminder that the pre-existing
frontiers had already been accepted on independence and now formed
an undeniable fact. However, a reference was also made in this connection to the Committee of Eleven formed at the inaugural meeting in
Addis Ababa to study further measures for strengthening and promoting
unity and solidarity between African states. Mentioning that committee,
which was to placate the radical African leaders, was a symbolic gesture
intended to forestall opposition to the Cairo Resolution.

The stressing of 'the imperious necessity of settling, by peaceful means
and within a strictly African framework, all disputes between African

---

[52] Reproduced in Ian Brownlie, *Basic Documents on African Affairs* (Oxford University
Press 1971) 360.

[53] See generally Touval, *Boundary Politics* 99 ff.

States' confirms mediation as the preferred African mechanism for handling boundary disputes.

The last preambular phrase of the Resolution reminds the African states of the pledge they made, under Article VI of the OAU Charter, to observe scrupulously the principle in Article III(3).[54] Even if Article VI refers to all principles mentioned in Article III, the preamble of the Cairo Resolution singles out paragraph 3 of that article. Paragraph 3 is the core of the implicit undertaking to respect the status quo and as such deserved specific reference as the paragraph subject to elaboration and further development in the Cairo Resolution.

The preamble of the Cairo Resolution is followed by two operative paragraphs. The First Paragraph reaffirms the strict respect for Article III(3) that implicitly confirms the status quo. The Second Paragraph declares explicitly that 'all Member States pledge themselves to respect the borders existing on their achievement of national independence'. The word pledge appearing in the OAU Charter is also used in the Cairo Resolution and in the same sense of accentuating that a pre-eminent commitment belonging to the entire continent is undertaken.[55]

Simple in statement and dispositive in effect, the Cairo Resolution proclaimed that all the borders existing on independence were to be invariably respected *in perpetuum*.

The Cairo Resolution is sometimes referred to as stating the principle of the inviolability of African frontiers. The UN Security Council Resolution 1234 (1999) on the situation in the DRC referred to the Cairo Resolution as 'the principle of the inviolability of national frontiers of African states'.[56] A *sine qua non* of accepting to respect the territorial status quo is to also recognize that existing boundaries are inviolable. Yet, as explained above, the distinct norm explicitly introduced by the Cairo Resolution is that the territorial status quo is not to be changed, not that boundaries should not be militarily violated. The Resolution is not stressing the doctrine of inviolability of frontiers or any other existing law doctrine.

---

[54] The text of the Cairo Resolution published on the AU official website refers mistakenly to Article IV instead of Article VI. For the correct text see Brownlie, *Basic Documents* 360.

[55] Cf. Lalonde, who suggests that the word 'pledge' indicates that the Resolution was not intended as a statement of a legal rule, Lalonde, *Determining Boundaries* 136.

[56] UNSC Res 1234 (9 April 1999) UN Doc S/RES/1234. Likewise, OAU Resolution AHG/Res 158 (XXII) (30 July 1986) refers to the 'inviolability of the borders in conformity with OAU resolution AHG/16 (I) adopted by the Cairo Summit in 1964'. Rule 14 of the OAU Rules of the Mechanism for Conflict Prevention, Management and Resolution, 1993, also referred to this African rule as 'the inviolability of borders inherited from colonialism'.

In his Separate Opinion in the *Frontier Dispute (Burkina Faso/Niger)*
Judge Yusuf found that the Cairo Resolution was an arrangement that
merely put the inherited boundaries in a 'holding pattern' and implies
temporary prohibition of the use of force. He stated:

> [I]t may be said that the principle of respect for boundaries in the Cairo
> Resolution places the boundaries existing at the time of independence in
> a 'holding pattern', particularly to avoid armed conflict over territorial
> claims, until a satisfactory and peaceful solution is found by the Parties
> to a territorial dispute in conformity with international law, or until such
> time as closer integration and unity is achieved among African States in
> general, or between the neighbouring countries in particular, in keeping
> with the Pan-African vision. As such, it implies a prohibition of the use of
> force in the settlement of boundary disputes and an obligation to refrain
> from acts of seizure of a portion of the territory of another African State.[57]

Judge Yusuf depended for arriving at this finding on the reference in the
preamble of the Cairo Resolution to the Committee of Eleven. Because
of that reference he perceived that in the Cairo Resolution the preservation of the boundaries was somehow balanced by the continued efforts
towards political integration undertaken by the Committee of Eleven.
The Committee of Eleven was required to receive from Member States
suggestions that 'may promote the unity and solidarity of the African
continent',[58] not projects for political integration involving dismantling
the boundaries as Yusuf presumes. Even on that limited mandate, the
Committee failed to present its report.[59]

A conclusion that a particular boundary arrangement is temporary
should not be easily drawn. Such proposition fails to take full account
of the settled doctrine of continuity and finality of boundaries, which
forms a general principle of law and 'constitutes one of the more fundamental and important precepts in the corpus of the rules relating to
boundaries'.[60] In the *Temple Case*, the ICJ had clarified that: 'In general,
when two countries establish a frontier between them, one of the primary

---

[57] Separate Opinion of Judge Yusuf, *Frontier Dispute (Burkina Faso/Niger)* (Judgment)
[2013] ICJ Rep 1, page 5 of the Separate Opinion.

[58] OAU CM/Res 20 (II) (29 February 1964).

[59] In the Lagos session of the OAU Council of Ministers, February 1964, the Council
decided to give the Committee of Eleven more time and included its report as an agenda
item in its next session. Because the Committee received no proposals from African
states and prepared no report, that agenda item did not appear in the following session.
Since then the Committee of Eleven has been completely forgotten.

[60] Kaiyan Homi Kaikobad, 'Some Observations on the Doctrine of Continuity and Finality
of Boundaries' (1984) 54 *British YBK Int'l L* 119, 120.

objects is to achieve stability and finality. This is impossible if the line so established can, at any moment, and on the basis of a continuously available process, be called in question'.[61] As such, a presumption arises that the object of boundary arrangements is finality, unless it is established otherwise. Consequently, when African states met in Cairo in July 1964 to adopt a Resolution on boundaries, it was presumed that they intended to conclude stable, continuous, and final arrangements. With the benefit of hindsight, it is indeed now clear that the intention of African states in 1964 was to make sure that the boundary issue was finally put to rest. African states would find it incredible to be told that the only achievement of the OAU founding fathers who converged in Cairo in July 1964 was to put African boundaries on a 'holding pattern'.

The Cairo Resolution was fatally misdiagnosed by the ICJ Chamber in the *Frontier Dispute*. In that case, it is held that the Cairo Resolution is a mere reinstatement of *uti possidetis*. This point is examined in the following section.

### 3.2.2.   *The status quo versus* uti possidetis

The ICJ Chamber in the *Frontier Dispute* found that the OAU Charter and the Cairo Resolution confirmed the principle of *uti possidetis*. The Court concluded:

> The Charter of the Organization of African Unity did not ignore the principle of *uti possidetis*, but made only indirect reference to it in Article 3, according to which member States solemnly affirm the principle of respect for the sovereignty and territorial integrity of every State. However, at their first summit conference after the creation of the Organization of African Unity, the African Heads of State, in their Resolution mentioned above (AGH/Res. 16 (1)), adopted in Cairo in July 1964, deliberately defined and stressed the principle of *uti possidetis juris* contained only in an implicit sense in the Charter of their organization.[62]

Contrary to this finding, *uti possidetis* was not referred to implicitly in the OAU Charter. Nor was it stressed explicitly in the Cairo Resolution. To be sure, a principle constrained temporally to the moment of independence has nothing to do with those two instruments intended to prevent future boundary changes.

---

[61]   *Temple of Preah Vihear Case* (Merits) [1962] ICJ Rep 6, 34.

[62]   *Frontier Dispute (Burkina Faso/Mali)* (Judgment) [1986] ICJ Rep 554, 565–6.

Shaw clarified that 'The principle of *uti possidetis juris* developed as an attempt to obviate territorial disputes by fixing the territorial heritage of new States at the moment of independence and converting existing lines into internationally recognized borders, and can thus be seen as a specific legal package, anchored in space and time.'[63] Consequently, it might be excusable to confuse the African practice of respecting the pre-existing frontiers on independence with *uti possidetis*. This is because the African practice takes place within the same time frame of independence and provides a doctrine for setting boundaries that are to be subject to international recognition. Yet, it is implausible to read *uti possidetis* in an instrument expressing the decision of African states not to change the borders existing on their achievement of national independence. Indeed, Shaw stresses that *uti possidetis* should not be understood as stipulating that boundaries are unchangeable. He states:

> It is important not to overstate the import of the principle of *uti possidetis*. It does not posit that the boundaries existing at the moment of independence are immutable and incapable of change. That can happen. What it does say is that without evidence to the contrary, then the boundary that continues is the one that was in evidence at independence, and that any alteration thereto must be demonstrated and proved by acceptable evidence.[64]

Shaw emphasized on another occasion that 'While it "freezes" the territorial situation during the movement to independence, *uti possidetis* does not prescribe a territorial boundary which can never be changed. It is not intangible in this sense'.[65]

In similar vein, Tomuschat opined:

> *Uti possidetis* is important when a State becomes independent. Its boundaries will be determined by the previous boundaries as they exist at that moment. Thereafter, a State which has emerged from colonial rule is a State like any other State. After having served its purpose, the principle of *uti possidetis* becomes irrelevant. Whether the territory of a new State

---

[63] Malcolm Shaw, 'The Heritage of States: The Principle of Uti Possidetis Juris Today' (1996) 67 British YBK Int'l L 75, 76; see also 95, 152. Interestingly, the ICJ Chamber arrives at its conclusion that the Cairo Resolution reinstates *uti possidetis* despite confirming that 'The essence of the principle [of *uti possidetis*] lies in its primary aim of securing respect for the territorial boundaries *at the moment* when independence is achieved' (emphasis added) *Frontier Dispute* (n 62) 566.

[64] Shaw, 'The Heritage of States' 141.

[65] Malcolm Shaw 'Peoples, Territorialism and Boundaries' (1997) 8 *EJIL* 478, 495.

may change by increasing or decreasing in size is determined by the rules which are applicable on a world-wide scale.[66]

*Uti possidetis* is indeed irrelevant to what takes place after independence. Nor is there any law doctrine of international applicability in this regard. Contrary to what Tomuschat assumes, there are no international rules 'applicable on a world-wide scale' for increasing or decreasing territory. Actions of individual states leading to altering boundaries or ceding or annexing territory attract no international law principle, as long as those exercises are consensual and peaceful. What African states did in the OAU Charter and the Cairo Resolution is that they enunciated new doctrine *in vacuo* to govern, or rather to preclude, those actions in Africa.

This conclusion raises a question as to how this new doctrine binds African states. Key to answering this question is determining whether the Cairo Resolution is a political statement, as scholars argue, or a legally binding instrument. We now turn to this point.

### 3.2.3.    *The legal force of the Cairo Resolution*

A number of scholars thought of the Cairo Resolution as a mere political statement devoid of any legal force. Brownlie concluded that the Cairo Resolution 'had no binding effect in terms of international law'.[67] Shaw stated somewhat ambivalently that the Cairo Resolution is 'a political statement of the highest order and one with important juridical associations'.[68] Chukwurah found that 'At best the OAU Resolution on Border Disputes as formulated represents a code of conduct of boundaries of the New States of Africa. Nothing more'.[69] Lalonde asserted that it is 'a statement of policy' that 'has undoubtedly had a considerable impact, but its legal effect is questionable'.[70] Naldi maintained, somewhat paradoxically, that the Resolution 'if non-binding, nevertheless reflects customary international law'.[71] Apart from the finding of Brownlie, all statements

---

[66] C. Tomuschat, 'Secession and Self-determination' in M. G. Kohen (ed.), *Secession: International Law Perspectives* (Cambridge University Press 2006) 38. See also Antonello Tancredi, 'A Normative "Due Process" in the Creation of States through Secession' in Marcelo G. Kohen (ed.), *Secession: International Law Perspectives* (Cambridge University Press 2006) 192.

[67] Brownlie, *African Boundaries* 11.

[68] Shaw, 'The Heritage of States' 103.

[69] A. O. Chukwurah, 'The Organization of African Unity and African Territorial and Boundary Problems: 1963–1973' (1973) 13 *Indian JIL* 176, 182.

[70] Lalonde, *Determining Boundaries* 136.

[71] Naldi, *The Organization of African Unity* 57.

above were made after the *Frontier Dispute* and apparently influenced by its categorical denial of the possibility of the emergence of African custom in this regard. Far from being a policy statement or merely hortatory, the Cairo Resolution was a legal instrument of immediate binding effect and significant subsequent implications.

It is by no means possible to set aside the Cairo Resolution as a political statement. A resolution of political disposition is typically articulated in programmatic language, contingent on the political situation prevailing at its adoption, and could hardly survive the circumstances of its birth.[72] The Cairo Resolution avoided the language of plans and intentions, and rather used the most stringent obligatory terms possible. With the benefit of hindsight, it did not depend on the political situation that existed on its adoption. Nor did subsequent political changes lead to abandoning its principle. As such, an initial presumption that the Cairo Resolution is of legal character arises.

While the Cairo Resolution imposes no new obligation on African states, it amplifies an implicit undertaking made in the OAU Charter. This means it belongs to the category of Resolutions that are interpreting treaty obligations. In UN practice, Resolutions of the General Assembly that interpret or concretize the principles of the UN Charter are considered to form evidence of law, and as such considered binding on Member States.[73] Schachter clarifies that the formal source of authority of those Resolutions is the UN Charter.[74] Vallat also states that such Resolutions are binding because they are 'strong evidence of the proper interpretation of the Charter'.[75] Consequently, an analogy with the UN law should lead to a conclusion that the Cairo Resolution is binding on African states because it is declaratory of law, being an authentic interpretation of the OAU Charter. The fact that the Cairo Resolution was not unanimous does not affect this finding. In UN practice, despite the controversy as to whether Resolutions that were not unanimous were accepted as binding

---

[72] Oscar Schachter, *International Law in Theory and Practice* (Kluwer 1991) 97–8.

[73] Schachter, *International Law in Theory and Practice* 86; see generally O. Y. Asamoah, *The Legal Significance of the Declarations of the General Assembly of the United Nations* (Martinus Nijhoff 1967); an example of such resolutions is the Declaration on Principles of International Law Concerning Friendly Relations and Cooperation among States in Accordance with the Charter of the United Nations, UNGA Res 2625 (XXV) (24 October 1970).

[74] Schachter, *International Law in Theory and Practice* 86.

[75] F. A. Vallat, 'The Competence of the United Nations General Assembly' (1959 II) 97 *Recueil Des Cours de l'Académie de Droit International* 203, 231.

or not, declaratory Resolutions that fell short of unanimity but considered to have been generally approved were accepted as binding.[76]

Yet, the UN system is not analogous to the OAU system. While in UN law the General Assembly is the organ with recommendation powers, at the OAU the Assembly of Heads of State and Government, which issued the Cairo Resolution, is the 'supreme organ of the Organization'. Elias explained that the Assembly of Heads of State and Government is the body to issue final decisions within the OAU on the basis of the recommendations of the Council of Ministers.[77] Nonetheless, it is not clearly stated in the OAU Charter that the Resolutions of the Assembly are binding, and hence the issue was unsettled.

Elias argued: 'The Resolutions of the Assembly of Heads of State and Government are binding upon the several Member States on the ground of the obligation they have voluntary assumed under the Charter of the Organization of African Unity'.[78] Naldi disagrees, contending that the Assembly Resolutions have no binding force.[79] Naldi added that although the Assembly requires a two-thirds majority to act, it normally acts by consensus.[80] This observation does not assist Naldi's argument. Even if the requirement of consensus makes it difficult for the OAU Assembly to adopt a Resolution, those difficulties end at that stage. When extensive support sufficient for adopting a consensual Resolution materializes, that consensus helps to attract universal adherence at the implementation phase.[81] This makes abiding by the OAU Assembly Resolutions the pattern rather than the exception. Certainly, the binding nature of the Resolutions of the OAU Assembly was not questioned within the OAU.

In contrast, the OAU Council of Ministers, being the body with recommendation powers similar to the UN General Assembly, was criticised for purporting to adopt a Resolution with binding effect.[82] Resolution 13 (VI), adopted by the OAU Council of Ministers on 5 December 1965, required

---

[76] An example of those Resolutions is General Assembly Resolution 1761 on the Policies of Apartheid, which was objected to by South Africa, UNGA Res 1761(XVII) (6 November 1962).

[77] Elias, *Africa and the Development of International Law* 136.

[78] *Ibid.* 154.

[79] Naldi, *The Organization of African Unity* 19.

[80] *Ibid.*

[81] Currently Articles 9(1)(e) and 23(2) of the AU Constitutive Act 2000 empower the AU Assembly to ensure compliance with its decisions, whether adopted by consensus or by two-thirds majority, and to subject Member States to sanctions if they fail to comply.

[82] Elias, *Africa and the Development of International Law* 136, 155; Naldi, *The Organization of African Unity* 21.

OAU Member States to sever relations with the UK if by 15 December 1965 the UK did not crush a rebellion in Southern Rhodesia and prepare for majority rule.[83] The Council of Ministers was criticised for adopting that Resolution because the Council is not empowered to issue binding decisions, and was supposed in that instance to make a recommendation to the Assembly.[84] If it were the OAU Assembly that issued Resolution 13 (VI) (1965), as was the case with the Cairo Resolution, the Assembly would not have been blamed for claiming to bind Member States.

Furthermore, while the competence of the General Assembly to interpret the UN Charter is highly debatable,[85] the OAU Assembly was explicitly assigned with the role of interpreting the OAU Charter. Article 27 of the OAU Charter empowers the Assembly to decide any question that may arise concerning the interpretation of the OAU Charter by a vote of two-thirds of the Assembly.[86] In view of the power of interpreting the OAU Charter accorded to the OAU Assembly, it is not unreasonable to argue that the Cairo Resolution forms a subsequent agreement interpreting the OAU Charter. According to Article 31(3) of the Vienna Convention on the Law of Treaties, any subsequent agreement regarding the interpretation or application of a treaty shall be taken into account together with the context of that treaty.

The maxim *pacta sunt servanda,* which encapsulates the sanctity of obligations, invariably underlies the above interpretations that confer legal force on the Cairo Resolution. This is because, according to those interpretations, the legal force of the Cairo Resolution is treaty-based, emanating from the binding obligation in the OAU Charter. However, this maxim is not the only viable source of the legal force of the Cairo

[83] OAU ECM/Res 13 (VI) (5 December 1965).
[84] Elias, *Africa and the Development of International Law* 148–59.
[85] See generally G. Arangio-Ruiz, 'The Normative Role of the General Assembly of the United Nations and the Declaration of Principles of Friendly Relations' (1972 III) 137 *Recueil Des Cours de l'Académie de Droit International* 419, 503 ff; L. B. Sohn, 'The UN System as Authoritative Interpreter of its Law' in O. Schachter and C. Joyner (eds.), *United Nations Legal Order*, vol. I (Cambridge University Press 1995) 203ff; Benedetto Conforti and Carlo Focarelli, *The Law and Practice of the United Nations* (4th edn, Martinus Nijhoff 2010) 16–19.
[86] Elias, *Africa and the Development of International Law* 147. Elias clarifies that in the early stages of drafting Article 27 a provision was made for a reference to the ICJ for interpretation, but it was finally decided that interpretation should be the prerogative of the Assembly. Currently Article 26 of the AU Constitutive Act seizes the African Court with matters of interpreting the Constitutive Act. Pending the establishment of the African Court, it is provided that the Assembly shall continue to decide such matters by a two-thirds majority.

Resolution. Bowett clarified that the maxim *pacta sunt servanda* 'is supplemented by the doctrine of estoppel in that statements of fact which condition and render meaningful these obligations are, by that doctrine, deemed to be binding on the parties to the agreement'.[87] Accordingly, the doctrine of estoppel which works in tandem with the maxim *pacta sunt servanda* stresses that the obligations undertaken in the Cairo Resolution could not be denied. This point is expanded below.

### 3.2.4.   *The estoppel created by the Cairo Resolution*

The doctrine of estoppel is well established in law.[88] In the *Eastern Greenland Case*, Denmark contended that various bilateral and multilateral treaties to which Norway was a party and which described Greenland as a Danish colony or as part of Denmark precluded Norway from contesting Danish sovereignty over Greenland. This contention was upheld by the PCIJ.[89]

The statement of fact contained in the Cairo Resolution that forms a representation and creates estoppel is the preambular declaration that 'the borders of African States, on the day of their independence, constitute a tangible reality'. States that voted for the Cairo Resolution are estopped by that Preambular Paragraph, read together with the Second Paragraph of the Resolution, from denying that they acknowledged independence borders as the tangible reality that they undertake to respect.

The fact that the statement in question is made in the preamble of the Resolution does not negate the possibility of creating estoppel. In the law of treaties it is established that the text of a treaty includes its preamble and annexes.[90] Pellet concludes that the ICJ has constantly treated the preamble as part of the context relevant to the interpretation of a treaty.[91] It is not unreasonable to draw parallels in this regard between the Cairo Resolution and a treaty.

As an authentic interpretation of the OAU Charter, the Cairo Resolution binds all OAU members including Morocco and Somalia despite the fact

---

[87]  D. W. Bowett, 'Estoppel before International Tribunals and its Relation to Acquiescence' (1957) 33 *British YBK Int'l L* 176, 181.

[88]  See generally *ibid.*

[89]  *The Legal Status of Eastern Greenland (Denmark/Norway)* [1933] PCIJ Rep Series A/B No 53, 70–1.

[90]  Article 31(2) of the Vienna Convention on the Law of Treaties 1969.

[91]  Alain Pellet, 'Article 38' in A. Zimmermann, C. Tomuschat and K. Oellers-Frahm (eds.), *The Statute of the International Court of Justice: A Commentary* (Oxford University Press 2006) 804.

that they did not vote for the Cairo Resolution. This is because in this case the obligation emanates from the OAU Charter to which they are parties. However, the Cairo Resolution does not bind those two states by way of estoppel, since they did not join the acclamation of adopting the Cairo Resolution. Bowett explained that 'It is, of course, clear that an estoppel will normally have effect only between the parties to the treaty which contains the representation'.[92]

The fact that the Cairo Resolution is not a treaty does not prevent the creation of estoppel. All types of representation regardless of the form they take could create estoppel. In the *Eastern Greenland Case* an oral declaration made by Norway to Denmark, the Ihlen Declaration, was found to have created estoppel. The Ihlen Declaration was the reply of M. Ihlen, the Norwegian Foreign Minister, given orally on 22 July 1919 to the Danish Minister accredited to Norway declaring that 'the Norwegian Government would not make any difficulty' concerning the Danish claim over Greenland.[93] The PCIJ found that as a result of the undertaking involved in the declaration 'Norway is under an obligation to refrain from contesting Danish sovereignty over Greenland as a whole, and *a fortiori* to refrain from occupying a part of Greenland'.[94]

In addition to its immediate legal force that obligated African states by convention and by estoppel, the Cairo Resolution generated in due course a customary rule specific to Africa that binds all African states. The following Chapter 4 shows how the Cairo Resolution gave rise to the customary rule of the status quo.

---

[92] Bowett, 'Estoppel before International Tribunals' 182.
[93] *Denmark/Norway* (n 89) 73.
[94] *Ibid.*

# 4

# The customary rule of respecting the territorial status quo

## 4.1. The norm-creating character of the Cairo Resolution

### 4.1.1. The concept of norm-creating character

It was established in the *North Sea Continental Shelf Cases* that a treaty provision can generate binding practice 'partly because of its own impact, partly on the basis of subsequent State practice'.[1] To be of this particular quality, a treaty provision needs to be of norm-creating character.

In the *North Sea Continental Shelf Cases* Denmark and the Netherlands argued that Article 6 of the Geneva Convention on the Continental Shelf, 1958, passed into the general *corpus* of international law as a customary rule. The ICJ found this process possible in principle. The Court added that for a provision to give rise to customary rule it shall evince a norm-creating character.[2] To meet this description, the provision should satisfy the following three requirements:

a) It 'could be regarded as forming the basis of a general rule of law'.[3]
b) There shall be no 'notion of special circumstances relative to the principle' embodied in the provision raising 'doubts as to the potentially norm-creating character of the rule'.[4]

---

[1] *North Sea Continental Shelf Cases (Federal Republic of Germany/Denmark, Federal Republic of Germany/Netherlands)* (Judgment) [1969] ICJ Rep 3, 41.
[2] *Ibid.* 189–91; cf. Akehurst who thinks that subsequent acceptability of a rule laid in a treaty is a matter of fact and that 'No useful purpose is served by trying to make *a priori* distinctions between rules which are capable of ripening into customary rules and rules which do not have that capacity', Micheal Akehurst, 'Custom as a Source of International Law' (1974–75) 47 *British YBK Int'l L* 1, 50.
[3] *North Sea Continental Shelf Cases* (n 1) 41–2.
[4] *Ibid.* 42.

c) There shall be no provision in the instrument that incorporates the principle for a faculty of making reservations that denies the principle the attribute of 'being eventually received as general law'.[5]

On applying those requirements to Article 6 of the Geneva Convention on the Continental Shelf it was found that the article fails on all three counts.

The relevant part of Article 6 of the Geneva Convention reads as follows: 'In the absence of agreement, and unless another boundary line is justified by special circumstances, the boundary is the median line, every point of which is equidistant from the nearest points of the baselines from which the breadth of the territorial sea of each State is measured'. The Court found that even if the equidistance principle, considered *in abstracto*, might be said to satisfy the first requirement, in the particular form in which it is embodied in Article 6 this must be open to some doubt. The Court found that 'Article 6 is so framed as to put second the obligation to make use of the equidistance method, causing it to come after a primary obligation to effect delimitation by agreement'. The Court concluded: 'Such a primary obligation constitutes an unusual preface to what is claimed to be a potential general rule of law.'[6] As to the second requirement, the Court found that 'the part played by the notion of special circumstances relative to the principle of equidistance as embodied in Article 6, and the very considerable, still unresolved controversies as to the exact meaning and scope of this notion, must raise further doubts as to the potentially norm-creating character of the rule'. Article 6 failed also regarding the third requirement because of the faculty of making reservations to Article 6.[7]

### 4.1.2.   Attesting the norm-creating character of the Cairo Resolution

The finding in the *North Sea Continental Shelf Cases* that a treaty provision can generate binding practice also applies to UN Resolutions.[8] By extension, the same rule applies to make it possible for OAU Resolutions to generate African state practice. Consequently, the test applied by the

[5] *Ibid.* For a slightly different reading of those guidelines see Jo Lynn Slama, 'Opinio Juris in Customary International Law' (1990) 15 *Oklahoma CULR* 603, 649–51.
[6] *North Sea Continental Shelf Cases* (n 1) 42.
[7] *Ibid.*
[8] Mark E. Villiger, *Customary International Law and Treaties: A Study of their Interactions and Interrelations with Special Consideration of the 1969 Vienna Convention on the Law of Treaties* (Martinus Nijhoff 1985) 192.

ICJ to a provision in the Geneva Convention on the Continental Shelf to establish its norm-creating faculty is applicable to the Cairo Resolution.

The paragraph of the Cairo Resolution that could be viewed as containing the norm-creating attribute is the Second Paragraph of the Resolution. This paragraph reads 'all Member States pledge themselves to respect the borders existing on their achievement of national independence'. The respect of the borders existing on independence is the primary obligation of this paragraph. It is stated as secondary to no other obligation. The obligation to respect the independence boundaries would have been secondary only if it applied in the event of the failure of the concerned states to agree on another boundary. Taken in abstract, as well as in the particular form in which it is enunciated, the Second Paragraph of the Cairo Resolution clearly forms the basis of a general rule of law.

The notion of special circumstances embodied in Article 6 of the Convention on the Continental Shelf is not implicated by the Second Paragraph of the Cairo Resolution. This is because the paragraph applies to all African borders in all circumstances. In the context of the Cairo Resolution if a compromise were reached with Morocco and Somalia, leading to exempting cases of pre-colonial empires (Morocco) or of national self-determination (Somalia) from the Resolution, then the Resolution would be applicable bar special circumstances.

The last requirement of the *North Sea Continental Shelf Cases* is the absence of a reservation clause. Resolutions, as opposed to treaties, do not foresee reservations. Notably, the Cairo Resolution states unusually that the pledge under it is undertaken by '*all* Member States'. The objection made by Morocco and Somalia at the adoption of the Cairo Resolution is of no relevance to the norm-creating character of the Resolution. It is the faculty of making reservations that denies the instrument its norm-creating feature; not the fact that reservations were actually made. Judge Lachs clarified in his dissenting opinion in the *North Sea Continental Shelf Cases* that 'there is evidence that reservations made to important law-making or codifying conventions have not prevented their provisions from being generally accepted as law'.[9]

---

[9] Dissenting Opinion of Judge Lachs, *North Sea Continental Shelf Cases* (n 1) 224–5. Judge Lachs mentioned as examples to this the Fourth Hague Convention (1907), to which five states made reservations, and the Geneva Convention on the High Seas (1958), among others.

After establishing that the Cairo Resolution is of norm-creating character, we now turn to examining the state practice and the *opinio juris* it generated.

## 4.2.  African state practice in line with the status quo

According to Baxter, the usual manner for establishing the existence of a rule of international law grounded in practice accepted as law is 'to adduce in an essentially undifferentiated way all of the evidence in support of the rule that may be found in the practice of States'.[10] This methodology was famously adopted in the *Paquete Habana* case. In that case, the US Supreme Court cited at length precedents and authorities to support the existence of a rule of international customary law that exempts fishing vessels from prize capture at the time of war.[11] The usage of the OAU/AU and African states forming the status quo practice could be tabulated and examined in a similar way. For the sake of clarity the African practice is categorized in four groups.

### 4.2.1.  *The practice of involvement in favour of the parent state*

In this category of African practice, when the territorial status quo is openly challenged by a secessionist movement, the OAU/AU and African states get directly involved supporting the parent state against the secessionists. The acts of the OAU/AU and African states during the secession attempts of Biafra, Anjouan and Azawad illustrate this practice.

#### The attempted secession of Biafra

Biafra's secession was declared unilaterally on 30 May 1967, triggering a war between the Nigerian Federal Government and the Biafran secessionists.[12] The matter was immediately taken up by the OAU at its next ordinary summit in Kinshasa in September that year.

In the Kinshasa Resolution, the African leaders resolved to send a Consultative Mission to the Head of the Federal Government of Nigeria 'to assure him of the Assembly's desire for the territorial integrity, unity

---

[10] R. A. Baxter, 'Multilateral Treaties as Evidence of Customary International Law' (1965–66) 41 *British YBK Int'l L* 275, 275.

[11] *The Paquete Habana; The Lola* (1900)175 US 677, 687–713.

[12] See Saadia Touval, *The Boundary Politics of Independent Africa* (Harvard 1972) 95–8; Bolaji Akinyemi, 'The Organization of African Unity and the Concept of Non-Interference in Internal Affairs of Member States' (1972–73) 46 *British YBK Int'l L* 393.

and peace of Nigeria'.[13] The carefully worded Resolution shows how the OAU was keen to express its support for the territorial unity of a Member State in the face of an *internal* attempt at secession.[14] Fearing to create an impression that Biafra has a status equal to Nigeria at the OAU, the OAU Mission to Nigeria visited Lagos but it did not visit Biafra.

After its visit to Nigeria, the OAU Mission issued a communiqué calling for a solution on the basis of 'the preservation of Nigeria's unity and territorial integrity'.[15] On receiving the progress report of the Consultative Mission the OAU Assembly of Heads of State and Government issued a resolution in which it appealed 'solemnly and urgently to the two parties involved in the civil war to agree to preserve in the overriding interest of Africa, the unity of Nigeria and accept immediately suspension of hostilities and the opening without delay, of negotiations intended to preserve unity of Nigeria'.[16] When Biafra ultimately surrendered in January 1970, the Biafran leader considered his decision an acceptance of 'the OAU Resolution'.[17]

When the war between Nigeria and the Biafra secessionists intensified, and the humanitarian tragedy aggravated, sympathy for the Biafran cause mounted the world over. At that time, four African states, namely Tanzania, Gabon, Ivory Coast, and Zambia, recognized Biafra as an independent state.[18] Although all other African states maintained their steadfast position against the Biafran secession,[19] the dissenting position taken by those four states raises the question as to whether a practice that was not observed or accepted by every state gives rise to custom or not.

As a matter of principle Oppenheim clarified that uniform acceptance of a practice is not a precondition to custom creation.[20] In the *Case Concerning Military and Paramilitary Activities in and against Nicaragua (Nicaragua/United States of America)*, the ICJ concluded:

> The Court does not consider that, for a rule to be established as customary, the corresponding practice must be in absolutely rigorous conformity

---

[13]  OAU AHG/Res 51 (IV) (14 September 1967).

[14]  Touval, *Boundary Politics* 96.

[15]  *Ibid.* 97.

[16]  OAU AHG/Res 58 (VI) (10 September 1969).

[17]  *Ibid.* 98.

[18]  Britain-Biafra Association, *Statements by Tanzania, Gabon, Ivory Coast & Zambia on Their Recognition of Biafra* (Britain-Biafra Association 1968).

[19]  Touval, Boundary Politics 97.

[20]  Lassa Oppenheim, *International Law* ed. by Robert Jennings and Arthur Watts (9th edn, Oxford University Press 1992) 29.

with the rule. In order to deduce the existence of customary rules, the Court deems it sufficient that the conduct of states should in general be consistent with such rules, and that instances of state conduct inconsistent with a given rule should generally have been treated as breaches of that rule, not as indication of a recognition of a new rule.[21]

Consequently, the failure of those four states to conform does not affect the establishing of the customary rule in question. Notably, the four states did not take their position in defiance of the status quo and were prompted by fears that the Ibos of Biafra were being massacred and subjected to extermination.[22] As such their stand was perceived within a humanitarian context.[23] Instead of weakening the African custom the isolated action of the four states forms a rare exception from an otherwise stringently followed practice.[24]

### The attempted secession of Anjouan

The State of Comoros consists of four islands, Grande Comore, Mohéli, Anjouan, and Mayotte. After a referendum, three of the islands became independent in 1975, while the fourth, Mayotte, remains under French administration.[25] Decision-making in Comoros has been centralized on Grande Comore and has allegedly led to the favouring of this bigger island over the others. Disaffected Anjouan and Mohéli declared secession unilaterally in August 1997 and managed in September to repel a forceful attempt by Grand Comore to restore unity.[26] Failing to suppress the separatists in Anjouan, which became the locus of secessionist activity, the central government invited the OAU to help.

In June 1998, the OAU Council of Ministers issued a decision stressing the need for the Anjouanese Party to commit itself to dialogue 'on

---

[21] *Case Concerning Military and Paramilitary Activities in and against Nicaragua (Nicaragua/United States of America)* Merits [1986] ICJ Rep 14,98.

[22] See the statements of Tanzania and Gabon at www.biafraland.com/biafra_recognized_by_tanzania.htm, and www.biafraland.com/biafra_recognised_by_Gabon.htm (accessed 12 March 2015).

[23] Malcolm Shaw, *Title to Territory in Africa: International Legal Issues* (Clarendon 1986) 209.

[24] See Touval, *Boundary Politics* 97.

[25] The OAU persistently objected to annexing Mayotte to France and issued a number of resolutions in this regard. See for instance EX CL/Dec 488 (XIV) (30 January 2009); EX CL/Dec 632 (XVIII) (28 January 2011).

[26] For the separatist action of Anjouan see generally G. J. Naldi, 'Separatism in the Comoros: Some Legal Aspects' (1998) 11 *Leiden JIL* 247; Emma Svensson, *The African Union's Operations in the Comoros: MAES and Operation Democracy* (FOI, Swedish Defence Research Agency, 2008); H. A. Hassan, 'The Comoros and the Crisis of Building a National State' (2009) 2 *CAA* 229.

the basis of the respect for the principle of the unity and territorial integrity of the Comoros'.[27] In April 1999, the OAU convened a conference in Madagascar that produced the Antananarivo Agreement, which contained the three OAU principles for resolving the crisis. These were: a) the unity and territorial integrity of the Comoros; b) a unified solution based on inclusivity of all parties and interest groups from the three islands; and c) a return to constitutional order. The Anjouanese Movement refused to sign the Antananarivo Agreement.[28] This led the OAU Council of Ministers to issue another decision recommending to the OAU Assembly of Heads of State and Government the endorsement of a proposal on military-related measures against the Anjouanese separatists.[29]

Following the death of the elected President of Comoros, a coup d'état took place on 30 April 1999 led by Colonel Azali. This complicated further the Antananarivo Accord process. Pursuant to the OAU 1999 Algiers Declaration on Unconstitutional Changes of Government, the OAU was obligated not to recognize Colonel Azali's Government. In July 2000 the OAU Assembly issued a resolution in which it reiterated its commitment to the unity and territorial integrity of the Comoros and approved the proposals of the Council of Ministers aimed at intervening militarily to put an end to the separatist crisis in Anjouan through military measures.[30]

Hard pressed by the OAU and isolated by the international community, Colonel Azali recognized the separatists and signed on 26 August 2000 an Agreement with Colonel Abeid of Anjouan despite the OAU stand. Additionally, in November 2000 Colonel Azali visited Tripoli, Libya, and issued a joint communiqué with Colonel Qaddafi who expressed support for 'Colonel Azali's efforts to end the crisis in the separatist island of Anjouan'.[31] Fearing that the recognition of the accord of August 2000 by African states might mount and lead to a legalizing of the separation, the OAU convened a Ministerial Meeting for the countries of the region on 29 December 2000 in Pretoria and rejected the Azali/Abeid accord.[32]

Subsequently the OAU sent a negotiation/mediation team to the Comoros to conclude the Framework Agreement for Reconciliation

---

[27] CM/Dec 405 (LXVIII) (June 1998).

[28] Available at www.dfa.gov.za/foreign/Multilateral/profiles/como.htm (accessed 11 March 2015).

[29] Decision on the Comoros (CM/2164 (LXXII) –c) (8 July 2000).

[30] OAU AHG/Dec 149 (XXXVI) (12 July 2000).

[31] All Africa.com, http://allafrica.com/stories/200011190043.html (accessed 11 March 2015).

[32] Available at www.dfa.gov.za/foreign/Multilateral/profiles/como.htm (accessed 11 March 2015).

in the Comoros signed in Fomboni, Comoros, on 17 February 2001, which confirmed the OAU principles as contained in the Antananarivo Agreement. Because the three principles of the OAU were guaranteed in the Fomboni Agreement, the OAU Council of Ministers, meeting in Tripoli, Libya from 24 to 26 February 2001 decided to immediately suspend the measures taken by the OAU against the secessionists. In June 2001 the OAU sent to Comoros a Ministerial delegation of the countries of the region and the OAU Troika 'to assist the Comorian Parties in their efforts towards the restoration of the unity and territorial integrity of the country'.[33] The separatists were thus forced to withdraw their territorial claim and accept a federal system in which the Presidency was decided to be rotational between the three islands.

The position taken by Libya shortly before the OAU managed to push through its agenda is reminiscent of the position taken by the four states that recognized Biafra. Rather than being seen as an indication of a new trend, Libya's attitude was viewed by other African states as a dangerous breach. This motivated the OAU to bring all Comorian parties together to conclude the Fomboni Agreement. Libya soon joined the African consensus and convened the summit at which the collective African decision of lifting the sanctions formerly imposed on the secessionists was taken.

## The Unilateral Declaration of Azawad

The Tuareg Saharan region in Northern Mali witnessed three bouts of war in 1962–4, 1990–5, and 2006–9 that were ended by short-lived peace agreements focused on the age-long demands of the Tuareg for autonomy and participation in the central government and the military.[34] However, no claims for secession were ever made until 2012.

After the downfall of Qaddafi in October 2011 in neighbouring Libya, which is home to a small Tuareg community, the National Movement for the Liberation of Azawad (known as MNLA as per its French name) was launched. Benefiting from the return of the well-trained and well-armed Malian Tuareg soldiers, who were employed in the Libyan army,[35] the MNLA stepped up a liberation struggle and controlled the entire territory of Northern Mali. On 6 April 2012, the 'Independent State of Azawad' was announced.[36]

---

[33] CM/Dec 11 (LXXIV) (8 July 2001).

[34] Stephen A. Emerson, 'Desert Insurgency: Lessons from the Third Tuareg Rebellion' (2011) 22 *Small Wars & Insurgencies* 669, 672.

[35] See 'Ex-Gaddafi Tuareg Fighters Boost Mali Rebels' BBC, 17 October 2011, at www.bbc.co.uk/news/world-africa-15334088 (accessed 11 March 2015).

[36] BBC Report at www.bbc.co.uk/news/world-africa-17635437 (accessed 11 March 2015).

The AU Assembly issued in July 2012 a decision reiterating 'the indefectible commitment of the AU to the respect of the national unity and territorial integrity of Mali, which are non-discussable and non-negotiable'.[37] The AU Assembly of Heads of State and Government also issued in July 2012 a Solemn Declaration on Mali 'noting that the situation in Mali calls into question some of the most basic principles of the AU, notably the respect of the national unity and territorial integrity of Member States'.[38] The Declaration reaffirmed 'the unflinching commitment of the AU and that of all its Member States to the national unity and territorial integrity of the Republic of Mali ... and Africa's determination to spare no effort to ensure their preservation'.[39] Notably the AU Declaration stated conditions for the negotiation with the rebels, which included 'the respect of the unity and territorial integrity of Mali'.[40]

Following UNSC Resolution 2085 (2012), France led a military operation, Operation Serval, against the MNLA as a counter-terrorism measure.[41] As a result, the MNLA military grip over Northern Mali weakened and its unilateral declaration of independence had been aborted. On 23 May 2014, a Ceasefire Agreement was concluded and complemented on 24 July 2014 by a Declaration of Cessation of Hostilities. Under the mounting pressure of the AU and the international community, the MNLA recognized the territorial integrity of Mali and settled to claiming an autonomous status for Northern Mali under the name 'Azawad'.[42] A mediation process led by Algeria, with the backing of the UN and the AU, was soon started with the announced goal of arriving at a political settlement preserving the unity of Mali. On 11 February 2015, the AU Peace and Security Council sent a Field Mission to Mali, jointly with the European Union (EU), within a broad context of supporting a comprehensive political deal of a united Mali.[43] The UN Security Council was

---

[37] Doc Assembly/AU/6 (XIX) (16 July 2012).
[38] Assembly/AU/Decl1 (XIX) (16 July 2012).
[39] *Ibid.*
[40] In recognition of African custom, the UNSC Res 2085 (20 December 2012) UN Doc S/RES/10870 confirmed the AU conditions.
[41] UNSC Resolution 2085 (20 December 2012).
[42] Press TV report at www.presstv.ir/detail/2013/06/19/309728/mali-signs-ceasefire-deal-with-tuaregs/ (accessed 11 March 2015); *Guardian* report at www.guardian.co.uk/world/2013/jun/19/mali-peace-deal-tuareg-insurgents-aid (accessed 11 March 2015).
[43] See Communiqué of the AUPSC 486th Meeting at www.peaceau.org/en/article/joint-field-mission-of-the-peace-and-security-council-of-the-african-union-and-the-european-union-political-and-security-committee-to-mali-10-14-february-2015 (accessed 11 March 2015).

also openly supportive of the announced objective of the political process. In a Presidential Statement, the UN Security Council called on the
Malian parties 'to make the necessary concessions, while respecting the
sovereignty, unity and territorial integrity of the Malian State'.[44]

On 1 March 2015, an agreement was finalized and signed by the Malian
Government and some of the movements in Northern Mali. Notably, the
1 March agreement confirmed the unity of Mali but did not recognize
the autonomous status that the MNLA demanded. The agreement does
not acknowledge the term 'Azawad' as an alternative for 'Northern Mali'.
However, it is conceded that Azawad is 'a human, sociocultural, memorial and symbolic reality shared by different populations of the north'. On
3 March 2015, the Chairperson of the AU Commission issued a statement
welcoming the agreement, stating that 'this document constitutes a balanced compromise taking into account the concerns of all the parties, on
the basis of the scrupulous respect of the unity, territorial integrity and
sovereignty of Mali'.[45] Apparently, for the AU any unity-compliant deal
is considered balanced and welcome regardless of the details. The MNLA
could not sign the 1 March agreement immediately and asked for time to
consult its grass roots.[46] It remains to be seen whether this agreement will
be joined by the MNLA and other main rebel groups to put to an end the
Azawad claim for secession.

### 4.2.2.   *The practice of the 'black wall of silence'*

While states that fail to crush secession movements, like Comoros and
Mali, welcome the full involvement of the OAU/AU, states that are willing to contend with their secessionists are normally sceptical about any
such role. The reason for this reluctance is that engagement of the regional
organization is feared to give the secessionists *de facto* recognition and
equal standing with the parent state.

Throughout the Biafran crisis, Nigeria was objecting to the OAU
involvement, contending that the conflict was an internal Nigerian

---

[44]   Available at www.un.org/press/en/2015/sc11771.doc.htm (accessed 11 March 2015).
[45]   Available at www.aps.dz/en/algeria/6267-au-welcomes-signing-in-algiers-of-peace,-
reconciliation-agreement-in-mali (accessed 11 March 2014).
[46]   Available at www.aps.dz/en/algeria/6267-au-welcomes-signing-in-algiers-of-peace,-
reconciliation-agreement-in-mali (accessed 11 March 2015). On 5 March the UN
Security Council also issued a welcoming statement, see https://minusma.unmissions.
org/en/press-statement-unsc-president (accessed 11 March 2015).

affair.[47] The Nigerian Head of Government General Gowon was disinclined to see the committee of African leaders who visited Nigeria. When he finally met the leaders, he told them that: 'the OAU has rightly seen our problem as a purely domestic affair and, in accordance with the OAU Resolution, your Mission is not here to mediate'.[48]

Likewise, the Congolese authorities were not willing to cooperate with the OAU initiative in the Katanga crisis, fearing that any OAU mediation would give the Katanga secessionists access to the African forum.[49] The same attitude was followed by other African states including Ethiopia and Sudan. This led the OAU/AU to respect the wishes of the parent state when the latter asserts that a secession situation within her jurisdiction is an internal affair that is not to surface as an agenda item at the OAU meetings.

In addition, in Africa secessionists normally disguise their secession claim as we shall see in Chapter 6. When a secessionist movement does not call openly for secession, the OAU/AU finds it difficult to follow the practice of direct involvement in favour of the parent state.

As a result another usage, forming a second category of African state practice, appeared.

Under this category, referred to herein as the practice of the 'black wall of silence',[50] when a secessionist movement starts its activities, regardless of whether it announces a unilateral declaration or not, the OAU/AU imposes on the movement blanket diplomatic isolation. This is done by formally ignoring the secession and not allowing it to appear on the agenda of OAU/AU official meetings. Individual African states take part in the practice when they consciously avoid recognizing the unilateral declaration made by the secessionists or the secession situation in its entirety. Moreover, African states avoid expressing concern or criticising the parent state as to the way it deals with the secessionist movement.

---

[47] Touval, *Boundary Politics* 96.

[48] Akinyemi, 'The Organization of African Unity' 398.

[49] The practice of the OAU in dealing with the aftermath of the Katanga secession is not part of the practice under the Cairo Resolution because the Katanga secession was considered by the UN Security Council to have been 'with the aid of external resources and manned by foreign mercenaries', see UNSC Res 161 (21 February 1961) UN Doc S/RES/4741 and UNSC Res 169 (24 November 1961) UN Doc S/RES/5002. The OAU Resolution ECM/Res 7 (IV) (21 December 1964) and the OAU Kinshasa Resolution of 1967 were in response to the appeal of the UN Security Council to support the central government of the Congo.

[50] The author finds this practice analogous to the usage termed the 'blue wall of silence' that takes place when police officers act on the assumption that there is an unspoken rule that they would watch each others' backs and remain silent to protect of a colleague at fault.

Additionally, in recognition of this African custom, the United Nations and the international community refrain from dealing with the secessionist movement or the state that it declares.[51]

Being all about silence, the practice of the 'black wall of silence' raises the issue of whether an omission or abstinence, as opposed to an act, could form a 'practice' in the technical sense of the word. In the *Lotus Case*, France drew the attention of the Court to the fact that 'questions of jurisdiction in collision cases, which frequently arise before civil courts, are but rarely encountered in the practice of criminal courts'. France deduced from this that 'in practice, prosecutions only occur before the courts of the State whose flag is flown and that that circumstance is proof of a tacit consent on the part of States'.[52] The Court found that this conclusion was unwarranted:

> [B]ecause absence of criminal prosecution in the circumstances would merely show that States had often, in practice, abstained from instituting criminal proceedings, and not that they recognized themselves as being obliged to do so; for only if such abstention were based on their being conscious of having a duty to abstain would it be possible to speak of an international custom.[53]

Akehurst considered this finding 'a clear inference that omissions accompanied by *opinio juris* can give rise to a rule of customary law'.[54] Villiger also adheres to the view that 'qualified passive conduct may constitute part of general practice and thus contributes towards the formation or continuous existence of a customary rule'.[55] On this basis it is concluded that conscious omission of the OAU/AU and African states out of a belief that there exists a duty to abstain forms state practice.

We now turn to examining how this practice unfolds. Because in some cases the African practice succeeds in isolating the secessionist situations to the extent of making them almost unknown,[56] the cases studied here, of Eritrea, South Sudan, and Somaliland, are the high-profile instances of this practice.

---

[51] J. Klabbers and R. Lefeber, 'Africa: Lost between Self-determination and Uti Possidetis' in C. Brolmann (ed.), *Peoples and Minorities in International Law* (Martinus Nijhoff 1993) 69.

[52] *Case of the SS 'Lotus'* [1927] PCIJ Rep Series A No 10, 28.

[53] *Ibid.*

[54] Akehurst, 'Custom as a Source of International Law' 10.

[55] Villiger, *Customary International Law and Treaties* 18.

[56] Examples of little known secessionist movements include the Caprivi Liberation Army, Caprivi Namibia; FLEC of Kabinda, Angola; and MFDC in Casamance, Senegal.

## The secession of Eritrea

Eritrean secessionists were of the opinion that the Ethiopian Emperor became active in creating the OAU after incorporating Eritrea in Ethiopia mainly to establish a regional body to ratify that incorporation.[57] As a matter of fact, throughout its long liberation struggle that continued from 1961 to 1991 Eritrea had no African forum to express its grievances and was neglected by the OAU.[58] No single OAU Resolution was issued regarding Eritrea.

Shaw commented as follows on the practice of neglect and silence that was followed with regard to Eritrea:

> African attitudes towards the Eritrea issue reflected the concern for the territorial integrity of the independent African States that had proved so potent on the continent … The OAU itself has been noticeably reluctant to criticize Ethiopia and the overall African position remains that of support for the territorial integrity of that country.[59]

Iyob stressed that the apathy of the African states towards the Eritrean cause was to be attributed to the role played by the Ethiopian military and diplomacy. She said:

> At best, it would be naïve, or at worst, condescending, to assume that African leaders were ignorant about the Eritrean-Ethiopian conflict, although they were certainly misinformed. In any case, it appears that their silence on the issue was a function both of Ethiopian military prowess and effective diplomatic leverage strong enough to block any official recognition.[60]

If it were not for the OAU indifference, no Ethiopian diplomatic dexterity or military prowess would have brought about that utter neglect by the entire African continent. However, Iyob's statement attests the practice of silence and omission.

When on the success of its liberation struggle Eritrea was eventually admitted to the African organization, the Eritrean President Isaias

---

[57] Paul H. Brietzke, 'Ethiopia's "Leap in the Dark": Federalism and Self-determination in the New Constitution' (1995) 39 *JAL* 19,116–17; Eritrean Department of Foreign Affairs (ed.) *Eritrea: Birth of a Nation* (1993), pages unnumbered.

[58] See Ruth Iyob, *The Eritrean Struggle for Independence: Domination, Resistance, Nationalism, 1941–1993* (Cambridge University Press 1997) 47–60; generally Dan Connell, *Against All Odds: A Chronicle of the Eritrean Revolution* (Red Sea 1993); Brietzke, 'Ethiopia's "Leap in the Dark"' 112–19; Antonio Cassese, *Self-determination of Peoples: A Legal Appraisal* (Cambridge University Press 1995) 218–22.

[59] Shaw, *Title to Territory in Africa* 212.

[60] Iyob, *The Eritrean Struggle* 52.

Afewerki criticised bitterly the role played by the OAU during the long Eritrean war. In his debut speech at the Harare Summit in 1996, he accused the OAU of doing too little not only for Eritrea but for Africa as a whole.[61]

The same practice of utter neglect was also followed regarding the two wars of South Sudan of 1955–70 and 1983–2005.

### The secession of South Sudan

When the OAU was founded in 1963, South Sudan's first civil war, fought by the Anya-Nya movement, was eight years old. When secession was openly claimed by the Anya-Nya, the OAU and African states officially ignored the war despite the sympathy of some sub-Saharan states with South Sudan. Shaw concluded that the African attitude towards the first civil war of Sudan ranged between indisposition to support the Anya-Nya, attempting to influence it, and compromise. He stated:

> Although some African States were sympathetic to the struggle of the Anya-Nya and Uganda appeared to tolerate the existence of its bases on its territory, there was never any support at governmental level for the proposed secession. Uganda and other concerned African States directed their influence primarily at an attempt to convince the separatists to compromise with the Sudanese authorities.[62]

The OAU followed the same policy of neglect with regard to the second civil war, despite avoiding an open call for secession by the Sudan Peoples' Liberation Movement (SPLM). However, during the second war the Government of Sudan was hard pressed by internal and international backing for the South Sudan right to a referendum. Sudan resorted in 1994 to a sub-regional organization, the Inter-Governmental Authority for Development (IGAD), preferring it to the OAU in order not to give the SPLM equal standing at the regional organization.[63] On its part, the OAU pursued its practice and formally ignored the IGAD mediation. No reference was made to the war or the mediation process by the OAU/AU

---

[61] Connell, *Against all Odds* 282–3.

[62] Shaw, *Title to Territory in Africa* 211.

[63] For Sudan peace-making efforts at the IGAD see J. Young, 'Sudan: A Flawed Peace Process Leading to a Flawed Peace' (2005) 32 *Review APE* 99; J. Young, *The Fate of Sudan: The Origins and Consequences of a Flawed Peace Process* (Zed Books Ltd 2012); Hilde F. Johnson, *Waging Peace in Sudan: The Inside Story of the Negotiations that Ended Africa's Longest Civil War* (Sussex Academic Press 2011).

until Khartoum agreed in the Machakos Protocol of 20 July 2002 to give South Sudan the right to self-determination. In the Maputo Resolution of 2003, the OAU welcomed 'the significant progress made in the Sudan peace talks under the auspices of IGAD and with the support of the international community'. No specific reference was made to the Machakos Protocol itself or the principle it contains.[64]

## The case of Somaliland

The current case of Somaliland is another example of how the OAU and the African states adhere to the status quo by omission. Somaliland became an independent state on 26 June 1960, and joined Somalia on 1 July 1960 to create the Somali Republic.[65] On finding that Southern Somalis monopolized power in the merged state, Somalilanders soon regretted their hasty decision.[66] In the referendum of June 1961, Somalilanders rejected the unitary constitution and soon started a rebellion to restore their independence. Eventually, the Somalilanders' action was one of the reasons for the collapse of Somalia.[67] When the central government crumbled in Mogadishu, Somaliland declared in Hargeisa in May 1991 its unilateral secession from Somalia.[68]

Since then, Somaliland has been administered autonomously and is more peaceful when compared to its war-ridden parent state.[69] However, up to now no African state has recognized the independence of Somaliland and the AU has never included the secession of Somaliland as an official agenda item. In 2005, the AU sent a mission to Somaliland on the insistence of the government of the region.[70] However, the report of that mission was not formally tabled before the AU Council of Ministers and no action was taken upon it.[71]

The silence surrounding Somaliland became deafening ever since the 2005 Somali process of reconciliation, which is intended to re-establish the central government of Mogadishu, started to appear as a permanent

---

[64] Doc EX/CL/42(III) (8 July 2003).
[65] I. M. Lewis, 'Somali Republic' in Colin Legum (ed.), *Africa: A Handbook* (2nd edn, Anthony Blond Ltd 1965) 83.
[66] I. M. Lewis, *A Modern History of the Somali* (4th edn, East African Studies 2002) 173–8.
[67] *Ibid.* 173–8.    [68] *Ibid.* 265–6.    [69] *Ibid.*
[70] ICG, *Somaliland: Time for African Union Leadership* (Africa Report No 110, 2006) 2.
[71] *Ibid.* For the OAU/AU denial of the *de facto* state of Somaliland see Aaron Kreuter, 'Self-Determination, Sovereignty, and the Failure of States: Somaliland and the Case for Justified Secession' (2010) 19 *Minessota JIL* 363; Alison K. Eggers, 'When is a State a State: The Case for Recognition of Somaliland' (2007) 30 *Boston College ICLR* 211.

agenda item in the AU summits.[72] Despite the recurrence of the issue over long years, none of the numerous AU resolutions, decisions, and statements on the Somali reconciliation process alludes to the fact that Somaliland political actors desist from taking part in the process because of the Hargeisa unilateral declaration. The AU sometimes condemns in general terms 'all attempts aimed at undermining the ongoing peace and reconciliation process in Somalia', but without mentioning Somaliland by name.[73] Even if the threat to the unity of Somalia posed by the *de facto* independence of Somaliland is unmistakable, the AU avoids referring to this state of affairs in the infrequent resolutions in which it reaffirms the unity of Somalia. On 31 May 1997, the OAU adopted a resolution to assert 'the sovereignty, unity and territorial integrity of Somalia as one and indivisible State'.[74] Again, on 20 February 2015, the AU Peace and Security Council (AUPSC) adopted a decision on the situation in Somalia that 'further reiterates [AUPSC] commitment to the unity, territorial integrity and sovereignty of Somalia'.[75] It is not clarified in any of those statements why the AU finds such occasional reiterations required.[76]

### 4.2.3.   The practice of rejecting state-to-state territorial claims

A territorial claim made by an African state against another is the mischief that the entire African territorial regime is created to eliminate. Consequently, the reaction of the OAU towards such claims takes the

---

[72] AU Resolutions Assembly AU/Dec 65 (IV) (31 January 2005); Assembly/AU/Dec 142 (VIII) (30 January 2007) and Assembly AU Dec 193(XV) (27 July 2010). From 2008 the situation in Somalia became a regular item in the annual report of the AUPSC on its Activities and the Status of Peace and Security in Africa, also without making reference to Somaliland.

[73] Assembly AU/Dec 193 (XV) (27 July 2010).

[74] CM/Dec 357 (LXVI) (31 May 1997).

[75] Available at www.peaceau.org/en/article/communique-487th-peace-and-security-council-of-the-african-union-meeting-on-the-situation-in-somalia#sthash.AHE61WGX.x2VmOHLQ.dpuf (accessed 14 March 2015).

[76] The issue of Somaliland attracted some attention in legal literature. Writers argued that Somaliland satisfied the conventional requirements of recognition provided for in Article I of the Montevideo Convention on the Rights and Duties of States of 1933. See A. Carroll and B. Rajagopal, 'The Case for the Independent Statehood of Somaliland' (1992) 8 *Am UJ Int'l L & Pol'y* 653,678; Eggers, 'When is a State a State' 214–17; Deon Geldenhuys, *Contested States in World Politics* (Palgrave 2009) 135. Kreuter suggested that the Somaliland case justifies the recognition of a right to secede from a failed state, see Kreuter, 'Self-Determination, Sovereignty, and the Failure of States'.

most extreme form of decided rejection. There are two examples for this practice.

### Admission of SADR to the OAU

Morocco and Mauritania laid their territorial claims on Western Sahara well before the departure of the Spanish administration, thus complicating the independence of that African country.[77] The Twenty-fifth Session of the OAU Council of Ministers, Kampala, July 1975, 'was unable to produce an acceptable resolution or recommendation on the question'.[78] When the UN General Assembly tabled the matter at the ICJ for Advisory Opinion, the OAU decided to await that opinion to illuminate its way.[79] After the ICJ finding that the Moroccan and Mauritanian claims were without merit,[80] the OAU's Fifteenth Summit, convened in Khartoum, Sudan, in July 1978, confirmed the right of the people of Western Sahara to self-determination and decided that an extraordinary summit on the Western Sahara should be convened.[81] It soon became clear that the self-determination referendum was unlikely to take place because of the Moroccan and Mauritanian complicating factor.

Frustrated by those negative actions, African states sympathized with the Western Saharan liberation movement, the Polisario. The Polisario invested that compassion in a diplomatic campaign for independence to win by 1980 the recognition of thirty-five African states.[82] During the OAU Seventeenth Ordinary Summit in Freetown, Sierra Leone, in June 1980, the Polisario presented an application for membership of the Sahrawi Arab Democratic Republic (SADR) in the OAU.[83] As a result of the mounting African support of the Polisario, Mauritania backed down. However, Morocco decided to continue to the bitter end.

Knowing that her claim might incur wrath rather than support if presented openly, Morocco preferred to object to the admission of SADR on

---

[77] For the right of Western Sahara to self-determination and how its exercise was affected by the claims of those states see Joshua Castellino, *International Law and Self-determination: The Interplay of the Politics of Territorial Possession with Formulations of Post-Colonial National Identity* (Martinus Nijhoff 2000) 180–211.

[78] OAU AHG/Res 75 (XII) (1 August 1975).

[79] *Ibid.*

[80] *Western Sahara* (Advisory Opinion) [1975] ICJ Rep 12, 47–9.

[81] OAU AHG/Res 92 (XV) (22 July 1978).

[82] For the support for the Polisario and the division it caused within the OAU see Gino J. Naldi, *The Organization of African Unity: An Analysis of Its Role* (2nd edn, Mansel 1999) 58–70.

[83] *Ibid.* 66.

procedural, as opposed to substantive, grounds and raised two issues. First, according to the OAU Resolution AHG/Res 92 (XV) adopted in Khartoum the matter of the Western Sahara was referred to an extraordinary summit, and hence could not be determined by the Seventeenth Ordinary Summit in Freetown. Second, according to Article IV of the OAU Charter, only independent sovereign states are entitled to membership of the OAU, and SADR did not fulfil this condition. In addition, Morocco threatened that it would withdraw from the OAU if the Polisario were seated.[84] No decision was taken on the matter in Freetown. However, in the Twentieth Assembly of Heads of State and Government in Addis Ababa, November 1984, the OAU decided to seat the Polisario. Morocco was left with no option but to act upon its threat and quit the OAU.[85]

Even though the decision to seat the Polisario was in accordance with the Cairo Resolution, the OAU did not invoke that Resolution explicitly. The reason for that is to be found in the guarded approach taken by Morocco of avoiding to advance her territorial claim on its merits. Conversely, when Libya made no secret of her claims on the territory of Chad, the OAU invoked the Cairo Resolution expressly, as we shall presently see.

## Libya's territorial claim against Chad

In 1973, Libya occupied the Aouzou strip along its border with Chad and annexed it without officially acknowledging its action.[86] When in 1977 Chad protested that act to the OAU, the OAU Assembly of Heads of State and Government formed an ad hoc mediation committee.[87]

In 1986, Libya advanced new claims to territories beyond the Aouzou strip to include the Chadian regions of Borkou, Ennedi and Tibesti. This changed the nature of the Libyan claim from a vertical claim to a horizontal claim. Instead of a claim rooted in a different perception as to where the independence boundary runs, Libya's second claim was for the establishment of a new boundary on the strength of an amalgam of arguments that were acknowledged not to have been the base of the independence boundary.[88] Consequently, and instead of a claim to a boundary strip, the second claim was to half of the Chadian territory. The new Libyan claim

---

[84] *Ibid.*     [85] *Ibid.* 70.

[86] Gino J. Naldi, 'The Aouzou Strip Dispute: A Legal Analysis' (1989) 33 *JAL* 72, 72.

[87] OAU AHG/DEC 108 (XIV) (22 July 1977); this Resolution was confirmed a year later by OAU AHG/Res 94 (XV) (22 July 1978).

[88] *Territorial Dispute (Libyan Arab Jamahiriya/Chad)* (Judgment) [1994] ICJ Rep 6, 16–20. See generally R. McKeon, 'The Aouzou Strip: Adjudication of Competing Territorial Claims in Africa by the International Court of Justice' (1991) 23 *Case Western Reserve Journal of International Law* 147.

was obviously indistinguishable from the Moroccan and Somali claims. An alarmed OAU Assembly of Heads of State and Government moved quickly to adopt on 30 July 1986 a resolution reaffirming 'the territorial integrity of Chad and inviolability of the borders'.[89] Despite the pressure exerted by Libya, the OAU Assembly maintained its course persistently and reaffirmed in a number of resolutions the status quo of the Chadian borders in accordance with the Cairo Resolution.[90]

The OAU position towards the claims made by Libya in 1986 stands in direct contrast with its position to the Libyan claims before that year. With regard to Libya's boundary claim on the Aouzou Strip an unperturbed OAU merely called upon the two states to resort to mediation to resolve their differences. In contrast, when Libya advanced its territorial claim the OAU stand amounted to utter denial of the Libyan right to make such claims to the territories of another African state.

### 4.2.4.   Embodying the status quo custom in treaty provisions

The rule of perpetuating the territorial status quo was enshrined in due course in OAU and AU instruments. The reference to a customary practice in treaty provisions constitutes part of state practice and is considered to form evidence of the customary status of the rule in question.[91]

The first OAU treaty that included the status quo rule was the Rules of the Mechanism for Conflict Prevention, Management and Resolution, 1993.[92] The principle of 'the inviolability of borders inherited from colonialism' was included in Rule 14 as a guiding principle of the Mechanism. Even as the African rule is referred to in the Rules of the Mechanism as 'the principle of inviolability of frontiers', the reference denotes the African custom of respecting the territorial status quo. The Rules of the Mechanism of Conflict Prevention have since lapsed with other OAU instruments. Yet, the reference in these Rules to the African custom passes as state practice.

---

[89]   OAU AHG/Res 158 (XXII) (30 July 1986). Notably, Libya had recorded a reservation to this Resolution.

[90]   OAU AHG/Res 167 (XXIII) (29 July 1987); and OAU AHG/Res 200 (XXVI) (11 July 1990).

[91]   Baxter, 'Multilateral Treaties' 277.

[92]   OAU Rules of the Mechanism for Conflict Prevention, Management and Resolution, 1993, available at www.peaceau.org/uploads/ahg-decl-3-xxix-e.pdf (accessed 11 March 2015); for the status of those rules within the OAU see Shadrack B. O. Gutto, 'The New Mechanism of the Organization of African Unity for Conflict Prevention, Management and Resolution, and the Controversial Concept of Humanitarian Intervention in International Law' (1996) 113 *South Africa LJ* 314.

The main treaty reinstatement for the African customary rule is Article 4(b) of the AU Constitutive Act 2000. In almost a verbatim reproduction of the Second Paragraph of the Cairo Resolution, Article 4(b) provides for the principle of 'respecting the borders existing on achievement of independence' among the guiding principles of the AU. In *Benin/Niger*, the ICJ had an opportunity to comment on Article 4(b) of the AU Constitutive Act. However, the ICJ merely reiterated its orthodox position and considered this provision as reflecting *uti possidetis*. The Court stated:

> As the Chamber formed in the case concerning *the Frontier Dispute (Burkina Faso/Republic of Mali)* had occasion to state, the existence of this principle has been recognized on several occasions in the African context; it was recognized again recently, in Article 4(b) of the Constitutive Act of the African Union.[93]

It has been explained in Chapter 3 that the Cairo Resolution is concerned with perpetuating the territorial status quo by preventing boundary changes and all forms of horizontal territory transfer.[94] When the African leaders met in Lome, Togo, in July 2000 to adopt the constituent instrument for the new incarnation of their organization, they found the rule laid down in Cairo in 1964 still relevant. If the Cairo Resolution was all about stressing the principle of *uti possidetis*, the African states would not have needed to recall it forty years after the completion of African independence.

The status quo rule was also inscribed in the Protocol Relating to the Establishment of the Peace and Security Council of the African Union 2002. Article 4(i) of the Protocol included the 'respect of borders inherited on achievement of independence' among the guiding principles of this important organ of the AU.[95]

Those provisions impose no new treaty obligations on African states. They merely reiterate the customary obligation that existed before the conclusion of the above-mentioned treaties.[96] The inclusion of those provisions in the AU Constitutive Act and the Protocol of the AUPSC evidences the acceptance by African states of the status quo rule as part of African customary international law.

---

[93] *Frontier Dispute (Benin/Niger)* (Judgment) [2005] ICJ Rep 90, 108; see also *Frontier Dispute (Burkina Faso/Niger)* (Judgment) [2013] ICJ Rep 1, 32.

[94] Section 3.2.1, text to footnotes 53–61.

[95] Availble at www.au.int/en/sites/default/files/Protocol_peace_and_security.pdf (accessed 11 March 2015).

[96] Baxter, 'Multilateral Treaties' 300.

### 4.2.5.    Assessment of African Practice

Akehurst opined that 'one can never prove a rule of customary law in an absolute manner but only in a relative manner – one can only prove that the majority of the evidence available supports the alleged rule'.[97] If Akehurst had had the opportunity to canvass the evidence of the African practice examined above, he would not have been as categorical in his denial of the possibility of absolute attestation of custom. Far from being relative, the evidence adduced for establishing the practice of perpetuating the territorial status quo is certainly absolute. Two reasons could be cited in support of this argument.

First, Waldock opined that 'where the occasions for acting only arise spasmodically, the density required for the practice will obviously be less'.[98] Having in mind the occasional recurrence of the incidents of secession and territorial claims in international discourse, the density of the African practice is remarkable.

Second, the African practice evidenced above is extraordinarily consistent. In the *Asylum Case* the ICJ described typically inconsistent evidence as disclosing 'so much uncertainty and contradiction, so much fluctuation', and 'so much influenced by considerations of political expediency in the various cases, that it is not possible to discern ... any constant and uniform usage, accepted as law'.[99] The standard stated by Villiger for consistent practice is that 'the instances of practice of individual States, and of States in general, circumscribe, apply, or refer to, and thereby express, the same customary rule'.[100] The evidence examined above establishes that the African practice is exceptionally uniform, constant and not subject to political considerations, and, as such, meets the standard for consistent practice.

Being remarkably dense and at the same time invariably consistent is a measure of an unqualified standard. Evidence that meets this exceptional description could by no means be considered less than absolute.

However, the reservation made by Morocco to the OAU Charter, its failure along with Somalia to join the acclamation of the Cairo Resolution, as well as the determined opposition of those two states to maintaining the

---

[97]  Akehurst, 'Custom as a Source of International Law' 13.
[98]  Humphrey Waldock, 'General Course on Public International Law' (1962) II *Recueil des Cours de l'Académie de Droit International* 1, 44.
[99]  *Colombian-Peruvian Asylum Case* (Judgment) [1950] ICJ Rep 266, 277; see Villiger, *Customary International Law and Treaties* 22.
[100]  Villiger, *Customary International Law and Treaties* 22.

inherited boundaries raise a question as to whether their position affects the African custom in any sense. While both states manifestly objected to the status quo rule at the initial stages, as explained above, they parted ways further down the line.

Morocco had withdrawn from the OAU in 1984 in protest to the seating of the Polisario. It is established that a state that persistently objected to a rule is not bound by it, so long as the objection was made manifest during the process of the rule's emergence.[101] In the *Fisheries Case (United Kingdom/Norway),* the Court held that even if there was a rule prohibiting the enclosure of bays by baselines exceeding ten miles in length, Norway would not be bound by it, since Norway had persistently objected to that rule.[102] Consequently, while the persistent objection of Morocco does not affect the emergence of the African customary rule, it means that Morocco is not bound by that rule.

Conversely, Somalia changed its position and is no longer objecting to the status quo rule. Somalia signed the AU Constitutive Act 2000 and joined the Protocol Relating to the Establishing of the Peace and Security Council 2002. Both instruments include articles that reiterate the African customary rule as explained earlier. Currently, Somalia is taking part in the practice of the 'black wall of silence' deployed against Somaliland for the benefit of the territorial unity of Somalia. As a result, the failure of Somalia to persist in its objection means that Somalia is now fully bound by the status quo rule despite its initial position.

### 4.3.    The *opinio juris* accompanying the status quo practice

#### 4.3.1.    *The standard of the* opinio juris

Because many consistent usages between states that are of habitual or ceremonial character qualify as settled practice, for establishing custom the emphasis is always laid on the subjective criteria or the *opinio juris.* The ICJ concluded in *the North Sea Continental Shelf Cases* that:

---

[101] Ted L. Stein, 'The Approach of the Different Drummer: The Principle of the Persistent Objector in International Law' (1985) 26 *Harv ILJ* 457, 458. See generally, David A. Colson, 'How Persistent Must the Persistent Objector Be?' (1986) 61 *Washington LR* 957; I. C. MacGibbon, 'Customary International Law and Acquiescence' (1957) 33 *British YBK Int'l L* 115, 118.

[102] (Judgment) [1951] 116, 131.

Not only must the acts concerned amount to a settled practice, but they must also be such, or be carried out in such a way, as to be evidence of a belief that this practice is rendered obligatory by the existence of a rule of law requiring it. The need for such a belief, i.e. the existence of a subjective element, is implicit in the very notion of the *opinio juris sive necessitatis*. The states concerned must therefore feel that they are conforming to what amounts to a legal obligation.[103]

In the *Lotus Case*, the failure to prove that the postulated abstention from instituting criminal proceedings was based 'on states being conscious of having a duty to abstain' was damaging to the case of France.[104]

The rule regarding the *opinio juris* pronounced in the *North Sea Continental Shelf Cases* was with respect to general custom. This raises the question as to whether the same standard is also required for special custom or not. The finding in the *Asylum Case* in relation to special custom that 'any feeling of legal obligation is sufficient'[105] was interpreted to mean that 'unlike the case of general custom, the *opinio juris* attached to [special custom] is of a consensualist nature'.[106] The correct reading of the *Asylum Case* does not support this interpretation. The standard required from Colombia was not less than that of general custom. Colombia was asked to show that the rule of unilateral and definitive qualification, which she alleged to exist, was 'exercised by the States granting asylum *as a right* appertaining to them and respected by the territorial States *as a duty* incumbent on them'.[107] Exercising a rule as a right or respecting it as a duty evidences a belief that it is obligatory. As such, the normal obligatory standard of general custom was applied.

---

[103] *North Sea Continental Shelf Cases* (n 1) 42.

[104] *Lotus Case* (n 52) 28. This raises the chicken and egg question of how states should regard conduct as obligatory before it becomes obligatory. Akehurst opined that this dilemma reveals 'the weakness of the traditional theory of *opinio juris*', Akehurst, 'Custom as a Source of International Law' 34–5; Thirlway suggested that the state that initiates the practice acts under the influence of an *opinio necessitatis* and when the rule comes into being states which act subsequently act in accordance with the *opinio juris*, H. W. A. Thirlway, *International Customary Law and Codification: An Examination of the Continuing Role of Custom in the Present Period of Codification of International Law* (Martinus Nijhoff 1972) 53–4. D'Amato used this weakness as a springboard for attacking the traditional theory of *opinio juris*, Anthony A D'Amato and RA Falk, *The Concept of Custom in International Law* (Cornell 1971) 67–8.

[105] *Asylum Case* (n 99) 286.

[106] Alain Pellet, 'Article 38' in A. Zimmermann, C. Tomuschat and K. Oellers-Frahm (eds.), *The Statute of the International Court of Justice: A Commentary* (Oxford University Press 2006) 764.

[107] *Asylum Case* (n 99) 277.

However uniform and extensive were the activities of the African states, the *opinio juris* is an additional requirement that could not be replaced by them. In the *North Sea Continental Shelf Cases,* it was concluded that 'State practice ... should have been both extensive and virtually uniform ... and should have moreover occurred in such a way as to show general recognition that a rule of law or legal obligation is involved'.[108] Referring to this requirement of establishing the *opinio juris* independently and separate from state practice, Akehurst posited that 'probably the only way such a requirement could be satisfied is by citing express statements by the States concerned'.[109] By insisting on citing express statements Akehurst contradicts his own approach of including omissions within state practice as well as his finding that 'there is a clear inference that omissions accompanied by *opinio juris* can give rise to a rule of customary law'.[110] The *opinio juris* accompanying omission is verifiable even if it does not take express form, as we shall presently see.

### 4.3.2.   The opinio juris *for the practice of the 'black wall of silence'*

The *opinio juris* accompanying the practice of the 'black wall of silence' could be established by the following five sources.

First, omission draws meaning from the legal background against which it takes place. The PCIJ found in the *Lotus Case* that abstention by states from instituting criminal proceedings 'based on their being conscious of having a duty to abstain' would have led to creating international custom.[111] It was difficult for France in the *Lotus Case* to prove its case because it was not possible to draw such inference from omission in the circumstances. The same difficulty does not arise in the case of the African practice of the 'black wall of silence'.

The prevailing legal culture exempts 'expressing concern' from the duty not to interfere. Cassese explained that the principle of non-interference does not bind states 'to remain silent, regardless of how a government behaves towards the peoples within its jurisdiction'.[112] He clarifies further that states are entitled to denounce the repressive measures of a government and 'publicly expose how it treats those subjected to its authority'.[113]

---

[108]  *North Sea Continental Shelf Cases* (n 1) 43.
[109]  Akehurst, 'Custom as a Source of International Law' 50 fn 4.
[110]  *Ibid.* 10.
[111]  *Lotus Case* (n 52) 28.
[112]  Cassese, *Self-determination of Peoples* 176.
[113]  *Ibid.*

When African states choose deliberately to remain silent while a secessionist movement is dealt with harshly, their departure from the lawful tradition of voicing concern denotes a conscious belief of having a duty to abstain.

Second, the OAU/AU occasionally issues wide-ranging resolutions that denounce secession in general terms, not confined to a particular instance. The first of such statements is possibly the Kinshasa Resolution on Biafra in which the African leaders reiterated 'their condemnation of secession in any Member States'.[114] The denouncement of the OAU Mission to Biafra of 'all secessionist attempts in Africa' is another example.[115] The most elaborate declaration in this regard is the recent decision of the AU Assembly of Heads of State and Government adopted in July 2012 during the crisis of Azawad. While discussing a report of the AUPSC on the crisis, the AU Assembly availed itself of the opportunity to 'condemn the secessionist tendencies observed in some parts of the Continent'. The Assembly underscored 'the unalloyed commitment of the AU to the principle of inviolability of borders inherited by African countries at independence, as well as the respect of the national unity and territorial integrity of Member States'.[116] Furthermore, the Assembly requested the AU Commission 'to submit concrete recommendations on how best to address the scourge of armed rebellion and secessionist demands' in the continent in general.

It is inconceivable that the Organization of American States or the European Union would issue similar statements. Hence, silence of those regional organizations, when secession is in issue in their respective jurisdictions, is construed as part of the international neutrality towards secession. Conversely, the occasional issuance of the statements referred to above by the OAU/AU shows that its silence is a conscious omission with the belief that it is obligatory to stand against secession in Africa.

Third, in some instances of secession or attempted secession the OAU/AU issues a resolution breaking its long silence and betraying that the African Organization is conscious of its omission. When the referendum of South Sudan, conducted on 9–12 January 2011, favoured secession the AU stressed in a resolution that the said development is specific to the Sudan. The OAU clearly expressed its concern about 'the sacrosanct principle of respect of borders' indicating that this was the reason behind its

---

[114] OAU AHG/ 51 (IV) (14 September 1967).
[115] Touval, *Boundary Politics* 97.
[116] Doc Assembly/AU/6 (XIX) (16 July 2012).

omission from issuing any resolution regarding the South Sudan conflict. At its Sixteenth Ordinary Session, 30–31 January 2011 in Addis Ababa, Ethiopia, the AU Assembly stated:

> We acknowledge that Sudan represents an exceptional case, which, in no way, calls into question the sacrosanct principle of respect of borders inherited at the accession of African countries to independence. We reaffirm our determination to ensure full respect of this principle and to forge ahead with our agenda of integration and greater unity among our countries, as foreseen by the founding fathers of the OAU and as enshrined in the AU Constitutive Act.[117]

Likewise, the AU reaffirmed on a number of occasions the unity of Somalia without explaining why the AU finds that necessary.[118] This shows that the AU silence towards the unilateral declaration of Somaliland is underlined by a position that denies that declaration.

Fourth, because the intention behind the OAU/AU omission is clear for African secessionists, and because it is futile to stand against the African central rule, secessionists normally adopt a cause alternative to the call for outright secession. This happened in the cases of Eritrea, South Sudan and Somaliland. All different liberation movements of Eritrea argued that their struggle is for reviving Eritrea's right to colonial self-determination.[119] The SPLM called itself 'the *Sudan* [not South Sudan] Peoples' Liberation Movement', and claimed that it was fighting to liberate the entire country.[120] Somalilanders claimed that they were calling for reviving the boundaries of their state that were once internationally recognized.[121] This aspect of African secessionism is examined in detail in Chapter 6. What matters here is that the secessionists' behaviour shows that they understand what the African silence entails.

Fifth, the international recognition of the African custom shows that the international community is aware of what the African omission means. When in December 2005 Somaliland applied to join the UN the United States and the United Kingdom, deferring to the African practice,

---

[117] Assembly/AU/Dec 338 (XVI) (31 January 2011).
[118] See: CM/Dec 357 (LXVI) (31 May 1997); AUPSC Decision on the Situation in Somalia adopted on 20 February 2015.
[119] Iyob, *The Eritrean Struggle for Independence* 127.
[120] F. M. Deng, *War of Visions: Conflict of Identities in the Sudan* (Brookings 1995) 19–20 and 234–5.
[121] Geldenhuys, *Contested States* 132; Lewis, *A Modern History of the Somali* 282.

announced that recognition of Somaliland is a matter for the African Union.[122]

### 4.3.3.    *The* opinio juris *for other categories of African practice*

The *opinio juris* in categories of African practice other than the 'black wall of silence' is revealed in the more direct form of express statements.

As to the first category of direct involvement favouring unity, OAU/AU resolutions mostly state in no uncertain terms the rules that African states believe should be respected. The communiqué of the OAU Mission to Nigeria called for a solution on the basis of 'the preservation of Nigeria's unity and territorial integrity'.[123] The OAU faced the attempted secession of Anjouan at a time when the Moroni Government was either unable or unwilling to protect the territorial integrity of the country. African states believed that it was their duty to preserve the territorial unity of the Comoros regardless of what the Comorian Government was willing or unwilling to do. The OAU principles enshrined in the Antananarivo Agreement, and later in the Fomboni Framework, are unequivocal in expressing that maintenance of the territorial unity of Comoros was the duty of the whole continent. The decisions of the OAU Council of Ministers on the Comoros, particularly the Lome Decision of 2000 and the Lusaka Decision of 2001, included specific statements regarding the obligation believed to exist with regard to the preservation of the territorial unity of the Comorian islands. Likewise, in the case of Azawad, where the Malian Government was obviously unable to deter the military threat of the MNLA unassisted, the AU Solemn Declaration on Mali, July 2012, referred to 'the respect of the unity and territorial integrity of Mali' as the condition for negotiations with the rebels. This condition was to be respected by both parties, the government as well as the rebels. The statement of the President of the African Commission considering the 1 March Agreement balanced on account of its 'scrupulous respect of the unity, territorial integrity and sovereignty of Mali' betrays that the AU

---

[122] *Financial Times*, 'Somaliland Seeks US Help in Battle for Recognition' (24 August 2006) 8, available at www.ft.com/cms/s10/90e4f022-330d-11db-87ac-0000779e2340.html#axzz3iRLxkg9F (accessed 16 June 2015). Notably, for the USA, in accordance with the principle established by the US Supreme Court, Somaliland had satisfied the standard of 'ultimate success' required for recognition, *Williams v Bruffy* (1877) 96 US 176,185–6; see also Klabbers and Lefeber, 'Africa: Lost between Self-determination and Uti Possidetis' 69.

[123] Touval, *Boundary Politics* 97.

is not simply a mediator. The AU is in fact a principal stakeholder with genuine interest in the preservation of the unity of Mali.

With regard to the third category, which is the practice of rejecting state-to-state territorial claims, the admitting of SADR to the OAU before it had attained independence expresses an element of *opinio juris*. It indicates that African states believe that they were bound to admit SADR by a substantive rule that trumps the procedural technicality of formal independence. Even as in this instance there was no statement by the OAU to express the *opinio juris*, the readiness of the OAU General Assembly to go to the extent of violating procedural rules to admit SADR evinces the *opinio juris* required. As to the Libya/Chad dispute, the affirmation in Resolution AHG/Res 158 (XXII) of July 1986, and in resolutions that followed, of the territorial integrity of Chad and inviolability of its borders in conformity with the Cairo Resolution forms an express statement of the *opinio juris*.

In the fourth category, that of embodying the African customary rule in treaty provisions, while the letter of the provisions inscribing the rule counts as state practice, the broader custom found to underlie those texts is the subjective criterion. On one hand, the *usus* of this practice, i.e. the evidence of the existence of the African custom, are the texts of Rule 14 of the Rules of the Mechanism for Conflict Prevention 1993, Article 4(b) of the AU Constitutive Act 2000, and Article 4(i) of the Protocol of the AUPSC 2002.[124] On the other hand, the *opinio juris*, is the customary rule that those provisions, regardless of any discrepancies in their language, uniformly evince.[125] While the *opinio juris* is independent of the wording of any text concluded subsequent to the creation of the custom, it is also not expressed by the letter of the antecedent text, being in this case the Cairo Resolution, the 'generator' and nucleus of the new customary rule.[126] The *opinio juris* is the authoritative change in international law that the custom made.

In conclusion, Chapter 2 and Chapter 4 have established that the unanimous acceptance of the inherited boundaries by African states on

---

[124] Baxter, 'Multilateral Treaties' 277.

[125] *North Sea Continental Shelf Cases* (n 1) 41; However, Villiger opines that the *opinio juris* in question must coincide with the 'generator', being the *jus scriptum*, Villiger, *Customary International Law and Treaties* 193, 197.

[126] The term 'generator' was used in reference to initiating custom by a written rule by Humphrey Waldock, 'Sixth Report on the Law of Treaties' (1966) II *YBK Int'l LC* 51, 74, paragraphs 1 and 3, the *North Sea Continental Shelf Cases* (n 1) 41, then by Villiger, *Customary International Law and Treaties* 193 and 198 fn 1.

independence and the multifarious types of practice generated by the Cairo Resolution, together with accompanying *opinio juris*, gave rise to two customary rules. The rule of intangibility of inherited frontiers and the rule of respecting the territorial status quo, thus created, made wide-ranging changes in international law as it applies to Africa. The following chapter explores those changes.

# 5

## The changes made in international law by African custom

The customary rules of intangibility of inherited frontiers and respecting the territorial status quo introduced significant changes in international law as it applies to Africa. In particular, two peremptory norms of prohibiting the redrawing of boundaries and proscribing secession are created. In addition, African custom reformulates the concept of the critical date as it applies to Africa. Furthermore, the African law regime approaches differently a number of matters of the law of territory, including: the source of legal force of treaty-based boundaries together with the legal mechanism for upgrading such boundaries to international frontiers. Admissibility of post-colonial subsequent conduct, estoppel, sovereignty over islands not connected to the coast, and deciding disputes *ex aequo et bono* are also treated differently in the African paradigm. These issues are examined in this chapter.

### 5.1.  The African *jus cogens*

The possibility of regional *jus cogens* is accepted in law. Schwarzenberger acknowledged that nothing prevents states at any level from 'establishing unequivocal *jus cogens* in a manner corresponding to written constitutions taking precedence over conflicting prior or subsequent treaties'.[1] It would be illogical to assume that all regional international law principles are *jus dispositivum*, while at international level there are peremptory norms that could not be excluded by treaties and at domestic level *ordre public* restrains the freedom to contract.[2] International *jus cogens* is defined by the ICJ as norms in which 'States do not have any interest of

---

[1] Georg Schwarzenberger, 'International Jus Cogens' (1964) 43 *Tex L Rev* 455, 460.
[2] See generally: Alfred Verdross, 'Jus Dispositivum and Jus Cogens in International Law' (1966) 60 *AJIL* 55; Egon Schwelb, 'Some Aspects of International Jus Cogens as Formulated by the International Law Commission' (1967) 61 *AJIL* 946; Christos L. Rozakis, *The Concept of Jus Cogens in the Law of Treaties* (North-Holland Publishing Company 1976); Anthony D'Amato, 'It's a Bird, It's a Plane, It's Jus Cogens' (1990) 6 *Connecticut J Int'l L* 1.

their own; they merely have, one and all, a common interest, namely, the accomplishment of those high purposes'.[3] By analogy, the same standard applies to elevating to regional *jus cogens* norms in which states of a particular region do not have any interest other than a profound commonly shared goal.

In Africa, when it became clear that the situation of newly independent states would border on chaos if boundary alterations were allowed, great store was laid on the common interest and the nexus between rights and order. States accepted to refrain from doing two things: first, pursuing their individual interest of carrying out post-independence border changes, and, second, allowing ethnic groups to claim secession. African states accepted that weighty obligation as a matter of common interest from which no derogation is permitted.

Shortly after establishing the OAU, Bowett took note of the OAU agreement to prohibit 'movement towards the revision of frontiers' as well as 'movements for secession', because such movements run counter to the common aims of African states. He stated that the OAU agreed that 'any general movement towards the revision of frontiers would create havoc and endless inter-state strife amongst African nations; that movements for secession run contrary to the aims of these states to create a free, multi-racial society which will cut across religious, ethnic and linguistic barriers'.[4] In the early 1970s, a distinguished political scientist, Onyeonoro Kamanu, read the same signs. He opined that African respect of the status quo is expected to lead to proscribing (i) 'irredentist demands at the level of inter-state relations', and (ii) 'secessionist attempts by purely domestic groups'. He stated:

> As a matter of political realism, after independence, African governments were virtually unanimous in agreeing that respect for existing European-delineated boundaries should be a guiding principle in inter-African relations ... However, over time it has been extended to rule out even those territorial changes that may originate from conflicts internal to individual states. In other words, the principle of respect for the geographical status quo is now expected to proscribe not only irredentist demands at the level of inter-state relations, but also secessionist attempts by purely domestic groups.[5]

---

[3] *Reservations to the Convention of Genocide* (Advisory Opinion) [1951] ICJ Rep15, 23.

[4] D. W. Bowett, 'Self-determination and Political Rights in the Developing Countries' (1966) 60 *PASIL* 129, 130.

[5] Onyeonoro S. Kamanu, 'Secession and the Right of Self-Determination: An OAU Dilemma' (1974) 12 *The Journal of Modern African Studies* 355, 356.

The African state practice that unfolded thereafter, as clarified in Chapters 2, 3, and 4, attests the vision of Bowett and Kamanu.

Fifty years on, the prohibition against redrawing of boundaries is holding and has never been relaxed anywhere in Africa. Likewise, movements for secession are vehemently opposed on principle. With this in mind, it is concluded that those two restrictions are exceptionally entrenched in the African territorial regime as matters in which Africa has paramount common interest to the extent that they form unequivocal peremptory norms. These two norms of African *jus cogens* are examined below.

### 5.1.1.   The prohibition against the redrawing of boundaries

It was explained in Chapter 1 that in the practice of Spanish America, the *uti possidetis* boundary of 1810 was considered to form the default position.[6] The treaties concluded by Spanish-American republics normally stipulate that while the republics adhere to the *uti possidetis* of 1810 they reserve the right to determine their final boundaries by agreement.[7] Conversely, in Africa adherence to the rule of intangibility of inherited frontiers means that African states sanctified the existing colonial boundaries. Additionally, by virtue of the rule of respecting the territorial status quo African states conceded indefinitely their right to redraw boundaries by agreement. As a result, the universal liberty of altering boundaries enjoyed by states elsewhere is the first rule of international law that the African territorial regime changes.

When only one of two states sharing a boundary wishes to alter it, while the other refuses, the OAU/AU stands decidedly by maintaining the inherited boundary. We have seen this in the strict position taken by the OAU regarding the territorial claims made by Libya against Chad.[8] This also happened when Morocco disputed its boundary with Algeria[9] and when Somalia unilaterally denounced the treaty that delimited the Somali boundary with Ethiopia and the Anglo-Italian Treaty on the boundaries of Somalia with Kenya.[10] The Moroccan and Somali appeals for starting processes leading to the redrawing of boundaries were not heeded by the OAU.[11] Instead, the OAU Assembly resorted to mediation

---

[6]  Section 1.2.2, text to footnotes 72–83.
[7]  *Ibid.*
[8]  Section 4.2.3, text to footnotes 86–90.
[9]  Section 3.1.4, text to footnotes 41–43.
[10]  *Ibid.*, text to footnotes 44–50.
[11]  In particular, the Somali Government pleaded with the UN and the OAU that the concerned states 'resort to the policy of pacific settlement of disputes between States as laid

on the basis of the OAU Charter to dissuade the two states from pursuing that course of action.[12]

While it is clear that when one of the two states sharing a boundary declines to renegotiate it the OAU/AU sides with the declining state, it is not clear what position the OAU/AU would take if both states sharing a boundary wanted to change it by agreement. Up to now, no treaty for *changing* the inherited boundary *per se* has ever been signed between two African states. The agreements concluded by African states relevant to their boundaries are demarcation treaties intended to establish the inherited frontier, as opposed to altering it. The testimony to this is that for fifty years the African map has not changed except for the creation of Eritrea and South Sudan. If an agreement drastically changing the inherited boundary were concluded between two African states, the AU would most likely pursue a plan similar to that used regarding secession agreements. Precisely, the African Organization would ignore the boundary redrawing and would not take part in mediating the process. If boundaries were finally altered, the AU would mostly reaffirm the pledge of respecting the boundaries achieved on independence and assert that the redrawing instance forms a special case.

The AU is not expected to object to a treaty slightly altering the status quo concluded by constitutional governments and endorsed by democratically elected parliaments. However, it is most unlikely that the OAU/AU would sanction a drastic boundary alteration made in questionable circumstances. Because of the African rule against secession, a right to change boundaries by treaty, permanently available, is open to abuse. A scenario of secessionists, somehow managing to control power in their parent state, signing a treaty with a neighbouring state for ceding a disputed region could not be ruled out in its entirety. We have at least seen a manifestation of this scenario in the Comoros in the form of the Azali/Abeid accord of 26 August 2000. When Colonel Azali took over in Moroni by a coup d'état and conceded Anjouan to the secessionists, the AU rejected the Azali/Abeid accord and worked with the parties to conclude the Fomboni Agreement, which confirmed the unity of Comoros.[13] The OAU would have had stronger reason to object if that accord were a treaty concluded with a neighbouring state to cede Anjouan. Consequently, it

down in the Charter of the United Nations and in the Charter of the Organization for African Unity'. See Official Records of the General Assembly, Twenty-seventh Session, Plenary Meetings, 209, 1st meeting, para 9 ff.

[12] Section 3.1.4.

[13] Section 4.2.1, text to footnotes 30–33.

should not be the ordinary course for the Court to give automatic effect to a treaty changing the inherited boundary in Africa. However, the ICJ Chamber in the *Frontier Dispute* was of a different mind.

In the *Frontier Dispute,* a question about whether the inherited administrative boundary of 1932 might have been altered by a treaty signed in 1965, i.e. concluded after independence, was raised. The Court found:

> Admittedly, the Parties could have modified the frontier existing on the critical date by a subsequent agreement. If the competent authorities had endorsed the agreement of 15 January 1965, it would have been unnecessary for the purpose of the present case to ascertain whether that agreement was of a declaratory or modifying character in relation to the 1932 boundaries.[14]

For a Court applying *uti possidetis* it is indeed possible that the 'Parties could have modified the frontier existing on the critical date by a subsequent agreement'. This is because in the context of *uti possidetis* when a treaty establishes the general character of a frontier the *uti possidetis* line will no longer be applicable and the Court should act on the basis of the treaty.[15] However, in applying the rule of intangibility of inherited frontiers, the Court's task is confined only 'to indicat[ing] the line of the frontier inherited by both States from the colonizers on their accession to independence',[16] nothing more. Even if the disputant states were specifically referring to a post-independence treaty the Court would not be bound to apply that treaty. An international convention establishing rules expressly recognized by the contesting states is applicable only if it does not violate peremptory norms.[17] A treaty that provides for redrawing the inherited boundary falls short of this standard because it violates the African *jus cogens.*

### 5.1.2.   *The prohibition against secession*

It is established that international law has no rules to regulate secession and no reason to interfere in secession matters. Akehurst had it that: 'there is no rule of international law, which forbids secession from an existing state; nor is there any rule which forbids the mother state to crush the

---

[14]  *Frontier Dispute (Burkina Faso/Mali)* (Judgment) [1986] ICJ Rep 554, 632–3.
[15]  M. Shaw, *International Law* (6th edn, Cambridge University Press 2008) 528–9.
[16]  *Frontier Dispute* (n 14) 632.
[17]  See Alain Pellet, 'Article 38' in A. Zimmermann, C. Tomuschat and K. Oellers-Frahm (eds.), *The Statute of the International Court of Justice: A Commentary* (Oxford University Press 2006) 800–9.

secessionary movement, if it can. Whatever the outcome of the struggle, it will be accepted as legal in the eyes of international law'.[18] This neutrality towards secession is the second rule of international law that the African custom changes.

In accordance with the African territorial regime, secession from an existing independent state is forbidden. This rule against secession is a consequence of the status quo rule. Because in Africa the law states that boundaries inherited on independence are to be respected indefinitely, a claim for secession runs counter to this doctrine. When secession claims are made, the OAU/AU typically warns the parties involved that it is imperative on the secessionists as well as the parent state 'to agree to preserve in the overriding interest of Africa, the unity of' their country regardless of their own cause or reason.[19] The parent state is under a duty to face any secessionist movement within its inherited boundaries. If the parent state fails, it is incumbent on the OAU/AU and other African states to assist, and see to it that the territorial status quo is respected.[20] If nonetheless a unilateral declaration of secession is made, the secessionist state is neither welcome at the African level nor recognized internationally.[21]

Moreover, when secession takes place with the agreement of the parent state, the OAU/AU organs refrain from taking part in the process until secession becomes a reality. The OAU/AU did not contest the agreement of May 1991 between Ethiopia and the Eritrean People's Liberation Front (EPLF) allowing Eritrea to secede, or the 20 July 2002 Machakos Protocol granting Southern Sudan the right to self-determination. However, the OAU/AU organs did not take part in

---

[18] M. Akehurst, *A Modern Introduction to International Law* (Routledge 1970) 72. See also Lee Buchheit, *Secession: The Legitimacy of Self-determination* (Yale University Press 1978) 45; James Crawford, *The Creation of States in International Law* (Oxford University Press 1979) 268; Antonio Cassese, *Self-determination of Peoples: A Legal Appraisal* (Cambridge University Press 1995) 340; Malcolm Shaw, 'The Heritage of States: The Principle of Uti Possidetis Juris Today' (1996) 67 *British YBK Int'l L* 75 143–4; *Accordance with International Law of the Unilateral Declaration of Independence in Respect of Kosovo* (Advisory Opinion) [2010] ICJ Rep 403, the Written Statement of the United Kingdom, which asserts that 'from the standpoint of international law there was, and is, no prohibition *per se* of secession' 87.

[19] OAU AHG/Res 58 (VI) (10 September 1969) addressed to the Government of Nigeria and the Biafran secessionists.

[20] See the reaction of the AU to Azali/Abeid accord conceding the Comorian island of Anjouan, Section 4.2.1, text to footnotes 30–33.

[21] See: the reaction of the AU to the unilateral declaration of Azawad, Section 4.2.1, text to footnotes 34–46; the AU reaction to the unilateral declaration of Somaliland, Section 4.2.2, text to footnotes 65–76.

enforcing those agreements.[22] Additionally, the OAU/AU issued resolutions stating clearly that the African rule against secession remains
unaffected by the agreements or instances to the contrary.[23] When the
eminence of a doctrine is not subject to challenge by private agreements
to the contrary, and when such agreements are unenforceable by the
relevant common body, this doctrine displays features of *jus cogens*. In
clarifying the meaning of *jus cogens* Schwarzenberger found that *jus
cogens* rules 'remain unaffected by agreements to the contrary between
private persons', and that such private agreements are 'at least unenforceable by community organs'.[24]

However, Kamanu saw in this emergent African attitude an 'apparent contradiction between African support for self-determination under
colonialism, and opposition to the application of the same principle in
a post-colonial setting'.[25] Kamanu is not alone in perceiving that the
African respect of colonial boundaries is incompatible with the right
to self-determination. The ICJ Chamber found in the *Frontier Dispute*
that the African decision entails a different interpretation of the right
to self-determination as it applies to Africa. The relevant part of the ICJ
dictum reads:

> The essential requirement of stability in order to survive, to develop and
> gradually to consolidate their independence in all fields, has induced
> African States judiciously to consent to the respecting of colonial fron-
> tiers, and to take account of it in the interpretation of the principle of
> self-determination of peoples.[26]

In principle, the right to self-determination is of international *jus cogens*
and hence could not be abridged by special custom. However, it is not
true that the choice of African states, which led to curtailing the right
to redraw boundaries and to denying secession, contradicts the right
to self-determination as Kamanu observes, or entails special interpretation as the ICJ Chamber in the *Frontier Dispute* found. Nor does this
choice consolidate the application of the principle of territorial integrity
in Africa. It is to this point that we now turn.

---

[22] Section 4.2.2, text to footnotes 57–61, 62–64.
[23] See AU Assembly Decision, Assembly/AU/Dec 338(XVI) (31 January 2011), stating that
South Sudan secession 'in no way, calls into question the sacrosanct principle of respect
of borders inherited at the accession of African countries to independence'.
[24] Schwarzenberger, 'International Jus Cogens' 456.
[25] Kamanu, 'Secession and the Right of Self-determination' 355.
[26] *Frontier Dispute* (n 14) 567.

### 5.1.3.    *African* jus cogens *versus self-determination and territorial integrity*

The requirements of legitimacy and recognition had prompted African states on independence to adhere to the colonial alignments as explained in Chapter 2. No African state availed itself of the right to subdivide the colonial unit, available to newly independent states as part of their right to colonial self-determination. However, by deciding to respect the pre-existing frontiers, African states exercised their right to colonial self-determination in full and as they deemed it appropriate. The right to colonial self-determination, which could be exercised by dismantling the pre-existing boundaries, could equally be exercised by deciding freely to respect those boundaries.

By exercising their right to colonial self-determination, African states had extinguished their one-off right to *external* self-determination. Cassese opined that 'once a people has exercised its right to external self-determination, the right expires'.[27] African states are currently entitled to exercise the *internal* right of self-determination available to 'all peoples' of the world. One feature of the version of the right to self-determination presently available is that it can only be exercised within the boundaries of existing states. In other words, it creates no positive entitlement for sub-national groups to challenge boundaries. In *the Reference Re Secession of Quebec* the Supreme Court of Canada was asked if there is 'a right to self-determination under international law that would give the National Assembly, legislature or government of Quebec the right to effect the secession of Quebec from Canada unilaterally'. The Canadian Court found that as a general rule 'international law expects that the right to self-determination will be exercised by peoples within the framework of existing sovereign states and consistently with the maintenance of the territorial integrity of those states'.[28] The international law of self-determination that applies to Quebec applies equally to Africa.[29] As such, African ethnic groups are entitled to no right of self-determination

---

[27] Cassese, *Self-determination of Peoples* 73.
[28] 1998 SCJ No 61, 29 para 122.
[29] The author is aware of the argument that the legal regime of self-determination lacks universality and applies only to states parties to the two UN Covenants on Human Rights; Cassese, *Self-determination of Peoples* 330. However, even if this argument is valid, self-determination applies to the entire African continent because all African states are parties to the 1966 UN Covenants. See treaty status http://treaties.un.org/pages/ViewDetails.aspx?src=TREATY&mtdsg_no=IV4&chapter=4&lang=en (accessed 17 February 2013).

exercisable beyond existing state frameworks even if no African prohib-ition of secession was imposed.[30] Drawing on Hohfeld's scheme of jural relations, rather than stipulating that there is *no right* where the inter-national law of self-determination provides for a *right*, the African regime creates on the part of African states a *duty* of proscribing secession while, at international level, there is *liberty* to secede.[31]

In the proper construction, the African territorial regime is a regime that precludes the making and conceding of territorial claims. It enjoins African states not to advance territorial claims against one another. Equally, it proscribes the entertainment of territorial claims made by seces-sionist groups. By operating exclusively in the field of the law of territory, the African territorial regime involves no inconsistency with the right of self-determination. Consequently, the current African territorial regime does not stand in contrast to the historical African support for the right to colonial self-determination. Nor does it oppose the application of the right of self-determination currently available in the post-colonial setting. Indeed, the *African decision* alluded to in the *Frontier Dispute*, regardless of whether the Chamber refers to the decision of inheriting the colonial boundaries taken on independence or the decision of respecting the status quo, involves no interpretation of the right of self-determination that could be calculated as abridging what this right has to offer on a worldwide scale.

Additionally, the rules of the African territorial regime do not dupli-cate the principle of territorial integrity, as we shall now see.

Lea Brilmayer stated in her scholarly article on secession and self-determination that:

> [C]ontrary to popular assumptions, the difficult normative issues arising out of secessionist claims do not involve an incompatibility of the terri-torial integrity and rights of peoples arguments. In fact, these arguments do not pose the inconsistencies normally assumed of them. Secessionist claims involve, first and foremost, disputed claims to territory.[32]

[30] The ACHPR in the *Katangese Peoples' Congress* echoed the finding of the Canadian Supreme Court, concluding that the people of Katanga are 'obligated to exercise a variant of self-determination that is compatible with the sovereignty and territorial integrity of Zaire', *Katangese Peoples' Congress v Zaire* (2000) AHRLR 72 (ACHPR 1995) para 5.

[31] W. N. Hohfeld, 'Some Fundamental Legal Conceptions as Applied in Judicial Reasoning' (1913) 23 *Yale LJ* 16, 28–33; W. W. Cook, 'Hohfeld's Contributions to the Science of Law' (1919) 28 *Yale LJ* 721, 723–5.

[32] L. Brilmayer, 'Secession and Self-determination: A Territorial Interpretation' (1991) 16 *Yale JIL* 177, 178. Cf Castellino, who suggests that a different relation exists between ter-ritorial claims and self-determination in the context of the rights of indigenous peoples, arguing for a consent-based determination of the fate of territory that 'could be offered to territorially based indigenous people living in contiguous zones or homogenous

The argument of Brilmayer, that secession claims do not involve rights of peoples, is in line with the above supposition that preventing secession in Africa does not contradict the right to self-determination. In keeping with the same position, territorial claims in general and secession claims in particular do not involve the principle of territorial integrity. Singularly, the prohibition of secession in Africa is a denial of the existence of a right on the part of sub-units of the African state to make territorial claims, not an assertion of the right of the African state to territorial integrity. Proscribing the making of claims to territory within an individual state does not as such enhance the principle of territorial integrity.[33] Shaw clarifies this point as follows:

> Where the boundaries of an independent State are altered by the secession of part of that State and a third State is involved in circumstances amounting to intervention, then the principle of respect for the territorial integrity of States at least will be breached. However, where no third State has intervened in the situation, no rule of international law as such is offended.[34]

Consequently, the reference to the principle of territorial integrity in the OAU Charter and in the Cairo Resolution does not change the way this principle applies to Africa. Equally, this reference does not make the African customary rule a mundane repetition of the principle of territorial integrity. As it stands, a secession claim with no external support, and as such not involving any incompatibility with the principle of territorial integrity, is nonetheless prohibited in Africa.[35]

In addition to these two peremptory norms, the African custom has introduced changes in other areas of international law. Notably, in the African territorial regime the concept of the critical date gained meaning

---

pockets', Joshua Castellino, 'Territorial Integrity and the Right to Self-Determination: An Examination of the Conceptual Tools' (2007) 33 *Brook J Int'l L* 503, 557 and generally 552–61.

[33] See Rosalyn Higgins, 'Postmodern Tribalism and the Right to Secession: Comments' in Catherine Brolmann, Rene Lefeber and Marjoleine Zieck (eds.), *Peoples and Minorities in International Law* (Martinus Nijhoff 1993) 34.

[34] Shaw, 'The Heritage of States' 143–4.

[35] A statement by Shaw reads that 'Practice in Africa has reinforced the approach of emphasising the territorial integrity of the colonially defined territory, witness the widespread disapproval of the attempted creation of secessionist states whether in the former Belgian Congo, Nigeria or Sudan', Shaw, *International Law* 524. This passage could not be reconciled with the pronounced opinion of Shaw stated in elaborate writings on the subject unless it is understood that in this text Shaw refers to 'territorial unity' not to 'territorial integrity'.

and implications that were not attached to it before. The following section shows how this concept is reformulated to fit the African context.

## 5.2.   The critical date in the African regime

The term 'critical date' is relatively new, and was first used in 1928 by Judge Huber, the sole arbitrator in the *Island of Palmas* case, in reference to the date of conclusion and coming into force of the Treaty of Paris of 10 December 1898.[36] Under that treaty, Spain ceded territories to the United States. The arbitrator had to determine whether on concluding the treaty the Island of Palmas (or Miangas) was under Spanish sovereignty, and as such ceded among others to the USA, or whether it was in Dutch possession.[37] Influenced by this leading case, Sir Gerald Fitzmaurice defined the critical date as 'the date on which the situation is deemed to have become crystallized',[38] or 'the date after which the actions of the parties can no longer affect the issue'.[39] This conventional use, however, is not the only use for the critical date. After the *Rights of Passage* and *The Minquiers and Ecrehos* were determined, Goldie identified two more uses for the critical date.

First, the jurisdictional critical date. This excludes the ICJ's jurisdiction on the ground that the dispute in question arose before adhesion to the Optional Clause of the ICJ Statute. In the *Rights of Passage* case the Court identified the facts 'which must be considered as being the source of the dispute' in order to determine whether they fall before or after the jurisdictional critical date.[40]

Second, the consolidational critical date. This is the date that closes the period of consolidation of an historical title.[41] It was introduced by the Counsel of France in *The Minquiers and Ecrehos Case (United Kingdom/France)*, who argued that the critical date for the case was connected with the consolidation or perfection of legal titles.[42] In his individual opinion,

---

[36] *Island of Palmas (Netherlands/USA)* (1928) II RIAA 829, 845 and 864.

[37] *Ibid.*

[38] *The Minquiers and Ecrehos Case (United Kingdom/France)* (Pleadings VII) [1953] ICJ Rep 47 61.

[39] Sir Gerald Fitzmaurice, 'The Law and Procedure of the International Court of Justice 1951–54: Points of Substantive Law Part II' (1951–54) 32 *British YBK Int'l L* 20, 21. See L. F E. Goldie, 'The Critical Date' (1963) 12 *ICLQ* 1251, 1254.

[40] *Case concerning Right of Passage over Indian Territory* (Merits) [1960] ICJ Rep 4, 35.

[41] Goldie, 'The Critical Date' 1266–7; See the Statement of Sir Percy Spender in the *Right of Passage* case (n 40) 108–10.

[42] *The Minquiers and Ecrehos Case* (n 38) 51.

Judge Basdevant also used the term in reference to the point of consolidation of title.[43] In this sense, the critical date is 'the terminal point of
a period of limitations or set[s] a term to the prescriptive acquisition of
title to land in municipal private law'.[44] Unlike the conventional and jurisdictional critical date, the consolidational critical date is not related to
the crystallization of the dispute and concerned solely with the process of
consolidating title.

In addition to those three categories, two other types of the critical date
are identifiable. These are: the possession-related critical date of *uti possidetis* and the recognition-related critical date of the rule of intangibility
of inherited frontiers.

### 5.2.1.    The possession-related critical date

Even if the term 'critical date' was not known as a term of art when the
principle of *uti possidetis* was articulated in the Spanish-American context early in the eighteenth century, a cut-off date was inherent to the
idea of *uti possidetis*. The term '*uti possidetis* of 1810' was widely used in
a number of South-American treaties, confederation projects, and constitutions of the new republics to refer to the year 1810 as the year marking the respective territories that each Spanish republic had the right to
possess.[45] According to Alvarez: 'The term *uti possidetis* of 1810, is generally understood to mean the territory which the respective countries
had the right to possess according to the Spanish administrative divisions obtaining at that date, the date of the beginning of the movement
for emancipation.'[46] This sets the *uti possidetis* date for South-American
republics as 1810. Likewise, the year 1821 was chosen for the *uti possidetis*
of Central-American republics.[47]

---

[43]  Individual Opinion of Judge Basdevant, *The Minquiers and Ecrehos Case* 76 ff.
[44]  Goldie, 'The Critical Date' 1260.
[45]  The determination of the year 1810 as the *uti possidetis* year was the subject of a debate
      in Spanish America that ran parallel to the better-known *de jure* and *de facto* debate.
      Castellino and Allen referred to this debate as 'more within the "critical date" discus-
      sion with the year being identified as 1810', Joshua Castellino and Steve Allen, *Title to
      Territory in International Law: A Temporal Analysis* (Ashgate 2003) 75.
[46]  A. Alvarez, 'Latin America and International Law' (1909) 3 *AJIL* 269, 290. Also see John
      Bassett Moore, *Costa Rica-Panama Arbitration 1911: Memorandum on Uti Possidetis*
      (The Commonwealth Company 1913).
[47]  Moore, *Costa Rica-Panama Arbitration 1911* 47–8; *Case concerning the Land, Island and
      Maritime Frontier Dispute (El Salvador/Honduras: Nicaragua intervening)* (Judgment)
      [1992] ICJ Rep 315, 380.

The choice for those years was indisputably meant to refer to the time when *possession* of territory by the new republics was determined, not the date of crystallization of the dispute, setting of jurisdiction, or consolidation of title. To be sure the *uti possidetis* of 1810 is the date critical to determining possession on the basis of the time-honoured interdict '*uti possidetis ita possideatis*'.

However, definition of territories in possession depends on verifying title to those territories. To achieve this result, title to every parcel of territory needed to be established separately. A methodology for validating title to multiple territories possessed by a particular republic was developed. In *El Salvador/Honduras*, the ICJ described the procedure followed in this regard:

> The location of boundaries seemed often, in the arguments of the Parties, to be incidental to some 'claim', or 'title', or 'grant', respecting a parcel of territory, within circumambient boundaries only portions of which are now claimed to form an international boundary. It is rather as if the disputed boundaries must be constructed like a jig-saw puzzle from certain already cut pieces so that the extent and location of the resulting boundary depend upon the size and shape of the fitting piece.[48]

The aforementioned jigsaw puzzle construction process required using mini-critical dates of consolidation to verify title and to determine claims to tracts of territory under possession by each republic. Those intermediary critical dates functioned as cut-off points for acts performed *à titre de souverain* by Spanish-American republics subsequent to the *uti possidetis* year.

The ICJ explained in *Nicaragua/Honduras* that in the context of applying *uti possidetis* acts performed *à titre de souverain* are valid as *effectivités* unless they are 'carried out by a State which, already having claims to assert in a legal dispute, could have taken those actions strictly with the aim of buttressing those claims'.[49] A cut-off point between actions aimed at buttressing a claim and actions that were not, is a critical date in the conventional sense of the term. Actions after this critical date are generally considered meaningless as *effectivités*,[50] unless they form 'normal

---

[48] *El Salvador/Honduras* (n 47) 388.
[49] *Territorial and Maritime Dispute between Nicaragua and Honduras in the Caribbean Sea (Nicaragua/Honduras)* (Judgment) [2007] ICJ Rep 659, 697–8.
[50] *Ibid.*

continuation of prior acts and are not undertaken for the purpose of improving the legal position of the Party which relies on them'.[51]

As a result, the consolidational critical date was introduced to Spanish America to supplement the possession-related *uti possidetis*. It is not uncommon in Spanish-American disputes that one or more consolidation critical date(s) are recognized alongside the *uti possidetis* possession-related critical date. Not only that, those mini-critical dates are indeed allowed to overrule the possession-related mini-critical date of *uti possidetis* of 1810. This is because the *uti possidetis* line simply forms a starting point, as explained in Chapter 1.

While this was the Spanish-American outlook regarding the critical date, the African approach to the matter is different altogether.

### 5.2.2.  *The recognition-related critical date*

It is explained above that in Spanish America the new republics were constituted by allocating territories out of the common Spanish inheritance. Conversely, African states were constituted by international recognition that upgraded colonies into sovereign states. While the issue at point in Spanish America is the determining of the territory in possession, what is crucial in Africa is the identification of the recognized boundary. As such, in the African paradigm the independence day, by virtue of being the day on which recognition takes effect, is *ipso jure* the critical date for boundary disputes. The reference in the Cairo Resolution to the boundaries of states 'existing on their achievement of national independence' as the boundaries to be respected shows the importance attached by African states to the independence date as the cut-off date.

The ICJ and international tribunals, even though they were applying *uti possidetis*, recognized the significance of independence as the cut-off date for African boundaries. In the *Frontier Dispute*, the ICJ Chamber found that what mattered for both parties is 'the frontier which existed at the moment of independence'.[52] In *Cameroon/Nigeria*, the ICJ obviously worked on the basis that the date of independence of Nigeria was the day on which Nigeria had presumably acknowledged the sovereignty of Cameroon over the disputed Bakassi Peninsula.[53] In the *Frontier Dispute*

---

[51]  *Sovereignty over Pulau Ligitan and Pulau Sipadan (Indonesia/Malaysia)* (Judgment) [2002] ICJ Rep 625, 682.

[52]  *Ibid.* 570.

[53]  *Land and Maritime Boundary between Cameroon and Nigeria (Cameroon/ Nigeria: Equatorial Guinea intervening)* (Merits) [2002] ICJ Rep 303, 410–12.

*(Benin/Niger)* the ICJ Chamber found that the dispute 'is set within a historical context marked by the accession to independence of the territories in question'.[54] The Chamber noted the agreement of the parties to take into account their respective independence dates for determining the boundaries. The ICJ Chamber went on to state that 'these territorial boundaries were no more than delimitations between different administrative divisions or colonies subject to the same colonial authority. Only at the moment of independence, also called the "critical date", did these boundaries become international frontiers'.[55] Shaw opines that with regard to Africa 'it thus appears obvious that the moment of independence is the critical date'.[56]

The independence day is not the conventional critical date defined by Sir Gerald Fitzmaurice as the date 'on which the situation is deemed to have become crystallized'.[57] This is simply because in the case of Africa the situation of the boundary in question crystalizes, or rather materializes, on a date other than the critical date. The materialization date could be the date of concluding a treaty or of drawing an administrative division on which the future boundary is based. As such, the materialization of a boundary takes place way before the critical date. In the *Frontier Dispute*, while the disputant states attained independence in 1965, the date on which the situation was deemed to have materialized was 31 December 1932. Consequently, even as the ICJ Chamber was requested to establish the boundaries inherited on independence it found that it had to delineate the administrative boundary lines drawn on 31 December 1932. The ICJ Chamber clarified its task as follows:

> It should again be pointed out that the Chamber's task in this case is to indicate the line of the frontier inherited by both States from the colonizers on their accession to independence. For the reasons explained above, this task amounts to ascertaining and defining the lines which formed the administrative boundaries of the colony of Upper Volta on 31 December 1932.[58]

Nor is the African critical date 'the date after which the actions of the parties can no longer affect the issue'. This is because the parties to an African dispute were non-existent at the material time of their dispute. Hence,

---

[54] *Frontier Dispute (Benin/Niger)* (Judgment) [2005] ICJ Rep 90, 107–8.
[55] *Ibid.* 120.
[56] Shaw, 'The Heritage of States' 130.
[57] *The Minquiers and Ecrehos Case* (n 38) 47, 61.
[58] *Frontier Dispute* (n 14) 632.

they did not affect the issue in the past Additionally, the African states would not do so in the future. This is because the African states acquire the faculty of performing acts *à titre de souverain* on their independence day, i.e. exactly when the time for affecting the issue lapses. Consequently, the African critical date could not be defined in terms of when the actions of the parties can or cannot affect the dispute.

It is also obvious that the independence day is not marking the culmination of a gradual process of consolidating title similar to that referred to in *Minquiers and Ecrehos*.

This means in Africa, the independence day is the critical date in a different sense. We now turn to examining the new meaning that the term critical date acquires in the African context.

### 5.2.3.   The function of the recognition-related critical date

It was explained earlier that the recognition-related critical date is the cut-off date for defining the boundary laid irretrievably to the new African state on the achievement of national independence. Unlike its Spanish-American counterpart, the recognition-related critical date is the date on which the final boundary is defined in unalterable terms.

It was also clarified that in Spanish America mini-critical dates for verifying the consolidation of title apply beside the *uti possidetis* critical date. Equally, in Africa the boundary line materializes on date(s) other than the critical date. However, the relation between the African critical date and the materialization date(s) is not similar to that of *uti possidetis* and the consolidation cut-off date(s). While in Spanish America the date of verifying the consolidation of title to a particular tract in possession overrides the *uti possidetis* date, in Africa the materialization date is subordinate to the critical date. In other words, the materialization date cannot confer rights irreconcilable with the boundary line laid down on independence. Nor is the materialization date the yardstick for determining the territory that was the subject of the sovereign transfer on the critical date. This role is for the recognition-related critical date, which is the date that determines the territory devolved to African states, as we shall presently see.

The role played by the UN General Assembly in the recognition of newly independent states in Africa cannot be overemphasized. International recognition normally takes place at the behest of the General Assembly and for the colony or trust territory defined by the UN. Even as it is unusual for a process of boundary delimitation to draw upon UN Resolutions, in the African context it is unrealistic to ignore this important tool. When it is remembered that UN General Assembly Resolutions were the mechanism for conferring legality on the new African state, it becomes obvious that those resolutions are critical for defining the limits of the territory subject to recognition. The Court and tribunals currently set the independence day as the critical date for African disputes. Yet, they soon forget about that date and barely try to establish the limits of the territorial transfer that was obtained on the achievement of independence. As soon as they get hold of a materialization date and embark on 'ascertaining and defining the lines which formed the boundary' at that materialization date, they do not foresee any role for what they earlier called the critical date. As such, cases are exclusively determined on the basis of the materialization date utterly ignoring the limits of the territory internationally recognized as devolved on independence. Setting the independence day as the critical date is, therefore, shorn of any practical significance. The critical date is denied its pivotal role of determining the extent of the territory that was the subject of international recognition. The ICJ Chamber in the *Frontier Dispute* would have ignored the critical date it had already set if the agreement of 15 January 1965 had been found binding on the parties.[59] Two more examples are found in the cases of the *Territorial Dispute (Libya/Chad)* and *Cameroon/Nigeria*. In addition to demonstrating the function of the critical date in Africa, the two cases also show the role played by the UN General Assembly Resolutions in determining the territory transferred to the newly independent state.

In *Libya/Chad*, the Court summarized the nature of the dispute as follows:

> Libya proceeds on the basis that there is no existing boundary, and asks the Court to determine one, while Chad proceeds on the basis that there is an existing boundary, and asks the Court to declare what that boundary is. Libya considers that the case concerns a dispute regarding attribution of territory, while in Chad's view it concerns a dispute over the location of a boundary.[60]

Under this pretext, Libya claimed three regions of Chad, Borkou, Ennedi, and Tibesti, which are referred to by Libya as the 'Borderlands'.

The starting point for resolving this dispute should have been the determining factor in general terms of whether the territories internationally recognized for Libya on its independence included the Borderlands or

---

[59] *Frontier Dispute* (n 14) 632–3.
[60] *Territorial Dispute (Libyan Arab Jamahiriya/Chad)* (Judgment) [1994] ICJ Rep 6, 14–15.

not. General Assembly Resolution 289 (IV) defined the territorial units of Libya for the purpose of independence. As such, it forms the incontestable evidence as to the territorial status quo of Libya on the achievement of independence. Yet, the Court mentioned that Resolution only in passing.

The background to this Resolution goes to the Treaty of Peace signed by the Four Allied Powers with Italy on 10 February 1947. In accordance with Article 23 of that Treaty, Italy renounced rights and title to Libya among its other African possessions.[61] On the failure of the Allied Powers to agree on the future of the Italian former possessions, the matter was referred to the General Assembly as stipulated in the treaty.[62] The General Assembly adopted Resolution 289 (IV), which, *inter alia*, specified the territories that form Libya. Resolution 289 (IV) reads in part 'With Respect to Libya, recommends: That Libya, comprising Cyrenaica, Tripolitania and the Fezzan, shall be constituted an independent and sovereign State.'[63] Evidently, the claimed 'Borderlands' were not included within this conclusive territorial definition of Libya.[64]

Resolution 289 (IV) was accepted by the Four Allied Powers as binding.[65] Libya attained independence as per the plan enunciated in this Resolution. General Assembly Resolution 515 (VI) of 1 February 1952 recognized Libya, as formed by Resolution 289 (IV), as an independent state and admitted her to the membership of the United Nations.[66]

Chad also went through the same international process of decolonization and recognition. General Assembly Resolution 1485 (XV) of 20 September 1960 recognized Chad as territorially defined on its independence on 1 August 1960 and admitted her to UN membership.[67] The so-called Borderlands formed part of the Chadian territory recognized as per Resolution 1485 (XV).

---

[61] See J. L. Kunz, 'Nationality and Option Clauses in the Italian Peace Treaty of 1947' (1947) 41 *AJIL* 622, 624–5.

[62] See Geoffrey Marston, 'Termination of Trusteeship' (1969) 18 *ICLQ* 1, 9; C. Seton-Watson, 'Italy's Imperial Hangovers' (1980) 15 *Journal of Contemporary History* 169, 171–3.

[63] UNGA Res 289 (IV) (21 November 1949).

[64] See also UNGA Res 387 (V) (17 November 1950). De Candole clarified that the provinces of Cyrenaica, Tripolitania, and the Fezzan 'throughout history have sometimes been united and sometimes artificially divided' and referred to as Libya 'ever since historical records began', E. A. De Candole, 'Libya' in Colin Legum (ed.), *Africa: A Handbook* (2nd edn, Anthony Blond Ltd 1965) 35.

[65] F. A. Vallat, 'The Competence of the United Nations General Assembly' (1959 II) 97 *Recueil Des Cours de l'Académie de Droit International* 203, 223 ff.

[66] UNGA Res 515 (VI) (1 February 1952).

[67] UNGA Res 1485 (XV) (20 September 1960).

Although the ICJ did not take full account of Resolutions 289 (V) and 1485 (XV), the Court referred to the reports submitted to the General Assembly by France, which included the Borderlands within the total area of Chad. The ICJ stated:

> Libya achieved its independence nearly nine years before Chad; during that period, France submitted reports on this territory to the United Nations General Assembly. The report for 1955 shows the area of Chad's territory as 1,284,000 square kilometres, which expressly includes 538,000 square kilometres for the BET [Borderlands]. Moreover United Nations publications from 1960 onward continued to state the area of Chad as 1,284,000 square kilometres. As will be clear from the indications above as to the frontier resulting from the 1955 Treaty (paragraph 63), the BET is part of the territory of Chad on the basis of that frontier, but would not be so on the basis of Libya's claim.[68]

This observation by the ICJ is very much pertinent to determining the extent of the territory that was the subject of the transfer on the critical date. It also shows that, in addition to UN Resolutions, there are other sources for garnering authoritative information on the limits of the area that was the subject of international recognition as the territory of a particular state on its independence.

However, what was in point for the ICJ in the above passage was that Libya did not protest to the inclusion of the Borderlands within the area of Chad, rather than the fact that the reports of France were evidence to the extent of the territory devolved to Chad on the critical date. The Court stated at the end of the above quote that 'Libya did not challenge the territorial dimensions of Chad as set out by France'. Judge Ajibola also made a similar comment in his separate opinion. He opined that the recognition of Chad at the UN General Assembly 'was a unique opportunity for Libya to protest the boundary of Chad as presented by France to the United Nations. But on the contrary, all that Libya did was to welcome Chad into the fold of independent States – there was no protest of any kind'.[69] It is not true that on the reporting by France or at the admittance of Chad, Libya could have protested the placement of the Borderlands within the territories of Chad. This is because by then Libya had already attained independence with recognized international boundaries that did not include the Borderlands. What was open for Libya to do on those occasions was simply to make sure that the boundaries of Chad as presented

---

[68] *Libya/Chad* (n 60) 36 (references omitted).
[69] The Separate Opinion of Judge Ajibola, *Libya/Chad* (n 60) 82.

by France were conterminous with the boundaries accepted by Libya and recognized for her on independence. The proposition that the boundaries that obtain on two different independence dates are presumed to be conterminous will be clarified in Section 5.2.4.

In *Cameroon/Nigeria*, Cameroon filed an application to the Court instituting proceedings against Nigeria in respect of a dispute described as 'relat(ing) essentially to the question of sovereignty over the Bakassi Peninsula'.[70] In its request Cameroon stated that Bakassi is an integral part of the territory of Cameroon. For Cameroon, Nigeria violated the fundamental principle of respect for frontiers inherited from colonization, and should withdraw its troops from the Cameroonian Peninsula.[71] On its part, Nigeria replied that sovereignty over the peninsula was vested in Nigeria because title to it lay in 1911 with the Kings and Chiefs of Old Calabar, and was retained by them until the territory passed to Nigeria upon independence.[72] The Court dismissed this argument on the basis that there was no evidence that Nigeria thought upon independence that it was acquiring Bakassi from the Kings and Chiefs of Old Calabar.[73] The ICJ clarified that neither the League of Nations nor the United Nations considered that to be the position.

It is clear from the above that the Court found the independence date to be the date significant for constituting Nigeria as a state and as such for determining the dispute. Additionally, the Court rightly pointed to the decisive role of UN recognition in determining the extent of the Nigerian territory as devolved on independence. However, the Court is to be blamed for dismissing the Nigerian Contention on the basis of lack of evidence when sufficient evidence was available. As a matter of fact, the UN General Assembly issued a number of resolutions regarding the Southern Cameroons, being the trust territory comprising the Bakassi Peninsula.[74] General Assembly Resolution 1608 (XV) of 21 April 1961, which endorsed the results of the plebiscites in the Northern Cameroons and the Southern Cameroons clarified that the people of the Southern Cameroons have decided to achieve independence by joining the independent Republic

---

[70] *Cameroon/Nigeria* (Merits) (n 53) 312.

[71] *Ibid*. 316–17.

[72] *Land and Maritime Boundary between Cameroon and Nigeria (Cameroon/Nigeria)* (Preliminary Objections) [1998] ICJ Rep 275, 400.

[73] *Ibid*. 410.

[74] UNGA Res 1282 (XIII) (5 December 1958); UNGA Res 1350 (XIII) (13 March 1959); UNGA Res 1352 (XIV) (16 October 1959); UNGA Resolution 1476 (XV) (20 September 1960); UNGA Res 1608 (XV) (21 April 1961).

of Cameroon. Accordingly, the Trusteeship Agreement of 13 December 1946 concerning the Cameroons under British administration was terminated with respect to the Southern Cameroons on 1 October 1961.[75] General Assembly Resolution 1608 (XV) ended the Trusteeship agreement of territorially defined trust territories and as such determines the limits of the territory granted independence by being transferred to the Republic of Cameroon. No mention was made in that resolution to any special case pertaining to Bakassi.

In addition, the situation of the trust territories of the British Cameroons, i.e. both the Northern Cameroons and the Southern Cameroons, received much attention from the Trusteeship Council of the United Nations and from the General Assembly itself.[76] The whole question of administration of the trust territories was over many years the subject of missions of the United Nations. If the Bakassi Peninsula were of special status, that status would have been clarified in the reports of those missions and the proceedings of the Trusteeship Council and the Fourth Committee of the General Assembly pertaining to the Southern Cameroons. Furthermore, the reports of the United Nations Plebiscite Commissioner who supervised the plebiscites held in the Trust Territory of the Southern Cameroons on 11 and 12 February 1961 examined in detail the situation of the Southern Cameroons without making any reference to the Bakassi Peninsula.[77]

However, the Court did not examine this evidence. Instead, it embarked on a lengthy discussion of the agreement signed between Great Britain and the Kings and Chiefs of Old Calabar in 1911. The Court found that this agreement created a form of indirect rule. On this basis, the Court concluded that 'under the law at the time, Great Britain was in a position in 1913 to determine its boundaries with Germany in respect of Nigeria, including in the southern section' in which the Bakassi Peninsula lies.[78] One wonders what would have been the conclusion of the Court if the transfer of title to Bakassi from the Kings and Chiefs of Old Calabar to Great Britain were not found defective under the law of that time.

Setting the independence day as the critical date invites two questions. First, what is the critical date of a boundary shared by two states that

[75] UNGA Res 1608 (XV) (21 April 1961) para 4.
[76] UNGA Res 1350 (XIII) (13 March 1959) para 4.
[77] For the UN activities in the Trust Territories of the Cameroons under British Administration see *Case concerning the Northern Cameroons (Cameroon/United Kingdom)* (Preliminary Objections) [1963] ICJ Rep 15, 22.
[78] *Cameroon/Nigeria* (Preliminary Objections) (n 72) 406–7.

attained independence on two different dates? This possibility was actually faced in the *Frontier Dispute* and in *Benin/Niger*. Second, what is the critical date for boundaries of states with no traditional 'independence' date? This issue faced the Eritrea-Ethiopia Border Commission and perplexed scholars who tried in vain to come up with an answer on the basis of the *uti possidetis* paradigm.

We will now turn to these two issues.

### 5.2.4.    *The possibility of two critical dates*

The litigants in the *Frontier Dispute* attained independence on two different dates: 20 June 1960 for Mali and 5 August 1960 for Burkina Faso. The Chamber reflected as follows the arguments that were advanced to address the issue of determining the critical date in such situations:

> In the opinion of Burkina Faso, the date to be taken into consideration is that of the accession of each Party to independence: 20 June 1960 for Mali and 5 August 1960 for Burkina Faso. In Mali's opinion, it is necessary to go back to the 'last date on which the French colonial authorities participated in the exercise of jurisdiction for administrative organization'.[79]

The ICJ Chamber found that this point was of no practical implications to the case and refrained from determining it.

The issue was brought up again in *Benin/Niger* where the two parties achieved independence on 1 and 3 August 1960 respectively. Once again, the ICJ avoided determining the issue assuming that 'there was no change in the frontier between those two close dates'.[80] The Chamber rather glossed over the issue and stated that 'the period between 1 and 3 August 1960 can be considered as the critical date'.[81]

Shaw proposes that 'Where there is more than one State involved, then logically it should be the date of first independence that will be important'.[82] While this proposal might be conducive to solving the problem where the two concerned states belong to the same colonial empire, it would encounter difficulties if two different colonial powers were involved. This is because in the latter case the solution proposed by Shaw leads to disregarding the colonial *effectivités* pertaining to the colony of second independence.

---

[79]  *Frontier Dispute* (n 14) 570.
[80]  *Benin/Niger* (n 54) 108.
[81]  *Ibid.* 120.
[82]  Shaw, 'The Heritage of States' 130.

The point of departure for resolving this issue is the observation made by the ICJ Chamber in the *Frontier Dispute* that 'the two parties both agree that when they became independent there was a definite frontier'.[83] By agreeing that there was a definite single frontier on either independence day, both states presume that their boundary line is conterminous. The presumption that the boundary line shared by any two states is conterminous is a consequence of the principle of the denial of *terra nullius*, as clarified by the tribunal in the *Rann of Kutch Arbitration*. In the *Rann of Kutch* it was found that the principle of *uti possidetis* does not apply to the boundary of India and Pakistan. Yet, it was concluded, one aspect of the principle, namely the denial of *terra nullius*, applies making it not possible for any area in the Indian-Pakistani border to be open for a claim by a third party.[84]

In the light of this principle, it would have been correct for the ICJ Chamber to accept the submission of Burkina Faso that 'the date to be taken into consideration is that of the accession of each Party to independence'. Although this means there will be two 'critical dates' for this dispute, no difficulty ensues as long as it is understood that the two dates ultimately yield a conterminous boundary line. In contrast, the submission of Mali, which presupposes that there is one critical date, being the last date of exercising administrative jurisdiction by the outgoing colonial power, is problematic. Evidently, this proposal was made on the assumption that there is one metropolitan state. When two colonial powers are involved the actions of both states need to be taken into account.

However, some African states have no classical independence dates similar to those of Burkina Faso and Mali. We now turn to determining the critical date in those anomalous cases.

### 5.2.5.  Anomalous African boundaries

Klabbers and Lefeber, on finding that the issue of the critical date was left open in the *Frontier Dispute*, raised the following point:

> Most of Africa became independent during the twentieth century, when, following the *Frontier Dispute case*, the *uti possidetis* principle undoubtedly was in force. The first question (at which date must 'the photograph' be taken?) may, however, still pose problems. It is for instance possible

---

[83]  *Frontier Dispute* (n 14) 570.

[84]  *The Indo-Pakistan Western Boundary (Rann of Kutch) between India and Pakistan* (1968) XVII RIAA 1,12, 60, 563.

that the date of decolonization does not entirely coincide with the date of independence, as is witnessed by the history of Eritrea. It could also be possible that, as was the case with Somalia, two former non-self-governing territories that were not decolonized on the same date, merge. Which date must then be deemed the 'critical date'? Unfortunately, although justified on the facts of that particular case, the Chamber dealing with *the Frontier Dispute case* left this question unanswered.[85]

There are two reasons why this question could not be answered under the supposition that 'the *uti possidetis* principle undoubtedly was in force'. First, the *uti possidetis* paradigm works on the basis of the 'possession-related critical date' which is of no relevance to Africa. Second, *uti possidetis* does not take into account the special role played by recognition in the African context. Whereas the first reason was explained earlier, the second reason is examined below.

It shall be remembered that the independence day is the watershed in the African territorial regime only because it is the day on which the African state acquired international recognition. When recognition materializes on another day, namely the status quo date, that day is the date critical for determining the boundary set to the new African state. Consequently, the date of recognition is the critical date for both Eritrea and Somalia, the two states mentioned by Klabbers and Lefeber, and for other anomalous African boundaries. We shall now see how this works.

Eritrea was born on the announcement of the result of its referendum on 27 April 1993,[86] while, for that matter, South Sudan was created on 9 July 2011, the date marking the expiry of the agreed interim period. After the recognition of Eritrea and South Sudan by their respective parent states, the two states were internationally recognized and subsequently admitted to the OAU/AU and the UN.[87] Consequently, the critical date for those two states is the date of their respective international recognition. In addition, the boundaries of those states have materialization dates that differ from the critical date for each state. For the boundaries of each state with the parent state, the function of the materialization date is the ascertaining of the lines that earlier formed the administrative boundaries

---

[85] J. Klabbers and R. Lefeber, 'Africa: Lost between Self-determination and Uti Possidetis' in C. Brolmann (ed.), *Peoples and Minorities in International Law* (Martinus Nijhoff 1993) 65.

[86] Ruth Iyob, *The Eritrean Struggle for Independence: Domination, Resistance, Nationalism, 1941–1993* (Cambridge University Press 1997) 140.

[87] UNGA A/RES/47/230 (28 May 1993) Admission of Eritrea to membership in the United Nations; UNGA A/RES/65/308 (14 July 2011) Admission of South Sudan to membership in the United Nations.

between the parent state and the seceding state. For the boundaries with other states, the materialization dates formerly applicable to the parent states apply to the seceding state. However, rather than being governed by the critical date of the predecessor state, which is no longer relevant, those boundaries will be subject to the extent of the sovereign territorial transfer made on the critical date of the successor state. Nonetheless, it is presumed that the limits of the horizontal territorial transfer that created the new state are conterminous with the limits of the vertical territorial transfer relevant to the parent state.

The case of the Republic of Somalia is the reverse. British Somaliland achieved independence on 26 June 1960 and Italian Somalia on 1 July 1960. The normal critical date for the boundaries of each of the two states is its respective independence day. However, when the two states merged on 1 July 1960, the Republic of Somalia was created and internationally recognized.[88] Subsequently, the African states pledged in the Cairo Resolution to respect the status quo boundaries of the Republic of Somalia, among others. The AU currently makes no mistake that the frontiers 'existing on the achievement of national independence' that shall be respected by African states in the face of the unilateral declaration of Somaliland are the internationally recognized boundaries of the Republic of Somalia. Those are the boundaries protected by the African status quo rule.[89] While the critical dates of British Somaliland and Italian Somalia do not apply, the materialization dates of the boundaries of the old units are still relevant. However, the date of the sovereign territorial transfer that took place on 1 July 1960, being the critical date for the Republic of Somalia, is the date that currently governs those materialization dates subject to the conterminous presumption.

In addition to the two examples for anomalous African boundaries mentioned by Klabbers and Lefeber, there is a third category. Namely, boundaries of states that were not colonized and as such have no classical independence dates. In this category, we have Ethiopia and Liberia. When African states pledged in Cairo on 21 July 1964 to respect 'the borders existing on their achievement of national independence' this undertaking was understood in respect of those two states to refer to their boundaries as they stood on the day of the African pledge, i.e.

---

[88] UNGA Res 1479 (XV) (20 September 1960) Admission of Somalia to the United Nations.
[89] A. Carroll and B. Rajagopal, 'The Case for the Independent Statehood of Somaliland' (1992) 8 *Am UJ Int'l L & Pol'y* 653, 660–1.

21 July 1964. As a result, African states did not recognize the Eritrean claims to secede from Ethiopia. Even though Eritrea was incorporated in Ethiopia barely two years before that pledge, on 21 July 1964, Eritrea was already encompassed within the boundaries recognized for Ethiopia.[90] In *Eritrea/Ethiopia*, the Commission had to determine the critical date for those two states of no conventional independence day. Rather than adopting a principled plan along lines similar to the above, the Commission invented an impromptu formula, as we shall see in section 5.3.2. Conversely, because SADR was not part of Morocco at the time of the African undertaking, the OAU supported the independence of SADR regardless of the Moroccan claims.[91]

In addition to the African *jus cogens* and the reformulation of the concept of the critical date, the African custom necessitates appraisal of numerous existing law principles. The following section explains how some international law norms are modified in relation to Africa.

## 5.3.   Norms reviewed under the African customary rules

### 5.3.1.   Boundaries born in treaties

Treaty-based boundaries of Spanish America and Africa were created in dissimilar circumstances. In Spanish America, all boundaries left by Spain were originally administrative lines that defined units of the Spanish Empire. After emancipation, most of those administrative divisions were accepted on a provisional basis and were eventually replaced by permanent boundaries drawn by treaties concluded between the republics. In Africa, whereas some of the boundaries left by colonial powers were of administrative origin, a greater number were born in treaties finalized by metropolitan states. On independence, African states left both types of colonial boundaries untouched and considered them to form the permanent unchangeable alignments. Despite the two dissimilar processes treaty-based boundaries currently form the majority in both continents. While boundaries based on post-emancipation treaties count for about 90 per cent in Spanish America, boundaries created

---

[90]  See generally G. H. Tesfagiorgis, 'Self-determination: its Evolution and Practice by the United Nations and its Application to the Case of Eritrea' (1987) 6 *Wisconsin ILJ* 75; Eritrean Department of Foreign Affairs (ed.) *Eritrea: Birth of a Nation* (1993); Iyob, *The Eritrean Struggle for Independence* 48–54.

[91]  See Section 4.2.3, text to footnotes 77–85.

by colonial treaties comprise nearly three quarters of African boundaries.[92] In the Spanish-American context, the boundary treaty is invariably drawn *after* the *uti possidetis* year, whereas in Africa, boundary treaties are consistently concluded *before* the independence day. Consequently, the *uti possidetis* rules developed in Spanish America regarding boundaries born in treaties were conceived to address a situation that has very little in common with the African context. The alternative African rules are clarified below.

As explained in Chapter 1, in Spanish America the *uti possidetis* boundary was the default position.[93] As a result, wherever a treaty delimiting the final boundary is agreed, the *uti possidetis* boundary ceases to be observed. This led to creating a subsidiary principle of *uti possidetis* to the effect that whenever a treaty applies, the *uti possidetis* boundary is excluded. Shaw explained that 'The principle of *uti possidetis* is not able to resolve all territorial or boundary problems. Where there is a relevant applicable treaty, then this will dispose of the matter completely'.[94] Additionally, in Spanish America on declaring the *uti possidetis* of 1810, or 1821, the former colonial administrative divisions are automatically upgraded to international boundaries.[95] Conferring legal force on formerly administrative boundaries by upgrading them into international frontiers by operation of *uti possidetis* is a second subsidiary principle of the Spanish doctrine. In applying *uti possidetis* to Africa, it was assumed by the ICJ Chamber in the *Frontier Dispute* that those two subsidiary principles apply by extension.

Regarding the first subsidiary principle, we have seen that the ICJ Chamber in the *Frontier Dispute* was ready to ignore the inherited boundary if the agreement of 15 January 1965 signed between Mali and Upper Volta (Burkina Faso) were found binding on the parties.[96] The boundary that obtained for Mali and Upper Volta on independence was not a default boundary to be subject to change by a subsequent treaty the way the *uti possidetis* boundaries were changed in Spanish America. The independence boundary is the boundary that the two states had accepted as

[92] Suzanne Lalonde, *Determining Boundaries in a Conflicted World: The Role of Uti Possidetis* (McGill-Queen's University Press 2002) 56; *Frontier Dispute (Burkina Faso/ Niger)* (Judgment) [2013] ICJ Rep 1, Separate Opinion of Judge Yusuf 4.

[93] Section 1.2.2, text to footnotes 72–83.

[94] Shaw, *International Law* 528–9.

[95] Moore, *Costa Rica-Panama Arbitration 1911* 20, 40; Shaw, 'The Heritage of States' 97; Lalonde, *Determining Boundaries* 104.

[96] *Frontier Dispute* (n 14) 632–3.

their international boundary on the basis of the rule of intangibility of inherited frontiers. Additionally, that boundary is the boundary of the achievement of independence, which the two states pledged in the Cairo Resolution to perpetuate rather than to alter. The 1965 agreement concluded subsequent to the critical date is not the type of treaty that should be taken into account in Africa. It has been shown earlier in this chapter that if the 1965 Agreement were intended to draw a new boundary it violates the African *jus cogens*.[97]

In *Libya/Chad*, and in the same vein as in the *Frontier Dispute*, the ICJ purported to ignore the boundary of *uti possidetis* because the Treaty of 1955 governed the dispute. The Court also decided that the Cairo Resolution did not apply to the case. The ICJ held:

> Moreover, in this case, it is Libya, an original party to the [1955] Treaty, rather than a successor State, that contests its resolution of the territorial or boundary question. Hence there is no need for the Court to explore matters which have been discussed at length before it such as the principle of *uti possidetis* and the applicability of the Declaration adopted by the Organization of African Unity at Cairo in 1964.[98]

Dismissing the Cairo Resolution, on equal footing with *uti possidetis*, takes little account of an important aspect. Namely, it attaches no legal implication to the fact that even as in Spanish America the treaties to be taken into account are drawn after the emancipation; in Africa the treaties that matter are the ones that define the boundaries on the achievement of independence. Consequently, while in Spanish America post-emancipation treaties trump *uti possidetis*, in Africa the Cairo Resolution overrules the equivalent post-independence boundary treaties. On comparing the Treaties in the *Frontier Dispute* and *Libya/Chad*, we find that while the Upper Volta/Mali Treaty of 1965 was subsequent to the independence of the two states, the France/Libya Treaty of 1955 was concluded before the independence of Chad. Consequently, the post-independence 1965 Treaty is immaterial as explained earlier, while the pre-independence 1955 Treaty is decisive, being for Chad the treaty that sets the boundaries on the achievement of independence. Pursuant to the conterminous principle, the boundary created for Chad by the 1955 Treaty is presumed to be the same as the boundary that Libya had gained earlier on her respective independence. Indeed, the Cairo Resolution, far

---

[97] Section 5.1.1.
[98] *Libya/Chad* (n 60) 38.

from being irrelevant as the ICJ found, forms the basis for determining this dispute.

Regarding the second subsidiary principle, the ICJ Chamber in the *Frontier Dispute* concluded that 'There is no doubt that the obligation to respect pre-existing *international* frontiers in the event of a State succession derives from a general rule of international law, whether or not the rule is expressed in the formula *uti possidetis*.'[99] The Chamber shied away from specifying that rule. In *Guinea-Bissau/Senegal*, the tribunal advanced another vague proposition to justify applying the principle of *uti possidetis* to boundaries that had already acquired international character during the colonial era. It concluded, 'In Africa, on the other hand, *uti possidetis* has a broader meaning because it concerns both the boundaries of countries born of the same colonial empire and boundaries which during the colonial era had already an international character because they separated colonies belonging to different colonial empires.'[100] The tribunal did not explain how *uti possidetis* acquired this broader meaning in Africa.

In his dissenting opinion in *Guinea-Bissau/Senegal*, Judge Bedjaoui addressed the issue from a perspective loyal to his hallmark conception of *uti possidetis* as a general principle that applies wherever independence occurs.[101] For him in Africa and elsewhere the principle of *uti possidetis* does not apply to boundaries born in treaties because there is no distinction, 'between a Latin-American *uti possidetis* and a *uti possidetis* which should be truly and specifically "African"'.[102] However, Bedjaoui did not spell out the source of the legal force of the treaty-born boundaries in Africa.

In Africa, the international recognition of the territorial definition of the new state does not differentiate between colonial boundaries that were administrative and those that were already international. Consequently, recognition forms the source of legal force of both types of boundaries. However, the ICJ Chamber in the *Frontier Dispute* and the arbitration tribunal in *Guinea-Bissau/Senegal* could have found an alternative explanation to the source of the legal force of the treaty-based African boundaries.

---

[99] *Frontier Dispute* (n 14) 566 (emphasis added).
[100] *Arbitral Award of 31 July 1989 (Guinea-Bissau/Senegal)* Annex to the Application instituting proceedings of the Government of the Republic of Guinea-Bissau [1995] ICJ Rep 1, 49.
[101] *Ibid.*, Dissenting Opinion of Judge Bedjaoui 89–90.
[102] *Ibid.* 92.

When African states found in the inherited boundaries a principle of legitimacy and a passport to recognition, those states preferred to stick to the boundary treaties regardless of the guaranteed right to declaring *tabula rasa*.[103] Although African states did not expressly accede to the boundary-establishing treaties, their conduct described in Chapter 2 is calculated to amount to the affirmation of the boundary treaties concluded by outgoing metropolitan administrations. According to Article 24(b) of the Vienna Convention on the Succession of States with Regard to Treaties, a bilateral treaty that at the date of a succession of states was in force is considered as binding between the newly independent state and the other state party. By extension, such treaty is binding among successor states when, because of the conduct of those states, they are to be considered as having so agreed. So even as the event of state succession was not, as such, the source of the legal force of treaty-based boundaries, the fact that in actuality African states adhered to those frontiers is an alternative source of legal force.

### 5.3.2.    Post-colonial subsequent conduct

At a worldwide level subsequent conduct is of great significance in establishing the agreement of the parties and interpreting treaties. Those two roles are stated in Article 31(3)(b) of the Vienna Convention on the Law of Treaties 1969. Regarding boundary-establishing treaties in Africa, which are *ipso facto* concluded by colonial powers, those two functions should be understood to apply to the subsequent conduct of the colonial administrations, not that of governments of successor independent states. This is because in Africa, the boundary is to be delimited *as inherited*, in contradistinction to *as subsequently adjusted*. As a consequence of the status quo rule the territory of the African state is static, coinciding always with the photographic snapshot taken on idependence. The title to such fixed territory is neither subject to forfeiture by adverse possession nor amenable to perfection by post-colonial *effectivités*. In an African boundary

---

[103] African states had availed themselves of the clean slate principle and declared *tabula rasa* regarding treaties other than boundary-creating treaties. The Nyerere Doctrine, which states that no colonial treaty becomes applicable unless the new state notifies its accession to it within a specified period of time, was largely followed. See E. G. Bello, 'Reflections on Succession of States in the Light of the Vienna Convention on Succession of States with Respect of Treaties 1978' [1980] 23 *German YBK Int'l L* 296, 298–9. For the practice of African states regarding treaties of predecessor states see *Yearbook of the International Law Commission*, vol. II, part I (1974) 188–92.

dispute, the parties would typically request the Court 'to ascertain what is the frontier which *was inherited* from the [colonial] administration'.[104] They would also require a tribunal to 'reaffirm the principle of respect for the borders *existing* at independence'.[105] Yet the ICJ and tribunals gave subsequent conduct in Africa a role that contravenes the intangibility of inherited frontiers and disregards considerations pertinent to the African context.

In *Kasikili/Sedudu (Botswana/Namibia)*, the Court was asked to determine on the basis of the Anglo-German Treaty of 1 July 1890 and the rules and principles of international law the boundary between Namibia and Botswana around Kasikili/Sedudu Island.[106] Namibia invoked, *inter alia*, the argument of subsequent conduct. Namibia contended that the continued control and use of the island by the people of Eastern Caprivi and the exercise of jurisdiction over the island by the governing authorities attributes Kasikili/Sedudu Island to Namibia.[107] The Court found that whereas it was asked to determine the dispute on the basis of the 1890 Treaty and the rules and principles of international law, the Court was not precluded from examining Namibia's prescription argument.[108] Consequently, the Court examined acts *à titre de souverain* performed way after termination of the mandate over Namibia in 1966. These included an incident between a patrol boat of the South African Defence Force and a unit of the Botswana Defence Force in October 1984. In Namibia's view that incident indicated that South Africa, to which Namibia was a predecessor, exercised state authority in respect of the island. The Court entertained Namibia's argument in principle and rejected it only on the basis that the conditions for acquiring title to territory by prescription were not satisfied.[109]

While the Mandate over Namibia was terminated in 1966, Namibia attained independence on 21 March 1990. Even though this complicates Namibia's case in particular, it shows the importance of restricting valid subsequent conduct to the recognized colonial era. The ICJ ruled on the presence of South Africa in Namibia during this prolonged interlude as illegal.[110] In the 1950 *Advisory Opinion on the International Status of South-West Africa*, the ICJ concluded that the rights of the peoples of that

---

[104]  *Frontier Dispute* (n 14) 570 (emphasis added).
[105]  *Decision Regarding delimitation of the Border between Eritrea and Ethiopia* (2002) XXV RIAA 83, 96 (emphasis added).
[106]  *Kasikili/Sedudu Island (Botswana/Namibia)* (Judgment) [1999] ICJ Rep 1045.
[107]  *Ibid*. 1093.    [108]  *Ibid*. 1102–3.    [109]  *Ibid*. 1105.
[110]  *The Legal Consequences for States of the Continued Presence of South Africa in Namibia (South West Africa) notwithstanding Security Council Resolution 276 (1970)* (Advisory Opinion) [1971] ICJ Rep 16, 65.

country could not be effectively safeguarded without international super-vision.[111] Consequently, it is erroneous of the Court in *Kasikili/Sedudu* to consider the actions of South Africa, which were undertaken without international supervision, as forming valid acts *à titre de souverain* that could have possible effect on the rights of Namibia and the interests of its population. Even though Namibia did not attain independence until 1990, subsequent conduct and *effectivités* that followed the termination of the Mandate in 1966 should not have been taken into account. The sound course for the ICJ to follow should have been to establish the agreement of the parties to the 1890 Treaty and interpret it in accordance with the legitimate colonial *effectivités* that took place until the termination of the Mandate in 1966.

Acquiescence to post-colonial *effectivités* was found in *Cameroon/ Nigeria* to form the basis for changing inherited frontiers. While con-sidering the frontier in the Lake Chad area, the ICJ noted that Nigeria performed acts *à titre de souverain* in areas where Cameroon had legal title. The Court concluded that 'as there was a pre-existing title held by Cameroon in this area of the lake, the pertinent legal test is whether there was thus evidenced acquiescence by Cameroon in the passing of title from itself to Nigeria'.[112] However, on the facts of the case the Court found that the acts of Nigeria and Cameroon, taken together, showed that there was no acquiescence by Cameroon in the abandonment of its title in that area in favour of Nigeria. Regarding the Sapeo area, the Court noted that the parties had accepted, contrary to the boundary line delimited by agreement, that this area lay within Nigerian territory.[113] Changing treaty title on the bases of acquiescence to post-colonial *effectivités* is an unlikely conclusion for a Court applying the rule of intangibility of inherited fron-tiers or recognizing the territorial status quo custom.

Evidence emanating from the governments of independent states also raises the same difficulties and attracts similar doctrine. This type of evidence presupposes that a boundary is subject to continuous change. In the African territorial regime, where the inherited frontier is intan-gible and preserved perpetually, this presumption does not arise. In the *Frontier Dispute (Benin/Niger)*, the two disputants differed with respect to the possibility of using maps after the date of independence. On the one

---

[111] *International Status of South-West Africa* (Advisory Opinion) [1950] ICJ Rep 128, 137.

[112] *Cameroon/Nigeria* (Merits) (n 53) 353.

[113] *Ibid.* 383. The 'test' referred to here by the Court is that for admitting colonial *effectivités* irreproachably set by the ICJ Chamber in the *Frontier Dispute* (n 14) 587. However, that test could not be applied with regard to post-colonial *effectivités*.

hand, Niger relied on such maps to establish the situation existing in the colonial era.[114] On the other hand, Benin considered that 'the Chamber should base its decision on research and documents prior to the critical date'.[115] The Chamber held that it could not exclude *a priori* the possibility that such maps may be relevant in application of the principle of *uti possidetis* in order to establish the situation that existed at the critical date. This finding should mean that the Court was to restrict admissibility of maps made by the parties to establishing the status quo. Yet, the ICJ Chamber added that the examination of the maps could lead to modification in the inherited boundary if such documents clearly express the parties' agreement to such change.[116]

In short, colonial *effectivités* play an important role in showing how the boundary set by the colonial powers was interpreted in practice by colonial administrations. What causes difficulty is taking account of post-colonial *effectivités*. This category of *effectivités* is incongruent with the African paradigm because it is based on the presumption that boundaries are subject to change by subsequent conduct of the disputant states.[117] A *conditio sine qua* of accepting that the inherited frontiers are intangible is to recognize that post-colonial *effectivités* are of no effect in determining boundaries. On demarcating African boundaries acts performed or acquiesced in by independence governments, as well as evidence created by national administrations, are inconsequential.

In addition to taking little account of the rule of intangibility of inherited frontiers, delimiting a boundary in Africa on the strength of post-colonial *effectivités* is practically unworkable and leads to harsh consequences. This is because post-colonial *effectivités* require cut-off dates, unrelated to the critical date, to differentiate between valid and self-serving sovereign actions. The unrelated cut-off dates are also used as the watershed for comparing the degree of display of sovereignty on each and every particular part of the boundary. This is what makes it possible elsewhere for every portion of the boundary to be adjudged separately on the basis of the strength of acts *à titre de souverain* performed by one party assessed in the light of the opposed claim.[118] In particular, this was the technique followed for introducing post-colonial *effectivités* in Spanish America. Such cut-off dates are not viable in the African context. This point is expanded below.

---

[114] *Frontier Dispute* (n 14) 587.
[115] *Ibid.*     [116] *Ibid.*
[117] Separate opinion of Judge Torres Bernardez, *El Salvador/Honduras* (n 47) 641, 643.
[118] *Legal Status of Eastern Greenland (Denmark/Norway)* [1933] PCIJ Rep Series A/B No 53, 45–6.

The rule of intangibility of inherited frontiers presupposes the existence of a single continuous boundary line delimiting the territory of the new African state. Conversely, *uti possidetis* assumes that swathes of territory were allocated out of the common inheritance as possessions of different Spanish-American republics. As such, in Spanish America a technique of mini-critical dates was required to determine disputes over title to tracts of territory. The reason why this methodology was required, and why it succeeded, in Spanish America is that the possession-related *uti possidetis* critical date is a general guideline that does not apply in a strict sense to each piece of land along the boundary.[119] Consequently, the title for each tract of territory was worked separately. This method was also introduced successfully to Asia because in Asia it is possible that the boundaries of one country or the islands that compose a particular country have different conventional critical dates that work as unrelated cut-off dates.[120] In contrast, because of adopting the independence day as the critical date it becomes impossible to invent unrelated intermediary cut-off dates in Africa to differentiate between valid and invalid post-colonial *effectivités*. For sure, there can be many materialization dates for one boundary. Yet, those dates could not function as intermediary cut-off dates because they are governed by the critical date and as such not unrelated. In fact those dates are mere tools for establishing the single boundary that was inherited on independence and shall be construed in line with the critical date of recognition. Notwithstanding, the methodology of unrelated mini-critical dates was applied in *Eritrea/Ethiopia*. The Eritrea-Ethiopia Border Commission treated the different materialization dates as unrelated, allowing for the possibility of identifying different cut-off dates for admitting post-colonial *effectivités*. This exercise ignored the critical date, eventually leading to disastrous consequences, as we shall presently see.

The Eritrean-Ethiopian dispute is a dispute between two states of no typical independence day, and, as such, of no conventional critical date. On facing this issue, the Eritrea-Ethiopia Border Commission concluded that the critical date was the date that developments subsequent to which 'are not to be taken into account save in so far as they can be seen as a continuance or confirmation of a line of conduct already clearly established, or take the form of express agreements between them'.[121] According to this formula, the boundary line laid down on recognition could be

---

[119]  *Nicaragua/Honduras* (n 49) 697–8, see Section 5.2.1 text to footnote 48 and below.
[120]  *Indonesia/Malaysia* (n 51) 682.
[121]  *Eritrea/Ethiopia* (n 105) 118.

changed in two instances: first, when developments subsequent to the critical date are a continuation of a line of conduct already established, and, second, when the subsequent conduct takes the form of express agreement between the parties. This test renders the concept of critical date of little authority and imparts no sanctity on the situation obtained on independence. In accordance with this approach, the Eritrea-Ethiopia Boundary Commission accepted post-colonial *effectivités* and created a chain of mini-critical dates on the basis of the colonial treaties of 1900, 1902, and 1908.

In the Eastern Sector, governed by the 1908 treaty, the Commission noted that the *effectivités* adduced for the period since the treaty essentially reinforced the geometric line.[122] However, on the basis of evidence presented by Eritrea of an agreement signed as recently as 1994 the Commission concluded that even as the line of the 1908 treaty placed Bure on the Ethiopian side 'both parties had agreed [in 1994] that their common border was placed at Bure'. Accordingly, a new boundary that 'passes equidistantly the checkpoints of the two parties' was drawn.[123]

In the Central Sector, of the treaty of 1900, the Commission depended on post-colonial *effectivités* to effect departure from the inherited boundary line in two places. First, the Commission adjusted the 1900 boundary line to place Zalambessa in Ethiopian territory.[124] This was done on the basis of a 'considerable number of significant administrative activities by Ethiopian authorities', coupled with Eritrean acknowledgement that the town falls within Ethiopia. Second, the treaty line was varied so as to place parts of the Endeli projection in Ethiopia. The Commission concluded that, although Ethiopia had presented the stronger evidence of administrative activity, the impact of Eritrean activity was stronger in the northern and western fringes of the Endeli projection and that Ethiopia had not established its effective sovereignty to the required degree over those areas.

When it came to the Western Sector of the 1902 treaty, the Commission did not vary the treaty line on the strength of post-colonial *effectivités*. The Commission considered a range of developments subsequent to the treaty that continued until the early 1930s and decided on the basis of

[122]  *Ibid.* 169.
[123]  *Ibid.* 171.
[124]  *Ibid.* 135–6.

no clear yardstick that the situation had largely crystallized.[125] Ethiopian claims that the boundary established by the colonial treaty of 1902 had been overridden by other factors, including *effectivités* on the ground in and around Badme, were rejected.[126] This meant that Ethiopia was to hand over the disputed town of Badme.

The dispute over Badme was the high point of the Eritrean-Ethiopian conflict.[127] The OAU Committee of Ambassadors found that 'Badme Town and its environs were administered by the Ethiopian authorities before 12 May, 1998'.[128] The OAU Decision on the Eritrea/Ethiopia Conflict demanded the Eritrean withdrawal from this area.[129] However, it was not immediately clear whether Badme falls in the Ethiopian or Eritrean side of the recognized international boundary. Therefore, the OAU stated in its decision that it is without prejudice to the final outcome of the delimitation.[130] Even if Ethiopia was bound to accept a finding that Badme falls in the Eritrean side of the inherited frontier should it be arrived at, the formula introduced by the Commission in other Sections relaxed the sanctity of the inherited boundaries, making it difficult for Ethiopia to accept such outcome.[131]

In addition to being the correct course of action to take, treating the inherited frontiers as subject to no possible variation has the advantage of being the only approach that could be pursued convincingly in Africa. If the Commission worked on the basis of this classical wisdom and made no changes in the inherited boundary line, the losing party would have most likely conceded the outcome. As a result of applying this unfamiliar principle the Eritrea-Ethiopia Border Commission failed in its principal function of resolving the Eritrean-Ethiopian dispute transparently in accordance with established tenets of international law.[132]

---

[125] *Ibid.* 162.    [126]    *Ibid.*

[127] The controversy over Badme town was the reason that triggered the border war of 1998 that killed 70,000 soldiers and displaced over a million people, see Christine Gray, 'The Eritrea/Ethiopia Claims Commission Oversteps Its Boundaries: A Partial Award?' (2006) 17 *EJIL* 699, 703.

[128] *Report on the Efforts made by the OAU High Level Delegation on the Dispute between Ethiopia and Eritrea* (Central Organ/MEC/AHG/2 (IV) Ouagadougou, December, 1998).

[129] See Gray, 'The Eritrea/Ethiopia Claims Commission Oversteps Its Boundaries' 701.

[130] *Ibid.*    [131]    *Ibid.* 707–9.

[132] See generally *ibid.* 707 ff; Aman Mahray McHugh, 'Resolving International Boundary Disputes in Africa: A Case for the International Court of Justice' (2005) 49 *Howard LJ* 209.

### 5.3.3.   Estoppel

The estoppel created by the Cairo Resolution plays an exceptional role in the African territorial regime of no equal in the *uti possidetis* prototype. This role stands in stark contrast to the restricted scope of subsequent conduct in Africa. Because of the representation made in the Cairo Resolution, all boundary-treaties that were not the basis of the boundaries inherited on independence could not be revived.[133] Successor states to those treaties are estopped from invoking those treaties to deny the status quo boundary. In the *Frontier Dispute*, and on the epitome of the African territorial regime, estoppel could have been successfully invoked against the application of the agreement of 15 January 1965 even if it were found valid.[134] This is because that agreement was not part of the legal framework of the boundaries inherited on independence. Likewise, in Cameroon/Nigeria, the principle of estoppel could have been successfully pleaded against the Treaty of Protection with the King and Chiefs of Old Calabar of 1884 claimed by Nigeria.[135]

### 5.3.4.   Sovereignty over islands

Denial of *terra nullius*, the underlying assumption of *uti possidetis*, did not afford the Spanish-American principle with the appropriate posture to develop rules regarding sovereignty over islands the way it did in relation to land. It is easy to prove whether a particular tract of land was subject to Spanish colonial rule or not, even if doubt exists as to the republic in which it was placed on the emancipation. Yet this is not necessarily the case with regard to islands not connected with the mainland. The ICJ found that the denial of *terra nullius* 'cannot bring within the territory of successor States islands not shown to be subject to Spanish colonial rule, nor *ipso facto* render as "attributed", islands which have no connection with the mainland coast concerned'.[136] On studying this aspect of the Spanish-American rule, Castellino concluded that *uti possidetis* provides no clear answer when the issue of sovereignty over islands is in question.[137]

It has been explained in Chapter 2 that denial of *terra nullius* is not among the reasons behind the African rule of intangibility of inherited

---

[133] Section 3.2.4.
[134] *Frontier Dispute* (n 14) 632–3.
[135] *Cameroon/Nigeria* (Preliminary Objections) (n 72) 410.
[136] *Nicaragua/Honduras* (n 49) 707.
[137] Castellino, *Territorial Integrity* 547–8.

frontiers.[138] Additionally, in the legal and historical circumstances that led to the creation of African colonies occupation of *terra nullius* was not required to establish sovereignty over islands.

Legally, during the scramble for Africa, territory was considered to form part of a particular colony or protectorate only if it satisfied the principles established in the Berlin Conference. Articles 34 and 35 of the General Act of the Berlin Conference 1885 contained two important principles. These are: first, the principle of notifying the contracting powers of any future taking of possession of territory on the coasts of Africa and, second, the principle of effective occupation of territory in the hinterland.[139] As such, the coast, together with islands, was to be included in the actual control of the colonial power by notification of the contracting powers of taking possession. Yet the hinterland falls in the hands of the colonial power only to the extent of effective occupation and with no need for notification.

Historically, the above rule takes full account of the political realities of Africa at that time. At the onset of the scramble for Africa, the focus of colonial powers in Africa was the coast, not the hinterland. In addition to being more known and easily accessible, African coasts were the most sophisticated and politically organized. Alexandrowicz observed that the Mediterranean Coast, the East African Coast of Islamic states, the states and chieftainships of West, Central, and South Africa Coasts 'could not, any more than Asian territory, be treated as *terra nullius* by the European newcomer'.[140] Hence, European powers had to first overwhelm the coastal rulers in order to establish their authority on the African interior. Before starting such coastal forays notification was required. When they are already established at the coast, determining the borderlines in the hinterland, even if effective occupation is required, was incidental to actual control of the coast and as such requires no fresh notification.

This background justifies why different approaches were taken in the two continents of Africa and Spanish America with regard to the application of the contiguity principle to the islands close to the mainland. In *Eritrea/Yemen*, where the very question at issue before the tribunal was to which coastal state the contested islands belonged, the tribunal found that: 'There is a strong presumption that islands within the

---

[138] Section 2.2.1, text to footnotes 38–39.
[139] C. H. Alexandrowicz, 'The Juridical Expression of the Sacred Trust of Civilization' (1971) 65 *AJIL* 149, 152.
[140] *Ibid.* 151.

twelve-mile coastal belt will belong to the coastal state, unless there is a fully-established case to the contrary'.[141] The dispute over the islands within the coastal belt of Eritrea was determined pursuant to this presumption. The tribunal unanimously found that the islands, islets, rocks, and low-tide elevations forming the Mohabbakah islands, within twelve miles from the territorial sea baseline, are subject to the territorial sovereignty of Eritrea, being appurtenant to the African coast.[142]

The contiguity presumption did not arise in Spanish America. In *El Salvador/Honduras* the Chamber of the Court found it necessary to consider whether it was 'possible to establish the appurtenance in 1821 of each disputed island to one or the other of the various administrative units of the Spanish colonial structure in Central America'. The Chamber did not consider the contiguity principle even if it faced difficulties with the evidence adduced by the parties. The ICJ Chamber concluded that 'The attribution of individual islands to the territorial administrative divisions of the Spanish colonial system, for the purposes of their allocation to the one or the other newly-independent State, may well have been a matter of some doubt and difficulty, judging by the evidence and information submitted.'[143]

In *Nicaragua/Honduras,* the Court declined to determine sovereignty over the islands in dispute on the basis of proximity. It was held:

> With regard to the adjacency argument, the Court notes that the independence treaties concluded by Nicaragua and Honduras with Spain … refer to adjacency with respect to mainland coasts rather than to offshore islands. Nicaragua's argument that the islands in dispute are closer to Edinburgh Cay, which belongs to Nicaragua, cannot therefore be accepted. While the Court does not rely on adjacency in reaching its findings, it observes that, in any event, the islands in dispute appear to be in fact closer to the coast of Honduras than to the coast of Nicaragua.[144]

The approach adopted in *Eritrea/Yemen* is more expressive of the African paradigm of inheriting the boundaries of the former colony. It takes into account the legal and historical realities that express the seaward orientation of the colonies. However, it shall be remembered that attribution of islands within the coastal belt of Africa in accordance with the contiguity principle is only a presumption. In *Eritrea/Yemen,* the

---

[141]  *Eritrea/Yemen Arbitration (Phase One: Territorial Sovereignty and Scope of Dispute)* [1996] 114 ILR 1, 132–3.

[142]  *Ibid.* 133.

[143]  *El Salvador/Honduras* (n 47) 558–9.

[144]  *Nicaragua/Honduras* (n 49) 709.

tribunal clarifies that this presumption could be rebutted by superior evidence. It is concluded that:

> And even if there were a presumption of coastal-state sovereignty over islands falling within the twelve-mile territorial sea of a coastal belt island, it would be no more than a presumption, capable of being rebutted by evidence of a superior title.[145]

### 5.3.5.    Ex aequo et bono

The approach of *uti possidetis* of determining title to tracts of land in possession led tribunals to apply 'considerations of equity and practical convenience'.[146] Because the purpose of the *uti possidetis* delimitation exercise was to allocate a territory vaguely defined, as opposed to delineating a precise boundary, it was illogical to exclude such considerations. As a result, in Spanish America arbitrators were normally empowered to decide boundary disputes *ex aequo et bono*.[147] Arbitration tribunals were frequently 'expressly authorized in the interests of justice, as disclosed by subsequent developments, to depart from the line of *uti possidetis* of 1821, even where that line is found to exist'.[148] Even in cases when the *compromis* did not provide for resort to equity, arbitrators 'declared the insufficiency of the *uti possidetis juris* and decided in equity'.[149] Conversely, African state parties to a dispute do not tend to empower a tribunal to decide as *amiable compositeur*.[150] This tallies with the supposition that in accordance with the rule of intangibility of inherited frontiers the laid boundary should be established as is.

Nonetheless, the ICJ Chamber in the *Frontier Dispute* acted *ex aequo et bono*, while apparently applying equity *infra legem*, to equitably divide the pool of Soum between the parties. In that case, the Chamber concluded that it 'must recognize that Soum is a frontier pool; and that, in the absence of any precise indication in the texts of the position of the frontier line, the line should divide the pool of Soum in two, in an equitable manner'.[151] This approach is not the appropriate course to take in the African context.

---

[145]  *Eritrea/Yemen* (n 141) 133.

[146]  Moore, *Costa Rica-Panama Arbitration 1911* 29.

[147]  Separate Opinion of Judge Torres Bernardez, *El Salvador/Honduras* (n 47) 633–4.

[148]  *Honduras Borders (Guatemala/Honduras)* (1933) II RIAA 1307, 1352.

[149]  Lalonde, *Determining Boundaries* 42–3, quoting P. De Lapradelle, *La Frontier: Etude de Droit International* (Les Editions Internationales 1928) 85.

[150]  The only exception in this regard in which the *compromis* empowered the Court 'in rendering its decision to take account of equitable principles' is the *Continental Shelf (Tunisia/Libyan Arab Jamahiriya)* (Judgment) [1982] ICJ Rep 18, 21. This is justifiable by the fact that equity plays an exceptional role in maritime and continental shelf delimitation.

[151]  *Frontier Dispute* (n 14) 633.

One of the uses of equity *infra legem* is to fill gaps in geographic data and the evidence adduced by the parties.[152] The sole arbitrator in *Guiana Boundary Case (Brazil, Great Britain)* resorted to this use.[153] The arbitrator, on finding that there was insufficient evidence to decide the controversy over certain parts of the disputed territory, decided to divide that territory equitably. However, even that task was rendered impossible by the insufficiency of geographic data. The arbitrator then concluded:

> [I]n the present state of the geographical knowledge of the region, it is not possible to divide the contested territory into two parts equal as regards extent and value, but that it is necessary that it should be divided in accordance with the lines traced by nature, and that the preference should be given to a frontier which, while clearly defined throughout its whole course, the better lends itself to a fair decision of the disputed territory.[154]

Applying equity *infra legem* in this sense could fit in Spanish America out of necessity where no definite boundaries were inherited and no sufficient geographic data is available. Nonetheless, resort to this form of equity is unwarranted in Africa. In the absence of sufficient evidence, the Court or tribunal applying the rule of intangibility of inherited frontiers should call into play the principle of the onus of proof. When the evidence adduced by the claimant state is not of *juris tantum* character such as to reverse the burden the issue should be determined in favour of the respondent state. Dividing a natural feature 'in an equitable manner' is implausible when the parties do not empower the Court to act *ex aequo et bono* and when a definite borderline is presumed to have been in existence.

Additionally, tribunals determining Spanish-American disputes were normally authorized to depart from the *uti possidetis* line when it resulted in inconvenience and to award compensation. In *Guatemala-Honduras Arbitration* Article V of the Treaty of Arbitration signed at Washington in 1930 provides that:

> If the Tribunal finds that one or both Parties, in their subsequent development, have established beyond that line, interests which should be taken into account in establishing the definitive boundary, the tribunal shall modify as it may see fit the line of the *uti possidetis* of 1821 and shall fix the territorial or other compensation which it may deem just that either party should pay to the other.[155]

---

[152] M. Akehurst, 'Equity and General Principles of Law' (1976) 25 *ICLQ* 801, 802–5.
[153] *The Guiana Boundary Case (Brazil/Great Britain)* (1904) XI RIAA 11.
[154] *Ibid.* 22.
[155] *Guatemala/Honduras* (n 148) 1322.

**Figure 1** The changes made in international law by the African territorial regime (*uti possidetis* v African customary rules)

**Uti possidetis** / **The African territorial regime**

| | *Uti possidetis* | The African territorial regime |
|---|---|---|
| | Applies automatically | Does not apply automatically |
| | No contiguity presumption arises | Contiguity presumption arises |
| Role of estoppel | Limited | Decisive |
| Post-colonial *effectivités* | Admissible | Inadmissible |
| Altering boundary by subsequent conduct | Possible | Not possible |
| Critical date | Possession-related, subject to consolidation cut-off dates | Recognition-related, dominating materialization date |
| Source of legal force for treaty-based boundaries | Not applicable | Recognition |
| Elevating administrative divisions to boundaries | By operation of *uti possidetis* | By recognition |
| Adherence to the inherited boundary | Flexible | Strict |
| Status of the inherited boundary | Default line | Final boundary |
| Secession | Neutral | Proscribed |
| Altering boundary by treaty | Possible | Not possible |

In contrast, African states do not provide for the possibility of territorial compensation in any hypothesis.[156] Even when maritime delimitations are undertaken, where the corrective-equity approach is inherent, the propriety of any equitable delimitation was questioned on the basis of its incompatibility with the status quo.[157] In *Cameroon/Nigeria*, when Cameroon claimed an 'equitable line' beyond point G, Nigeria contended that Cameroon was departing from the status quo rule.[158]

To conclude, this chapter has demonstrated that the African territorial regime introduced many changes to international law regarding Africa (see Figure 1). It reformulated the concept of critical date and put it to a different use. The African regime approaches differently the boundaries born in treaties. It has its own outlook as to understanding the source of their legal force and to what extent they are subject to changes by subsequent conduct or protected by estoppel. Issues of post-colonial subsequent conduct, sovereignty over islands, and *ex aequo et bono* are also viewed differently from the perspective of the African territorial regime.

Yet, the major change made by the African custom in international law is the creation of the African *jus cogens*. The prohibition of the redrawing of boundaries and the rule against secession are the most important features of the African territorial regime. In actuality, African states have managed to avoid redrawing boundaries and advancing state-to-state territorial claims. However, the African rule against secession has been occasionally violated. Because a secession claim violates a peremptory African norm, secession aspirants rarely admit their secessionist agenda or that they are making a simple claim to territory. In Africa, secession claims are always camouflaged by an argument believed to assign a semblance of legitimacy to an otherwise unlawful and denigrated course. These disguising arguments complicate further an already complex phenomenon of secession in Africa. Four arguments currently advanced for justifying secession in Africa are identified and studied in the following chapter.

---

[156] For Spanish-American provisions stating this possibility see Article V of the 1829 Treaty between Peru and Colombia, Moore, *Costa Rica-Panama Arbitration 1911* 23; Article XVI of the Definitive Treaty of Peace and Friendship between Bolivia and Peru (1831) 25; the award of King Alphonso III of Spain in the Boundary case between Honduras and Nicaragua, *The Border Dispute between Honduras and Nicaragua* (1906) XI RIAA 101,116. See also the Separate Opinion of Judge Torres Bernardez, *El Salvador/Honduras* (n 47) 633–4.

[157] Yoshifumi Tanaka, 'Reflections on Maritime Delimitation in the Cameroon/Nigeria Case' (2004) 53 *ICLQ* 369, 375–6.

[158] *Cameroon/Nigeria* (Preliminary Objections) (n 72) 422.

# PART II

## Towards an exception to the African rule against secession

To see a world in a grain of Sand
And a Heaven in a Wild Flower
Hold Infinity in the palm of your hand
And Eternity in an hour
A Robin Red breast in a Cage
Puts all Heaven in a Rage
A Dove house filld with Doves & Pigeons
Shudders Hell thr' all its regions
A dog starvd at his Masters Gate
Predicts the ruin of the State

*William Blake,*
*Auguries of the Innocence*

# 6

## Current justifications for secession in Africa

Advancing secession openly as a simple claim to territory is not the pattern in Africa. African secession claims are normally intertwined with excuses and shrouded with alternative arguments. Four such apologetic arguments are currently identifiable.

First, an argument for reviving the right to colonial self-determination or claiming a right to reversion for a particular unit.

Second, an argument for recognizing a constitutional right to self-determination either for a discrete region or for sub-national groups in a multi-ethnic state.

Third, an argument for remedial secession. This involves the contention that in the event of excessive human rights violations, coupled with non-representation in government, a right to secede accrues to the aggrieved section of the people.

Fourth, an argument for national self-determination. This argument alleges that historically Africa was composed of larger nation-like entities, and that it is possible to regroup the current states along the lines of those presumed nations.

Conceived with the premeditated intention to elude the African territorial regime, those arguments fail deliberately to take account of the common African interest. Moreover, the four arguments are conceptually flawed, as this chapter shows.

### 6.1.  Revivalist secession

Finding fault with the decolonization or merger process that led to the creation of the state against which a territorial claim is made is the preferred argument for disguising a secession claim. When it is found that in the historical context of a particular claim to secession it is possible to make such an argument, secessionists reformulate their secession claim to fit the revivalist mould. They argue that their entire action for secession is impelled by an altruistic motive to correct that particular historical

mistake. In the process, the real reason behind the secession call fades
away and is sometimes tabooed. Soon a revolutionary culture that fuses
the real cause with the excuse arises, making it difficult even for the secessionists themselves to disentangle their cause from the revivalist argument. Arguments for reviving the right to colonial self-determination or
sovereign statehood were made to justify the secession claims of Eritrea,
Southern Cameroons, and Somaliland.

### 6.1.1.   *The Eritrean argument for reviving a right to a referendum*

Eritrea presented its case for secession as a case of denied decolonization.
To understand the Eritrean call for revivalist secession we need to examine the historical background of the UN Resolution that annexed Eritrea
to Ethiopia.

In accordance with Article 23 of the 1947 Peace Treaty, concluded at
the end of the Second World War between the Allied Powers and Italy,
Italy renounced rights and title to Eritrea among its other possessions in
Africa. When the Allied Powers failed in 1949 to agree on what to do with
these possessions, they referred the matter to the UN General Assembly.[1]
The General Assembly recommended in Resolution 289 (IV) to refer
Eritrea to an Inquiry Commission.[2] The Commission, established of representatives of five states, failed to present an agreed report and, instead,
made three different proposals.[3] In December 1950, the UN General
Assembly adopted Resolution 390 (V) recommending that 'Eritrea shall
constitute an autonomous unit federated with Ethiopia under the sovereignty of the Ethiopian Crown'.[4] On the strength of this recommendation,
Eritrea was annexed to Ethiopia without conducting a plebiscite to ascertain the wishes of the Eritrean people.

Assessing the actions taken by the UN that led to this inauspicious outcome Cassese opined:

---

[1]  *UN Report of the United Nations Commission for Eritrea,* (UN Doc A/ 1285, 1950) 24.
[2]  UNGA Res 289 (IV) (21 November 1949). Conversely, that resolution recommended that
other Italian possessions, Libya and Somaliland, should be granted independence.
[3]  The representatives of Burma and South Africa recommended a federation with Ethiopia
under the Ethiopian Crown. The representatives of Guatemala and Pakistan proposed
complete independence for Eritrea after ten years of direct trusteeship under the United
Nations. The fifth representative, from Norway, advocated the complete reunion of Eritrea
with Ethiopia. *UN Report of the United Nations Commission for Eritrea* (n 1).
[4]  General Assembly Resolution 390 (V) of 2 December 1950 on the Report of the United
Nations Commission for Eritrea.

Where the UN action can be faulted is in its failure to organize a referendum in 1950 to establish the wishes of Eritreans. Actually the manner in which the five-member UN Commission ascertained the will of Eritreans is highly questionable. In short, it seems that political and strategic considerations took the upper hand, and self-determination – as the 'genuine and free expression of will' of a people – was set aside.[5]

The validity of Cassese's argument, that the UN General Assembly could be faulted for failing to organize a referendum for Eritrea, will be examined later.

It did not take the Eritreans long to find that under the Ethiopian Crown they were not equal compatriots with the Ethiopians. Additionally, the Ethiopian monarch rescinded the autonomous federal status of Eritrea and fully incorporated Eritrea in the Ethiopian Empire. Resentment mounted and the Eritrean elite started a movement to secede from Ethiopia. Mindful of the emergent African collective position against boundary revisionism, the Eritreans focused on criticising the historical circumstances that led to annexing their country to Ethiopia, which were still vivid in the memories of that generation. They portrayed Eritrea to have been singled out on decolonization and denied the exercise of the right to colonial self-determination granted to other colonial peoples. The year 1961 marked the start of the Eritrean civil war that continued for thirty years. A self-determination referendum was claimed to make up for the missed plebiscite. This referendum became the unrivalled objective of the Eritrean struggle.

In May 1991, the EPLF controlled the entire Eritrean territory. Ethiopia, under the rule of the Ethiopian People's Revolutionary Democratic Front (EPRDF), accepted the *de facto* independence of Eritrea.[6] All impediments preventing the secession of Eritrea were thus removed and there was no reason for the Eritreans not to declare their new state. If the ICJ were to provide an Advisory Opinion on the Eritrean situation, it would have mostly made a conclusion along lines similar to those of *the Kosovo Advisory Opinion*. Namely, on controlling the Eritrean soil in May 1991, a unilateral declaration of secession made by the EPLF would have offended no principle of international law. This is because for the ICJ, which does not as yet recognize the African territorial regime and its rule against secession, general international law applies to Africa. In the words of the

[5] Antonio Cassese, *Self-determination of Peoples: A Legal Appraisal* (Cambridge University Press 1995) 222.
[6] See generally Ruth Iyob, *The Eritrean Struggle for Independence: Domination, Resistance, Nationalism, 1941–1993* (Cambridge University Press 1997).

ICJ in *the Kosovo Advisory Opinion*, 'general international law contains no applicable prohibition of declarations of independence'.[7]

Nonetheless, the EPLF was unable to disentangle itself from three decades of revolutionary culture based on the ideal of reviving a right to a referendum. On overtaking Asmara, and as if turning back the clock, the EPLF put aside the liberation flag and hoisted instead the UN standard, which was used briefly by the UN Commission in 1950, to indicate that Eritrea was not yet decolonized. The EPLF insisted on the UN to return to Eritrea to organize a referendum.

The General Assembly accepted in December 1992 to simply send an observer mission to verify the referendum scheduled to take place in April 1993.[8] No reference was made in General Assembly Resolution 47/114 (1992) to Resolutions 1514 (XV) and 1541 (XV). It was rather clearly stated in Resolution 47/114 that the UN General Assembly was acting upon the request of 'the authorities directly concerned'; not upon an Eritrean right to colonial self-determination, as the EPLF would prefer. The UN Observer Mission to Verify the Referendum in Eritrea was not asked 'to ascertain the wishes of the Eritrean people', as would have been the case if the General Assembly was drawing on its now obsolete decolonization mandate. The role of the mission was restricted to monitoring the impartiality of the referendum, reporting claims of irregularities, verifying the counting and announcing the results. In April 1993, the referendum was conducted as scheduled. A total of 99.8 per cent of Eritreans voted for independence. Only on the announcement made by the UN Special Commissioner in April 1993 that the referendum was free and fair, was Eritrea declared independent.[9]

For the EPLF the Eritrean independence was a consequence of the April 1993 referendum. This exercise poses the question of whether the Eritrean referendum was a decolonization plebiscite, or at least a curative action in lieu of the decolonization plebiscite.

In the *Western Sahara Advisory Opinion*, the law that governs the exercise of self-determination upon decolonization was extensively discussed. It was found that the failure of the UN General Assembly to consult the inhabitants of a colony does not affect the legality of the exercise of colonial self-determination. The Court held:

---

[7] *Accordance with International Law of the Unilateral Declaration of Independence in Respect of Kosovo* (Advisory Opinion) [2010] ICJ Rep 403, 438.

[8] UNGA Res A/RES/47/114 (16 December 1992).

[9] *Ibid.* 140.

The validity of the principle of self-determination, defined as the need to pay regard to the freely expressed will of peoples, is not affected by the fact that in certain cases the General Assembly has dispensed with the requirement of consulting the inhabitants of a given territory.[10]

Consequently, the UN General Assembly could not be faulted even if it dispensed altogether with consulting the people in question. This means that, contrary to the supposition made by Cassese, General Assembly Resolution 390 (V) could not be questioned on not recommending a plebiscite for Eritrea. Nor is it possible to blame the UN Commission on the basis that in ascertaining the will of the Eritreans the Commission acted upon political and strategic considerations rather than on legal doctrine. The reason why the UN could not be faulted in this regard is that past actions of the General Assembly are finally consummated. Any alleged violations by the UN or shortcomings of its actions cannot be rectified, form the subject of reparation, or be the reason for reviving past rights. The ICJ clarified this rule in *Cameroon/United Kingdom*.

When the Republic of Cameroon objected to annexing the Northern Cameroons to Nigeria, Cameroon presented a plea to the UN General Assembly asking for the plebiscite to be declared null and void and for detaching the Northern Cameroons from Nigeria. The UN General Assembly rejected that plea.[11] In *Cameroon/United Kingdom*, the ICJ found, along lines similar to those of the General Assembly, that there is no such remedy available in law. In that case, the Republic of Cameroon asked the ICJ to declare that in the application of the Trusteeship Agreement for the Territory of the Cameroons the United Kingdom failed, with regard to the Northern Cameroons, to respect certain obligations flowing from that Agreement. Those obligations were related to the plebiscite that led to attaching the Northern Cameroons to Nigeria.

The Court found that 'the violations referred to have been finally consummated, and the Republic of Cameroon cannot ask for a *restitutio in integrum* having the effect of non-occurrence of the union with Nigeria'.[12] Further, the ICJ concluded that a judgment issued for the claimant state could not be enforced. This is because 'The decisions of the General Assembly would not be reversed by the judgment of the Court. The Trusteeship Agreement would not be revived and given new life by

---

[10] [1975] ICJ Rep12, 33.

[11] UNGA Res 1608 (XVI) (21 April 1961) paras 2 and 3.

[12] *Case concerning the Northern Cameroons (Cameroon/United Kingdom)* (Preliminary Objections) [1963] ICJ Rep 15, 31.

the judgment. The former Trust Territory of the Northern Cameroons would not be joined to the Republic of Cameroon'.[13] The Court added that it is not apparent how such a claim could be made against the United Nations.[14] The ICJ also clarified that it is not feasible to ask for reparation for not convening a referendum. A speculative claim arguing that if a particular referendum were conducted the objected annexation would have not taken place was found not to provide the required causal link between the failure to conduct the referendum and the annexation.[15] The Court clarified further that because 'it is physically impossible to undo the past', the Court would not issue 'more than a finding, with force of *res judicata*, that the Trusteeship Agreement has not been respected by the administering Power'.[16]

The finding in *Cameroon/United Kingdom* applies *mutatis mutandis* to all revivalist claims based on blaming actions taken by the UN General Assembly during decolonization. It shows the ineffectuality in law of the claim for a right to undo past actions and demonstrates that such a claim is devoid of any chance of satisfaction.[17] If Eritrea were the subject of an Advisory Opinion, similar to those of Namibia, Western Sahara, and Kosovo, the ICJ would have clarified that there is no base in law for a call for the revival of the right to a decolonization referendum. Yet that would not be the end of the surprises for the EPLF. In the hypothetical Advisory Opinion, two points would most likely be drawn.

First, whether the existence of legal ties for Eritrea with Ethiopia, of the type that involves sovereignty, affects the application of Resolution 1514 (XV) on Eritrea. In the *Western Sahara Advisory Opinion*, the Court held:

> [T]he Court's conclusion is that the materials and information presented to it do not establish any tie of territorial sovereignty between the territory of Western Sahara and the Kingdom of Morocco or the Mauritanian entity. Thus the Court has not found legal ties of such a nature as might affect the application of resolution 1514 (XV) in the decolonization of Western Sahara and, in particular, of the principle of self-determination through the free and genuine expression of the will of the peoples of the Territory.[18]

---

[13] *Ibid.* 33.    [14] *Ibid.* 34.

[15] *Ibid.* 32–3; see also the Separate Opinion of Judge Sir Gerald Fitzmaurice 99–100.

[16] *Cameroon/United Kingdom* (n 12) 31.

[17] See generally James Crawford, *The Creation of States in International Law* (2nd edn, Oxford University Press 1979) 584–5.

[18] Separate Opinion of Judge A Boni, *Advisory Opinion on Western Sahara* (n 10) 68.

While in the case of Western Sahara Morocco and Mauritania failed to establish legal ties of the type required to disapply Resolution 1514 (XV), it would have not been a problem for Ethiopia to establish such ties with respect to Eritrea. In fact, General Assembly Resolution 289 (IV) 1949 acknowledged that such ties existed. This resolution directed the Commission, while verifying the wishes of the inhabitants of Eritrea, to take account of 'The rights and claims of Ethiopia based on geographical, historical, ethnic or economic reasons, including in particular Ethiopia's legitimate need for adequate access to the sea.'[19] Resolution 390 (V) also stressed that the General Assembly had taken into consideration the Ethiopian rights and claims.[20] Consequently, because of the legal ties with Ethiopia the decolonization law might not have been applicable in its entirety to Eritrea.

Whether the doctrine of intertemporal law allows the disregarding of all the legal developments that took place since 1960, so that the decolonization law applies to Eritrea retrospectively in 1993. In 1993, Eritrea was no longer a trust territory to which Chapter XII of the UN Charter applies. The referendum ballot, which asked the voters to vote 'yes' or 'no' to the question of whether they 'approve Eritrea to become an independent sovereign state',[21] shows the difference between the 1993 referendum and the decolonization plebiscites. The options of free association or integration with an independent state, mentioned in Resolution 1541(XV), were not offered in the Eritrean referendum. Obviously, even if the EPLF were claiming that Eritrea was still a colonial country that should be offered the full menu, Ethiopia would not accept to be considered a metropolitan state. Nor would the UN General Assembly have entertained such an exercise.

### 6.1.2.  The Southern Cameroons' call for a third alternative of independence

The United Kingdom administered the Southern Cameroons separately while the Northern Cameroons was administered as part of Nigeria. Pursuant to the UN General Assembly Resolutions 1350 (XIII) of 13 March 1959 and 1352 (XIV) of 16 October 1959 the United Kingdom organized

---

[19]  UNGA Res 289 (IV) (21 November 1949).
[20]  UNGA Res 390 (V) (2 December 1950) Preambular Paragraph (c).
[21]  Iyob, *The Eritrean Struggle for Independence* 139.

plebiscites to ascertain the wishes of the inhabitants of the Cameroons under its administration. Parargraph 2 of Resolution 1352 offered the British Cameroons the right to choose between the two alternatives of either joining Nigeria or the formerly French Cameroon. This means the third option of independence was curtailed. Based on those plebiscites, the Northern Cameroons joined Nigeria and the Southern Cameroons joined the Republic of Cameroon. On 21 April 1961 the General Assembly endorsed the results of the plebiscites and adopted Resolution 1608 (XV) in which it was decided that the Trusteeship Agreement concerning the Cameroons under the United Kingdom's administration should be terminated.[22] A union was established in the Republic of Cameroon in which the Southern Cameroons enjoyed a semi-autonomous status. However, that status was soon abrogated.

The termination of the federal structure of the state, coupled with alleged cultural and economic marginalization of the Anglophone minority in the French-speaking Republic of Cameroon, led to political discontent and allegations of human rights violations. Southern Cameroonians gave up on the idea of continuing in the Republic of Cameroon and embarked on collective action to revive their right to a choice of independence.[23] In the 1990s, the Southern Cameroonians started challenging the decolonization plebiscite of 1961. The Southern Cameroonians blamed the annexation of their Anglophone region to a Francophone country on irregularities that marred the self-determination plebiscites of the British Cameroons.

The Southern Cameroons found fault with the United Nations and the United Kingdom on two counts.

First, General Assembly Resolution 1352 (XIV), October 1959, and the UN Trusteeship Council Resolution 2013 (XXIV) of 31 May 1960 offered the Southern Cameroonians a plebiscite that restricted them to the two

---

[22] See *Cameroon/United Kingdom* (n 12) 21–2. See also Albert W. Mukong, *The Case for the Southern Cameroons* (CAMFECO 1990); Frank M. Stark, 'Federalism in Cameroon: The Shadow and The Reality' [1976] *Canadian JAS* 423; Victor Julius Ngoh, *Constitutional Developments in Southern Cameroons, 1946–1961: From Trusteeship to Independence* (Pioneer 1990).

[23] P. Konings and F. B. Nyamnjoh, 'The Anglophone Problem in Cameroon' (1997) 35 *JMAS* 207, 207; *Southern Cameroons v Attorney General of the Federal Republic of Nigeria* The Federal High Court of Nigeria, Record of Proceedings, Suit No: FHC/ABJ/CS/30/2002 p 6 para 31; *Kevin Mgwanga Gunme et al on behalf of Southern Cameroons v The Republic of Cameroon* 2003 ACHRLR 266 (ACPHR 2003) paras 7–13 and 34–6; Nelson Enonchong, 'Foreign State Assistance in Enforcing The Right to Self-determination under the African Charter: Gunme & Ors v Nigeria' (2002) 46 *Journal of African Law* 246, 247.

choices of either joining Nigeria or the French Cameroon. It is contended that the plebiscite 'ignored a third alternative, namely the right to independence and statehood for Southern Cameroons'.[24]

Second, the termination of the trusteeship over the Southern Cameroons by the United Kingdom on 30 September 1961 without ensuring that the arrangements of the union contemplated under the plebiscite were implemented was a breach that made it possible for the Republic of Cameroon to annex the Southern Cameroons by force on 10 October 1961.[25]

In 1993, the Southern Cameroonians issued the Buea Declaration in which they announced their readiness to take part in constitutional talks with the Republic of Cameroon. The Declaration asserted that 'the only redress adequate to right the wrongs done to Anglophone Cameroon and its people since the imposition of the Unitary state is a return to the original form of government of the Reunified Cameroon'.[26] When that call was not heeded, Southern Cameroonians adopted the Bamenda Declaration on 1 May 1994 announcing that:

> Should the Government either persist in its refusal to engage in meaningful constitutional talks or fail to engage in such talks within a reasonable time, the Anglophone Council shall ... thereupon, proclaim the revival of the independence and sovereignty of the Anglophone territory of Southern Cameroon and take all measures necessary to secure, defend and preserve the independence, sovereignty and integrity of the said territory.[27]

The international community took the Bamenda Declaration seriously.[28] Nigeria, in particular, and in addition to its sympathies with its eastern Anglophone neighbour, had its own interest in the case of Southern Cameroons.

The Nigerian factor in the issue of the Southern Cameroons became clear after the institution by the Republic of Cameroon on 29 March 1994 of proceedings at the ICJ against Nigeria regarding the oil-rich Bakassi

---

[24] *Gunme/Cameroon* (n 23) para 4.
[25] *Ibid.* para 6.    [26] *Ibid.* para 14.
[27] *Ibid.* para 15.
[28] France, the former colonial power of the Republic of Cameroon, was the first to react. In 1996 the French President Jacques Chirac distanced France from the position of the Republic of Cameroon, recognized the problem of the Anglophone and proposed dialogue and a constitutional approach as solutions, Konings and Nyamnjoh, 'The Anglophone Problem' 223.

Peninsula.[29] Notably, the Bamenda Declaration was issued shortly after
Cameroon initiated the ICJ proceedings. On 14 February 2002, i.e. before
the ICJ judgment of 10 October 2002, the Federal High Court of Nigeria
allowed Southern Cameroonians to start proceedings against Nigeria.
Claiming that their right to self-determination under the African Charter
of Human and Peoples' Rights had been violated by their country, Gumne
and others required Nigeria, as a state party to the African Charter, to
present the case of the peoples of the Southern Cameroons before the
ICJ and the United Nations General Assembly.[30] Eventually, a 'settlement' was reached between the Government of Nigeria and the Southern
Cameroonians.

In that settlement, Nigeria agreed to institute a case before the ICJ
concerning three issues. First, whether the Union envisaged under the
Southern Cameroons Plebiscite of 1961 legally took effect as contemplated by the relevant United Nations Resolutions. Second, whether
the termination by the United Kingdom of its trusteeship over the
Southern Cameroons on 30 September 1961 without ensuring prior
implementation of the constitutional arrangements was not in breach
of the international obligations of the United Kingdom. Third, whether
the Southern Cameroonians were not entitled to self-determination
within their clearly defined territory.[31] Obviously, those issues were formulated with the intention of criticising the General Assembly and the
United Kingdom on grounds similar to those of 'the third alternative'
and 'the forceful annexation' arguments of the Southern Cameroonians
mentioned above.

The decision of the Nigerian High Federal Court was received 'with
a good deal of suspicion' in the Republic of Cameroon.[32] However, after
losing the case for the Bakassi Peninsula at the ICJ, no proceedings were
enunciated by Nigeria. Even as the ending of the Bakassi factor had
marked the termination of the sudden surge in the Nigerian involvement, it did not affect the endeavours of the Southern Cameroonians.

---

[29] *Land and Maritime Boundary between Cameroon and Nigeria (Cameroon/
Nigeria: Equatorial Guinea intervening)* (Merits) [2002] ICJ Rep 303. The Bakassi
Peninsula became part of the Republic of Cameroon by reason that it was part of the
Southern Cameroons. Although Nigeria cannot question the territorial status quo, it can
pre-empt the claim of the Republic of Cameroon to the Bakassi Peninsula if the Southern
Cameroons ceases to be part of the Republic of Cameroon.

[30] Enonchong, 'Foreign State Assistance' 246; *Gumne/Nigeria* (n 23).

[31] Enonchong, 'Foreign State Assistance' 250–1.

[32] *Ibid.* 255.

In 2003 the Southern Cameroonians tabled a petition with the African Commission on Human and Peoples' Rights (ACHPR).

The jurisdiction *ratione temporis* of the ACHPR is limited *in limine* to violations that occur after the entry into force of the African Charter of Human and Peoples' Rights on 18 December 1989.[33] In addition, it is doubtful that the jurisdiction *ratione materiae* of the African Commission would have allowed it to look into a claim for reviving a right to independence and sovereignty separate from allegations of human rights violations. Consequently, Cameroon argued that the African Commission is 'incompetent to handle the issue of the process of decolonization that took place in this State and under the auspices of the United Nations'.[34] The Commission concluded that it could not make a finding on those allegations since they fall outside its jurisdiction *rationae temporis*.[35]

The conflict between the claim of the Southern Cameroons and the African doctrine was brought into sharp focus by the ACHPR. The ACHPR asked the representatives of the Southern Cameroonians as to how they 'reconcile their claim to self-determination with the OAU Cairo Declaration of 1964 on the inviolability of boundaries inherited at independence?'[36] The Southern Cameroonians formulated a cautious answer that was reported as follows:

> The Complainants responded by confirming their total subscription to the terms of the OAU Cairo Declaration that States must respect the borders, which they inherited at the time they attained independence. Complainants called the Commission's attention to the fact that the Respondent State ... achieved independence on January 1, 1960 and was admitted to membership of the United Nations on September 20, 1960. At no time prior to or at the independence of the Respondent State or at the time of its admission to the United Nations was the Southern Cameroons ever a part of the Respondent State. The international law principle of *Uti Possidetis Juris* ordains that the boundaries of a colonial territory become frozen on the date of its attainment of independence. Respondent State's claim to territory outside the territorial framework it inherited on its attainment of independence could only be ... outlawed under international law.[37]

---

[33] *Gunme/Cameroon* (n 23) para 93.
[34] *Ibid.* para 153.    [35] *Ibid.* para 155.
[36] *Report on 'the Banjul Communiqué 37th Session of the African Commission on Human & Peoples Rights'* (Re: Communication No 266, 2003), available at www.unpo.org/article/2534 (accessed 17 March 2015).
[37] *Ibid.*

This response shows the extent to which secessionists go to avoid conflict with the norms of the African territorial regime. As resourceful as it could be, this argument is flawed. The African pledge of 1964 protects the boundaries of the Republic of Cameroon, as they stood on the decolonization of the entire territory of the Republic on 1 October 1961 and has nothing to do with the developments that led to this outcome. As to the effects of the UN admission, the Southern Cameroons could have made a better argument if the Southern Cameroons, not just the Republic of Cameroon, had been admitted to the UN before the merger, as will be explained in Section 6.1.3.

The legal flaws of the revivalist approach to secession, examined above in the context of the Eritrean call for a referendum, are also attendant in the case of the Southern Cameroons. To begin with, the finding in the *Western Sahara Advisory Opinion* that the validity of the actions of decolonization taken by the General Assembly is not affected by dispensing with the requirement of consulting the inhabitants of a given territory, is of direct consequence for the Southern Cameroons.[38] This finding means that the General Assembly could not be faulted for not offering the third alternative of independence to the Southern Cameroonians or for not waiting for the federal constitutional arrangements to be completed. Secondly, the conclusion of the ICJ in *Cameroons/United Kingdom* that Resolution 1608 (XV) could not be called into question with regard to the Northern Cameroons, means that the same Resolution 1608 (XV) could not be impugned in respect of the Southern Cameroons. The ICJ finding with regard to the Northern Cameroons that questioning General Assembly Resolution 1608 (XV) would 'introduce an element of uncertainty into a matter decided by the Assembly', applies to the Southern Cameroons.[39] Thirdly, along the lines clarified by the ICJ in *Cameroons/United Kingdom*, because the violations referred to had been finally consummated, the Southern Cameroonians could ask for non-occurrence of the union with the Republic of Cameroon.[40] Finally, the doctrine of intertemporal law precludes prospective application of the decolonization law to the modern-day Southern Cameroons, which is, in any case, no longer a trust territory.

---

[38] *Western Sahara Advisory Opinion* (n 10) 33.
[39] *Cameroon/United Kingdom* (n 12) 25.
[40] *Ibid.* 31.

### 6.1.3.   The Somaliland case for reversion

Before the independence of Somaliland and Somalia, on 26 June and 1 July 1960 respectively, it was decided in a conference convened in Mogadishu, 16–22 April 1960, that a merger agreement should be concluded by the two political units on 1 July 1961.[41]

On 27 June 1960, the Legislative Assembly of Somaliland passed 'the Union of Somaliland and Somalia Law.' Because the Somaliland Government did not sign that legislation into law,[42] the Legislative Assembly of Somalia approved, on 30 June 1960, another bill of its own making, the 'Act of the Union'.[43] Consequently, instead of one merger treaty, two different instruments were drawn up separately and were not exchanged.[44] To overcome this difficulty, on 31 January 1961, the National Assembly that was constituted of the two legislative bodies repealed 'the Union of Somaliland and Somalia Law', and decided that the 'Act of the Union' comes into effect retroactively as from 1 July 1960.[45]

One year later, in June 1961, the Constitution of the Somali Republic was presented in a referendum for public approval. However, because the draft constitution was negotiated only between Italy and the Government of Somalia, Somalilanders did not take part in drafting that constitution and decided to boycott the referendum.[46]

As of that early time, Somalilanders regretted their hasty move. Their loss was exacerbated by the evaporation of the dream of Greater Somalia. The situation worsened further because of the allegedly secondary status accorded to Somalilanders by the dominating Southern clans of the former Italian Somalia. Human rights violations were claimed particularly as of the military coup of Siad Barre in 1969.[47] However, Somaliland waited until 1991 when the implosion of Somalia and the associated anarchy

---

[41] Paolo Contini, *The Somali Republic: An Experiment in Legal Integration* (F Cass & Company 1969) 7.

[42] *Ibid.* 8–9.    [43] *Ibid.*

[44] *Ibid.* 9.    [45] *Ibid.*

[46] A. Carroll and B. Rajagopal, 'The Case for the Independent Statehood of Somaliland' (1992) 8 *Am UJ Int'l L & Pol'y* 653, 661; Deon Geldenhuys, *Contested States in World Politics* (Palgrave 2009) 133.

[47] Geldenhuys, *Contested States in World Politics* 130–1.

made it possible for them to attempt to be freed from the throes of a failed state. In May 1991, the Hargeisa unilateral declaration was announced.[48]

Wary of the African rule against secession, Somalilanders were keen – as Geldenhuys put it – 'to make the point that Somaliland was not conceived and born in secessionist sin but instead represented the restoration of its previous post-colonial status'.[49] Geldenhuys summarized as follows the revivalist case articulated by the Somaliland leaders: '[T]he territory's Foreign Minister declared in 2007, 'because Somaliland was a separate colonial entity from Somalia and was recognized previously as an independent state in 1960 before it joined the disastrous union with Somalia'. In like vein a Somaliland communiqué issued in 2007 stated that the Republic of Somaliland as reconstituted in May 1991 did not secede from the Somali Democratic Republic, but 'is a reversion to the independent state of Somaliland of 1960 within the same agreed borders of the 1960 state'.[50]

It is clear from the above that Somalilanders built their case on arguing that Somaliland, formerly a sovereign state, was entitled to withdraw from the union and to revert to its original international borders.[51]

This argument is patently devoid of legal substance. A claim of reversion, i.e. that a state that lost its sovereignty is entitled to restore it, is of no recognized status in law.[52] Crawford concluded that 'whatever the validity or usefulness of reversion as a political claim, there is little authority and even less utility for its existence as a legal claim'.[53] When a state merges with another, it cannot retrieve its sovereignty other than in accordance with the constitutive agreement of the union or pursuant to any other internal arrangement. As such, a decision to abrogate a union poses no question of international law. Abrogation of a union is a matter that falls, in accordance with Article 2(7) of the UN Charter, within the domestic jurisdiction of the union. Nonetheless, if the withdrawing state was formerly a member of the UN, the presumed continuity of

---

[48] I. Lewis, *A Modern History of the Somali* (4th edn, East African Studies 2002) 265–6; see generally Geldenhuys, *Contested States in World Politics* 132; Aaron Kreuter, 'Self-Determination, Sovereignty, and the Failure of States: Somaliland and the Case for Justified Secession' (2010) 19 *Minnesota JIL* 363.

[49] Geldenhuys, *Contested States in World Politics* 131.

[50] *Ibid.* (references omitted).

[51] See *ibid.* 133; see generally Carroll and Rajagopal, 'The Case for the Independent Statehood of Somaliland'.

[52] Charles Alexandrowicz, *New and Original States: The Issue of Reversion to Sovereignty* (1969) 45 *International Affairs* 465, 474.

[53] Crawford, *The Creation of States* 699.

its membership in the UN is an international law issue that might be of some consequence.

The UN Charter does not contemplate an end to membership in the international organization. Consequently, a state that joins the UN never loses that status even if it voluntarily decides to withdraw from the UN or to merge with another state.[54] This happened in the case of Syria when it merged with Egypt in 1958 and withdrew from the union in 1961. Because of the 1958 merger, Syria relinquished its seat in the UN General Assembly. When the union was dissolved and Syria applied to resume its membership in the international organization, Syria was readmitted by the General Assembly without the formality of a recommendation from the UN Security Council and without a formal decision under Article 4(2) of the UN Charter. The President of the General Assembly asked whether there were any objections to restoring the seat of Syria. When no objection was raised the Syrian delegation was simply invited to join the meeting.[55]

On applying this to Somaliland, the argument of a sovereign right to withdraw from the union would have had some legal significance if Somaliland were admitted to the UN during its short sovereign hiatus. Somaliland was recognized by about thirty-five states, including the five permanent members of the UN Security Council, during the few days of its independent existence.[56] As it was, Somaliland was preoccupied with the preparations for completing the merger with Somalia and did not join the United Nations.

Somalilanders also cite the irregularities that accompanied the merging process to argue that the union did not take place at all. This argument is self-defeating. As a matter of fact, the union was consummated and continued for three decades despite any irregularities. However, the argument was surprisingly given credence in the report of an AU Fact-finding Mission to Somaliland in 2005. The mission, which was sent to the territory on the request of the Somaliland government,[57] reported favourably on the Somaliland claim, concluding that:

---

[54] Simon Chesterman, Thomas Franck and David Malone, *Law and Practice of the United Nations: Documents and Commentary* (Oxford University Press 2008) 5–6.

[55] Benedetto Conforti and Carlo Focarelli, *The Law and Practice of the United Nations* (4th edn, Martinus Nijhoff 2010) 38. For the statement of the Assembly President readmitting Syria on 13 October 1961 see GAOR, 16th Sess, Pl Meet 1035th Meet No 1.

[56] Matt Bryden, 'The 'Banana Test': is Somaliland Ready for Recognition?' (2003) 19 *Annales d'Ethiopie* 341, 342; Geldenhuys, *Contested States* 129.

[57] ICG, *Somaliland: Time for African Union Leadership* (Africa Report No 110, 2006) 2.

> [T]he fact that the union was never ratified and also did not work to sat-
> isfaction while it lasted from 1960 to 1990, makes Somaliland's search
> for recognition historically unique and self-justified in African political
> history. As such the AU should find a special method of dealing with this
> outstanding case.[58]

Obviously, the sympathetic fact-finding mission chose to argue along those lines in a bid to furnish the AU with a revivalist excuse, hoping that this might make it possible to relax the African rule and recognize the independence of Somaliland. However, the AU did not consider the report.

Yet again, if the case of Somaliland were the subject of an Advisory Opinion, similar to that of Kosovo, a Court that does not recognize the African custom would find that 'general international law contains no applicable prohibition of declarations of independence' that would pre-clude the Hargeisa Declaration.

### 6.2.   Constitutional self-determination

Knowing that a call for secession does not resonate well with the OAU and a secession war would lead nowhere, the Tigray Liberation Front of Ethiopia and the SPLM of South Sudan found it feasible to champion the constitutionalization of a right to self-determination.

Under this pretext, instead of seeking recognition for a secession claim from the OAU/AU, recognition would be sought for a constitu-tional right to self-determination from the parent state. A broader goal of self-determination galvanizes wider support on the national scene and attracts less antipathy at the African level. With the wider backing of dis-affected groups hailing from all parts of the country, the OAU/AU found it difficult to intervene directly the way it did in the cases of Biafra, Anjouan, and Azawad. At the same time, when secession is not openly asserted, the OAU/AU strategy of 'the black wall of silence' becomes less effective.

In addition to escaping the OAU/AU doctrine and shoring up broader national support, the label 'self-determination' was found by the seces-sionists to have an added advantage. As Brilmayer rightly concluded, that tag afforded the 'secessionist claims an undeserved opportunity to stake out the high moral ground' of defending a human right.[59] Obviously, the term 'constitutional self-determination' is a misnomer. The right to *external* self-determination, which is the version of self-determination

---

[58] *Resume: AU Fact Finding Mission to Somaliland, 30 April to 4 May 2005* (Unpublished Report, 2005) para 8.

[59] L. Brilmayer, 'Secession and Self-determination: A Territorial Interpretation' (1991) 16 *Yale JIL* 177, 179.

normally wished for by the term 'constitutional self-determination', is an international law right that accrues only to non-self-governing peoples. Currently, the right to colonial self-determination, the only recognized instance of external self-determination, is largely obsolete and no longer relevant other than in the exceptional cases of the territories still considered non-self-governing by the UN General Assembly.[60] As such, the international law right to external self-determination could not be inscribed in the constitution of an independent state. Conversely, a right to secede, simpliciter, makes no claim to the undeserved panoply of the international right to self-determination pointed to by Brilmayer. Irrespective of its prospected implications to national processes of democracy and social cohesiveness, a simple right to secede is indeed capable of constitutionalization outside Africa. However, such right contravenes the African rule against secession and could not be invoked in the African context.

The constitutional right to self-determination became the clarion call for Ethiopian and South Sudan civil wars. It turned into the means for *liberation* and, at the same time, its ultimate goal. Eventually, the Constitution of the Federal Democratic Republic of Ethiopia 1995 and the Interim National Constitution of the Republic of Sudan 2005 enshrined this right. Unlike revivalist secession, which concerns only the territory making the claim, a constitutional right to self-determination is of consequence to every sub-national group in the country. As such, it challenges the overall durability of the entire state, as we shall now see on examining the two cases of Ethiopia and Sudan.

### 6.2.1.   The constitutional self-determination of Ethiopia

The EPRDF, which came to power in 1992, was of the ideological conviction that it is not possible to gloss over the ethnic reality of the African state and aspire to building a nation state modelled on the European example.[61] Consequently, a system of ethnic federalism in which the ethnic sub-national groups of Ethiopia were made part of the political process and granted the right to self-determination was established. The EPRDF divided Ethiopia into ethnic blocs and entrenched that structure in the Constitution.[62]

---

[60] For the UN list of non-self-governing territories entitled to the exercise of the right to colonial self-determination, see www.un.org/en/decolonization/nonselfgovterritories. shtml (accessed on 14 March 2015).

[61] See generally John Young, 'Regionalism and Democracy in Ethiopia' (1998) 19 *Third World Quarterly* 191.

[62] Articles 46 and 47 of the Ethiopian Constitution. See also J. Cohen "Ethnic Federalism" in Ethiopia' (1995) 2 *Northeast African Studies* 157.

The right to self-determination was enshrined in the long Article 39 of the Constitution of Ethiopia, entitled 'Rights of Nations, Nationalities, and Peoples'. Article 39(1) provides that 'Every Nation, Nationality and People in Ethiopia has an unconditional right to self-determination, including the right to secession'. Article 39(4) reads in part:

> [T]he right to self-determination, including secession, of every Nation, Nationality and People shall come into effect: (a) When a demand for secession has been approved by a two-thirds majority of the members of the legislative Council of the Nation, Nationality or People concerned; (b) When the Federal Government has organized a referendum which must take place within three years from the time it received the concerned council's decision for secession; (c) When the demand for secession is supported by a majority vote in the referendum.

Up to now, despite the temptation of statehood, no Ethiopian ethnicity has presented a 'demand' for secession to test whether the Ethiopian state is prepared to respect Article 39 of the Ethiopian Constitution or not. Indeed, it was hoped that the availability of a constitutional right to self-determination would make its exercise less likely.[63] This perceived benefit is uncertain and the risk taken to achieve it is inordinate.

In the international law of self-determination, the denial of internal self-determination is conceived to form the imperious precondition for any prospected right to external self-determination. Even if it is warned that inadequacy of political preparedness should not serve as a pretext for delaying independence, the requirement of progressive attainment of a full measure of self-government was intended to prepare trust and non-self-governing territories to exercise their right to colonial self-determination. Likewise, the alleged right to remedial secession is tied to the denial of representation in government and violation of human rights. Notwithstanding, the Ethiopian Constitution does not provide for the fulfilment of any condition or the denial of any entitlement as prerequisites for the right to self-determination. All that is required for the right to accrue to an ethnicity is 'a demand for secession' to be made by a two-thirds majority of the ethnicity's legislative council. However, the literal consequence of the article is not necessarily what is sensibly expected to happen. In realpolitik, while constitutional self-determination is the right of the empowered for the asking, less-privileged ethnic groups could not be reasonably expected to be able to invoke this right unreservedly. This means that, until Ethiopia is fully democratized, constitutional self-determination will be the means

---

[63] Paul H. Brietzke, 'Ethiopia's 'Leap in Dark': Federalism and Self-determination in the New Constitution' (1995) 39 *JAL* 19, 32. See generally B. Selassie 'Self-determination in Principle and Practice: The Ethiopian-Eritrean Experience' (1997–98) 29 *Columbia HRLR* 91.

for those in power to concentrate authority. Instead of being the ultimate guarantee for the marginalized against abuse, a constitutional right of self-determination permanently available for all might gradually turn into the Damoclean Sword of the advantaged.

Yet, it is difficult to evaluate the Ethiopian model because Ethiopia has not been tested on its generous offer to all ethnicities. In contrast, Sudan has guaranteed constitutional self-determination to one ethnicity and put that right into effect. This invites a different set of issues and considerations, as we shall now see.

### 6.2.2.   The region-specific constitutional self-determination of South Sudan

The multi-ethnic composition of Sudan was characterised by a rare singularity of north–south dichotomy. While the northern Sudan is predominantly Muslim, Arabic-speaking, and comparatively developed, the southern part of the country, which now forms the Republic of South Sudan, is largely non-Muslim, of no Arab affiliation, and quite underdeveloped.[64] The stark dissimilarity of the two regions, as well as their supervening juxtaposition in one state, was a result of geography and history rather than anything else.

Impassable Sudd vegetation barriers of the White Nile, abutting muddy planes, swampy marches of the Bahr-el-Arab river system and the hilly southern edge of Kordofan tightly sealed off the southern Sudan from its northern neighbour and the rest of the world.[65] As a result, while northern Sudan was the hub of the Napata and Meroe civilizations, 1070 BC– AD 350, identified respectively with the Pharaohs and the Ptolemies, and the hotbed of medieval Christian kingdoms and Islamic sultanates, fostered correspondingly by the Byzantines and the Ottomans,[66] the cloistered southern Sudan was virtually unknown and had to wait for the time of Livingstone, Baker, Speke, and Grant.[67]

---

[64] For background to the north–south dichotomy see M. O. Bashir, *The Southern Sudan: Background to Conflict* (Khartoum University Press 1979), and Francis Deng, *War of Visions: Conflict of Identities in the Sudan* (Brookings 1995).

[65] See R. Gray, *A History of Southern Sudan: 1839–1889* (Oxford University Press 1961) 9.

[66] For the making of northern Sudan see J. S. Trimingham, *Islam in the Sudan* (Oxford University Press 1949); A. J. Arkell, *A History of the Sudan to 1821* (University of London 1961); Yusuf F. Hasan, *The Arabs and the Sudan: from the Seventh to the Early Sixteenth Century* (Edinburgh University Press 1967).

[67] On the early history of South Sudan see R. Gray, *A History of Southern Sudan: 1839–1889*; R. O. Collins, *The Southern Sudan 1883–1898: A Struggle for Control* (Yale University Press 1962).

At the onset of the scramble for Africa, France withdrew from the Nile valley after the Fashoda incident in 1889, leading to the annexation of the upper reaches of the Nile to the Anglo-Egyptian Sudan rather than to the French Empire in Central and West Africa.[68] The United Kingdom was not sure whether to administer the newly acquired territory as part of East Africa or Sudan. Hence, an undecided plan of annexing southern Sudan to its northern neighbour, while preserving the traditional context of the south by isolating it from cultural and developmental influences, was pursued.[69] As ambivalent as it was, the southern Sudan policy had the far-reaching effect of nipping in the bud the opportunity of gradual acculturation and balanced development of the two regions.[70] When that policy was reversed in the Juba Conference, June 1947, the southern Sudan was allowed only eight years to integrate with a country that had over three millennia of sociocultural evolution, and which had benefited from half a century of modernization and development. A government report issued in 1956 described as follows how the north–south split loomed large in the year of Sudan independence:

> Firstly: ... there is very little in common between Northern and Southern Sudanese. Racially, the North is Arab, the South is negroid; Religiously the North is Muslim, the South is pagan; Linguistically the North speaks Arabic, the South some eighty different languages. This apart from the geographical, historical and cultural differences ... Secondly: ... for historical reasons the Southerners regard the Northern Sudanese as their traditional enemies ... Fourthly: ... for political, financial, geographical and economical reasons the Northern Sudan progressed quickly in every field ... whilst the Southern Sudan lagged far behind.[71]

In 1953, the United Kingdom and Egypt concluded the Anglo-Egyptian Agreement concerning self-government and self-determination for Sudan. The agreement confirmed 'the right of the Sudanese people to Self-Determination and the effective exercise thereof at the proper time and with the necessary safeguards'. Article 5 expresses that for the two

---

[68] See M. B. Giffen, *Fashoda: The Incident and its Diplomatic Setting* (The University of Chicago Press 1930) 4–6. See also Lam Akol, *Southern Sudan: Colonialism, Resistance and Autonomy* (Red Sea Press 2007) 15–19, 207–11.

[69] For the southern Sudan policy see K. D. D. Henderson, *Sudan Republic* (Ernest 1965) 161–96; Muddathir Abdel Rahim, *Imperialism & Nationalism in the Sudan* (Oxford University Press 1969) 70–83; Akol, *Southern Sudan* 23–5.

[70] See Tim Niblock, *Class and Power in the Sudan: The Dynamics of Sudanese Politics, 1898–1985* (State University of New York Press 1987) 156.

[71] Sudan Government, *Report of the Commission of Inquiry into the Disturbances in the Southern Sudan during August 1955* (McCorquedale 1956) 81.

contracting governments it was 'a fundamental principle of their common policy to maintain the unity of the Sudan as a single territory'.[72] For southern Sudan, this principle augurs impending incorporation into a country with which it has little in common. In August 1955, four months before independence, southern Sudan started its first war of separation.

Because in 1955 the African rule against secession was yet to develop, the Anya Nya Movement made no secret about the intention of southern Sudan to secede. The declared agenda of the struggle was 'a strenuous liberation war against Arab imperialism for complete independence of Southern Sudan'.[73] The political wing of the liberation movement was openly styled South Sudan Liberation Movement (SSLM). Before long the African rule against secession was created and vigorously demonstrated in the Biafra crisis 1967, and the reality gradually dawned on the southern Sudanese that their uncalculated call for secession would not take them far. In 1972, the SSLM signed the Addis Ababa Agreement that gave southern Sudan autonomous status. In May 1983, however, the Addis Ababa Agreement collapsed and the second bout of the southern Sudan conflict started.[74] Having benefited from the lessons of the former insurgency, the leaders of the 1983 movement preferred to hedge their bets. Instead of the outmoded claim for secession, a new cause was articulated for liberating the entire country to create a 'New Sudan', in which an African identity would replace the dominant Muslim-Arab identity. The organization put in place to achieve that ambitious goal was tellingly called the Sudan Peoples' Liberation Movement (SPLM).

In 1955, the reference to the Arab–African dimension of the north–south divide was the typical means for recalling the history of the deplorable slave trade of the Ottoman era of 1839–85. However, in 1983 that aspect of the divide was brought into sharp focus by the SPLM with the purpose of establishing that the prospect of future coexistence of the two parts of the country was uninviting unless the country was 'Africanized'. The SPLM found this argument opportune when the issue of the identity of Sudan became the subject of unending polemics, particularly after the promulgation of Islamic laws in September 1983. In that debate, the SPLM adopted an extreme position arguing for an African identity 'as the common denominator on which a united national identity

---

[72] Reproduced in Abdel Rahim, *Imperialism & Nationalism in the Sudan*, Appendix IX, 257.

[73] Akol, *Southern Sudan* 81.

[74] For the signing, implementation and failure of the Addis Ababa Agreement see *ibid.* 123–77.

can be based'.[75] Even as the 'New Sudan' was to be founded exclusively on the postulated African identity, it was portrayed as 'liberated from any discrimination based on race, ethnicity, [or] religion'.[76] Francis Deng, the most published scholar of the southern Sudan, explains as follows why the SPLM fought for a 'New Sudan' rather than separation:

> Although separation would be the first choice of most southerners, it is obvious that separation does not resonate well worldwide, and specially in Africa. The SPLM-SPLA leaders obviously realized that fighting for justice or equality is more likely to win sympathy and support than calling for secession ... Tactically, the leadership of the SPLM-SPLA is following a multifaceted policy that does not exclude and indeed discreetly prefers separation as the ultimate goal.[77]

Obviously, an exclusive African identity disregards the pluralistic character of the country. The Northern Sudanese found this postulation particularly threatening to the Muslim-Arab value system and outlook for the state. While the 'Civilization Scheme' advanced by the NCP was the antithesis of the SPLM approach,[78] alternative middle-ground proposals were explored. Unsurprisingly, all northern propositions, however liberal, were discredited by the southern elite as 'predominantly Arab'.[79] When dialogue proved

---

[75] Deng, War of Visions 22. The African identity vision was announced in Koka Dam, Ethiopia, in March 1986. On analysing the SPLM address to northern parties, Deng concluded: 'In the coded language of the North-South Sudanese political lexicon, Garang's words would be understood as advocating the Africanization of the country', ibid. 24–5.

[76] Ibid. 19–20.

[77] Ibid. 20. Deng also clarified: 'Separation as an objective would therefore benefit from the struggle for equality in unity. Should the ultimate goal for a new Sudan fail, the regional objective of liberating the South would have been accomplished in a practical way in the process', ibid. 234–5.

[78] The 'Civilization Scheme' vision was expressed in the 1998 Constitution (Articles 1 and 3), defining Sudan as an embracing homeland where Islam is the religion of the majority, Christianity and customary creeds have considerable followers, and Arabic is the official language.

[79] Mansour Khalid, a northern scholar and advisor to the SPLM leader, articulated an analogy of a 'microcosm of Africa'. On studying the linguistic and religious multiplicity of the country, Khalid found that 'All those diversities are evocative of the African continent'. He suggested: 'inhabitants [of Sudan] may call themselves Arabs, or Africans or, indeed Afro-Arabs or Arab-Africans', Mansour Khalid, The Government they Deserve: The Role of the Elite in Sudan's Political Evolution (Kegan Paul 1990) 4. Deng dismissed this conception as 'more open, but predominately Arab, at least in its cultural and linguistic orientation', Deng, War of Visions 24. Likewise, Deng set aside the analysis of Al-Tayeb Saleh, a prominent northern writer, as that of a person who 'has been concerned with the historical legacy of Northern identity', ibid. 23. The viewpoint of M. A. Abdel-Ghaffar, a distinguished northern academic, was disqualified as in agreement with the 'general theory that Arabism is cultural and not racial', ibid. 437. Southerners held to their position until the signing of the CPA in 2005, in which the SPLM recognized that Sudan

to be unproductive, the focus turned to the battlefield. As long as the war was waged against the north, the traditional enemy of southern Sudan, the SPLM did not find it difficult to convince its rank and file to fight for this complex strategy.

The second southern Sudan war continued, with different degrees of intensity, for more than two decades. Yet, the SPLM did not win its fight against the central government the way Eritrea did. Nor was military victory the goal of the southern Sudan. The SPLM strategy of struggle was to launch a war of attrition, forcing the north to accept the southern outlook. Deng clarified that the SPLM plan for the war was to bring the country to a point 'when the north will accept the need for radical changes that will lead to the restructuring of the national power process'.[80] Indeed, the fact that the southern Sudan warfare was sustained long enough to merit the unsavoury designation of the longest civil war in Africa was of consequence. In the northern Sudan, two generations born in intractable civil strife were keen not to be outlived by that conflict to cripple further the opportunity for democracy and development. From the 1990s, the northern political class found it agreeable to state in instruments of the highest order that 'The history and nature of the Sudan conflict demonstrate that a military solution cannot bring lasting peace and stability in the country'.[81] The southern Sudan war was no longer portrayed as a mere mutiny or rebellion. Yet, until the early 1990s the SPLM was not quite sure that its strategy functions. In 1991, Deng stated that despite the SPLM performance in the field 'the movement and most of the more politicized southern population believe that the point has not yet been reached when the north will accept the need for radical changes'.[82] However, things changed drastically when oil was struck by the Government and an export pipeline was built in 1999. Just at the time when

---

is a 'multi-cultural, multi-lingual, multi-racial, multi-ethnic, and multi-religious country' (Article 1.1 of the Sudan Interim Constitution). On the eve of secession, the AU was drawn into Sudan's identity debate to affirm that diversified Sudan forms the 'melting pot of Africa'. The AU Assembly emphasized that in the event of secession 'northern and southern Sudan will be equally African nations. The separation of southern Sudan, in no way, dilutes the African identity of northern Sudan' (Assembly/AU/Decl 3(XVI) 31 January 2011).

[80] Francis Deng, 'War of Visions for the Nation' in John Voll, *Sudan: State and Society in Crisis* (Indiana University Press 1991) 38.

[81] This statement forms Paragraph 1.1 of the Declaration of Principles 1994, and part of Paragraph A (10) of the Asmara Declaration 1995. Similar statements are also used in the Chapeau of the Sudan Comprehensive Peace Agreement (CPA), the Machakos Protocol, and the preamble of the CPA Power Sharing Protocol.

[82] Deng, 'War of Visions for the Nation' 38. In 1995, Deng's assessment of the situation was that 'It now seems clear that after decades of a debilitating civil war, the Sudanese are ready and eager for a solution.' *Ibid.* 513.

its strategy started to bear fruit, the SPLM realized that its protracted war was becoming less effective as the Sudanese Government drew increasing oil revenues.[83] By the turn of the century, a window of opportunity was opened for a political settlement between a wearied north and a worried south.

Until 1990, self-determination was not part of the official political narrative of the SPLM. Nor was it incorporated in the political packages presented by mediators.[84] In 1991, a group of senior SPLM commanders dissented and stressed the right to self-determination in a bid to embarrass the mainstream movement.[85] This led the SPLM to discard its nebulous agenda of nationwide liberation and to adopt the call for self-determination as its main objective. However, in order not to impinge on its national facade, 'the leadership of the SPLM/SPLA has consistently stood for the unity of the country'.[86]

Astonishingly, by the mid-1990s, acknowledging southern Sudan's right to self-determination became commonplace among all political parties of the country.[87] The coalition of the opposition parties of Sudan, the National Democratic Alliance (NDA), concluded on 23 June 1995 in Asmara, Eritrea, the Asmara Declaration on Fundamental Issues. The paragraph on self-determination reads in part:

1. The affirmation of the doctrine of the right to self-determination as an inherent, basic and democratic right of peoples.
2. Acknowledging that the exercise of the right of self-determination forms a solution for ending the raging civil war, and facilitates the restoration and entrenching of democracy, peace and development.
3. This right shall be exercised in an atmosphere of legitimacy and democracy under regional and international supervision.
4. ...

---

[83] See ICG Report, 'God, Oil and Country: Changing the Logic of War in Sudan' (Africa Report N°3928 January 2002).

[84] An 'American Initiative' presented by former US President Jimmy Carter in March 1990 provided that 'Sudan will remain united in a single nation', Lam Akol, *SPLM/SPLA: Inside an African Revolution* (Khartoum University Press 2001) 300.

[85] See generally Riek Machar, *South Sudan: A History of Political Domination – A Case of Self-Determination* (University of Pennsylvania African Studies Center 1995) at www.africa.upenn.edu/Hornet/sd_machar.html (accessed on 15 March 2015); P. A. Nyaba, *Politics of Liberation in South Sudan: An Insider's View* (Fountain Publishers 1997) 117.

[86] Deng, 'War of Visions for the Nation' 38. In 1993, the SPLM concluded in Washington a document with dissidents in which it was proclaimed that the official position of the SPLM was the unity of Sudan, see Nyaba, *Politics of Liberation in South Sudan* 179.

[87] See Machar, *South Sudan*.

5. The citizens of South Sudan, as per its boundaries of 1 January 1956, are entitled to exercise the right to self-determination before the end of the interim period.[88]

The Asmara Declaration 1995, which was adopted by all major political parties of Sudan bar the ruling National Congress Party (NCP), derives its importance from the wide support it garnered. Commenting on this aspect, the International Crisis Group (ICG) concluded that 'Given the number of participants [in the Asmara Conference], it could be seen as a mini national constitutional conference.'[89] However, the NCP, which had already indicated its readiness to consider self-determination in the Frankfurt Declaration of 1992 concluded with a southern dissenting faction, hardly needed more than a reassuring nod of national support. Following the Asmara Declaration, the Government acknowledged the right of southern Sudan to self-determination in the Political Charter of 10 April 1996 and the Khartoum Peace Agreement of 21 April 1997, both signed with dissident southern movements. Subsequently, the right was enshrined in Article 139(3)(g) of the Sudan Constitution 1998. Those commitments, concluded by different actors in the north and the south, were not acted upon. Yet, the fact that virtually no political or constitutional document concluded in the 1990s missed asserting the right of southern Sudan to self-determination shows the nationwide support drawn by the idea. Not long after the emergence of that national predisposition, the international community weighed in.

International pressure for offering southern Sudan a right to self-determination, surprisingly, started within the region itself. On 20 July 1994, the Inter-Governmental Authority for Development (IGAD), which comprises six states of East Africa, proposed a Declaration of Principles to form the basis of negotiations. Paragraph 2 of the Declaration provides for 'The right of self-determination of the people of south Sudan to determine their future status through a referendum'.[90] After 11 September 2001 the Bush Administration took official interest in ending

---

[88] The Asmara Declaration on Fundamental Issues, at www.umma.org/08/8,1b3.htm (accessed 17 March 2015).

[89] ICG Report, 'Sudan: Major Reform or More War' (Africa Report N°194 – 29 November 2012) 5.

[90] At www.issafrica.org/Af/profiles/sudan/DOP94.pdf (accessed on 17 March 2015). The Declaration of Principles call for self-determination resonates with an unbinding resolution adopted by the US Congress in 1993, stating that the 'southern Sudanese had the right to self-determination'. See Rebecca Hamilton, 'Special Report: The Wonks who sold Washington on South Sudan' (Reuters 11 July 2012) at

the war of southern Sudan, leading to increasing international pressure on the Government of Sudan.[91] As a result, the peace talks moderated by the IGAD were backed by a troika comprising the United States, United Kingdom, and Norway, to see that the process proceeded in earnest.

On 20 July 2002, the Government of Sudan signed the Machakos Protocol with the SPLM. In that Protocol, it was affirmed that 'the people of South Sudan have the right to self-determination, *inter alia*, through a referendum to determine their future status'.[92] This provision was later enshrined in Article 219 of the Sudan Interim National Constitution 2005. Additionally, Article 222 detailed this right as follows:

> Six months before the end of the six-year interim period, there shall be an internationally monitored referendum for the people of Southern Sudan organized by Southern Sudan Referendum Commission in cooperation with the National Government and the Government of Southern Sudan. The people of Southern Sudan shall either: (a) confirm unity of the Sudan by voting to sustain the system of government established under the Comprehensive Peace Agreement and this Constitution, or (b) vote for secession.[93]

The southern Sudan self-determination referendum was conducted on 9–15 January 2011. A resounding 98.8 per cent of South Sudanese favoured secession.[94] On 9 July 2011, the day marking the expiry of the agreed interim period, 'The Republic of the Sudan announces its acknowledgement of the establishment of the Republic of South Sudan as a sovereign state within the 1956 boundaries.'[95]

www.reuters.com/article/2012/07/11/us-south-sudan-midwives-idUSBRE86A0GC 20120711 (accessed 17 March 2015).

[91] Hilde Johnson, The Norwegian Minister accredited with putting together the international troika supporting South Sudan's right to self-determination, stated that: 'Developments in the late 1990s had laid the foundation for a serious effort to make peace in Sudan. But the most decisive factor was September 11', Hilde Johnson, *Waging Peace in Sudan: The inside Story of the Negotiations that ended Africa's Longest Civil War* (Sussex Academic Press 2011) 23. See also A. Huliaras 'Evangelists, Oil Companies, and Terrorists: The Bush Administration's Policy towards Sudan' (2006) 50 *Orbis* 709.

[92] Article 1.3 of the Machakos Protocol 2002, the Sudan Comprehensive Peace Agreement 2005, http://unmis.unmissions.org/Portals/UNMIS/Documents/General/cpa-en.pdf (accessed 17 March 2015).

[93] The Interim National Constitution of the Republic of Sudan 2005, www.unhcr.org/refworld/docid/4ba749762.html (accessed 15 March 2015).

[94] Results of Southern Sudan referendum, Southern Sudan Referendum Commission and Southern Sudan Referendum Bureau, http://southernsudan2011.com/ (accessed 15 March 2015).

[95] The official statement of recognition issued by the Sudan Minister for Presidential Affairs.

Two factors determined how the constitutional right to self-determination of South Sudan fared in practice. First, the mounting global political support to holding the referendum was the bulwark assuring the South Sudanese that Sudan would deliver on its promise. Second, because of the long civil war and the acrimonious six-year interim period, the vote for secession was a *fait accompli*. Relying on those two certainties of a guaranteed referendum and an obvious outcome, the South Sudanese lost the incentive to remain loyal to the Republic of Sudan. It was clear that they needed no more than the end of the six-year period before their glowing dream of independent statehood materialized. The SPLM leaders, who were holding senior Government posts including the First Vice President and the Minister of Foreign Affairs, used their positions to undercut the interests of the country they publically represented. When those officials visited Washington, they cared only for exempting their region from the American sanctions imposed on Sudan and ironically campaigned for keeping the country they represented on the US list of states sponsoring terrorism.[96] Likewise, northerners, who suddenly realized that it was finally possible to end the intractable southern war, ceased to consider southerners as compatriots. The Khartoum street clashes, triggered by the killing of the SPLM Chairman John Garang on 30 July 2005 in a plane crash, took decisive north–south allegiances despite fervent calls of the leaders of the two sides. Throughout the interim period, NCP leaders focused on cultivating the confidence of the northerners in the viability of the post-secession Sudan. A vision of a Muslim-Arab Sudan with no need to compromise any more on its identity became the subject of arousing official address.

As a result, during the interim period the prospects for compromise between the presumed partners of peace and unity, the NCP and the SPLM, were reduced drastically. On the one hand, the NCP had no reason to continue providing for South Sudan, already a *de facto* state. On the other hand, the SPLM introduced in every political decision considerations that were less loyal to the parent state.[97] The promise to make unity attractive, which the two parties made in the Machakos Protocol, turned

[96] Salva Kiir Mayardit, the First Vice President of Sudan, visited the United States and met President George W. Bush on 20 July 2006, and requested the exemption of South Sudan from US sanctions while sanctions on Sudan continue. Later that year the US President issued EO 13412 exempting the then regional government of Southern Sudan from most of the prohibitions under the Sudan Sanctions Program.

[97] J. Young, *The Fate of Sudan: The Origins and Consequences of a Flawed Peace Process* (Zed Books Ltd 2012) 197–205.

into a subject of ridicule and sarcasm. Yet, the separation process that followed the interim period proved to be even more difficult.

Despite the positive spirit that prevailed towards 9 July 2011 and culminated in the high profile participation of Sudan in the South Sudan independence celebrations, tension soon escalated between the two states. Border skirmishes started in March 2012, leading to intensified fighting from 13 to 20 April that involved the capture and recapture of Higleig, the main oilfield of Sudan. The possibility of full-blown war loomed large on the horizon. Resolution of unsettled separation issues came to a halt.[98] Fearing that the situation might degenerate further, the AU adopted on 24 April 2012 the Roadmap for Sudan and South Sudan that was endorsed by the UN Security Council Resolution 2046 of 2 May 2012. On 27 December 2012, and on the basis of the AU Roadmap, the two states concluded eight agreements that cover significant parts of the unresolved issues. While implementation of the concluded agreements is still awaited, further agreement on the remaining issues is imperative for reviving the bygone vision of two viable states living in peace.

Sudan guaranteed South Sudan a constitutional right to self-determination with the hope of exchanging land for internal peace. However, as soon as the right of South Sudan to secede was exercised, Sudan witnessed an ethnic backlash. Centrifugal trends mushroomed and the focus of interest for many Sudanese had shifted from national politics to ethnic causes. The crisis in Darfur, which arose suddenly after the signing of the Machakos Protocol, worsened. The conflicts of the Blue Nile and South Kordofan witnessed a new surge. On 12 November 2011, four months after the South Sudan secession, the Sudan Revolutionary Front (SRF), an alliance bringing together the insurgents of the three regions, was announced. A 'new southern Sudan' comprising the dominantly non-Arab fringe of the country is already up in arms. While the Sudan Government has not officially recognized the SRF, the AU is currently mediating the peace process with the SPLM-North of South Kordofan and the Blue Nile.[99] The declared goal of the SRF is, again, evolving

---

[98] For a tabulation of the post-secession outstanding issues see: The Cooperation Agreement between the Republic of the Sudan and the Republic of South Sudan, Addis Ababa 27 September 2012 at http://sites.tufts.edu/reinventingpeace/files/2012/09/The-Cooperation-Agreement-Between-Sudan-and-South-Sudan0001.pdf (accessed 20 March 2015).

[99] The African Union High-Level Implementation Panel (AUHIP), chaired by former South African President Thabo Mbeki, is mandated to mediate by UN Security Council Resolution 2046 (2012) 2 May 2012 (S/RES/2046(2012)). For examples of the AUHIP progress reports see PSC/AHG/COMM/2 (CCCXCVII) adopted at AUPSC 353rd meeting, Addis Ababa, 25 January 2013; PSC/AHG/COMM/1(CCCLIII) 397th meeting,

around the identity of the country and 'the restructuring of the national power process'. However, instead of making a call for an obviously outdated African vision, a 'pluralistic identity' is claimed. The epitome of restructuring the country is expressed in terms of a call to dismantle the one-party state, rather than the founding of a 'New Sudan'. An alliance between major armed groups and mainstream opposition political parties of Khartoum, termed 'the Sudan Call', is already sealed in the footsteps of the NDA.[100] A novel guise is being synthesized, and a new protracted war of attrition is in the offing. A serious plea for constitutionalizing a right to self-determination is not yet advanced. In addition to the difficulties associated with the African rule against secession and the assured AU opposition to a new secession call in Sudan, four disincentives that did not face South Sudan are decisive in the case of the three regions of Darfur, Blue Nile, and South Kordofan. First those regions are not exclusive 'African' zones in the way South Sudan is. All of these three regions are home to sizeable 'Arab' communities. Second, peoples of these regions are widely dispersed in the country, largely inter-married and economically integrated. Hundreds of thousands of enterprising Darfurians take Khartoum, Omdurman, Port Sudan, and other towns for their home and cannot be easily persuaded to return to Darfur, leaving behind their houses, farms, shops, jobs, and other means of sustenance the way the South Sudanese did. Third, the total collapse of the state in South Sudan dissuades inhabitants of the three regions from contemplating secession. Fourth, Khartoum, which had recently ceded a sizeable part of the country, would not easily reach again the point of entertaining a new secession claim. However, despite these disincentives a sense of déjà vu prevails, and the die is cast.

In South Sudan the old disguise started to unravel as soon as the lofty constitutional right was extinguished. Throughout the long years of the civil war, the compulsive ideal of extricating a constitutional right to secede mesmerized the South Sudanese and became their galvanizing and unifying factor. Because the SPLM was always aligning for achieving this paramount goal with northern opposition and northern areas, emphasizing aspects of internal cohesiveness of South Sudan was considered anti-revolutionary and positively forbidden.[101] The real reason

New York, 23 September 2013; PSC/PR/COMM(CDLVI) 456th meeting, Addis Ababa, 12 September 2014.

[100] See the 'Sudan Call Document', Addis Ababa, 3 December 2014, at www.altareeq.info/ar/call-sudan/#.VTxQGyGqpBc (accessed 15 March 2015).

[101] For instance, the SPLM rejected the Addis Ababa Agreement because it 'is guided by the old moulds that divide Sudan into South and North'. See 'Position of the SPLM/SPLA on the Charter of the National Democratic Alliance' reproduced in Akol, *SPLM/SPLA* 294.

behind the call for self-determination, which should have formed the core of national unity of South Sudan, was long since forgotten. The legitimacy of the 'liberation' was at the expense of the legitimacy of the unborn state. As soon as South Sudan seceded, the SPLM lost its enormous centripetal force. When the cause and moral authority of the SPLM had unexpectedly evaporated, the political class turned to their ethnic constituencies for a substitute source of political base. The SPLM was vertically riven along ethnic lines, basically of Dinka and Nuer proclivities, paving the way for episodes of fierce ethnic showdown that have unfolded since 16 December 2014.[102] Calls for constitutionalizing a right of self-determination to all South Sudan ethnicities, on a par with Ethiopian ethnic self-determination, were already made.[103] The AU set a Commission of Inquiry on South Sudan (AUCISS) to investigate the human rights violations and 'to make recommendations on how to move the country forward in terms of unity'. According to a draft report attributed to AUCISS, a High-Level Oversight Panel should be appointed by the AUPSC and mandated by the UN Security Council to run a transition in South Sudan.[104] It remains to be seen whether the UN and AU will act upon these recommendations, which effectively place South Sudan under a form of UN-AU Trusteeship. Notwithstanding, it is unquestionable that South Sudan is coming apart at the seams.

Even as both Sudan and South Sudan are reeling from the knockout effect of the constitutional right to self-determination, they are not the only sufferer. The African system is gradually realizing that by condoning constitutional self-determination it has compromised its central doctrine. In a bid to contain the situation, the AU asserted that the constitutional right accorded to South Sudan has nothing to do with the right to colonial self-determination enunciated in UN General Assembly Resolution 1514 (XV). In the resolution that welcomed the holding of the referendum of South Sudan, the AU Assembly stressed that the right to self-determination of people under colonial rule is no longer relevant to Africa:

---

[102] See UNMISS, 'Conflict in South Sudan: A Human Rights Report', (8 May 2014) at www.unmiss.unmissions.org/Portals/unmiss/Human%20Rights%20Reports/ UNMISS%20Conflict%20in%20South%20Sudan%20-%20A%20Human%20 Rights%20Report.pdf (accessed 20 March 2015).

[103] See John Young, 'Ethiopia Ethnic Federalism: A Model for South Sudan' (unpublished paper, March 2015).

[104] See paras 181–5 of the Draft Report attributed to AUCISS.

Drawing inspiration from Resolution 1514(XV) on the Declaration on the Granting Independence to Colonial Countries and Peoples, whose 50th anniversary has just been celebrated by the international community, we value and uphold the right of self-determination of peoples under colonial rule, which was indeed duly exercised by our own nations to achieve independence, and which continues to be relevant to the peoples of the non-self-governing territories listed as such by the United Nations General Assembly.[105]

Even if that pronouncement was not intended to dispute the South Sudan self-determination referendum, it indicates that the AU would be reluctant to accept constitutionalizing self-determination once again in Africa. In the same vein, the draft report attributed to AUCISS aptly observed that constitutionalizing self-determination has led to the creation of an external right vis-à-vis other states without guaranteeing internal self-determination within South Sudan. It states:

The Commission acknowledges that the exercise of self-determination is incomplete if understood in only its external aspect, i.e. the relationship between the independent state and other states in the international system. The Commission calls for an internal process of broad consultation and reform to realize internal self-determination.[106]

A constitutional right to secession, unlike the constitutional right to self-determination, which is thus far an exclusive African invention, is much debated in academic circles. Constitutional lawyers and political thinkers have warned of two unfavourable outcomes of constitutionalizing secession. While in established democracies a constitutional right to secede is feared to endanger democracy, in Africa that right is dreaded to fuel ethnic violence. Cass Sunstein, examining the threats contingent on a constitutional right to secede in the United States and the West, opined that:

A nation that recognizes this right, and is prepared to respect it, may true well find that it has thereby endangered ordinary democratic processes. A decision to allow a right of exit from the nation will divert attention from matters at hand, allow minority vetoes on important issues, encourage strategic and myopic behavior, and generally compromise the system of self-government.[107]

---

[105] Assembly/AU/Dec 338 (XVI) (31 January 2011).
[106] Para 191 of the Draft Report attributed to AUCISS.
[107] C. R. Sunstein, 'Constitutionalism and Secession' (1991) 58 *The University of Chicago Law Review* 633, 670.

Paul Brietzke, speaking of the Ethiopian context, concluded:

> A right of secession will stimulate a surge of nationalism, and it is incon-
> sistent with a competitive politics under federal arrangements: rather
> than practice the political art of compromise, some or most opposition
> parties will simply threaten to leave the state.[108]

While in the West a constitutional right to secede endangers democracy,
in Africa the exercise touches the raw nerve of state legitimacy and contradicts the basic doctrine of the African territorial regime. In the parent state,
when a particular group is accorded a right to quit, others will not settle
for less. Equally, in the seceding state a culture of constitutional secession
becomes entrenched. According to this culture, the right to constitutional
secession is perceived as the sublime political achievement that every ethnicity deserves. In both political units, constitutional secession turns into
a substitute for state building, federalism, and competitive politics. This
degrades important means of government and unleashes unbridled ethnic
aspirations. Governability of the parent state and viability of the seceding political unit are seriously jeopardized. By and large, the lessons learnt
from granting a right to constitutional self-determination in Africa are
mostly relevant to constitutionalizing secession in similar contexts.

## 6.3.    Remedial secession

### 6.3.1.    Remedial secession and Article 13(1) of the African Charter

In *the Katangese Peoples' Congress/Zaire*, the ACHPR considered remedial secession to form a viable alternative in Africa.[109]

The ACHPR was requested to recognize the Katangese Peoples'
Congress as a liberation movement entitled to profess its secessionist
agenda. The ACHPR was requested further to issue a finding in favour
of the recognition of Katanga and confirming Katanga entitlement to
OAU support and help in securing the evacuation of Zaire. The petition was brought under Article 20(1) of the African Charter on Human
and Peoples' Rights, which guarantees to all peoples the unquestionable
and inalienable right to self-determination. There were no allegations of

---

[108]   Brietzke, 'Ethiopia's "Leap in the Dark"'.

[109]   *Katangese Peoples' Congress/Zaire* (2000) AHRLR 72 (ACHPR 1995). In 1988, on the
occasion of the 25th anniversary of the OAU, An-Na'im made the first plea for recognizing remedial secession in Africa citing the cases of Eritrea and South Sudan. See
Abdullahi A An-Na'im, 'The OAU and the Right of Peoples to Self-determination: A
Plea for a Fresh Approach' (1988) 35 *Africa Today* 27, 31–32.

specific breaches of human rights apart from the claim of the denial of the right to self-determination. The Commission concluded that:

> In the absence of concrete evidence of violations of human rights to the point that the territorial integrity of Zaire should be called to question and in the absence of evidence that the people of Katanga are denied the right to participate in government as guaranteed by article 13(1) of the African Charter, the Commission holds the view that Katanga is obligated to exercise a variant of self-determination that is compatible with the sovereignty and territorial integrity of Zaire. For the above reasons, the Commission: Declares that the case holds no evidence of violations of any rights under the African Charter. The request for independence for Katanga therefore has no merit under the African Charter on Human and Peoples' Rights.[110]

On the basis of an *argumentum e contrario,* the Commission's finding means that the claim of the Katangese People's Congress for self-determination is of merit under the African Charter if two conditions are satisfied. First, if human rights of the Katangese People were violated to the point of calling into question the territorial integrity of Zaire. Second, if the people of Katanga were denied the right to participate in government pursuant to Article 13(1) of the African Charter. In effect, the ACHPR told the Katangese People's Congress that if they wanted to secede, rather than making a claim under Article 20(1), they should adduce 'concrete evidence of violations of human rights' coupled with denial of 'the right to participate in government' under Article 13(1). Human rights violations were not the cause that brought the Katangese to the ACHPR. Katanga started its secession endeavours hot on the heels of the Belgians before human rights violations were allegedly perpetrated by Kinshasa and even before any Congolese government was set. However, according to this finding the African Commission concludes that the Katangese, and by extension all secessionists in Africa, stand a better chance if they consider the remedial secession gambit and straitjacket their claims in this form.

It is surprising that the ACHPR, which did not find grounds for a claim to self-determination under Article 20(1), found that remedial secession is of positive standing under Article 13(1). Article 13(1) reads: 'Every citizen shall have the right to participate freely in the government of his country, either directly or through freely chosen representatives in accordance with the provisions of the law'. Far from supporting a right to remedial secession, Article 13(1) does not go beyond guaranteeing to every individual citizen the trite right to participate in electing his or her representative. The article does not hinge any consequence on denying the right

---

[110] *Ibid.* paras 2–6.

under it similar to the consequence perceived under Paragraph 7 of the Declaration on Friendly Relations among States. Article 13(1), which has no counterpart in the European Convention of Human Rights, is of close affinity to the more detailed Article 23 of the American Convention on Human Rights.[111] However, the Inter-American Commission of Human Rights did not interpret Article 23 of the American Convention as giving rise to remedial secession. That article is rather understood to provide for the right to take part in the conduct of public affairs.[112] Umozurike gives a similar interpretation to Article 13(1). In his commentaries on the African Charter on Human and Peoples' Rights, Umozurike clarifies that the thrust of Article 13(1) is to guarantee that representatives in government shall be freely chosen.[113] He went on to argue that the article was intended to impliedly prohibit the takeover of governments by the military.[114] In communications that followed *the Katangese People's Congress* the ACHPR interpreted the article along lines similar to those suggested by Umozurike and invoked it against violating the right of democratic participation by the military,[115] as well as the denial of that right by civilian governments.[116]

Yet, in *Gunme/Cameroon*, the ACHPR confirmed its erroneous finding in *the Katangese Peoples' Congress*. The Commission found in *Gunme/ Cameroon* that in order for human rights violations 'to constitute the basis for the exercise of the right to self-determination under the African Charter, they must meet the test set out in the Katanga case'.[117]

In addition to the implausibility of predicating a positive right to remedial secession in Africa on Article 13(1) of the African Charter, remedial secession is also of no recognized standing at international level.

---

[111] For a comparison of the three systems on this point see B. O. Okere, 'The Protection of Human Rights in Africa and the African Charter on Human and Peoples' Rights: A Comparative Analysis with the European and American Systems' (1984) 6 *HRQ* 141, 155–6.

[112] For instance in *Miguel Gonzalez and Andrea Fries v Chile* [2009] IACHR 406/03 the Inter-American Commission found a violation under Article 23 of the Inter-American Convention on the part of Chile. When Chile denied public access to environmental information Chile was found to be 'effectively denying its citizenry the right 'to take part in the conduct of public affairs', para 59.

[113] O. Umozurike, 'The African Charter on Human and Peoples' Rights' (1983) 77 *AJIL* 902, 905; O. Umozurike, *The African Charter on Human and Peoples' Rights* (Martinus Nijhoff 1997) 36.

[114] Umozurike, *The African Charter on Human and Peoples' Rights* (1997) 36.

[115] *Sir Dawda K Jawara v The Gambia* (2000) AHRLR 107 (ACHPR 2000).

[116] *Constitutional Rights Project and Another v Nigeria* (2000) AHRLR 191 (ACHPR 1998).

[117] *Gunme/Cameroon* (n 23) para 192.

### 6.3.2.   Remedial secession in general international law

It is clarified above that Article 13(1) of the African Charter provides no base for remedial secession in Africa. Equally, no rule of law exists at universal level that gives inhabitants of a sovereign independent state a positive entitlement to secede if their human rights are violated or if they are denied the right to participate in government.

Lee Buchheit claimed in 1978, the time he first coined the term 'remedial secession', that from the indications then available 'the concept of "remedial secession" seems to occupy a status as the *lex lata*'.[118] For him 'Remedial secession envisions a scheme by which, corresponding to the various degrees of oppression inflicted upon a particular group by its governing State, international law recognizes a continuum of remedies ranging from protection of individual rights, to minority rights, and ending with secession as the *ultimate remedy*.'[119] Even if Buchheit speaks often of oppression, he anchors remedial secession in denying representation in government.[120] His claim to a positive existence of remedial secession is based on the saving clause of Paragraph 7 of the Declaration on Principles of International Law concerning Friendly Relations. This paragraph reads:

> Nothing in the foregoing paragraphs shall be construed as authorizing or encouraging any action which would dismember or impair, totally or in part, the territorial integrity or political unity of sovereign and independent States conducting themselves in compliance with the principle of equal rights and self-determination of peoples as described above and thus possessed of a government representing the whole people belonging to the territory without distinction as to race, creed or colour.[121]

Buchheit argues that this paragraph stipulates that a state forfeits the protection accorded under international law to territorial integrity if it does not possess a representative government.[122]

---

[118] Lee Buchheit, *Secession: The Legitimacy of Self-determination* (Yale University Press 1978) 222. Before Buchheit invented the term remedial secession, Umozurike, obviously influenced by UN General Assembly Resolution 2526 (XXV) even if he did not refer to paragraph 7, argued for linking the respect of human rights to preserving the territorial integrity of a state, see O. Umozurike, *Self-determination in International law* (Archon Books 1972) 199.

[119] Buchheit, *Secession* 222 (emphasis in the original).

[120] Buchheit, *Secession* 221.

[121] UNGA Res 2625 (XXV) (24 October 1970).

[122] Buchheit, *Secession* 221.

Later, Paragraph 2 of the Vienna Declaration and Programme of Action 1993 restates Paragraph 7 of the Declaration on Friendly Relations almost word for word; altering only the 'distinction' proviso to read 'without distinction of any kind'. The confirmation of Paragraph 7 in the context of a comprehensive analysis of the international human rights system and the machinery for its protection ameliorated the antiquated status of Paragraph 7. This gave impetus to the argument that remedial secession forms the *lex lata*. Robert McCorquodale argued in 1994, on the basis of Paragraph 7 of the Declaration of Friendly Relations, that 'a government of a State which does not represent the whole population of its territory without discrimination ... cannot succeed in limiting the right of self-determination on the basis that it would infringe that State's territorial integrity'.[123] Without referring specifically to any of the two Declarations, Hurst Hannum asserted in 1996 that where violations of fundamental rights by the state occur secession can be justified.[124] More recently, Tomuschat stated that 'Given the special circumstances set out in that provision [Paragraph 7], the group concerned would legitimately pursue its aim of obtaining independence statehood'.[125] Since then the notion of 'remedial secession' has received wide support in legal literature and was argued as being of positive status.[126] Yet, remedial secession is not authoritatively pronounced upon. The Supreme Court of Canada and the ICJ declined to express themselves on the issue when it was considered in the cases of Quebec and Kosovo respectively.

In *the Reference re Secession of Quebec*, without using the term 'remedial secession', the Supreme Court of Canada described what the principle entails. Referring to Paragraph 2 of the Vienna Declaration the Court summarized as follows the remedial secession argument:

> [W]hen a people is blocked from the meaningful exercise of its right to self-determination internally, it is entitled, as a last resort, to exercise it by secession. The Vienna Declaration requirement that governments

---

[123] Robert McCorquodale, 'Self-Determination: a human rights approach' (1994) 43 *ICLQ* 857, 879–80.

[124] Hurst Hannum, *Autonomy, Sovereignty, and Self-Determination: The Accommodation of Conflicting Rights* (University of Pennsylvania Press 1996) 471.

[125] Christian Tomuschat, 'Secession and Self-determination' in Marcelo G. Kohen (ed.), *Secession: International Law Perspectives* (Cambridge University Press 2006) 44.

[126] For a list of some twenty writers supporting 'remedial secession' see Antonello Tancredi, 'A Normative "Due Process" in the Creation of States through Secession' in Marcelo G. Kohen (ed.), *Secession: International Law Perspectives* (Cambridge University Press 2006) 176, fn 13.

represent 'the whole people belonging to the territory without distinction of any kind' adds credence to the assertion that such a complete blockage may potentially give rise to a right of secession.[127]

However, the Supreme Court of Canada did not agree to this hypothesis. The Court concluded that 'it remains unclear whether this … proposition [of remedial secession] actually reflects an established international law standard'.[128]

In the *Kosovo Advisory Opinion* a number of states participating in the proceedings claimed that 'the population of Kosovo has the right to create an independent State either as a manifestation of a right to self-determination or pursuant to what they described as a right of "remedial secession"'.[129] Finding that the issue was 'beyond the scope of the question posed by the General Assembly', the Court refrained from determining this point.[130]

Courts shied away from making any pronouncement on remedial secession because the weak theoretical foundations of remedial secession make it hardly possible to arrive at any concrete conclusions.[131] The difficulty of accepting that such a groundbreaking trend in law would be introduced by a saving clause couched in the negative is manifest. Drawing attention to this weakness of the argument for remedial secession, Shaw stated:

> Such a major change in legal principle cannot be introduced by way of an ambiguous subordinate clause, especially when the principle of territorial integrity has always been accepted and proclaimed as a core principle of international law, and is indeed placed before the qualifying clause in the provision in question.[132]

It is true that the blurred and subservient status of the saving clause of Paragraph 7 is the major weakness of the argument of remedial secession. However, remedial secession could not be questioned on the basis of the principle of territorial integrity. This is because an argument for remedial secession does not involve this principle. The concept of remedial secession

---

[127]  1998 SCJ No 61 para 134.

[128]  *Ibid.* para 135.

[129]  *Kosovo Advisory Opinion* (n 7) 403; examples are: Written Statement of the United Kingdom 92–3, Written Statement of Switzerland 14–18, and Written Statement of the Netherlands 8.

[130]  *Ibid.* 438.

[131]  See Jure Vidmar, 'Remedial Secession in International Law: Theory and (Lack of) Practice' (2010) 6 *St Antony's International Review* 37.

[132]  Malcolm Shaw, 'Peoples, Territorialism and Boundaries' (1997) 8 *EJIL* 478, 498.

was initially perceived as a do-it-yourself remedy. Buchheit clarified that he understands the approach of the UN General Assembly in Paragraph 7 as 'international legitimation of a right to secessionist self-determination as a self-help remedy by the aggrieved group'.[133] Because 'the scope of the principle of territorial integrity is confined to the sphere of relations between states',[134] when remedial secession is prospected as an unassisted measure involving no inter-state relations, it does not violate the principle of territorial integrity.[135]

In addition to the drawbacks of the text of Paragraph 7 pointed to by Shaw, Paragraph 7 was originally intended to address the problem of domination of white minorities in racial settlements in Africa.[136] This is the reason why the paragraph insists on utter denial of representation in government as the benchmark required. As a result, the right to remedial secession predicated on that paragraph does not accrue unless it is proved that the group in question is barred from representation in government in a way similar to the circumstances during the Apartheid regime. Even if this yardstick was easy to satisfy during the racial regime of South Africa and the government of Ian Smith in South Rhodesia, it is almost impossible to be met in the modern world. What matters today is meaningful representation, not the simple occupation of government seats, which may no longer be denied anywhere.

While those are general reasons why remedial secession is of no positive standing in international law, there is a special reason pertaining to Africa that makes remedial secession out of the question for this continent in particular. The legal culture currently prevailing in Africa and parts of Asia holds liberation struggles in high esteem while vilifying secession struggles. Article 2(a) of the Arab Convention on the Suppression of Terrorism 1998, to which a number of African states are signatories, exempts from the definition of terrorism the activities of liberation movements. Simultaneously, Article 2(a) styles a struggle prejudicing the territorial integrity of any Arab state as a terrorist offence. The article reads: 'All cases of struggle by whatever means, including armed struggle, against foreign occupation and aggression for liberation and

---

[133] Buchheit, *Secession* 222.

[134] *Advisory Opinion on Kosovo* (n 7) 437.

[135] Consequently, the yardstick in *the Katangese Peoples' Congress* that 'In the absence of concrete evidence of violations of human rights to the point that *the territorial integrity of Zaire should be called to question*', is erroneously formulated.

[136] Georges Abi-Saab, 'Wars of National Liberation in the Geneva Conventions and Protocols' (1979) IV *Recueil des Cours de l'Académie de Droit International* 351, 394.

self-determination, in accordance with the principles of international law, shall not be regarded as an offence. *This provision shall not apply to any act prejudicing the territorial integrity of any Arab State*.[137] Likewise, Article 1(2) of the Convention of the Organization of the Islamic Conference on Combating International Terrorism 1999 includes acts 'threatening the stability, territorial integrity, political unity or sovereignty of independent States' within the treaty definition of terrorism.[138]

The provisions that equate secessionism with terrorism, quoted above, have no counterpart in multilateral treaties on combating terrorism at worldwide level. At international level, treaties against terrorism do not exempt liberation and self-determination struggles from the definition of the crime of terrorism. For instance, the International Convention against the Taking of Hostages 1979 and the Terrorist Bombing Convention 1997 have no provisions on liberation and self-determination struggles similar to those in the Arab and Organization of the Islamic Conference Conventions on combating terrorism. As such, those worldwide treaties do not need to pronounce themselves on secession struggles. As a result, while secession is vilified in Afro-Asia and specifically exempted from the tolerance afforded in this region to liberation and self-determination struggles, international law maintains its classical neutral posture towards secession.

## 6.4.   National self-determination

While in Africa the *status quo* rule excluded decisively all horizontal territory transfers, national self-determination was revived in Europe after the end of the cold war to result in substantial sovereign transfers. It achieved the reunification of Germany in 1990, the independence of the Baltic States in 1991, the emergence of fifteen independent states from the Soviet Union in 1991, and the break-up of Yugoslavia in 1992.[139] The doctrine used for those territorial transfers is indistinguishable from the 1919 Wilsonian principle employed to disintegrate the Austro-Hungarian and Ottoman Empires. It is understood that Africa missed out on this new

---

[137] www.unhcr.org/refworld/publisher,LAS,,,3de5e4984,0.html (accessed 9 June 2012) (emphasis added).

[138] www.oicun.org/7/38/ (accessed June 2012). Twenty-odd African states are signatories to this treaty.

[139] See Martti Koskenniemi, 'National Self Determination Today: Problems of Legal Theory and Practice' (1994) 43 *ICLQ* 241. See also Graham Smith, *The Baltic States: The National Self-determination of Estonia, Latvia, and Lithuania* (Palgrave Macmillan 1994); Reneo

wave of national self-determination, the way it missed out on the earlier wave that disintegrated the old empires, because, *inter alia*, Africa is a continent of ethnic communities not nations.[140] However, the euphoria of the post-Cold War nationalism of the mid 1990s prompted a distinguished African jurist, Makau Mutua, to propose national self-determination as an alternative solution for the crisis of legitimacy of the African state.

Mutua contended in a nonconformist article that the right to self-determination was not properly exercised by Africans because at independence the West, not the African people, decolonized the colonial state.[141] He made the following call for abolishing the inherited boundaries and reconfiguring African states along pre-colonial entities:

> I contend that foreign imposition of artificial states and their continued entrapment within the concepts of statehood and sovereignty are sure to occasion the extinction of Africa unless those sacred cows are set aside for now to disassemble African states and reconfigure them. I propose that pre-colonial entities within the post-colonial order be allowed to exercise their right to self-determination. Only this radical but necessary step can legitimize the African state and avoid its demise.[142]

Mutua argued that there are fourteen pre-colonial entities in Africa and contended that if self-determination were availed in Africa, Africans would voluntarily associate along the lines of those pre-colonial entities. He drew a sketch of the fourteen new African nation states, which he considered to form 'a starting point for more rigorous analyses on what a new map might look like'. He stated:

> Although my map compresses the 50-odd states in Africa today to only 14 larger entities, I want to emphasize that the eventual map should be arrived at through voluntary association and disassociation of precolonial entities, taking into account historical circumstances; population density; resources and economic viability; and cultural, ethnic, and geographic variables.[143]

Lukic and Allen Lynch, *Europe from the Balkans to the Urals: The Disintegration of Yugoslavia and the Soviet Union* (Oxford University Press 1996).

[140] In the only incident of its kind, in 1917–18 British Prime Minister David Lloyd George called for the application of national self-determination to the African territories taken over from Germany during the war with a view to legitimizing their retention by Great Britain. See H. W. V. Temperley, *A History of the Peace Conference of Paris*, vol. II (Oxford University Press 1920) 227.

[141] Makau wa Mutua, 'Why Redraw a Map of Africa: A Moral and Legal Inquiry' (1994–1995) 16 *Mich JIL* 1113, 1116–18.

[142] *Ibid.*    [143] *Ibid.* 1118 fn 13.

Mutua's proposal reveals many failings, as we shall now discuss.

First, in order to solve the problem of secessionists and some failed states, Mutua proposes a wholesale solution that applies indiscriminately to all Africa including states for which the consecration of the inherited boundaries has worked as an alternative principle of legitimacy. While the problem faced by the African state is currently restricted to addressing secession, Mutua's approach reopens the possibility of state-to-state territorial claims that Africa was about to forget. Egypt, for instance, already has her hands full and would not be exhilarated to add on top of that the problems of the conflict-ridden Sudan. Likewise, it is doubtful that Southern African or West African states would accept relinquishing their sovereignty and submit to potential dominance of South Africa or Nigeria, respectively, under any guise. Mutua is in essence prepared to destabilize all Africa because some African states are already destabilized. Wishing away individual secession claims currently advanced, Mutua provides a monolithic mask to obscure their distinctive features.

Second, it is widely accepted that unlike Europe, which is composed of dozens of nations, Africa is home to thousands of ethnic groups, formerly referred to as tribes.[144] Mutua did not clarify why he rejects this established thesis, arguing that Africa has only fourteen pre-colonial entities. Statistics normally give figures for the number of ancient African kingdoms higher than that claimed by Mutua. Hodgkin, for instance, gave a list and a map of twenty-eight pre-colonial African kingdoms in Sub-Saharan Africa alone.[145] Yet, those entities lack the essential sense of a nation that acts as 'the pole of attraction' to develop the necessary irredentist and unification sentiments.[146]

Third, the socio-political formation in Africa is the ethnic group, as opposed to the 'nation'. Mutua does not see any difference between the two. He specifically agrees with Hansen that 'ethnic groups (once called tribes) in Africa are also nations'.[147] He had the Masai community as an example of 'where European map-makers split one *nation* in two states'.[148]

---

[144] See generally Elizabeth Colson, 'African Society at the Time of the Scramble' in L. H. Gann and P. Duignan (eds.), *Colonialism in Africa*, vol. I (Cambridge University Press 1969) 27; Arnold Hughes, 'The Nation State in Black Africa' in Leonard Tivey (ed.), *The Nation State: The Formation of Modern Politics* (Martin Robertson 1981) 122; Thomas Hodgkin, *Nationalism in Colonial Africa* (Muller 1956).

[145] Hodgkin, *Nationalism in Colonial Africa*, introductory unnumbered pages.

[146] Saadia Touval, *The Boundary Politics of Independent Africa* (Harvard University Press 1972) 31.

[147] Mutua, 'Why Redraw a Map of Africa' 1145.

[148] *Ibid.* 1119 (emphasis added).

Political scientists stress that nations and ethnic groups are not the same geopolitical formation. Notably, the two entities respond differently to division. While nations struggle for unity ethnic groups do not have that as an ideal. Touval observed 'In Europe, nationalism was a political movement of ethnically homogenous nations. Where such nations did not possess their own states (nation-states), the nationalist movement waged a struggle for the creation of a nation-state'.[149] In comparison he added: 'Tribes may be possessed of a highly developed sense of group identity and be firecely engaged in the internal political struggle, yet be devoid of secessionist sentiments, and refrain from aiming at unity with kinsmen across the border'.[150] Large African ethnic groups, the perceptible form of Mutua's pre-colonial entities, did not persist in pursuing unification when they were divided between different states. The Ewe of British and French Togolands, the Masai of Kenya and Tanganyika, and the Bakongo who were divided between the Belgian Congo, the French Congo, and Angola, all worked for a form of unity at one stage or another only to finally give up. In the absence of a strong popular feeling for unification, the political leaders of those groups resigned themselves to working to attain independence within different colonial countries.[151] As such, the idea that African ethnic groups will behave like nations, and disassociate or associate along the lines proposed by Mutua is misconceived.

Fourth, Mutua cared little for the precepts of the current international law of self-determination and did not clarify how this right to external self-determination accrues outside the colonial context. Arguing normatively does not incorporate a licence to discard the current legal system in its entirety. The sweeping nature of Mutua's proposal is uncharacteristic of this field of law. By arguing for drastic change, Mutua's proposal violates 'a settled principle of the law of nations that a state of things which actually exists and has existed for a long time should be changed as little as possible'.[152]

## 6.5.   Conclusions and lessons learned

African secessionists were constrained to use the arguments explained above 'to make the point that [their cause] was not conceived and born

---

[149] Touval, *Boundary Politics* 27–8.
[150] *Ibid.* 29–30, 36.
[151] *Ibid.*
[152] *The Grisbadarna Case (Norway v Sweden)* (1909) Hague Court Reports 121, 130.

in secessionist sin'.[153] However, somewhere down the line the secessionists themselves get confused and could not differentiate between the real
cause and the guise. We have seen this in the cases of Eritrea, the Southern
Cameroons, and South Sudan.

This masquerading complicates the phenomenon of secession in
Africa. The late Ali Mazrui and Michael Tidy predicted that secessionist
civil wars were tending to become less frequent. He stated:

> Civil wars in Africa as a form of instability will continue to be a threat for
> the rest of this century. What may become less likely are secessionist civil
> wars. The failure of the Biafran bid to secede from Nigeria, and the les-
> sons of the Sudanese civil war add up to a major disincentive for would be
> secessionists in the future. We may have civil wars that seek to overthrow
> a government but not to carve out a new state.[154]

As we now know, this forecast did not materialize. The last decades of
the twentieth century that Mazrui and Tidy expected not to witness wars
for secession has seen the secessionist-related upheavals narrated above.
The towering African scholar and his colleague were placated by the successful application of the African rule to the cases of Biafra and the first
war of South Sudan. Additionally, an absence of open secessionism anywhere in the continent might have meant for them that the phenomenon
was waning.

Now, because Eritrea and South Sudan have managed to secede some
might easily jump to the conclusion that the 'successes' are providing
strong incentive to secession in Africa. There is more to secessionism in
Africa than the transient influence of what takes place next door. Again,
there is more to this phenomenon than what bubbles on the surface.
Unless and until secessionists speak their mind, African secessionism
will always be difficult to discern.

In addition to being disingenuous, the arguments presented to justify secession, examined above, are not unassailable. We have seen how
the revivalist and the remedial secession arguments are erroneous. The
risks contingent on constitutional and national secession were explained.
Furthermore, none of the arguments advanced to justify secession was
conceived while taking into consideration the wellbeing of Africa as
a whole. Those arguments veil only thinly the flagrant violation of the
African rule against secession and care little for its endurance. What

---

[153] Geldenhuys, *Contested States in World Politics* 131.
[154] Ali Mazrui and Michael Tidy, *Nationalism and New States in Africa* (Richard Clay Ltd
1989) 214.

matters for those arguments is how to outmanoeuvre the African regime, not how to preserve it.

Yet, the above arguments show that in Africa it is not feasible to simply advance a secession claim, the way things are done elsewhere. It must always be remembered that simple claims to statehood allowed under general international law are proscribed under the African territorial regime. However, while this prohibition should be generally observed there are exceptional circumstances in which it needs to be relaxed. This makes it imperative to identify an exception to the African rule against secession. In addition to the interests of the secessionists, this exception must cater for the parent state and take into account the interests of the African territorial regime in its entirety.

The following chapter argues that domination of one sub-national group by another within an independent African state should be recognized as an instance for a right to external self-determination. Along lines similar to those of *Reference re Secession of Quebec*, Chapter 7 argues that this right to external self-determination could be rooted in Paragraph 2 of the Declaration on Friendly Relations among States.

# Domination as a possible instance for a right to external self-determination

## 7.1. Why the exemption to the rule against secession should be rooted in self-determination

It has been explained in Chapter 5 that secession is in essence a simple claim to territory not involving the right to self-determination.[1] Even so, there is no reason why a particular claim to secession could not be furnished with an entitlement rooted in the right to self-determination.

The development of self-determination from a right of nationalities to their own states to a right of decolonization, and the current debate on remedial secession and other prospects of development, show that the potential of the right to self-determination is not yet exhausted.[2] In addition to its normative value, self-determination had singularly acquired *erga omnes* status making it possible for entitlements created under it to

---

[1] Section 5.1.3, text to footnotes 27–31.

[2] See generally Antonio Cassese, *Self-determination of Peoples: A Legal Appraisal* (Cambridge University Press 1995). For the historical background of self-determination see Alfred Cobban, *National Self-Determination* (Oxford University Press 1944); Erez Manela, *The Wilsonian Moment: Self-determination and the International Origins of Anticolonial Nationalism* (Oxford University Press 2007). For the decolonization phase of self-determination see Malcolm Shaw, *Title to Territory in Africa: International Legal Issues* (Clarendon 1986) 92–144; Cassese, *Self-determination of Peoples* 71–89. For the modern debate on remedial secession and related issues see Lee Buchheit, *Secession: The Legitimacy of Self-determination* (Yale University Press 1978); W. Michael Reisman, 'Sovereignty and Human Rights in Contemporary International law' (1990) 84 *AJIL* 866; T. M. Franck, 'Postmodern Tribalism and the Right to Secession' in Catherine Brolmann, Rene Lefeber and Marjoleine Zieck (eds.), *Peoples and Minorities in International Law* (Martinus Nijhoff 1993); Hurst Hannum, *Autonomy, Sovereignty, and Self-Determination: The Accommodation of Conflicting Rights* (University of Pennsylvania Press 1996); Joshua Castellino, *International Law and Self-determination: The Interplay of the Politics of Territorial Possession with Formulations of Post-Colonial National Identity* (Martinus Nijhoff 2000); F Francioni, 'Of War, Humanity and Justice: International Law after Kosovo' (2000) 4 *Max Planck UNYB* 107; Jan Klabbers, 'The Right to be taken Seriously: Self-determination in International Law' (2006) 28 *HRQ* 186; Jure Vidmar, 'Remedial Secession in International Law: Theory and (Lack of) Practice' (2010) 6 *St Antony's International Review* 37.

give rise to a claim for their execution that accrues to any individual member of the international community.[3] This particular aspect is of special significance in recognizing a right of secession under international law. A state cannot legitimately take interest in a secession claim advanced within another state unless there is reason to exclude that secession claim from the domestic jurisdiction of the state within which the claim is made. Self-determination provides third-party states and international organizations with the legal base required to validate their intervention in support of a right to secession.

Furthermore, there are also reasons to argue that self-determination is of particular relevance in the African context. Historically, Africa was closely associated with the right of self-determination. Nearly all African states were created through the application of the right to colonial self-determination. In contrast, other international law regimes that create rights for groups, such as the regime for the protection of minorities and the rights of indigenous peoples, are alien to Africa. It is next to impossible that any ethnicity in Africa would accept being characterized as a minority or as non-indigenous.[4]

Additionally, in the current human rights discourse, Africa is leading with regard to the concept of peoples' rights.[5] Rights that are enjoyed by the group are of special resonance and implication within the African culture of *ubuntu*.[6] The right of self-determination was particularly enriched by important elaborations in the African Charter of Human and Peoples'

---

[3] *The Barcelona Traction Case (Belgium/Spain)* ICJ Rep (1970) 3, 32; Cassese (n 2) 134.

[4] See ACHPR, Advisory Opinion of the African Commission on Human and Peoples' Rights on the United Nations Declaration on the Rights of Indigenous Peoples (41st Session, Accra, 2007) in which the ACHPR concluded that 'any African can legitimately consider him/herself as indigene to the Continent' 4; see also ACHPR, *Report of The African Commission's Working Group of Experts on Indigenous Populations/Communities* (28th session, 2005) in which it was found that all collective rights in the African Charter are applicable to the promotion and protection of the rights of indigenous peoples.

[5] Richard N. Kiwanuka, 'The Meaning of 'People' in the African Charter of Human and People's Rights' (1988) 82 *AJIL* 69.

[6] The concept of *ubuntu* is defined as 'the capacity in African culture to express compassion, reciprocity, dignity, harmony and humanity in the interests of building and maintaining community with justice and mutual caring'. The popular phrase 'I am what I am because of who we all are' is accepted as expressive of the moral value behind the concept. Even as this concept is theorized in South Africa it transcends the Bantu culture to all African traditional cultures. See Timothy Murithi, 'Practical Peacemaking Wisdom from Africa: Reflections on Ubuntu' (2006) 1 *The Journal of Pan African Studies* 25; Mluleki Mnyaka and Mokgethi Motlhabi, 'The African Concept of Ubuntu/Botho and its Socio-moral Significance' (2005) 3 *Black Theology: An International Journal* 215; Barbara Nussbaum, 'African Culture and Ubuntu' (2003) 17 *Perspectives* 1.

Rights, as Chapter 8 clarifies. This makes the African Charter, compared to other human rights instruments, the more conducive to creating a new entitlement under the right of self-determination.

Drawing on the law of human rights to sort out problems of statehood might sound out of the ordinary outside Africa. However, in Africa this has been the rule rather than the exception. The African Charter of Human and Peoples' Rights itself was originally conceived to assist in addressing the problems created by the status quo rule. The decision of the OAU Assembly of Heads of State and Government in 1979 to draft the African Charter was adopted in response to the atrocities perpetrated by Idi Amin of Uganda, Macias Nguema of Equatorial Guinea, and Jean Bedel Bokassa of the Central-African Republic.[7] The repression unleashed by those notorious dictators, abusing the concepts of absolute sovereignty and unquestionable territorial unity, distressed the continent as a whole and drew its attention to the possibility of exploiting the African territorial regime. The decision to draft the African Charter was an affirmation by the OAU that African governments, despite the requirements of the African territorial regime, should respect human rights.[8]

With this background in mind, it becomes logical to start the search for a viable exception to the African rule against secession by exploring the possibilities available under the law of self-determination.

## 7.2.    Domination as an instance for self-determination under Paragraph 2 of the Declaration on Friendly Relations

In *Reference re Secession of Quebec* the Canadian Supreme Court was asked 'whether there is a right to self determination under international law that would give the National Assembly, legislature or government of Quebec the right to effect the secession of Quebec from Canada unilaterally'. To answer this question, the Supreme Court conducted a survey of the possible sources of the law of self-determination that give rise to such right.[9] In its highly

---

[7] Decision 115 of the OAU Assembly of Heads of State and Government at its Sixteenth Ordinary Session, held in Monrovia, Liberia from 17 to 20 July 1979. See Bolaji Akinyemi, 'The Organization of African Unity and the Concept of Non-Interference in Internal Affairs of Member States' (1972–73) 46 *British YBK Int'l L* 393; B. O. Okere, 'The Protection of Human Rights in Africa and the African Charter on Human and Peoples' Rights: A Comparative Analysis with the European and American Systems' (1984) 6 *HRQ* 141, 144; Kofi Oteng Kufuor, *The African Human Rights System: Origin and Evolution* (Palgrave 2010).

[8] See Okere, 'The Protection of Human Rights in Africa' 143.

[9] 1998 SCJ No 61 paras 126–38.

regarded opinion the Canadian Court concluded that there are three possible circumstances for grounding an entitlement to unilateral secession in the right to self-determination. The first two of those circumstances are considered by the Court as 'recognized situations', whereas the third circumstance, of 'remedial secession', is found to be 'unclear'. We have already examined 'remedial secession' and ruled it out as a possible root for a right to secession in the African context.[10] As such, we will focus here on the other two situations.

The Supreme Court of Canada stated that the two instances are, first, 'The right of colonial peoples to exercise their right to self-determination by breaking away from the "imperial" power'.[11] The Court clarified that this right of decolonization is now undisputed, but was irrelevant to the reference in its hand. Second, 'The other clear case where a right to external self-determination accrues is where a people is subject to alien subjugation, domination or exploitation outside a colonial context'.[12] The Court explained that the source of this right is Paragraph 2 of the Declaration on Principles of International Law concerning Friendly Relations and Cooperation among States.

The first situation of colonial self-determination, found to be irrelevant in the context of Quebec, is also no longer relevant to post-colonial Africa. This means we are left only with the second situation as the possible root for an exception to the African rule against secession.

The Canadian Court then quoted Paragraph 2 of the Declaration in its entirety. Because of the centrality of Paragraph 2 in this inquiry, it is reproduced here:

> Every State has the duty to promote, through joint and separate action, realization of the principle of equal rights and self-determination of peoples, in accordance with the provisions of the Charter, and to render assistance to the United Nations in carrying out the responsibilities entrusted to it by the Charter regarding the implementation of the principle, in order:
>
> (a) To promote friendly relations and co-operation among States; and
> (b) To bring a speedy end to colonialism, having due regard to the freely expressed will of the peoples concerned;

---

[10] Section 6.3.1, text to footnotes 94–102.
[11] *Reference re Secession of Quebec* (n 9) para 132.
[12] *Ibid.* para 133.

and bearing in mind that subjection of peoples to alien subjugation, domination and exploitation constitutes a violation of the principle, as well as
a denial of fundamental human rights, and is contrary to the Charter.[13]

It is instructive that the Supreme Court of Canada considered that the
case of subjecting a people to alien subjugation, domination and exploitation, referred to at the bottom of Paragraph 2, forms an instance of
external self-determination 'outside a colonial context'. This means the
Supreme Court did not restrict the entire paragraph to the colonial circumstance referred to in sub-paragraph (b) that reads 'To bring a speedy
end to colonialism … etc'.

The reading of the Canadian Court is feasible only if Paragraph 2 is
understood to impose a duty on every state to promote the realization
of self-determination and to render assistance to the UN regarding its
implementation with a view to three distinct fields. Those are:

a)  to promote friendly relations,
b)  to bring a speedy end to colonialism, and
c)  *to avoid subjecting peoples to alien subjugation, domination and
    exploitation.*

This interpretation faces two difficulties. First, the bottom proviso of the
paragraph is not set separately as sub-paragraph (c). Second, the bottom
proviso is not formulated in obligatory language similar to that used in
sub-paragraphs (a) and (b). However, even if the interpretation of the
Canadian Supreme Court is not clearly discernable from the text, nothing
in that circuitous paragraph prevents that construction.

Regarding the first difficulty, although the proviso at the bottom is not
a separate sub-paragraph, it is not part of sub-paragraph (b). The draftsperson changed the style to indicate a clear break from sub-paragraph
(b). Consequently, it is not unreasonable to argue that the bottom proviso
provides for a distinct norm.

As to the second difficulty, even if the wording of the bottom proviso
is not obligatory the content of that proviso is clearly not hortatory. It is
emphasized towards the end that subjection of peoples to alien subjugation, domination, and exploitation 'constitutes a violation of the principle
[of equal rights and self-determination of peoples], as well as a denial of
fundamental human rights, and is contrary to the Charter'. When it is stipulated that a particular conduct violates the right to self-determination,
denies human rights, and is contrary to the Charter, states cannot argue

---

[13]  UNGA Res 2625 (XXV) (24 October 1970).

that because non-obligatory language is used they are not obligated to abstain from that conduct.

If it is possible to read the bottom proviso of Paragraph 2 the way the Supreme Court of Canada read it, the paragraph could be understood to identify the circumstance 'where a people is subject to alien subjugation, domination or exploitation outside a colonial context' as an instance of external self-determination. In this reading the term 'peoples' used in the bottom proviso does not necessarily denote the entire population of a state normally referred to by the term in the colonial context. The Supreme Court clarified as follows that it is not necessary to restrict the term 'people' to this meaning:

> It is clear that 'a people' may include only a portion of the population of an existing state. The right to self-determination has developed largely as a human right, and is generally used in documents that simultaneously contain references to 'nation' and 'state'. The juxtaposition of these terms is indicative that the reference to 'people' does not necessarily mean the entirety of a state's population.[14]

But is it possible to construe Paragraph 2 in this sense while Paragraph 7 of the Declaration forewarns that 'Nothing in the foregoing paragraphs shall be construed as authorizing or encouraging any *action* which would dismember or impair, totally or in part, the territorial integrity or political unity of sovereign and independent States'? Paragraph 7 clearly proscribes interpreting other paragraphs that precede it in a way that authorizes *action* that would lead to this fateful result. However, this does not mean that the preceding paragraphs cannot be construed to give rise to a *right* under 'the principle of equal rights and self-determination of peoples'. Paragraph 7 rather suggests that rights under the principle of equal rights and self-determination had been 'described above'.

Additionally, the duty not to construe the paragraphs that precede Paragraph 7 as authorizing or encouraging any *action* of secession is imposed on states. A state is not allowed to take actions that violate the territorial integrity of another state under the pretext that an interpretation of a paragraph that precedes Paragraph 7 authorizes that action. The Supreme Court of Canada clarified that: 'The international law principle of self-determination has evolved within a framework of respect for the territorial integrity of existing states'.[15] However, if Paragraph 2, as

---

[14] *Reference re Secession of Quebec* (n 9) para 124.
[15] *Ibid.* para 127.

well as any other paragraph preceding Paragraph 7, authorizes or encourages a *people*, as opposed to a state, to take action pursuant to the principle of equal rights and self-determination of peoples, Paragraph 7 does not prevent the people authorized as such from taking that action. This is because a self-help action taken by a people subjected to 'alien subjugation, domination and exploitation' to free itself from that domination does not violate the principle of territorial integrity.

The *travaux préparatoires* of Paragraph 2 help to confirm the interpretation advanced by the Canadian Supreme Court. Rosenstock, who participated in the drafting process of the Declaration on Friendly Relations among States, stated that there was a difference between states 'who argued that the principle [of self-determination] was universal in its application and those who sought to limit its application to colonial situations of the salt-water variety'.[16] So during the drafting process there was a trend pushing towards applying external self-determination outside the colonial context. The position of that trend is reflected, even if not in the clearest way possible, in the bottom proviso of Paragraph 2. Rosenstock clarified that: 'while the text of the principle of equal rights and self-determination contains some tortured phraseology and while it may not be set out in the most logical order, a careful reading of it will show it to be a moderate and workable text'.[17]

We saw above that the Supreme Court of Canada referred to the instance of subjecting people under Paragraph 2 as a 'clear case where a right to external self-determination accrues'. If the Canadian Court means by the term 'clear case' that an entitlement to external self-determination outside the colonial context already exists under Paragraph 2 as the *lex lata*, that finding would be difficult to defend. Paragraph 2 does not reflect existing customary international law. Although the Declaration's provisions on *internal* self-determination are argued to be of customary status, this is not the case with regard to the provisions on *external* self-determination outside the colonial context.[18] However, in determining that the instance

---

[16] R. Rosenstock, 'The Declaration of Principles of International Law concerning Friendly Relations: A Survey' (1971) 65 *AJIL* 713, 730.

[17] *Ibid.* 733.

[18] Cassese, *Self-determination of Peoples* 120. The reference in the Advisory Opinion on Kosovo to Resolution 2625(XXV) as reflecting customary international law is understood as a statement that the parts of the Resolution on the prohibition of the use of force are reflecting customary international law, see *Accordance with International Law of the Unilateral Declaration of Independence in Respect of Kosovo* (Advisory Opinion) [2010] ICJ Rep 403, 437; *Case Concerning Military and Paramilitary Activities in and against Nicaragua (Nicaragua/United States of America)* Merits [1986] ICJ Rep 14, 101–3.

under Paragraph 2 is a clear case of external self-determination, the Supreme Court of Canada might be in agreement with the position of Cassese, which restricts that instance only to the case of military occupation.

The Court cited in a preceding paragraph a quotation of Cassese that reads: 'the right to external self-determination, which entails the possibility of choosing (or restoring) independence, has only been bestowed upon two classes of people (those under colonial rule or foreign occupation)'.[19] Indeed elements of *opinio juris* and state practice in support of considering military occupation a positive instance of external self-determination outside the colonial context abound.[20] However, restricting the entire normative breadth of Paragraph 2 to 'foreign military occupation' is an erroneous assumption. The concept of foreign domination is not limited to military occupation. Nor is the right to external self-determination available under Paragraph 2 a correlative of the prohibition of the use of force in international law. We now turn to this point.

### 7.3.   Limiting Paragraph 2 of the Declaration on Friendly Relations to military occupation

In his seminal work on self-determination, Cassese surveyed cases in which UN Resolutions had demanded the right of self-determination of peoples under military occupation to be respected. On completing his survey, which started with the Soviet invasion of Hungary in 1956 and ended with the Iraqi invasion of Kuwait in 1990, Cassese found that:

> It is thus reasonable to conclude that the term 'alien domination' or 'subjugation' does not contemplate economic exploitation or ideological domination. Rather, 'alien subjugation; domination and exploitation' covers those situations in which any one Power *dominates* the people of a *foreign territory* by recourse to *force*. If this is correct, self-determination is violated whenever there is a military invasion or belligerent occupation of a foreign territory … The right to external self-determination is thus, in a sense the counterpart of the prohibition of the use of force in international relations.[21]

It is true that whenever one power dominates the people of another country the right to self-determination is violated. This forms the *lex lata*.

---

[19] Cassese, *Self-determination of Peoples* 334.
[20] *Ibid*. 93–9.
[21] *Ibid*. 99 (emphasis in the original).

However, it is not entirely true that the right to external self-determination is the counterpart of the prohibition of the use of force. The right to external self-determination is of normative potential that covers areas not linked to military occupation. Cassese arrived at his finding that the two norms are counterparts because for him the right to external self-determination is *limited* to military occupation. He states:

> Recent General Assembly resolutions on self-determination which characterize 'acts or threats of foreign military intervention and occupation' and 'foreign military intervention, aggression and occupation' as egregious infringements of the right of self-determination also suggest that, *in practice, States have agreed to limit the concept of 'foreign domination' to intervention by use of force and military occupation.*[22]

The cases surveyed by Cassese are instances where the UN confirmed the right to external self-determination available to occupied peoples under Paragraph 2 of the Declaration on Friendly Relations. However, they provide no evidence that *states have agreed to limit* the right of external self-determination available under Paragraph 2 only to those instances. First and foremost, the concept involved, as per the language of Paragraph 2, is 'domination', not 'foreign domination' as Cassese states. While external self-determination would be counterpart to the prohibition of the use of force if the practice censured by paragraph 2 is 'foreign' domination, this is not the case when the paragraph refers to domination generally. Moreover, what is limited is state practice pursuant to that concept, not the concept itself. For the time being, there is no state practice to support a contention that the concept of 'domination' in Paragraph 2 gives rise to a right to external self-determination beyond military occupation. However, there is no reason why such practice cannot take place in the future and give rise to an entitlement for external self-determination under Paragraph 2 in an instance other than military occupation. Cassese's argument is a typical example of an argument based on lack of evidence to the contrary. As the maxim of suppositional logic goes, absence of evidence is not evidence of absence.

Furthermore, by limiting Paragraph 2 of the Declaration on Friendly Relations to military occupation, Cassese ignores the historic origins of the trilogy 'alien subjugation, domination and exploitation', which also features in Protocol I Additional to the Geneva Conventions 1977 with a slight variation.[23]

---

[22] *Ibid.* 93 (emphasis added). For the survey see 93–9.

[23] Article 1(4) of Protocol I Additional to the Geneva Conventions 1977 reads: 'The situations referred to in the preceding paragraph include armed conflicts in which peoples are fighting against colonial domination and alien occupation and against racist regimes

## 7.4.    The history of the trilogy 'alien subjugation, domination and exploitation'

When the trilogy 'alien subjugation, domination and exploitation' was used in Paragraph 2 of the Declaration on Friendly Relations among States it was intended to capture the phenomenon of domination that was taking place within the white settlements in Africa. That phenomenon occurred where no classical colonialism of the typical form of *foreign* domination or military occupation was involved.

Georges Abi-Saab, who took part in drafting Protocol I Additional to the Geneva Conventions, clarified as follows the historical origins of the trilogy 'colonial domination, and alien occupation and against racist regimes' that appears in Article 1(4) of Protocol I:

> If the first category of this triptych is self-evident, the same cannot be said of the other two. Indeed, proceeding from the hard-core case of classical colonial rule, the concept of colonialism was refined and extended within the United Nations to include other varieties of colonization producing the same result of denial of self-determination to whole peoples, which have been designated as alien domination and racist regimes. In fact both partake of the same phenomenon of 'colonies of settlement', which are generally designated as 'alien domination' and of which the 'racist regimes' are a species or a special case.[24]

The short point of Abi-Saab is that the trilogy extends the definition of colonialism outside its traditional turf of *colonial* domination to include other forms of domination. As per Abi-Saab, Article 1(4) of Protocol I extends the right of self-determination that accrues in the instance of *colonial* domination to the two instances of *non-colonial* domination mentioned in the article, which are alien occupation and racist regimes. But while it is clear that the term 'racist regimes' denotes a form of non-colonial domination, it is not as clear that the term 'alien occupation' refers to a subset of the same phenomenon.

Abi-Saab clarified as follows that the term 'alien occupation', which appears in Article 1(4) of Protocol I, relates to the same phenomenon of non-colonial domination the way the term 'racist regimes' does. He

---

in the exercise of their right of self-determination, as enshrined in the Charter of the United Nations and the Declaration on Principles of International Law concerning Friendly Relations and Co-operation among States in accordance with the Charter of the United Nations'.

[24] Georges Abi-Saab, 'Wars of National Liberation in the Geneva Conventions and Protocols' (1979) IV *Recueil des Cours de l'Académie de Droit International* 351, 394.

clarified that the term 'alien occupation' was chosen in order to avoid using the term 'alien domination', feared to create confusion with the allegation of socialist movements in Latin America that particular governments affiliated to the West were under foreign domination. He narrated as follows the drafting history of this term:

> Article 1, paragraph 4, of Protocol I uses slightly different formula, namely 'armed conflicts in which peoples are fighting against colonial domination and alien occupation and against racist regimes'. In fact the formula of the United Nations resolutions was initially used in the Socialist amendment CDDH/I/5 as well as in the amalgamated one CDDH/I/41. But when the five Latin American Powers were preparing their initiative, they asked the sponsors of the amalgamated amendment CDDH/I/41 to change the term 'alien domination'. Their objection was not to the inclusion of the phenomenon of 'colonies of settlement' in the category of situations which can give rise to wars of national liberation, but to the words as such; and this for reasons which are particular to the Latin American context. It was to exclude any possible interpretaion of the amendment by dissident movements that certain governments are under 'foreign domination', hence armed insurrection against them constituted wars of national liberation.[25]

Abi-Saab added that 'The import of this episode of legislative history is that "alien occupation" in Article 1(4) has the same meaning as "alien domination" in the United Nations resolutions, namely colonies of settlement.'[26] In other words, domination targeted by the drafters when they coined the trilogy in both instruments was the white settlements domination taking place 'outside the colonial context' proper and without military involvement of a foreign power.

The white settlements domination was a type of domination to which one people is subjected by another of the same country. In this case, no classical colonialism was attendant and no foreign state was involved. Abi-Saab explained this point as follows:

> The main conceptual legal difficulty with colonies of settlement is that the colonial power and the colony are telescoped into the same territory. It is not the mere act of a group of people emigrating and settling in another country which constitutes the 'alien domination'; but it becomes so when the colonies of settlement are established to the detriment of local populations, i.e., when the settlers, while severing their formal ties with their mother countries, exercise a colonial policy vis-à-vis these populations which denies them their right to self-determination.[27]

---

[25] *Ibid.* 395.     [26] *Ibid.*     [27] *Ibid.*

Consequently, equating 'alien occupation and racist regimes' with colonial domination made it possible for the United Nations to apply the right of external self-determination available in the case of colonial domination to the white settlements.

However, this particular historical background of the trilogy does not mean that its usage should be limited only to the situation it was coined to address. Domestic legislations addressing exclusively a particular situation *ex post facto* are considered invalid for the reason of being *ad hominem*.[28] International instruments are not different in this regard. Texts that were intended to fight domination of one group by another within the white settlements are not dedicated exclusively to fighting that disgrace, and could now be used to address domination currently faced by sub-national groups within independent states. In 1970, when the Declaration on Friendly Relations among States was adopted, the international community was fighting domination within white settlements and that was the maximum the international community could foretell. However, as it was argued by Abi-Saab in a not dissimilar context, this does not mean 'that the clock has been stopped once and for all at that time and at that stage of legal evolution'.[29] As soon as the phenomenon of domination within independent states appears at a later stage in the development of the international community, there is no reason for the law to be stultified to the only shape of domination that humankind knew in 1970.

In addition to Abi-Saab, other jurists also argued that the historical context of those terms should not be allowed to detract from their general scope. Klabbers and Lefeber contend that references in the UN Charter, General Assembly Resolutions and ICJ case law to people under alien or foreign domination:

> were a sign of the times, but should not be invoked to deny the universal and perpetual scope of the right of self-determination. At any time, any people which had been subjected to foreign or alien domination is entitled to self-determination and to restoration of the territorial integrity if it had already achieved independence. Following this extensive interpretation, the restriction of the right of self-determination to peoples under foreign

---

[28] See *Liyanage v R* 1 [1966] 1 All ER 650, [1967] AC 259; *Kable v DPP* (NSW) (1996) 138 ALR 577.

[29] Abi-Saab, 'Wars of National Liberation' 397.

or alien domination would also not necessarily preclude the extension of
the right of self-determination to sub-national groups.[30]

In sum, the drafting history of Paragraph 2 of the Declaration on Friendly
Relations suggests strongly that the domination intended to give rise to
external self-determination is the domination that takes place in one
country outside the traditional colonial context. In addition to the *travaux
préparatoires*, scholarly support is plentiful to the notion of according
to a sub-national group dominated by another within an independent
multi-ethnic state a right to external self-determination. We now turn to
examining this secondary source of law.

### 7.5.   Support in legal literature for 'domination' as an instance for secession

The significance of the finding of the Supreme Court of Canada that there
is a clear instance of external self-determination under Paragraph 2 of
the Declaration on Friendly Relations cannot be overemphasized. Even
as that finding is not made by an international tribunal and is outside the
strict *ratio decidendi* it is of significance in legal literature and forms part
of the process leading to the creation of a new customary norm.[31]

Notwithstanding, considering domination to form an instance of
a right to external self-determination is by no means restricted to that
finding. Gros-Espiell, Franck, Klabbers and Lefeber, Bowett, Yusuf, and
Cassese, among others, had all expressed support for this idea one way
or another. However, the support given by those scholars to the idea of
recognizing a distinct right of *external* self-determination fails short of
identifying an appropriate root for this novel right outside the colonial
context. On facing this difficulty, scholars mostly preferred an expanded
interpretation of colonialism to a separate norm, as we shall presently see.

Gros-Espiell was ready to extend the purview of the concept of 'colonial and alien domination' to encompass cases that existed regardless of
the appearance of national unity. He stated: 'beneath the guise of osten-
sible unity, colonial and alien domination does in fact exist, whatever
legal formula may be used in an attempt to conceal it, the right of the

---

[30]   J. Klabbers and R. Lefeber, 'Africa: Lost between Self-determination and Uti Possidetis'
     in C. Brolmann (ed.), *Peoples and Minorities in International Law* (Martinus Nijhoff
     1993) 41.
[31]   Malcolm Shaw, 'Peoples, Territorialism and Boundaries' (1997) 8 *EJIL* 478, 512.

people concerned cannot be disregarded without international law being violated'.[32] Obviously, Gros-Espiell argues that domination within an independent state violates international law. However, to justify how international law would be violated in such instance Gros-Espiell draws upon the robust legal arsenal of decolonization by using the terms 'colonial and alien'. Along the lines argued in the previous section, the solution lies in throwing wider the net of the international law of self-determination, so that it encompasses domination that takes place within independent states, rather than squeezing modern-day domination into the straightjacket of colonialism.

Other lawyers also joined Gros-Espiell's call for a 'somewhat stretched definition of colonialism' to encompass domination in independent states. Franck argues that international law should assume a role within such independent context to 'decolonize' the group subjected to domination. Franck was referring to scenarios that he identifies as cases in which international law should depart from its conventional neutrality towards secession. He stated that the first among those arises 'when a minority within a sovereign state – especially if it occupies a discrete territory within that state – persistently and egregiously is denied political and social equality and the opportunity to retain its cultural identity'.[33] Rather than defining this type of inequality or domination by using taxonomy pertinent to independent statehood, Franck resorts to the more familiar turf of colonialism to further state: 'In such circumstances it is conceivable that international law will define such repression, prohibited by the Political Covenant, as coming within a somewhat stretched definition of colonialism. Such repression, even by an independent state not normally thought to be "imperial" would then give rise to a right of "decolonization"'.[34] When India intervened militarily to assist Bangladesh to free itself from the domination of Pakistan, India resorted to the classical argument of colonialism instead of citing domination within an independent state as the reason for its intervention. At the UN Security Council, India argued that Bangladesh was in effect a non-self-governing territory that became a victim of Pakistan colonial rule.[35] India resorted to this exaggerated characterization because unless the situation is considered colonial, India

---

[32] H. Gros-Espiell, *The Right to Self-determination: Implementation of United Nations Resolutions: Study* (United Nations 1980) 10, 14.

[33] Franck, 'Postmodern Tribalism' 13–14.

[34] *Ibid.* (emphasis in the original).

[35] UN Doc S/PV 1606, 1971, p 16; T. M. Franck and N. S. Rodley, 'After Bangladesh: The Law of Humanitarian Intervention by Military Force' (1973) 67 *AJIL* 275, 276.

would have no right in law to intervene. Franck endorsed the Indian hyperbole, along the lines stated above, and criticised India only in acting unilaterally. He stated that: 'What may have been fallible in India's case was not so much its assertion of a new right of a people to rebel against new colonialism but, rather, its claim to be entitled to act unilaterally as that population's vindicator'.[36]

Remarkably, before the Declaration on Friendly Relations was adopted, and hence before the 'colonial settlement' culture proliferated, Bowett was prepared to assert the existence of a right of sub-national groups to external self-determination without seeking refuge in the decolonization nomenclature. He opined that when a people of a definable area clearly wishes freedom the group in question should not be allowed to either be subjected or annihilated simply because the classical salt-water, pigmentation or proximity test does not apply. He stated:

> I would also suggest that factors of geographical proximity, ethnic or religious affiliation (or lack of it) are not conclusive, for we are talking about something which is essentially a political right. If regardless of such factors, a substantial majority of the people of a definable area express a clear, political decision on their future, I am not sure by what right a state can compel them to remain within its jurisdiction. The choice between subjection and annihilation is not one which a state ought to be permitted to offer to human beings, however 'irrational' that state might regard their wish for freedom.[37]

It is clear from the above that Gros-Espiell, Klabbers and Lefeber, Franck, and Bowett were all speaking of a situation of subjecting a sub-national group to domination in an independent state regardless of whether that state is possessed of a representative government or not. This situation unmistakably pertains to Paragraph 2 of the Declaration on Friendly Relations as opposed to Paragraph 7. Yet, Yusuf spoke of the possibility of addressing domination also under Paragraph 7. Referring to Paragraph 7 as 'the clause' he stated:

> However, the clause in its latter part implies that if a state fails to comport itself in accordance with the principle of equal rights and self-determination of peoples, an exceptional situation may arise whereby the ethnically or racially distinct group denied internal self-determination may claim a right of external self-determination

---

[36] Franck, 'Postmodern Tribalism' 14; Franck and Rodley, 'After Bangladesh' 276.
[37] D. W. Bowett, 'Self-determination and Political Rights in the Developing Countries' (1966) 60 *PASIL* 129, 131–2.

or separation from the state which could effectively put in question the state's territorial unity and sovereignty. Indeed as pointed out above, the equal rights of peoples makes it legally impermissible that one people should dominate or oppress another people, even in those cases where both peoples are part of the same state. The domination or oppression by one people by another within the boundaries of the state does not legally differ from oppression across the oceans (or saltwater domination) insofar as it constitutes an infringement of the equal rights of peoples.[38]

Yusuf preferred to consider 'The domination or oppression by one people by another within the boundaries of the state' under Paragraph 7 possibly because he is influenced by the misconception that Paragraph 2 is limited to military occupation. It is difficult, though, to agree that Paragraph 7, which is hinged on the concept of denial of the right to participate in government, could be used to address the situation of domination. Nevertheless, Yusuf joins the scholarly consensus that domination taking place in an independent state is impermissible under international law.

The views studied above are expressed somewhat parenthetically. Notwithstanding, Cassese advanced a comprehensive normative blueprint for addressing domination within independent states. The backdrop for this project is Cassese's understanding of the instance of external self-determination under Paragraph 2 as being limited to military occupation. We now turn to examining that proposal.

## 7.6.   Cassese's blueprint for addressing domination

Cassese was dismayed at the UN performance in addressing domination within independent states. He opined that if the UN indifference towards the predicament of minorities and oppressed groups during the period 1945–65 could be excused because at that time the international organization was preoccupied with dismantling colonialism, this excuse is no longer valid.[39] He explained how internal self-determination, in the form of participation in government and autonomy, which represents the maximum that the UN system currently offers, provides no answer to 'the plight of oppressed ethnic groups'.[40] In his proposal for future reform of the law of self-determination, which he gave the title 'From *lex lata* to *lex*

---

[38] Abdulqawi Ahmed Yusuf, 'The Role that Equal Rights and Self-determination of Peoples can Play in the Current World Community' in Antonio Cassese (ed.), *Realizing Utopia: The Future of International Law* (Oxford University Press 2012) 381–2.

[39] Cassese, *Self-determination of Peoples* 341.

[40] *Ibid.* 362.

*ferenda*: a blueprint for action',[41] Cassese conceived of two instances for the exercise of external self-determination by sub-national groups. The first is the outbreak of armed conflict in a multinational state, and the second is oppression by central authorities. He stated:

> Allowance should nevertheless be made for exceptional cases where factual conditions render internal self-determination impracticable. When in a multinational State armed conflict breaks out and one or more groups fight for secession, it may be that it is too late to plead for a peaceful solution based on internal self-determination. Similarly when the central authorities of a multinational State are irremediably oppressive and despotic, persistently violate the basic rights of minorities and no peaceful and constructive solution can be envisaged, it seems difficult to imagine that those central authorities would be willing to grant autonomy, or participatory rights.[42]

It is respectfully submitted that this proposal is misguided.

As to the first instance of considering outbreak of armed conflict a reason for external self-determination, no recipe could be advantageous to proliferating conflict throughout the world more than this one. If it were accepted that when armed conflict erupts in a multi-ethnic state the concerned ethnicity acquires a passport to external self-determination civil wars would multiply. Affected ethnic groups in Africa will be more inclined to take up arms when they realize that external self-determination passes through the barrel of a gun. Self-determination would be a source of conflict and fragmentation rather than an agent of stability and solidarity. In the heyday of national self-determination, the US State Secretary Robert Lansing, alarmed by unwarranted expectations aroused by the new principle, warned in an often quoted expression that self-determination was 'simply loaded with dynamite'.[43] If Cassese's proposal were accepted as law, it would turn the modern right of self-determination into an ethnic bomb, the way the unstructured Wilsonian self-determination was feared to be.

In his second instance, though less explosive than the first, Cassese misdiagnosed the oppression that ethnic groups face. In characterizing the phenomenon of domination, Cassese opines that it takes place 'when *the central authorities* of a multinational State are irremediably oppressive and despotic'. The persistent problem faced since the days of the trilogy

---

[41] *Ibid.* 341.    [42] *Ibid.* 359.
[43] R. Lansing, *The Peace Negotiations: A Personal Narrative* (Houghton Mifflin Company 1921) 97.

introduced by Paragraph 2 of the Declaration on Friendly Relations and Article 1(4) of Protocol I Additional to the Geneva Conventions was the subjugation of one people by another as opposed to oppression by the central authorities. Nor is repression by the central authorities the appropriate yardstick for gauging this form of domination. Moreover, actions or inactions of a despotic government, however repressive, do not warrant invoking the extreme measure of external self-determination. When a tyrant is oppressive the solution is not in dividing the state between him/her and the oppressed group.

Even if Cassese's blueprint falls short of providing a solution to the problem of domination within multi-ethnic independent states, it draws attention to this gaping lacuna in the international law of self-determination.

In conclusion, this chapter has explored the possibility of an entitlement within the right to self-determination that could serve as an exception to the African rule against secession. It is obvious from the survey thus made that the potential of the right to self-determination is not yet exhausted. In particular, a right to external self-determination in the instance where one people is subjected to domination by another in an independent multi-ethnic state is intensely debated and drawing wide support. The Supreme Court of Canada had identified Paragraph 2 of the Declaration on Friendly Relations as a clear case for a right to external self-determination outside the colonial context. While currently, this right exists as the *lex lata* only in the case of military occupation, the breadth of Paragraph 2 allows for a right to external self-determination to accrue in the instance of domination when no military occupation is involved. Scholarly writings agree that domination exists behind the mask of independence, and that there is no reason why a people subjected as such should not be allowed to set itself free. Yet, for addressing this abomination scholars prefer an expanded definition of colonialism to initiating a separate norm. They occasionally limit that potential right to instances where repression by central authorities is established or simply adhere to the outdated formula of a lack of representative government.

In Africa the possibility of domination by one ethnicity over another cannot be ruled out in many multi-ethnic states. African states that have not succeeded over the last fifty years to convince their different ethnicities to coexist have failed to draw legitimacy from their inherited boundaries. Rather than allowing these states to consider people-to-people domination a viable substitute, they should be provided with a framework for introspection. Consequently, the instance identified by the Supreme Court of Canada as available under Paragraph 2 could be of special relevance to Africa and possibly serve as an exception to the African rule against secession. Even if Africa is the continent having the most recent experience of imperialism, arguing for banishing this modern-day depravity by an extended definition of colonialism is not feasible. The international community had gone a long way in eliminating present-day eyesores with bespoke measures and should not continue to hide behind this vestigial lexicon. As such, it is imperative to identify a root for this new right to external self-determination clearly outside the colonial context. The following chapter argues that Articles 19 and 20(22) of the African Charter on Human and Peoples' Rights, read together with Paragraph 2 of the Declaration on Friendly Relations, are normatively capable of giving rise to the required norm. The right to egalitarian self-determination, which would as such be conceptualized, is the sought-after exception to the African rule against secession.

# 8

## Towards a right to egalitarian self-determination

### 8.1. The egalitarian rights

Article 19 and Article 20(2) of the African Charter on Human and Peoples' Rights are unique in recognizing entitlements under the right of self-determination that have no counterpart in the 1966 UN Covenants, or in the American and European Conventions on Human Rights. By comprising those *sui generis* rights the two articles furnish the African Charter with what would give rise to a right to egalitarian self-determination.

We shall first examine the rights under Article 19 and then move to Article 20(2).

#### 8.1.1. The egalitarian rights under Article 19 of the African Charter

Article 19 is the first of the six articles on peoples' rights in the African Charter and arguably states the principle that permeates the articles that follow.[1] It provides that 'All peoples shall be equal; they shall enjoy the same respect and shall have the same rights. Nothing shall justify the domination of a people by another'.

The drafting of the this article, and indeed the whole Charter, took place a few years after the Burundi massacre of 1972–73, in which over 100,000 Hutu were killed by the Tutsi and an equal number was forced to take refuge in neighbouring states.[2] This is a strong indication as to what the drafters of Article 19 had in mind, and a lead that this article was intended to introduce a set of rights customized to address the African problem

---

[1] Clive Baldwin and Cynthia Morel, 'Group Rights' in Rachel Murray and Malcolm Evans (eds.), *African Charter on Human and Peoples' Rights: The System in Practice, 1986–2000* (Cambridge University Press 2002) 250.

[2] B. O. Okere, 'The Protection of Human Rights in Africa and the African Charter on Human and Peoples' Rights: A Comparative Analysis with the European and American Systems' (1984) 6 *HRQ* 141, 146.

of community suppression within multi-ethnic states. Against this background and giving ordinary English words their ordinary meaning, four distinct rights are identified under this article. These are the right of all peoples:

a) to be equal,
b) to enjoy the same respect,
c) to have the same rights, and
d) to non-domination by another people.

Those four rights, in addition to another right under Article 20(2) that will be examined later, are referred to hereinafter as the egalitarian rights.

This textual reading of Article 19, which gives words their plain meaning and takes account of the intention of the draftsperson, is not what all scholars accept. Commentators argue that the rights guaranteed under Article 19 are a humdrum elaboration of other recognized peoples' rights and are of no new normative substance.

Rose M. D'Sa states: 'Thus, the principle of non-discrimination against individuals in Article 2 [of the African Charter], is extended by Article 19 to "all peoples" who are to also enjoy the same rights and are not to be dominated by any other people'.[3] For D'Sa, Article 19 simply extends to groups the individual right of non-discrimination under Article 2 of the African Charter. Article 2 reads: 'Every individual shall be entitled to the enjoyment of the rights and freedoms recognized and guaranteed in the present Charter without distinction of any kind such as race, ethnic group, colour, sex, language, religion, political or any other opinion, national and social origin, fortune, birth or any status'. While adhering to the *individual* right of non-discrimination solidifies respect of the *collective* egalitarian rights provided for by Article 19, this does not mean that the collective rights under Article 19 merely duplicate the individual right under Article 2. Whereas the individual right under Article 2 is enjoyable by the individual as an individual, the collective rights under Article 19 are further rights that accrue to the group as a group. The ACHPR had succinctly clarified as follows the interdependence between the individual and collective rights in the African Charter: 'The minimum that can be said of peoples' rights is that, each member of the group carries with him/her the individual rights into the group, on top

³ Rose M. D'Sa, 'Human and People's Rights: Distinctive Features of the African Charter' (1985) 29 JAL 72, 77.

of what the group enjoys in its collectivity'.[4] Baldwin and Morel rightly stated: 'The difference between Article 19 and Article 2 is a difference between individual and group rights'.[5] Individual rights and collective rights mirror each other like the right and left hands. Yet, like the right and left hands, they are not interchangeable.

D'Sa is not alone in thinking that Article 19 merely elaborates another human right. Murray and Wheatley had understood Article 19 as amplifying the right to participation in government stated in Paragraph 7 of the Declaration on Friendly Relations among States. They said:

> This point [of representative government] is made in the General Assembly's Declaration on Principles of International Law Concerning Friendly Relations: States conducting themselves in compliance with the principle of self-determination of peoples should be 'possessing a Government representing the whole people belonging to territory, without distinction as to race, creed or colour.' This aspect of self-determination is further reflected in Article 19 of the ACHPR.[6]

Article 13(1) of the African Charter elaborates the right to participation in government that arises under Paragraph 7 of the Declaration on Friendly Relations. Article 13(1) provides for the right of every citizen to participate freely in the government of his country directly or through chosen representatives. In a number of communications, the ACHPR interpreted Article 13(1) of the African Charter as the article that enunciates the right to participation.[7] Consequently, the African Charter does not need to repeat that right in Article 19.

Additionally, the rights in Article 19 are conceptually different from the right under Paragraph 7 of the Declaration on Friendly Relations. While the right in Paragraph 7 takes the shape of a claim against a government that is not representative of a particular segment of society, the egalitarian rights under Article 19 are a claim against another people. The confusion between Article 19 and the concept of representative government of Paragraph 7 led Murray and Wheatley to argue incorrectly that for a

---

[4] *Kevin Mgwanga Gunme et al on behalf of Southern Cameroons/The Republic of Cameroon* 2003 ACHRLR 266 (ACHPR 2003) para 176.

[5] Baldwin and Morel, 'Group Rights' 253.

[6] Rachel Murray and Steven Wheatley, 'Groups and the African Charter on Human and Peoples' Rights' (2003) 25 *HRQ* 213, 230.

[7] *Katangese Peoples' Congress/Zaire* (2000) AHRLR 72 (ACHPR 1995) para 6; *Sir Dawda K Jawara/The Gambia* (2000) AHRLR 107 (ACHPR 2000) para 67; *Constitutional Rights Project and Another/Nigeria* (2000) AHRLR 191 (ACHPR 1998) para 50; *Gunme/ Cameroon* (n 4) paras 143–4.

finding of violation of equality and non-domination to be substantiated under Article 19 it should be proved that the government is unrepresentative and that there exists a deliberate state policy of exclusion.[8] While those could be the typical symptoms of subjecting one people by another of the same country, they are not the condition precedent to a finding of domination under Article 19. Among the paragraphs of the Declaration on Friendly Relations, Article 19 is of close affinity to Paragraph 2 that provides for the avoidance of *'subjection of peoples* to alien subjugation, domination and exploitation', as explained at length in the previous chapter.

Kiwanuka presented a more pertinent reading for Article 19. He stated that: 'by the injunction of Article 19 that "Nothing shall justify the domination of a people by another", the Banjul Charter proscribes external and internal forms of colonialism'.[9] In this statement, Kiwanuka agrees that Article 19 is of an exclusive normative value. He did not confuse the rights guaranteed under Article 19 with any other human right. For him the thrust of Article 19 is the proscribing of domination of a people by another within the post-colonial context. However, Kiwanuka is to be criticised for using colonial taxonomy. While he was obviously addressing domination that takes place within independent states, Kiwanuka referred to that phenomenon as 'internal' colonialism.

Baldwin and Morel advocated that Article 19 should be seen in its proper context of addressing internal domination of one people by another within an African state:

> Article 19 must be seen in the context of internal inequality and domination of peoples by others within a State. Apartheid in South Africa serves as one of the most extreme forms of domination of a people over another. The genocide in Rwanda in 1994 also brought into sharp focus how domination of one people by another in violation of one Charter right (Article 19) may lead to the systematic elimination of another people's right to existence, and thus violating another (Article 20).[10]

The reference to apartheid in South Africa and genocide in Rwanda as examples of the types of domination captured by Article 19, shows that Baldwin and Morel identified the singular normative content of Article

---

[8] Murray and Wheatley, 'Groups and the African Charter on Human and Peoples' Rights' 231.

[9] Richard N. Kiwanuka, 'The Meaning of "People" in the African Charter of Human and People's Rights' (1988) 82 *AJIL* 69, 90.

[10] Baldwin and Morel, 'Group Rights' 251–2.

19. However, on studying Baldwin and Morel more closely, it becomes clear that they fail to extricate people-to-people domination from the concept of representation in government. The two authors agree with Murray and Wheatley that domination exists only when the government is unrepresentative and where deliberate state policy of exclusion exists.[11] Domination under Article 19 could exist even if a government is superficially representative. A deliberate state policy of exclusion, in the context of violating the egalitarian rights, rather than signifying the onset of domination, means that domination has become endemic. While domination could reach the extent of hijacking the government by one ethnic group and turning it into a device for subjecting other groups, a finding that this happened in actuality is not required for establishing that Article 19 is violated.

Two opportunities were presented to the ACHPR to make a pronouncement on Article 19. On both occasions, the African Commission entertained the proposition that Article 19 is of distinctive normative value focused on 'equality of peoples'.

In *Malawi African Association and other/Mauritania* the Commission concluded:

> At the heart of the abuses alleged in the different communications is the question of the domination of one section of the population by another. The resultant discrimination against Black Mauritanians is, according to the complainants, the result of a negation of the fundamental principle of the equality of peoples as stipulated in the African Charter and constitutes a violation of Article 19.[12]

The African Commission did not disagree with the complainants that 'negation of the fundamental principle of equality of peoples' constitutes a violation of Article 19. However, on the merits of the case the Commission found that no violation of the right under the article had occurred. In *Gunme/Cameroon*, the complainants claimed that 'Article 19 places an absolute ban on the domination of one people by another.'[13] The ACHPR did not find that understanding objectionable and declined to determine that point only because it falls outside the jurisdiction *rationae temporis* of the Commission. However, where the jurisdiction of the Commission allowed, the Commission found that certain economic measures taken

---

[11] *Ibid.* 252–3.
[12] *Malawi African Association and Others/Mauritania* (2000) AHRLR 149 (ACHPR 2000) Para 142 (references omitted).
[13] *Gunme/Cameroon* (n 4) para 152.

by the Government of Cameroon that favour the Francophone part of Cameroon over the Anglophone part violated the right of equality among the two peoples under Article 19.[14] The Commission stated 'the relocation of business enterprises and location of economic projects to Francophone Cameroon, which generated negative effects on the economic life of Southern Cameroon constituted violation of Article 19 of the Charter'.[15]

It should be clear from the above that Article 19 is of normative content that focuses on guaranteeing equality of peoples in a sense that is unique to the African Charter.

### 8.1.2. *The egalitarian right under Article 20(2) of the African Charter*

In addition to the four rights guaranteed under Article 19, Article 20(2) of the African Charter adds a fifth egalitarian right. The article states that 'Colonized or oppressed peoples shall have the right to free themselves from the bonds of domination by resorting to any means recognized by the international community'. Again a textual reading of this article leads to a plain conclusion: the article accords to oppressed peoples, as well as colonized peoples, an entitlement to free themselves from domination by resorting to any means recognized by the international community.

Unlike Article 19, Article 20(2) attracted little attention among commentators. The reason for the lack of interest is that writers tend to consider the term 'oppressed' synonymous with the term 'colonized'. While the right of colonized people to freedom hardly raises an eyebrow, the article becomes spirited if it is understood to guarantee the same right to oppressed peoples outside the colonial context. This understanding, however unconventional, forms the only plausible interpretation of Article 20(2).

To clarify how the right guaranteed under Article 20(2) accrues to 'oppressed peoples' in marked differentiation with and in addition to 'colonized peoples', we need to determine the holders of the egalitarian rights. In other words, we should find out what is meant by the terms 'all peoples' and 'oppressed peoples' that appear in Articles 19 and 20(2) respectively.

---

[14] Cf. the conclusion of Cassese that 'It is thus reasonable to conclude that the term "alien domination" or "subjugation" does not contemplate economic exploitation or ideological domination', Antonio Cassese, *Self-determination of Peoples: A Legal Appraisal* (Cambridge University Press 1995) 99.

[15] *Gunme/Cameroon* (n 4) para 162.

## 8.2. Holders of the egalitarian rights

Despite its wide currency in legal usage, the term 'people' is not defined in international law instruments. Arguing for a less formalistic approach towards using and understanding the term 'people' and all related idioms, Brownlie contended:

> It is my opinion that the heterogeneous terminology which has been used over the years – the references to 'nationalities', 'peoples', 'minorities', and 'indigenous populations' – involves essentially the same idea. Nor is this view based upon a theoretical construction. Once a member of a people or community is expressing political claims in public discourse in Geneva, New York, Ottawa or Canberra, and using the available stock of concepts so to do, it seems to me that the type of political consciousness involved is broadly the same.[16]

Africa bears out the judiciousness of this approach. In Africa the terms 'people', 'nation', 'minority', and 'indigenous population', are new and sound contrived and alien as opposed to the term 'ethnic group', formerly 'tribe', which defines the only socio-political reality that Africa knows. However, the term 'people' soon stood out and became of particular resonance in Africa.

During the decolonization process, the term 'people' was associated with the entire population of the colonial political unit attaining independence. In this context, the terms 'indigenous population' and 'minority' were considered divisive and incompatible with the concept of nation building. When either of these two terms is considered to form the standard for guaranteeing rights, Africa is alarmed. In 2007, the UN adopted the Declaration on the Rights of Indigenous Peoples, which states in Article 3 that indigenous peoples have the right to self-determination. The AU Assembly, 'concerned at the political, economic, social and constitutional implications of the Declaration on the African Continent', issued a decision affirming the Cairo Resolution and announcing that 'the vast majority of the Africans are indigenous to the African continent'.[17] Likewise, when an ethnic group in Africa becomes politically conscious it normally refers to itself as a 'people', not a minority, and claims all rights that are available to 'peoples' in international law.

---

[16] Ian Brownlie, 'The Rights of Peoples in Modern International Law' (1985) 9 *The Bulletin of Australian Society of Legal Philosophy* 104, 108.

[17] Assembly/AU/Dec 141(VIII) (30 January 2007).

The African Charter on Human and People's Rights, despite being notable for using the word 'people' in its title and notwithstanding its large claim that African collective values inspire and characterize its approach, provides no clue as to who is entitled to the numerous peoples' rights it includes.[18] Whereas the words 'nations', 'minorities', and 'indigenous populations' appear nowhere in the Charter, the word 'people' is frequently used, and with various meanings. Half of the forty-four instances in which the term 'people' appears in the African Charter are in the context of the broad reference to 'human and peoples' rights'. The rest, bar the usages in Articles 19 and 20, are mundane references to the state itself or its population in its entirety. The ACHPR concluded that 'the drafters of the Charter refrained deliberately from defining' this term.[19] The reason behind that abstention is possibly that the drafters of the African Charter faced the age-old problem alluded to by Brownlie and encountered by all drafters of human rights instruments, which is that the term 'people' is incapable of one standard definition and not always distinguishable from interrelated idioms.[20] This makes it imperative for an understanding of the term 'people' in any provision of the African Charter to read the term within the context in which it appears.

Crawford argues for a context-dependent approach for interpreting the term 'people' wherever it appears in international law instruments. He found it particularly objectionable to insist that a people is always nothing but the entire population of a state.[21] Remarkably, the example cited by Crawford for a provision that requires context-dependent interpretation was Article 20(2) of the African Charter.[22] Cassese agrees with this approach. He objects to the idea of coining a general definition for the term 'people', arguing that such definition will be exceedingly vague and controversial. He added: 'the lack of the formal legal definition [of the term people] does not entail that the interpreter cannot deduce such definitions from the context of the existing legal framework. Indeed, it is easy to infer such definitions'.[23] The context-dependent approach, advanced by Crawford and Cassese, is apt in determining the meaning of the terms 'all

---

[18]  See generally Kiwanuka, 'The Meaning of "People"'.
[19]  *Gunme/Cameroon* (n 4) para 169.
[20]  Brownlie, 'The Rights of Peoples' 108.
[21]  James Crawford, 'Some Conclusions' in James Crawford (ed.), *The Rights of Peoples* (Clarendon 1988) 169.
[22]  *Ibid*. 170.
[23]  Cassese, *Self-determination of Peoples* 327.

peoples' and 'oppressed peoples' that appear in Articles 19 and 20(2) of the African Charter respectively.

There are only two possible meanings of the term 'all peoples' in Article 19. That term could refer to the entire population of a state or, alternatively, to a sub-national group within the state.[24] In the context of a human rights instrument, it does not make sense to argue that the rights guaranteed under Article 19 accrue to the entire population of the state. Such interpretation would lead to a conclusion that the article is amplifying the principle of sovereign equality of peoples.[25] It was explained in *Reference re Secession of Quebec* in no dissimilar context that:

> To restrict the definition of the term to the population of existing states would render the granting of a right to self-determination largely duplicative, given the parallel emphasis within the majority of the source documents on the need to protect the territorial integrity of existing states, and would frustrate its remedial purpose.[26]

Conversely, if the term 'all peoples' is read as referring to sub-national groups within the state, this interpretation assigns content and consequence to the rights enunciated in the article. The ACHPR guidelines and practice agree with this understanding. The ACHPR 'Guidelines for National Periodic Reports under the African Charter' requests governments presenting their initial reports under Article 19:

> to state the constitutional and statutory framework which seeks to protect *the different sections of national community*. Any administrative regulations with the same intention as well as judicial decisions intended to establish the same rights. Precautions taken to proscribe any tendencies *of some people dominating another as feared by the article*.[27]

---

[24] Baldwin and Morel, 'Group Rights' 247–8.

[25] Hence, the present writer disagrees with the finding of the ACHPR in *Democratic Republic of Congo/Burundi, Rwanda, Uganda* (1999) AHRLR 227 (ACHPR 1999) that the armed aggression perpetrated by Burundi, Rwanda, and Uganda on DRC violates Article 19.

[26] 1998 SCJ No 61 para 124.

[27] Guidelines for National Periodic Reports, Second Annual Activity Report of the African Commission on Human and Peoples' Rights 1988–1989, ACHPR/RPT/2nd, Annex XII (emphasis added). The author is aware that these guidelines were superseded by a subsequent summary adopted in 1997. However, the guidelines continued to be distributed to states to elaborate the summary. See Malcolm Evans, Tokunbo Ige and Rachel Murray, 'The Reporting Mechanism of the African Charter on Human and Peoples' Rights' in Rachel Murray and Malcolm Evans (eds.), *African Charter on Human and Peoples' Rights: The System in Practice, 1986–2000* (Cambridge University Press 2002) 49.

Furthermore, the African Commission confirmed this understanding more authoritatively in two communications.

In *Malawi African Association/Mauritania*, a petition was presented by Mauritanian black communities claiming that following a coup d'état that brought Ould Sid Ahmed Taya of the Moors to power in 1984 the black ethnic groups of Mauritania had been marginalized.[28] The ACHPR accepted that the matter was a 'question of the domination of one section of the population by another'.[29]

In *Gunme/Cameroon*, the ACHPR was faced with the denial of Cameroon that the Southern Cameroonians are 'people' entitled to the rights guaranteed to 'peoples' under the African Charter. Cameroon argued that the specificities of the Southern Cameroons stemmed solely from the heritage of the British administration and that no ethno-anthropological argument could be put forward to determine the existence of a people of the Southern Cameroons.[30] Although the contention of the Republic of Cameroon was made in response to a claim under Article 20(1), the ACHPR found that limiting the term 'people' to the ethnic meaning advanced by Cameroon was not feasible for any of the rights under Articles 19 to 24 of the African Charter.[31] The ACHPR stated: 'Collective rights enumerated under Articles 19 to 24 of the Charter can be exercised by a people, bound together by their historical, traditional, racial, ethnic, cultural, linguistic, religious, ideological, geographical, economic identities and affinities, or other bonds'.[32] In Africa, those who are normally bound together by such characteristics and similarities are sub-national groups, not the entire populations of states. For the ACHPR, however, ethno-anthropological attributes are an added feature of a people that cannot be used as the only determinant factor that qualifies a group for the enjoyment of a peoples' right.[33] Based on this conclusion, the Commission held that 'the people of Southern Cameroon can legitimately claim to be a "people". Besides the individual rights due

---

[28] *Malawi African Association/Mauritania* (n 12).

[29] *Ibid*; *see* Baldwin and Morel, 'Group Rights' 252–3.

[30] *Gunme/Cameroon* (n 4) para 168.

[31] Unlike Article 19 and Article 20(2), Article 20(1) of the African Charter is obviously applicable to the entire people of a state, see *Jawara/The Gambia* (n 7); see also AHG/222 (XXXVI) Annex IV Page 50, Resolution on the Western Sahara, The African Commission on Human and Peoples' Rights, at its 27th Ordinary Session held in Algiers, from 27 April to 11 May 2000.

[32] *Gunme/Cameroon* (n 4) para 171.

[33] *Ibid*.

to Southern Cameroon[ians], they have a distinct identity which attracts certain collective rights'.[34]

In light of the above, it is concluded that the term 'all peoples' in Article 19 refers to sub-national groups within one multi-ethnic state. We now turn to the holders of the right under Article 20(2).

The right under Article 20(2) is accorded to two different categories of peoples, namely 'colonized peoples' on the one hand and 'oppressed peoples' on the other hand. By alternating the two categories Article 20(2) went a long way in clarifying that the right it articulates accrues to two different categories: one under colonial rule and the other in independent states. The usage of the disjunctive 'or' in the phrase 'colonized or oppressed peoples' grammatically indicates alternation between the two words as opposed to coordination which would have been achieved if the conjunctive 'and' was used instead. Crawford agrees to this interpretation. He states: 'Paragraph 2 [of Article 20] refers to "colonized or oppressed peoples" (there is no reason to suggest that the term "oppressed" is coextensive with "colonized")'. [35] Consequently, the two terms are not synonymous. While a 'colonized people' is the entire population of a colony, an 'oppressed people' is a sub-national group within an independent state. Recognizing external self-determination for 'oppressed peoples', as a distinct category, leads to extending the right under Article 20(2) to groups in multi-ethnic states. According to this understanding of the article, oppressed peoples have the right to free themselves from domination 'by resorting to any means recognized by the international community'.

The guidelines given by the African Commission to the states for reporting under Article 20 did not adopt a plan requiring separate reporting for each of the three sub-articles of Article 20. As a result, the guidelines confused the right of oppressed peoples 'to free themselves from the bonds of domination by resorting to any means recognized by the international community', under Article 20(2), with the right to assistance accorded only to liberation struggles against foreign domination under Article 20(3).[36] For this reason, the ACHPR guidelines are not helpful in drawing a distinction between oppressed peoples and colonized peoples.

---

[34] *Ibid.* para 178.

[35] Crawford, 'Some Conclusions' 169.

[36] The guidelines read: '(ii)Provide information on any form of assistance rendered to dominated people, in their liberation struggle against foreign domination be it political, economic or cultural; (iii) Information on assistance in any form given to colonised or oppressed peoples to help them free themselves'.

Yet, the ACHPR found in *Gunme/Cameroon* that it is possible to establish oppression within an independent African state. In this communication, the ACHPR found that oppression is a condition that could be established under Article 20(2) outside the colonial context. The ACHPR concluded that 'when a Complainant seeks to invoke Article 20 of the African Charter, it must satisfy the Commission that the two conditions under Article 20.2 namely oppression and domination have been met'.[37]

It is clear from the above that Article 20(2) accords to 'oppressed peoples' as distinct from 'colonized peoples' the right to free themselves from domination by resorting to any recognized means.

By arriving at these conclusions, it becomes obvious that the holders of the rights guaranteed under Articles 19 and 20(2) are sub-national groups within independent African states. This finding is of momentous implications. By reading the two articles together, if the egalitarian rights guaranteed under Article 19 were violated, an oppressed people would be entitled under Article 20(2) to free itself from domination by resorting to all means recognized by the international community. This raises an important question. Do those 'means' include secession? We now turn to this point.

## 8.3.   The right to egalitarian secession

### 8.3.1.   Unavailability of a right to secession as the lex lata

In the *Katangese Peoples' Congress*, the complainant alleged that a right to external self-determination exists under Article 20(1) of the African Charter. The ACHPR rejected the claim, concluding that the Commission is 'obligated to uphold the sovereignty and territorial integrity of Zaire, a member of the OAU and a party to the African Charter of Human and Peoples' Rights'.[38] Likewise, in *Gunme/Cameroon* the Commission found that 'the people of Southern Cameroon cannot engage in secession, except within the terms expressed hereinabove, since secession is not recognised as a variant of the right to self-determination within the context of the African Charter'.[39]

---

[37]   *Gunme/Cameroon* (n 4) para 197.
[38]   *Katangese Peoples' Congress/Zaire* (n 7) para 5.
[39]   *Gunme/Cameroon* (n 4) para 200.

The terms referred to by the ACHPR in *Gunme/Cameroon* are those formerly stated in the *Katangese Peoples' Congress* to the effect that the territorial integrity of a state should be called into question when human rights violations reach a point that justifies this measure and when the government of that state is not representative. Indeed, 'secession is not recognized as a variant of the right to self-determination' in the African Charter and the Commission's findings cannot be faulted in this regard. However, the ACHPR was mistaken in stating parenthetically that 'within the terms expressed hereinabove' secession is recognized.

This interpretation does not take full account of Article 20(2) under which the claim in *Gunme/Cameroon* was presented. Article 20(2) clearly stipulates that oppressed peoples shall have the right to free themselves from domination 'by resorting to any means *recognized by the international community*'. As yet the international community has not recognized any positive right that entitles oppressed groups to secede. Hence, secession is not currently available within the means referred to by Article 20(2). The African Commission was not justified in telling the Southern Cameroonians that 'Secession was the last option after the demands of Buea and Bamenda Conferences were ignored by the Respondent State'.[40]

Likewise, in accordance with extant laws, the Katangese are obligated to exercise a variant of self-determination that is compatible with the sovereignty and territorial integrity of Zaire even if they are oppressed or dominated by another sub-national group. Until the international community recognizes the right of an oppressed people to free itself by secession, violations of human rights to whatever point, even if coupled with a denial of the right to participation in government, would not make it possible to claim a right to external self-determination.

The proposition by the African Commission that secession is available in Africa within the terms stipulated in the *Katangese Peoples' Congress* is typical of the liberal attitude followed by the ACHPR in construing the African Charter. While in so many respects the ACHPR was commended for reinventing the African Charter and compensating for its flaws, it has been occasionally criticised for purporting to introduce some inventions that would need an amendment to the Charter.[41] Within a regional regime that is built on preserving the territorial status quo, unless the text

---

[40] *Ibid.* 198.
[41] Christof Heyns, 'African Regional Human Rights System: In Need of Reform' (2001) 1 *AHRLJ* 155, 157–8; Kofi Oteng Kufuor, *The African Human Rights System: Origin and Evolution* (Palgrave 2010) 76.

expressly says otherwise, no provision should be interpreted as involving a right to secession. Additionally, it is doubtful that the jurisdiction *ratione materiae* of the African Commission would allow it to go to the extent of considering petitions for secession even when its test in the *Katangese Peoples' Congress* is satisfied.[42]

In short, secession is not currently available within the means to which an oppressed people can resort under the African Charter. Nonetheless, Article 20(2) of the African Charter is amenable to including secession within such means if a right to external self-determination is recognized by the international community in the instance of domination. Whenever the international community recognizes any measure as available, that measure would be automatically included within the means to which oppressed peoples in Africa could resort. The reason why Article 20(2) is open to such development is that it does not include a paragraph similar to Paragraph 7 of the Declaration on Friendly Relations. To be more clear, a saving clause that reads 'nothing in the foregoing shall be construed as authorizing or encouraging any action which would dismember or impair totally or in part the territorial integrity or political unity of sovereign and independent state', is missing in Article 20(2).

As such, a question arises as to how the 'international community' can recognize a right to egalitarian secession to be included within the means available for oppressed peoples under Article 20(2) of the African Charter.

### 8.3.2.    How the 'international community' can recognize egalitarian secession

International law norms are created either by custom or by treaties. We shall start by considering the possibility of recognizing a customary right to egalitarian secession.

It has been clarified in Chapter 7 that Paragraph 2 of the Declaration on Friendly Relations among States considers the subjection of peoples to alien subjugation, domination, and exploitation a violation of the right to self-determination, a denial of human rights and contrary to the UN Charter. Paragraph 2 was construed by the Supreme Court of Canada as providing a clear case for a right to external self-determination outside the colonial context.[43] It is indeed 'clear' that military occupation,

---

[42]  Heyns 158.
[43]  Section 7.2, text to footnotes 9–20.

which forms one type of domination outside the colonial context is now an established instance under Paragraph 2. Yet, subjugation of one people by another within an independent state is not recognized as giving rise to a right to external self-determination. However, the paragraph and the Court's finding are part of the process of creating a new customary norm. While it takes a long time for this gradual process to culminate and lead to a recognition of a customary right of external self-determination in the event of domination, that possibility remains valid.

An act of secession that takes place accompanied by the appropriate belief that it is justified under Paragraph 2, counts as state practice. As such, it would add to the emergence of a new customary norm. However, such an act will not give rise to custom unless its exercising as being warranted under Paragraph 2 is not met with protest by other states.[44] The test laid by Sir Humphrey Waldock to the effect that less practice is required where occasions arise spasmodically obviously entails minimal practice with respect to secession. Yet, one act of secession is not enough to give rise to custom.[45] Repetition is inherent in the notion of custom, and apparently more than one act is required as evidence of settled state practice. This conclusion generally represents the recognized tradition for generating custom in international law.[46]

The alternative paradigm proposed by D'Amato dispenses with the need for repetition as a requirement of custom generation and cares little for gradual norm creation. In accordance with this model, Paragraph 2 of the Declaration on Friendly Relations forms an 'articulation'.[47] What is missing for 'domination' to give rise to customary entitlement of external self-determination is an 'act' pursuant to this articulation. According to

---

[44] Dissenting Opinion of Judge Ad Hoc Sørensen, *North Sea Continental Shelf Cases (Federal Republic of Germany/Denmark, Federal Republic of Germany/Netherlands)* (Judgment) [1969] ICJ Rep 3, 246.

[45] Humphrey Waldock, 'General Course on Public International Law' (1962) II *Recueil des Cours de l'Académie de Droit International* 1, 44.

[46] See generally H. W. A. Thirlway, *International Customary Law and Codification: An Examination of the Continuing Role of Custom in the Present Period of Codification of International Law* (Martinus Nijhoff 1972); Micheal Akehurst, 'Custom as a Source of International Law' (1974–75) 47 *British YBK Intl L* 1; Mark E. Villiger, *Customary International Law and Treaties: A Study of their Interactions and Interrelations with Special Consideration of the 1969 Vienna Convention on the Law of Treaties* (Martinus Nijhoff 1985); Alain Pellet, 'Article 38' in A. Zimmermann, C. Tomuschat and K. Oellers-Frahm (eds.), *The Statute of the International Court of Justice: A Commentary* (Oxford University Press 2006) 677.

[47] Anthony A. D'Amato and R. A. Falk, *The Concept of Custom in International Law* (Cornell 1971) 75.

this approach, a solitary act of secession based on a claim by a sub-national ethnic group that it is subjected to 'alien subjugation, domination and exploitation' under Paragraph 2 creates custom. The caveat that such act would not give rise to custom if it were met with protest by other states applies. However, D'Amato's approach is not yet accepted as representative of mainstream jurisprudence.

Custom is not the only means for international law to recognize a right to egalitarian secession. International law is currently developed by treaties more than any other source of law. On comparing treaties to custom Shaw found that treaties 'are a more direct and formal method of international law creation'.[48] While custom is inimical to instantaneous norm creation, treaties provide a prompt means for effectively addressing pressing situations before it is too late. In particular, human rights norms are mostly created by treaties not customary rules.

Notably, a treaty providing for the right to egalitarian secession should state specifically the exclusive content of this new right and the distinctive elements that need to be met before a finding of community domination could be made. These characteristics are clarified below.

### 8.3.3.   The normative content of egalitarian secession and elements of 'community domination'

The egalitarian rights enunciated in Article 19 of the African Charter are the entitlement of each sub-national group in a multi-ethnic state against the other. Those rights are denied when one ethnic group subjugates another. As such, the domination in question is 'community domination', i.e. people-to-people domination. In *Gunme/Cameroon*, the African Commission confirmed that this type of domination exists in post-colonial Africa and leads to civil wars and conflicts. The ACHPR stated:

> The Commission is aware that post-colonial Africa has witnessed numerous cases of domination of one group of people over others, either on the basis of race, religion, or ethnicity, without such domination constituting colonialism in the classical sense. Civil wars and internal conflicts on the continent are testimony to that fact.[49]

It is important to differentiate between community domination and two other types of domination. First, community domination should be distinguished from government discrimination provided for in Paragraph

---

[48]   Malcolm Shaw, *International Law* (6th edn, Cambridge University Press 2008) 902.
[49]   *Gunme/Cameroon* (n 4) para 181.

7 of the Declaration. While in the case of government discrimination the perpetrator is the central authority, in community domination the culprit is another community. Second, community domination differs from 'structural domination' conceptualized by Tomuschat as the form of domination that takes place where the individual citizen is discriminated against by another community to which that citizen is not a member.[50] Obviously, it is a form of domination pertaining to the individualist West, where individuals belonging to dominant communities could target individual citizens from non-dominant communities. In community domination, which is more relevant to communal Africa, an entire community, as opposed to individual members, is subjugated. This differentiation between community domination and the other two types of domination is of consequence as to the suitability of the remedies currently available in international law.

Government discrimination and structural domination are both conceived to give rise to a right to secession. As to government discrimination, Buchheit envisions 'a scheme by which, corresponding to the various degrees of oppression inflicted upon a particular group by its governing State, international law recognizes a continuum of remedies ranging from protection of individual rights, to minority rights, and ending with secession'.[51] Likewise, Tomuschat posits that 'international law must allow the members of a community suffering structural discrimination – amounting to grave prejudice affecting their lives – to strive for secession as a measure of last resort after all other methods employed to bring about change have failed'.[52] The remedy for government discrimination of Paragraph 7 is not in dividing the state between the tyrant and the oppressed. A colourful array of internal self-determination mechanisms, which range from democracy to autonomy, is already available in international law for facing problems of under-representation in government and violation of human rights. Likewise, structural domination targeting the individual citizen could be remedied through guaranteeing respect for individual human rights rather than by granting secession. Yet, in communal Africa where the phenomenon takes the decided form of people-to-people domination the measures of internal self-determination and

---

[50] Christian Tomuschat, 'Secession and Self-determination' in Marcelo G. Kohen (ed.), *Secession: International Law Perspectives* (Cambridge University Press 2006) 41.

[51] Lee Buchheit, *Secession: The Legitimacy of Self-determination* (Yale University Press 1978) 222.

[52] Tomuschat, 'Secession and Self-determination' 41.

protection of individual human rights presently available are insufficient. In the case of community-to-community domination, the entire subjugated community needs to be furnished, as a collectivity, with a people's right that enables it to rise up to the challenge. This unique attribute forms the normative content of the new right of egalitarian self-determination and justifies why a new remedy of egalitarian secession should be availed in international law. We now move to identifying the elements required for establishing community domination.

Typically, community domination occurs when the dominated sub-national group is denied the egalitarian rights enunciated in Article 19 of the African Charter. More plainly, community domination occurs when one group does not accept another group as equal in status, has no respect for the other group, and denies rights for that group. These physical elements differentiate community domination from the underdog status that might lamentably attach to one community because the opponent community prevails in terms of demographic or economic factors. When compared to misfortunes attributed to circumstances of nature, community domination is embedded in society. Even if geography and history are still defining the advantage in Africa, with increasing human and material development, the role of those factors is rapidly diminishing. Consequently, socio-political supremacy connected with those transient considerations should not be sufficient to satisfy the physical element of community domination.[53]

For this type of domination to exist, the physical acts described above should be accompanied with an appropriate mental element. An *animus* of prejudiced, spiteful, and malevolent ill will on the part of the dominating people proving that it acted with the intent to bring about a certain consequence of inequality, lack of respect or denial of community rights needs to be established as underlying the physical act. The existence of this mental element is necessary for a conclusion that the relation between the two peoples concerned degenerated to the level of 'subjugation, domination and exploitation' of one people by another. Paragraph 2 of the Declaration on Friendly Relations considers the subjection of peoples to domination a violation of the principle of self-determination, a denial of fundamental human rights, and contrary to the Charter. No conduct that lacks the *animus* above could merit those grave consequences attached by

---

[53] Compare to the anti-caste principle proposed by Sunstein for constitutional democracies: C. R. Sunstein, *Designing Democracies: What Constitutions Do* (Oxford University Press 2003) 155–82.

Paragraph 2. In the absence of this *animus,* it would be inconceivable to find that the attitude attributed to the dominating sub-national group is comparable, even if not necessarily equal, to the behaviour characterizing the white settlement domination. Casual, reckless, and uncalculated ethnic behaviour, which sadly abounds in Africa, does not satisfy this mental element. In a continent where vast sections of the population are, regrettably, illiterate and secluded from modern trends, inconsiderate ethnic attitudes should be corrected through exposure, awareness, education, and appropriate administrative measures, rather than being allowed to lead to secession.

In the law of self-determination, an entitlement to a right of *external* self-determination should typically accrue when there has been a denial of the rights afforded in the context of *internal* self-determination. The same measure applies in the context of the right to egalitarian self-determination. The right to egalitarian self-determination comprises two entwined parts, the egalitarian rights under Article 19 and the egalitarian secession under Article 20(2). Whereas resorting to Article 20(2) would be a measure of external self-determination, the protection of the rights under Article 19 is the prerequisite form of internal self-determination. Even when community domination is established efforts to guarantee and enhance the egalitarian rights are to be given a real opportunity to succeed before allowing egalitarian secession as a last resort. Indeed, the existence of the right to egalitarian secession is hoped to improve the respect for the egalitarian rights under Article 19 and to serve as a deterrent against their violation. The right to egalitarian self-determination should ultimately lead to the creation of a culture of egalitarianism not a cult of secessionism. When the right to egalitarian self-determination is recognized, the measure of achievement should not be the number of communities freeing themselves under Article 20(2) of the African Charter. What really matters is the enjoyment of the egalitarian rights under Article 19, and the improvement made in the lives and status of oppressed communities because of the protection of those rights.

Finally, it must be remembered that the right to egalitarian self-determination is conceptualized as an exception to the African rule against secession. An exception should ideally lead to respect for the general rule rather than the negation of its central doctrine. This is indeed where the excuses currently advanced for secession fail. When compared to these excuses, egalitarian self-determination addresses the

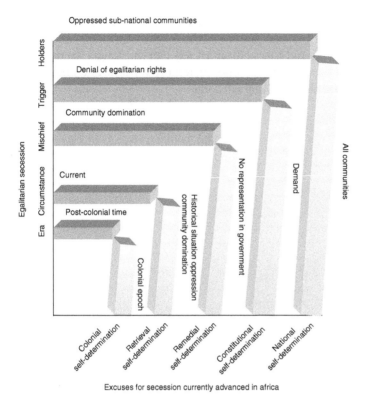

**Figure 2**  Comparing egalitarian secession with current excuses for secession

phenomenon of secession in Africa while having in mind the wellbeing of the African territorial regime. Additionally, while the excuses approach secession evasively, the right to egalitarian self-determination seizes of the phenomenon on its merits. The alternatives tried in Africa are confined to attempting in vain to reverse past acts of decolonization, desperately clinging to an amorphous concept of remedying violations, or triggering impulsively on simple demand. Conversely, egalitarian secession faces squarely the modern-day abomination that befalls parts of Africa as we speak, draws on a wide array of contemporary human rights jurisprudence, and kicks in when specific egalitarian rights designed to protect targeted groups are violated (see Figure 2). While upholding the egalitarian rights provides the African regime with an integral mechanism to prevent the abuse of sovereignty, the availability of a right to egalitarian secession precludes the exploitation of the African customary rule. The net result is that the right to egalitarian self-determination strengthens the African territorial regime by making it more versatile and prepares it to function for another fifty years to come.

# 9

## Conclusion

### 9.1. The significance of this study

This study has arrived at the following eight conclusions:

1. *Uti possidetis* is not a general principle of law that applies wherever the phenomenon of independence occurs. It is not applicable to Africa. Nor does it give rise to the concept of intangibility of inherited frontiers. In this regard, the finding to the contrary in the *Frontier Dispute* is erroneous.

2. African states were not bound on independence by *uti possidetis* or any other law principle to respect the pre-existing frontiers. As they decided to adhere to those frontiers, their uniform practice generated a new customary rule *in vacuo*. The rule of intangibility of inherited frontiers thus created, as opposed to *uti possidetis*, is the rule that governed the vertical territory transfers on independence and applies to the delimiting of African boundaries.

3. While the rule of intangibility of inherited frontiers is constrained to the moment of independence, the Cairo Resolution obligated the African states, by convention, as well as by estoppel, to perpetuate the territorial status quo beyond independence. Subsequently, the Resolution generated state practice and *opinio juris* that gave rise to customary rule binding on African states. The status quo rule enjoins African states to preserve the territorial status quo indefinitely.

4. The above-mentioned customary rules made extensive changes in international law with respect to Africa. Because of those rules, African boundaries are fixed and cannot be redrawn by treaties. Furthermore, even as international law is neutral towards secession, secession is proscribed in Africa. Those two norms are of African *jus cogens*. In addition, the concept of critical date and a number of other principles of the law of territory are approached differently in the African paradigm.

5. The African rule against secession made it implausible in Africa to advance simple secession claims. In order not to be criticised for violating the central African rule against secession, secessionists in Africa predicated their arguments for secession on revivalist, constitutional, or remedial causes. National self-determination was also considered. Those arguments face multiple legal and practical difficulties and, as they take little account of the common African interest, none of them provides a viable exception to the African rule against secession.

6. An exemption to the African rule against secession geared towards facing community domination is feasible. Subjugation of one people by another within an independent state forms a circumstance that gives rise to external self-determination under Paragraph 2 of the Declaration on Principles Concerning Friendly Relations. Normatively, this instance is neither limited to the historic context of colonial settlements nor to the recognized form of military occupation.

7. Articles 19 and 20(2) of the African Charter of Human and Peoples' Rights, in their proper construction, embody *sui generis* egalitarian rights guaranteed for sub-national groups within multi-ethnic states. Those are the rights of all sub-national groups to be equal, to enjoy the same respect, to have access to the same rights, not to be dominated by another group, and to free themselves from domination by resorting to any means recognized by the international community.

8. When domination within independent states is recognized by the international community as an instance for external self-determination under Paragraph 2 of the Declaration on Friendly Relations, Article 20(2) of the African Charter would give rise to a right to secession if egalitarian rights under Article 19 were violated. The right to egalitarian self-determination addresses the scourge of people-to-people domination and forms a viable exception to the blanket prohibition of secession in the African territorial regime.

These conclusions are of significant consequence. When this study was started, the finding in the *Frontier Dispute* that *uti possidetis* applied to Africa and that the Cairo Resolution did not give rise to African custom was accepted as unquestionable dogma. This finding led to a misunderstanding of both the principle of *uti possidetis* and the African territorial regime. In addition to forming the basis for introducing *uti possidetis* to Africa, the ruling led to the invoking of *uti possidetis* without agreement on a worldwide scale, and applying *uti possidetis* to situations outside the decolonization context. Conclusions 1 to 4 listed above refute this finding and question applying *uti possidetis* to Africa or to anywhere else in the world.

Additionally, at the start of this study, Paragraph 2 of the Declaration on Friendly Relations was understood to be constrained to just one instance outside the colonial context, which is the case of military occupation. Indeed, no other instance exists as the *lex lata*. However, this study establishes that normatively Paragraph 2 is not limited to military occupation and could give rise to a right to external self-determination in the instance of community domination taking place outside the colonial context. Likewise, it is now established that Articles 19 and 20(2) of the African Charter of Human and Peoples' Rights could engender a right to egalitarian self-determination to serve, *inter alia*, as an exception to the African rule against secession.

## 9.2.   The main arguments of this study

The conclusions above were arrived at as a result of establishing four arguments: (1) *uti possidetis* is not a general principle of law; (2) state practice and *opinio juris* generated by the Cairo Resolution gave rise to customary rule; (3) African custom made substantial changes in the law regarding Africa, including the creation of peremptory norms; and (4) the right to egalitarian self-determination forms a viable exemption to the African rule. These arguments are summarized below.

### 9.2.1.   Uti Possidetis *is not a general principle of law*

The origins of *uti possidetis* were studied to show that it initially appeared as special custom limited only to parts of Latin America under the Spanish Crown. The findings in the *Beagle Channel* and the *Guatemala and Honduras Boundary Dispute* questioning the applicability of the doctrine even to Spanish America in its entirety were cited. The conclusion that the principle operated only on the basis that both states involved were part of the Spanish colonial regime was highlighted. The supposition made by Waldock in 1948 that the principle of *uti possidetis* could not be drawn upon by Argentina and Chile in their dispute with the United Kingdom over the Falkland Islands was examined. The applicability of the principle outside Spanish America without agreement was contested, citing authority from *Belgium/Netherlands* and *the Rann of Kutch Arbitration*. The study then moved from examining the geneses of the principle to state practice.

It was argued that state practice does not support the finding that *uti possidetis* was a general principle of law at the time of African decolonization. The instances of state practice listed by Naldi in support of the ruling were examined, arguing that they do not substantiate the finding in the *Frontier Dispute*. The Helsinki Final Act 1975, the Vienna Convention on the Law of Treaties 1969, the Vienna Convention on Succession of States in Respect of Treaties 1978, the *Temple Case*, and the *Rann of Kutch Arbitration*, were not found to form the instances of application of *uti possidetis* argued by Naldi. Additionally, it was clarified that the landmark *Aaland Case* is open to no interpretation other than that *uti possidetis* was not a general principle of law at the time when the Aaland dispute was determined.

The approach of Shaw and Ratner of attributing normative value to *uti possidetis* regardless of its customary status was examined. It was clarified that the ICJ Chamber in the *Frontier Dispute* acted on the basis that *uti possidetis* was already a general principle of law at the time of the African decolonization and required no evidence to overturn any existing norm. Additionally, the three arguments advanced in this regard by Shaw and Ratner were found to be misplaced. First, while it was possible for the ICJ Chamber to employ the methodology of inductive reasoning for the purposes of verifying the pertinence of the Spanish-American *uti possidetis* to Africa, as it stands, the ICJ Chamber did not adopt this methodology. The Chamber analysed in great detail the original scenario of Spanish America but it did not examine the African set of facts to find out whether they were analogous to that scenario or not. Second, no law principle could be of positive standing unless its customary or conventional status is established. *Uti possidetis* could not be argued to form the *lex lata* before its credentials are attested. Third, it is not true that there are no legal norms contradictory to *uti possidetis*. The right to colonial self-determination and the clean slate principle entitle the colonial people to disregard pre-existing boundaries.

It was also argued in this connection that in its Spanish-American cradle *uti possidetis* did not lead to consecrating pre-existing frontiers as intangible, and as such did not form the root for the legal doctrine of intangibility of inherited frontiers. It was clarified that the paramount purpose behind the principle of *uti possidetis* was to assert the denial of *terra nullius* in Spanish America, not to sanctify pre-existing boundaries. The commitments made in the Treaty of Confederation 1848 and other Spanish-American treaties to respect the territorial integrity were found, along the lines established in the *Beagle Channel*, to aim at confirming the denial of *terra nullius*. The *Colombian-Venezuelan Frontier, El Salvador/ Honduras* and *Nicaragua/Honduras* were cited to establish that the key aspect of *uti possidetis* was the denial of *terra nullius*. In practice, the Spanish-American boundaries were not definite and Spanish-American republics considered the *uti possidetis* line to form a default position, not the final boundary. When agreements to change the inherited boundary line were not reached in many cases the republics abandoned the *uti possidetis* line and resorted to war. Additionally, the demarcation commissions treated the *uti possidetis* line as a general basis of settlement and did not adhere to it meticulously.

While they were not bound by the principle of *uti possidetis*, African states were not obligated by the right to colonial self-determination to respect the colonial boundaries. The right to colonial self-determination as expressed in UN General Assembly Resolution 1514 (XV) entitled the colonial peoples to subdivide their country if that was their choice. Likewise, the law of state succession did not bind African states to abide by the colonial boundary-creating treaties. The clean slate principle enabled newly independent states to declare *tabula rasa* on state succession to avoid succeeding to boundary treaties.

On the basis of the foregoing, it was clarified that the practice of accepting the inherited boundaries by African states led to the emergence of the African customary rule of intangibility of inherited frontiers. The unanimous participation in this practice forms uniform conduct evidencing the *opinio juris*. By 1961, the period of time required for a customary rule to emerge was satisfied. The *Advisory Opinion on the Free City of Danzig* and the *North Sea Continental Shelf Cases* were cited to justify the possibility of emergence of custom within comparable periods.

### 9.2.2.    The Cairo Resolution gave rise to custom

The status of the Cairo Resolution as a legal instrument of immediate binding force was explained. It was argued that in the OAU law, the Cairo Resolution, which was adopted by the Assembly of Heads of State and Government, binds African states as an authoritative interpretation of the provisions of the OAU Charter. The statement made in the Resolution estops African states from denying that they pledged to perpetuate the boundaries obtained on independence.

The customary standing of the status quo rule was proved in three steps. First, it was established that the Cairo Resolution was of norm-creating character and could as such be regarded as forming a basis of a rule of law. This characteristic of the Resolution was substantiated in accordance with the guidelines in the *North Sea Continental Shelf Cases.*

Second, the usages forming the practice of respecting the territorial status quo were canvassed in four categories to establish the objective criteria required. Those categories are: (a) the practice of active involvement favouring the parent state, as in the cases of Biafra, Anjouan, and Azawad; (b) the practice of the 'black wall of silence' followed regarding Eritrea, Southern Sudan, and Somaliland; (c) the practice of outright rejection of state-to-state territorial claims demonstrated by the admission of SADR to the OAU and the stand against the Libyan claim to Chadian territories; and (d) embodying the African rule in OAU/AU treaties notably the AU Constitutive Act 2000.

Third, the *opinio juris* required to give rise to customary rule was shown to be independent of the aforementioned practice. In addition to the express statements that are available for the three categories of the practice other than the 'black wall of silence', five sources were identified for the *opinio juris* of the fourth category of omission.

### 9.2.3.   The changes made in the law by African custom

It was clarified that right from the beginning, as observed by Bowett and Kamanu, African states resolved to prohibit the revision of frontiers and to proscribe secession. In due course, customary rules were generated. Adherence to the rule of intangibility of inherited frontiers and the rule of respecting the territorial status quo meant that African states conceded indefinitely the right to redraw boundaries and proscribed secession. Those particular changes in the law are argued to be of African *jus cogens* as no derogation from them is allowed.

Other changes introduced in the law regarding Africa include the concept of the critical date. In Africa, the independence day is the critical date because it is the date on which the boundaries of the new state were recognized. The function of this recognition-related critical date is to determine in general terms the territory devolved on independence. This role differs substantially from that of the conventional critical date of marking the consolidation of title or crystallization of a dispute. Yet, a role similar to the one played by the conventional critical date is accorded in Africa to another cut-off date, which is the materialization date. The materialization date is the date on which the boundary finally materialized before it was inherited by the newly independent state. The critical date is superior to and governs the materialization date. The supposition of the recognition-related critical date makes it possible to address the problem posed when the disputed states are of different independence dates. It also resolves the question of anomalous African boundaries with no conventional independence dates. Likewise, the African paradigm approaches boundaries born in treaties in a way that takes into account the special legal and historical conditions that rendered those boundaries respected. The source of the legal force of those boundaries and to what extent they are subject to change by subsequent conduct or protected by estoppel are issues that are treated differently in the African territorial regime. It is clarified further that the African custom led to different approaches with respect to issues of post-colonial *effectivités*, acquiescence, evidence emanating from the parties, sovereignty over islands not connected to the coast, and *ex aequo et bono*.

### 9.2.4.   A right to egalitarian self-determination is viable

Four different arguments were advanced in Africa to avoid being blamed for flouting the African rule against secession. First: a claim for reviving the right of colonial peoples to self-determination was advanced by Eritrea and the Southern Cameroons. In a similar vein, Somaliland claimed a right to reversion. Second: in the cases of Ethiopia and Sudan a right to self-determination was constitutionalized to provide an exit for all ethnicities in the case of Ethiopia and to a particular region in the case of Sudan. Third: in the *Katangese Peoples' Congress* remedial secession was considered a viable option if violations of human rights reached a critical point coupled with a denial of representation in government. Fourth: self-determination along national lines of pre-colonial African entities was propagated by Mutua. It was explained that those four arguments, in addition to being of no sound base in law, fail to take account of the overall African interest. As such, none of those suppositions forms a viable exception to the African rule against secession.

A possible exception to the African rule against secession is argued *de lege ferenda* to be feasible under Paragraph 2 of the Declaration on Friendly Relations among States. Subjecting a people to alien subjugation, domination, and exploitation outside the colonial context is found in *Reference re Secession of Quebec* to form a clear case for external self-determination. It is further argued that even as the instance of external self-determination under Paragraph 2 of the Declaration is not yet of standing in customary international law, it is erroneous to limit the normative breadth of Paragraph 2 to military occupation. Nor is it defensible to limit the trilogy 'alien subjugation, domination and exploitation' to the only historical form of white settlements' domination that took place in Africa. It was found that while there is no element of state practice or *opinio juris* to support considering domination an instance of external self-determination within an independent multi-ethnic state, there is significant support for this notion in legal literature.

The egalitarian rights accorded under Article 19 of the African Charter, which are the rights of peoples to be equal, enjoy the same respect, have the same rights, and not to be subjected by another people, are argued to be of singular normative content. Those rights are found to accrue to sub-national groups in multi-ethnic African states. When it is accepted by the international community that domination gives rise to a right to external self-determination, this makes it possible for violations of the egalitarian rights under Article 19 to give rise to an entitlement to egalitarian secession under Article 20(2) of the African Charter. Recognition of that right by the international community could be either on a customary basis or by convention. It was clarified that the characteristic feature of the right to egalitarian secession is that it accrues when people-to-people domination, as opposed to government-to-people domination, occurs. An *animus* to proximate this domination with the subjugation and exploitation defining the white settlements' domination needs to be established. Finally, it was stressed that the right to egalitarian self-determination is intended to augment the African territorial regime by protecting egalitarian rights. Consequently, it is a right that encourages egalitarianism rather than secessionism. Egalitarian secession is conceived as a remedy of last resort that will accrue only when egalitarian rights are incurably denied.

## 9.3.   Concluding remarks

This study conveys four messages, each to a different interest group.

First, establishing the positive existence of the customary African territorial regime is twenty-five years overdue. Within this period, the ICJ and arbitration tribunals have endorsed the erroneous ruling in the *Frontier Dispute* time and again. Examples of the wandering for the quarter of a century that followed the *Frontier Dispute* include: (1) the decision in the *Territorial Dispute (Libya/Chad)* that the Cairo Resolution is inapplicable to that case of unmasked territorial dispute; (2) the acceptance of post-colonial *effectivités* in *Kasikili/Sedudu, Ethiopia/Eritrea,* and *Cameroon/Nigeria*; (3) the finding in *Guinea-Bissau/Senegal* that boundaries already of an international character during colonialism are also the subject of an African version of *uti possidetis*; (4) the possibility of taking into account post-colonial maps raised in the *Frontier Dispute (Benin/ Niger)*; and (5) the possibility of admitting treaties counter to the status quo implicated in *Ethiopia/Eritrea* and *Cameroon/Nigeria*.

Yet, the findings in this study are not too late. The ICJ could benefit from the absence of *stare decisis* in international law and accept that 'a principle of customary international law, limited in its impact to the African continent', as has previously been the case with regard to Spanish America, had indeed emerged. The ICJ should draw a line and turn the page on the deviation that the *Frontier Dispute* started. The Separate Opinion of Judge Yusuf in the *Frontier Dispute (Burkina Faso/Niger)* that the Cairo Resolution did not reinstate *uti possidetis* is a light at the end of the tunnel. Africa now looks towards the ICJ rather than side-stepping it. The recent Declaration of the AU Assembly of 31 January 2014 on the implementation of the Bakassi judgment, commending the wisdom of the Heads of State of Cameroon and Nigeria when they seized the ICJ of the matter, would have been unthinkable fifty years ago. It is now time for an ICJ change of heart. Nonetheless, Africa is poised to establish its own Court of Justice, which is expected to contribute immensely to clarifying African customary rules on the law of territory. This is the message of this study to the ICJ and to the forthcoming African Court of Justice and Human Rights.

Second, this study shows that the African customary regime is functioning despite the Judas kiss delivered by the ruling in the *Frontier Dispute*. Before the judgment, we saw the OAU prevailing on Morocco and Somalia to tone down their territorial claims. SADR was admitted in the face of the ardent Moroccan objection. The Biafran crisis was faced on principle. The secessionists of Eritrea and the first war of South Sudan were isolated. After the ICJ ruling, the African customary regime continued unperturbed. In 1986–7 the OAU opposed strongly the Libyan claims against Chad. In 2000, when Africa reinvigorated its regional organization the status quo rule was embodied in the AU Constitutive Act. The secessionists of Somaliland, Anjouan, and Azawad were encountered with the same vigor with which earlier secessionists were faced. The African states that celebrated the golden jubilee of the OAU in 2013 had reason to be proud of their customary regime. Yet they also have reason to worry about its future versatility.

The African territorial regime had indeed managed to control state-to-state territorial claims. However, intra-state territorial claims advanced by sub-national groups have proved to be disruptive and need to be addressed on merits. When fifty years down the line some African states are still facing a deepening crisis of legitimacy, those states should be advised to consider fostering egalitarian rights instead of insisting merely on the inherited frontiers. When a segment of the inhabitants of a state is actively challenging the territorial status quo, giving up altogether on the idea of sharing the country with another particular sub-national group, protecting the egalitarian rights of that segment becomes the path to unity and stability. Insisting on a hopeless façade of illusive national unity would produce only civil wars, agony, and genocide. Nonetheless, if the egalitarian rights of such people are not respected, egalitarian secession should be available as an option of last resort. Likewise, multi-ethnic states that have passed the test of national unity over the previous decades should now be aware that guaranteed continuance of their political unity, ethnic diversity, and social coherence hinges critically on promoting the egalitarian rights of their sub-national groups. This message is for the AU and individual African states.

Third, it is not the ICJ and Africa alone that are supposed to act. The development of a doctrine that 'domination' is an instance of external self-determination depends largely on what the international community would make of the suggestive Paragraph 2 of the Declaration on Friendly Relations. The African regime is part of and not apart from international law. It was the close oversight of the UN and the exceptional prowess of the General Assembly during the decolonization era that made it possible for this regime to develop. Moreover, the African regime depends now for its reinforcement on recognizing domination as an instance for external self-determination. Recognition of this new instance by the international community is the key to introducing the right to egalitarian self-determination and to renewing the legitimacy of the African state. This is the message of this project to the international community.

Fourth, this project raises important inquiries of a jurisprudential nature, judicial significance, and human rights implications. Four areas are identified below:

a) The dependence of African states for their very existence on a regional territorial regime raises questions as to the suitability of the Westphalia paradigm for studying the African state. But was it not clarified by Kelsen that the international legal order may determine and restrict the validity of the national legal order? Is this not the trend in international relations nowadays rather than the exception? Don't we see more and more limitations imposed on the conventional concept of state sovereignty? Does this simply mean that we agree to Jackson's supposition that the African state is a 'juridical' state? To put this question differently, does the African territorial regime paradigm, despite capturing important dimensions, end up relegating the African state to a quasi-state? Does the end result expose weaknesses in the phenomenon studied or does it rather reveal deficiency in the perspectives and standards employed? Does this mean that the difference between the African state and its Western counterpart is a difference of quantity as opposed to a simple difference of quality? Yet, if in Europe territorial sovereignty is the reason that brings territory within state jurisdiction, as Judge Huber stated in *the Island of Palmas,* did the territory come first in creating the African state and was the sovereignty born later? Does this conception entail a different configuration of the relation between the African state and the territory it occupies? If in Europe the emphasis is on the *dominium* and states can exercise supreme authority with regard to their territory without being impugned, is the state jurisdiction in Africa equally exclusive? If not, does this tilt the balance to the *imperium* conception of the relation between state and territory? Are the state and territory one and the same in Africa, rendering any disposition of territory a violation of the state itself? Those jurisprudential inquiries are of no mean value to understanding the African state, comprehending how it functions within its own territorial regime, and finding out how it relates to the outside world. Unless straitjacketing the African state in readymade moulds stops, the legal nature of the African state will not be properly appreciated.

b) The issue of *continuum juris* that was once raised in the African context by Abi-Saab in his separate opinion in the *Frontier Dispute* was recently revisited in the Declaration of Judge Bennouna in the *Frontier Dispute (Burkina Faso/Niger).* Both jurists agree that no judicial relay should take place between the colonial law and international law in order not to legitimize the colonial institution. However, while Abi-Saab argues that the solution is in equity *infra legem,* for Bennouna the emphasis should be on the second limb of the doctrine of intertemporal law. The question is still open. Now the hypothesis of the African territorial regime presupposes that the rule of intangibility of inherited frontiers was an African creation and a result of a well-considered and conscious African move that knowingly consecrated the colonial alignments. Did this achieve the required epistemological dichotomy making it morally irreprehensible to draw on the colonial heritage? Or would Africa continue to be haunted forever by its despicable experience? This issue of serious judicial implications needs to be clarified if adjudication under the international law of territory should be predictable for African states and with foreseeable outcomes.

c) If *uti possidetis* is not a general principle of law, this means it no longer applies anywhere outside Spanish America. Questions arise as to what law principles govern situations similar to those addressed by Opinion No III of the Badinter Commission. Whether *uti possidetis* had indeed been received in Europe or elsewhere as a result of the developments that took place since the 1990s is a matter that needs to be considered anew.

d) Subjecting sub-national groups to domination by other sub-national groups is not limited to Africa. Hence, the egalitarian rights developed in the African context are of relevance elsewhere. If much has been said since the 1970s about remedial secession and Paragraph 7 of the Declaration on Friendly Relations, more needs to be said now about egalitarian self-determination and Paragraph 2 of that Declaration. Unshackling the trilogy 'alien subjugation, domination and exploitation' from the vestiges of the white settlements, the outdated jargon of colonialism and the misconceived dogma of military occupation would revitalize Paragraph 2 and pave the way to a new age of egalitarianism. There is rich legal literature on the prevalence of domination in independent states. The appearance of territorial unity and the veneer of national sovereignty are abused more often than not. Nonetheless, ideas on how to actually face this post-colonial scourge with post-colonial means are very much lacking. Despite falling short of advancing a comprehensive scheme, Cassese has aptly identified this area in his blueprint for reforming the law of self-determination. More blueprints are indeed in high demand.

In sum, although this study focuses on the African territorial regime, it did not clarify it in full. Nor did it address all its problems. What this study claims to have achieved is that it attests to the gradual emergence of a special customary law order in Africa, and opens the door wide for recognizing it for what it is. Yet, and regardless of its limited scope, this project is of universal implication. In the international law of territory, it shows the imperious need for charting the way beyond *uti possidetis*. It is time indeed to grow out of the fixation with this fetish. Likewise, in the field of international human rights law this study is the opening salvo for a new age of egalitarianism. A generation of egalitarian rights, much needed for facing the endemic people-to-people domination in multi-ethnic independent states, is waiting to be ushered in. This is the message of this study for future researchers.

# BIBLIOGRAPHY

Abdel Rahim M., *Imperialism & Nationalism in the Sudan* (Oxford University Press 1969)

Abi-Saab G., 'Wars of National Liberation in the Geneva Conventions and Protocols' (1979) IV *Recueil des Cours de l'Académie de Droit International* 351

Abun-Nasr J. M., *A History of the Maghrib in the Islamic Period* (Cambridge University Press 1987)

Akehurst M., *A Modern Introduction to International Law* (Routledge 1970)
'Custom as a Source of International Law' (1974–75) 47 *British YBK Intl L* 1
'Equity and General Principles of Law' (1976) 25 *ICLQ* 801

Akinyemi B., 'The Organization of African Unity and the Concept of Non-Interference in Internal Affairs of Member States' (1972–73) 46 *British YBK Intl L* 393

Akol L., *Southern Sudan: Colonialism, Resistance, and Autonomy* (Red Sea Press 2007)
*SPLM/SPLA: Inside an African Revolution* (Khartoum University Press 2001)

Alexandrowicz C., *The European-African Confrontation: A Study in Treaty Making* (A. W. Sijthoff 1973)
'The Juridical Expression of the Sacred Trust of Civilization' (1971) 65 *AJIL* 149
'New and Original States: The Issue of Reversion to Sovereignty' (1969) 45 *Intl Affairs* 465

Alvarez A., *American Problems in International Law* (Baker, Voorhis 1909)
'Latin America and International Law' (1909) 3 *AJIL* 269

American Law Institute, *1 Restatement (Third) of the Foreign Relations Law of the United States* (American Law Institute 1987)

American Law Institute, (ed.) *Restatement of the Law, Foreign Relations Law of the United States (Revised): Tentative Draft I* (American Law Institute 1980)

An-Na'im, Abdullahi A., 'The OAU and the Right of Peoples to Self-determination: A Plea for a Fresh Approach' (1988) 35 (*Africa Today* 27)

Anghie A., 'The Evolution of International Law: Colonial and Postcolonial Realities' (2006) 27 *Third World Quarterly* 739

Arangio-Ruiz G., 'The Normative Role of the General Assembly of the United Nations and the Declaration of Principles of Friendly Relations' (1972) 137 III *Recueil Des Cours de l'Académie de Droit International* 419

Arechaga E. D., 'Boundaries in Latin America: Uti possidetis Doctrine' in R. Bernhardt (ed.), *Encyclopedia of Public International Law*, vol. VI (Oxford University Press 1984) 45

Arkell A. J., *A History of the Sudan to 1821* (University of London 1961)

Asamoah O. Y., *The Legal Significance of the Declarations of the General Assembly of the United Nations* (Martinus Nijhoff 1967)

Atkins G. Pope, *Encyclopaedia of the Inter-American System* (Greenwood 1997)

Aust A., 'Limping Treaties: Lessons from Multilateral Treaty-Making' (2003) 50 *Netherlands International Law Review* 243

Baldwin C. and Morel C., 'Group Rights' in R. Murray and M. Evans (eds.), *African Charter on Human and Peoples' Rights: The System in Practice, 1986–2000* (Cambridge University Press 2002) 244

Baldwin S., 'The International Congresses and Conferences of the Last Century as Forces Working Towards the Solidarity of the World' (1907) 1 *AJIL* 808

Bashir M. O., *The Southern Sudan: Background to Conflict* (Khartoum University Press 1979)

Baxter R., 'Multilateral Treaties as Evidence of Customary International Law' (1965–66) 41 *British YBK Intl L* 275

Bello E., 'Reflections on Succession of States in the Light of the Vienna Convention on Succession of States with Respect of Treaties 1978' [1980] 23 *German YBK Intl L* 296

Bodansky D. and Watson J., 'State Consent and the Sources of International Obligation' (1992) 86 *PASIL* 108

Bowett D., 'Estoppel before International Tribunals and its Relation to Acquiescence' (1957) 33 *British YBK Intl L* 176

'Self-determination and Political Rights in the Developing Countries' (1966) 60 *PASIL* 129

Bradely C. A. and Gulati M., 'Withdrawing from International Custom' (2010) 120 *Yale LJ* 202

Brierly J., *The Law of Nations: An Introduction to the International Law of Peace* ed. by H. Waldock (6th edn, Oxford University Press 1978)

Brietzke P. H., 'Ethiopia's "Leap in the Dark": Federalism and Self-determination in the New Constitution' (1995) 39 *JAL* 19

Brilmayer L., 'Secession and Self-determination: A Territorial Interpretation' (1991) 16 *Yale JIL* 177

Britain-Biafra Association, *Statement by Tanzania, Gabon, Ivory Coast & Zambia on Their Recognition of Biafra* (Britain-Biafra Association 1968)

Brownlie I., *African Boundaries: A Legal and Diplomatic Encyclopedia* (1st edn, University of California 1979)

*Basic Documents on African Affairs* (Oxford University Press 1971)

*Basic Documents in International Law* (4th edn, Clarendon 1995)

*Principles of Public International Law* (6th edn, Oxford University Press 2003)

'The Rights of Peoples in Modern International Law' (1985) 9 *The Bulletin of Australian Society of Legal Philosophy* 104

Bryden M., 'The "Banana Test": Is Somaliland Ready for Recognition?' (2003) 19 *Annales d'Ethiopie* 341

Buchheit L., *Secession: The Legitimacy of Self-determination* (Yale University Press 1978)

Carroll A. and Rajagopal B., 'The Case for the Independent Statehood of Somaliland' (1992) 8 *Am UJ Int'l L & Pol'y* 653

Cassese A., *Self-determination of Peoples: A Legal Appraisal* (Cambridge University Press 1995)

Castellino J., *International Law and Self-determination: The Interplay of the Politics of Territorial Possession with Formulations of Post-Colonial National Identity* (Martinus Nijhoff 2000)

'Territorial Integrity and the Right to Self-Determination: An Examination of the Conceptual Tools' (2007) 33 *Brook J Int'l L* 503

Castellino J. and Allen S., *Title to Territory in International Law: A Temporal Analysis* (Ashgate 2003)

Charpentier J., 'Le Problème des Enclaves' in *Société Française pour le Droit International Colloque de Poitiers, La Frontière* (A. Pedone 1980) 41

Cheng B., *Custom: The Future of General State Practice in a Divided World in the Structure and Process of International Law: Essays in Legal Philosophy Doctrine and Theory*, ed. by R. St. J. Macdonald and D. M. Johnston (Martinus Nijhoff 1983)

'United Nations Resolutions on Outer Space: "Instant" International Customary Law?' (1965) 5 *Indian JIL* 23

Chesterman S., Franck T., and Malone D., *Law and Practice of the United Nations: Documents and Commentary* (Oxford University Press 2008)

Chukwurah A., 'The Organization of African Unity and African Territorial and Boundary Problems: 1963–1973' (1973) 13 *Indian JIL* 176

Clapham C., 'Post-war Ethiopia: The Trajectories of Crisis' (2009) 36 *Review APE* 181

Cobban A., *National Self-Determination* (Oxford University Press 1944)

Cohen J. M., '"Ethnic Federalism" in Ethiopia' (1995) 2 *Northeast African Studies* 157

Collins R. O., *The Southern Sudan 1883–1898: A Struggle for Control* (Yale University Press 1962)

Colson D. A., 'How Persistent Must the Persistent Objector Be?' (1986) 61 *Washington LR* 957

Colson E., 'African Society at the Time of the Scramble' in L. Gann and P. Duignan (eds.), *Colonialism in Africa*, vol. I (Cambridge University Press 1969) 27

Conforti B. and Focarelli C., *The Law and Practice of the United Nations* (4th edn, Martinus Nijhoff 2010)

Congress US and others, *A Decade of American Foreign Policy: Basic Documents, 1941–49* (US Govt Print Off 1950)

Congress US and others, *Documents of the United Nations Conference on International Organization, San Francisco, 1945*, vol. III (United Nations Information Organizations 1945)

Connell D., *Against all Odds: A Chronicle of the Eritrean Revolution* (Red Sea 1993)

Contini P., *The Somali Republic: An Experiment in Legal Integration* (F. Cass & Company 1969)

Cook W., 'Hohfeld's Contributions to the Science of Law' (1919) 28 *The Yale LJ* 721

Cordier A. and Harrelson M. (eds.), *Public Papers of the Secretaries General of the United Nations: U Thant*, vol. VII: 1965–1967 (Columbia University Press 1977)

Corten O. and Klein P., *The Vienna Conventions on the Law of Treaties: A Commentary* (Oxford University Press 2011)

Craven M., 'The European Community Arbitration Commission on Yugoslavia' (1995) 66 *British YBK Intl L* 333

Crawford J., *The Creation of States in International Law* (Oxford University Press 1979)

'Some Conclusions' in J. Crawford (ed.), *The Rights of Peoples* (Clarendon 1988) 159

D'Amato A. A., 'The Concept of Special Custom in International Law' (1969) 63 *AJIL* 211

*International Law Process and Prospect* (Transnational Publishers 1987)

'It's a Bird, It's a Plane, It's Jus Cogens' (1990) 6 *Connecticut J Int'l L* 1

D'Amato A. A. and Falk R., *The Concept of Custom in International Law* (Cornell 1971)

D'Sa R. M., 'Human and People's Rights: Distinctive Features of the African Charter' (1985) 29 *JAL* 72

De Candole E. A., 'Libya' in C. Legum (ed.), *Africa: A Handbook* (2nd edn, Anthony Blond Ltd 1965) 35

De Lapradelle P., *La Frontier: Etude de Droit International* (Les Editions Internationales 1928)

De la Reza G. A., 'The Formative Platform of the Congress of Panama (1810–1826): The Pan-American Conjecture Revisited' (2013) 56 *Revista Brasileira de Politica Internacional* 5

Deng F., *War of Visions: Conflict of Identities in the Sudan* (Brookings 1995)

'War of Visions for the Nation' in John Voll (ed.), *Sudan: State and Society in Crisis* (Indiana University Press 1991) 24

Djonovich D. J. (ed.) *United Nations Resolutions: Series 1 Resolutions Adopted by the General Assembly*, vol. VIII (Oceana Publications 1973)

Dugard J., *Recognition and the United Nations* (Cambridge University Press 1987)

Dworkin R., *The Philosophy of Law* (Oxford University Press 1977)

*Taking Rights Seriously* (Duckworth 1977)

East W. G. and Moodie A. E., *The Changing World, Studies in Political Geography* (George G. Harrap 1956)

Eggers A. K., 'When is a State a State: The Case for Recognition of Somaliland' (2007) 30 *Boston College ICLR* 211

Elias T., *Africa and the Development of International Law* (A. W. Sijthoff 1972)
'The Charter of the Organization of African Unity' (1965) 59 *AJIL* 243
'The Commission of Mediation, Conciliation and Arbitration of the Organization of African Unity' (1964) 40 *British YBK Intl L* 336
'The Doctrine of Intertemporal Law' (1980) 74 *AJIL* 285
*Problems Concerning the Validity of Treaties* (A. W. Sijthoff 1972)

Emerson R., *From Empire to Nation: The Rise to Self-assertion of Asian and African Peoples* (Harvard University Press 1960)
'Self-determination' (1971) 65 *AJIL* 459

Emerson S. A., 'Desert Insurgency: Lessons from the Third Tuareg Rebellion' (2011) 22 *Small Wars & Insurgencies* 669

Englebert P., *State Legitimacy and Development in Africa* (Lynne Rienner 2002)

Enonchong N., 'Foreign State Assistance in Enforcing the Right to Self-determination under the African Charter: Gunme & Ors v Nigeria' (2002) 46 *Journal of African Law* 246

Eritrean Department of Foreign Affairs (ed.) *Eritrea: Birth of a Nation* (1993)

Evans M., Ige T., and Murray R., 'The Reporting Mechanism of the African Charter on Human and Peoples' Rights' in R. Murray and M. Evans (eds.), *African Charter on Human and Peoples' Rights: The System in Practice, 1986–2000* (Cambridge University Press 2002) 49

Fenwick C., 'The Third Meeting of Ministers of Foreign Affairs at Rio de Janeiro' (1942) 36 *AJIL* 169

*Financial Times*, 'Somaliland Seeks US Help in Battle for Recognition' (24 August 2006) available at www.ft.com/cms/s10/90e4f022-330d-11db-87ac-0000779e2340.html#axzz3iRLxkg9F (accessed 16 June 2015)

Fisher F., 'The Arbitration of the Guatemalan-Honduran Boundary Dispute' (1933) 27 *AJIL* 403

Fitzmaurice G., 'The Law and Procedure of the International Court of Justice, 1951–54: General Principles and Sources of Law' (1953) 33 *British YBK Intl L* 1
'The Law and Procedure of the International Court of Justice 1951–54: Points of Substantive Law Part II' (1951–54) 32 *British YBK Int'l L* 20
'The Law and Procedure of the International Court of Justice: Treaty Interpretation and Certain other Treaty Points' (1951) 28 *British YBK Intl L* 1Francioni F., 'Of War, Humanity and Justice: International Law after Kosovo' (2000) 4 *Max Planck UNYB* 107

Franck T. and Rodley N., 'After Bangladesh: The Law of Humanitarian Intervention by Military Force' (1973) 67 *AJIL* 275

Franck T. M., 'Postmodern Tribalism and the Right to Secession' in C. Brolmann, R. Lefeber, and M. Zieck (eds.), *Peoples and Minorities in International Law* (Martinus Nijhoff 1993) 3

　　*Recourse to Force: State Action against Threats and Armed Attacks* (Cambridge University Press 2002)

Geldenhuys D., *Contested States in World Politics* (Palgrave 2009)

Ghali B. B., 'The Addis Ababa Conference' (1963–65) 35 *International Conciliation* 5

Ghebrewebet H., *Identifying Units of Statehood and Determining International Boundaries* (Peter Lang GmbH 2006)

Giffen M. B., *Fashoda: The Incident and its Diplomatic Setting* (The University of Chicago Press 1930)

Goldie L., 'The Critical Date' (1963) 12 *ICLQ* 1251

Goodrich L., Hambro E., and World Peace Foundation, *Charter of the United Nations: Commentary and Documents* (World Peace Foundation 1949)

Gray C., 'The Eritrea/Ethiopia Claims Commission Oversteps its Boundaries: A Partial Award?' (2006) 17 *EJIL* 699

　　*International Law and the Use of Force* (Oxford University Press 2000)

Gray R., *A History of Southern Sudan: 1839–1889* (Oxford University Press 1961)

Gros-Espiel H, 'Self-Determination and Jus Cogens', in A. Cassese (ed.), *UN Law/ Fundamental Rights: Two Topics in International Law* (Martinus Nijhoff 1979) 167

Guest A., 'Logic in the Law' in A. Guest (ed.), *Oxford Essays in Jurisprudence: A Collaborative Work* (Oxford University Press 1961) 176

Gutelius D., 'Islam in Northern Mali and the War on Terror' (2007) 25 *Journal of Contemporary African Studies* 59

Gutto S. B., 'The New Mechanism of the Organization of African Unity for Conflict Prevention, Management and Resolution, and the Controversial Concept of Humanitarian Intervention in International Law' (1996) 113 *South Africa LJ* 314

　　*The Right to Self-determination: Implementation of United Nations Resolutions: Study* (United Nations 1980)

Halleck H. W., *International Law* (Bancroft 1861)

Halper T., 'Logic in Judicial Reasoning' (1968) 44 *Indiana LJ* 33

Hamilton R., 'Special Report: The Wonks who sold Washington on South Sudan' (Reuters 11 July 2012) at www.reuters.com/article/2012/07/11/us-south-su dan-midwives-idUSBRE86A0GC20120711

Hannikainen L., *Peremptory Norms (Jus Cogens) in International Law: Historical Development, Criteria, Present Status* (Lakimiesliiton Kustannus 1988)

Hannum H., *Autonomy, Sovereignty, and Self-Determination: The Accommodation of Conflicting Rights* (University of Pennsylvania Press 1996)

Hargreaves J., *Prelude to the Partition of West Africa* (Macmillan & Co 1963)

　　'Towards a History of the Partition of Africa' (1960) 1 *JAH* 97

Harris D. J., *Cases and Materials on International Law* (6th edn, Sweet and Maxwell 2004)

Hasan, Y. F. *The Arabs and the Sudan: from the Seventh to the Early Sixteenth Century* (Edinburgh University Press 1967)

Hassan H., 'The Comoros and the Crisis of Building a National State' (2009) 2 *CAA* 229

Henderson K. D. D., *Sudan Republic* (Ernest 1965)

Heyns C., 'African Regional Human Rights System: In Need of Reform' (2001) 1 *AHRLJ* 155

Higgins R., 'Postmodern Tribalism and the Right to Secession: Comments' in C. Brolmann, R. Lefeber, and M. Zieck (eds.), *Peoples and Minorities in International Law* (Martinus Nijhoff 1993) 29

*Problems & Process: International Law and How We Use It* (Clarendon 1994)

Hodgkin T., *Nationalism in Colonial Africa* (Muller 1956)

Hohfeld W. N., 'Some Fundamental Legal Conceptions as Applied in Judicial Reasoning' (1913) 23 *The Yale LJ* 16

Hughes A., 'The Nation State in Black Africa' in L. Tivey (ed.), *The Nation State: The Formation of Modern Politics* (Martin Robertson 1981) 122

Huliaras A., 'Evangelists, Oil Companies, and Terrorists: The Bush Administration's Policy towards Sudan' (2006) 50 *Orbis* 709

Hyde C. C., *International Law Chiefly as Interpreted and Applied by the United States*, vol. I (Brown Little 1922)

International Law Commission, *Yearbook of the International Law Commission, Summary Records of the Twentieth Session 27 May–2 August 1968*, vol. I (1968)

Irele A., 'The Crisis of Legitimacy in Africa' [1992] *Dissent* 296

Iyob R., *The Eritrean Struggle for Independence: Domination, Resistance, Nationalism, 1941–1993* (Cambridge University Press 1997)

Jackson R. H., 'Juridical Statehood in Sub-Saharan Africa' (1992) 46 *Journal of Int'l Affairs* 1

Jenks C., 'State Succession in Respect of Law-Making Treaties' (1952) 29 *British YBK Intl L* 105

Jennings R. Y., *The Acquisition of Territory in International Law* (Manchester University Press 1963)

Johns M., 'Does Democracy have a Chance' (1991) The World and I

Johnson H. F., *Waging Peace in Sudan: The Inside Story of the Negotiations that Ended Africa's Longest Civil War* (Sussex Academic Press 2011)

Kaikobad K. H., 'Some Observations on the Doctrine of Continuity and Finality of Boundaries' (1984) 54 *British YBK Intl L* 119

Kamanu O. S., 'Secession and the Right of Self-Determination: An OAU Dilemma' (1974) 12 *The Journal of Modern African Studies* 355

Kapil R. L., 'On the Conflict Potential of Inherited Boundaries in Africa' (1966) 18 *World Politics* 656

Keltie J., *The Partition of Africa* (2nd edn, Edward Stanford 1895)

Khalid M., *The Government they Deserve: The Role of the Elite in Sudan's Political Evolution* (Kegan Paul 1990)

Kindiki K., 'The Proposed Integration of the African Court of Justice and the African Court of Human and Peoples' Rights: Legal Difficulties and Merits' (2007) 15 *AJICL* 138

Kiwanuka R. N., 'The Meaning of 'People' in the African Charter of Human and Peoples' Rights' (1988) 82 *AJIL* 69

Klabbers J., 'The Right to be Taken Seriously: Self-determination in International Law' (2006) 28 *HRQ* 186

Klabbers J. and Lefeber R., 'Africa: Lost between Self-determination and Uti Possidetis' in C. Brolmann (ed.), *Peoples and Minorities in International Law* (Martinus Nijhoff 1993) 37

Kohn M., 'Colonialism' in The Stanford Encyclopedia of Philosophy (Spring 2014)

Konings P. and Nyamnjoh F., 'The Anglophone Problem in Cameroon' (1997) 35 *JMAS* 207

Koskenniemi M., 'National Self Determination Today: Problems of Legal Theory and Practice' (1994) 43 *International and Comparative Law Quarterly* 241

Kreuter A., 'Self-Determination, Sovereignty, and the Failure of States: Somaliland and the Case for Justified Secession' (2010) 19 *Minnesota JIL* 363

Kufuor K. O., *The African Human Rights System: Origin and Evolution* (Palgrave 2010)

Kunz J., 'Guatemala v Great Britain: in Re Belice' (1946) 40(2) *AJIL* 383
    'Nationality and Option Clauses in the Italian Peace Treaty of 1947' (1947) 41 *AJIL* 622

Lalonde S., *Determining Boundaries in a Conflicted World: The Role of Uti Possidetis* (McGill-Queen's University Press 2002)

Langille B., 'It's "Instant Custom": How the Bush Doctrine became Law after the Terrorist Attacks of September 11' (2001) 26 *Boston College ICLR* 145

Lansing R., *The Peace Negotiations: A Personal Narrative* (Houghton Mifflin Company 1921)

Lauterpacht E., Schwebel S., Rosenne S., and Vicuña F. O., *Legal Opinion on Guatemala's Territorial Claim to Belize* (2001)

Lauterpacht H., *The Development of International Law by the International Court* (Grotius Publications 1982)
    *Recognition in International Law* (Cambridge University Press 1947)

Legum C., *Pan-Africanism: A Short Political Guide* (Praeger 1962)

Levi E., 'The Nature of Judicial Reasoning' (1965) 32 *The University of Chicago Law Review* 395

Lewis I., *A Modern History of the Somali* (4th edn, East African Studies 2002)
    'Somali Republic' in C. Legum (ed.), *Africa: A Handbook* (2nd edn, Anthony Blond Ltd 1965)

Library of Congress, *Documents of the United Nations Conference on International Organization, San Francisco, 1945*, vol. III (United Nations Information Organizations 1945)

Lim C. and Elias O., 'Withdrawing from Custom and the Paradox of Consensualism in International Law' (2010–11) 21 *Duke JCIL* 143

Lister M., 'The Legitimating Role of Consent in International Law' (2010–11) 11 *Chicago JIL* 663

Lukic R. and Lynch A., *Europe from the Balkans to the Urals: The Disintegration of Yugoslavia and the Soviet Union* (Oxford University Press 1996)

MacGibbon I., 'Customary International Law and Acquiescence' (1957) 33 *British YBK Intl L* 115

Machar R., *South Sudan: A History of Political Domination – A Case of Self-Determination* (University of Pennsylvania African Studies Center 1995)

Manela E., *The Wilsonian Moment: Self-determination and the International Origins of Anticolonial Nationalism* (Oxford University Press 2007)

Marston G., 'Termination of Trusteeship' (1969) 18 *ICLQ* 1

Mazrui A., *The Africans: A Triple Heritage* (Little, Brown & Co 1986)
   'Planned Governance and the Liberal Revival in Africa: The Paradox of Anticipation' (1992) 25 *Cornell ILJ* 541

Mazrui A. and Tidy M., *Nationalism and New States in Africa* (Richard Clay Ltd 1989)

McCorquodale R., 'Self-Determination: A Human Rights Approach' (1994) 43 *ICLQ* 857

McHugh A. M., 'Resolving International Boundary Disputes in Africa: A Case for the International Court of Justice' (2005) 49 *Howard LJ* 209

McKeon R., 'The Aouzou Strip: Adjudication of Competing Territorial Claims in Africa by the International Court of Justice' (1991) 23 *Case Western Reserve Journal of International Law* 147

McNair A., *The Law of Treaties* (Clarendon 1961)

McWhinney E., *Declaration on the Granting of Independence to Colonial Countries and Peoples* (UN Audiovisual Library of International Law 2008)

Mendelson M., 'The Cameroon-Nigeria Case in the International Court of Justice: Some Territorial Sovereignty and Boundary Delimitation Issues' (2004) 75 *British YBK Intl L* 223

Miller D. H., *The Drafting of the Covenant*, vol. I (Johnson Reprint Corp 1969)

Mnyaka M. and Motlhabi M., 'The African Concept of Ubuntu/Botho and its Socio-moral Significance' (2005) 3 *Black Theology: An International Journal* 215

Moore J. B., *Costa Rica-Panama Arbitration 1911: Memorandum on Uti Possidetis* (The Commonwealth Company 1913)

Mukong A. W., *The Case for the Southern Cameroons* (CAMFECO 1990)

Munya P. M., 'The Organization of African Unity and its Role in Regional Conflict Resolution and Dispute Settlement: A Critical Evaluation' (1999) 19 *Boston College Third World Law Journal* 537

Murithi T., 'Practical Peacemaking Wisdom from Africa: Reflections on Ubuntu' 1 *The Journal of Pan African Studies* 25

Murphy S., 'Democratic Legitimacy and the Recognition of States and Governments' (1999) 48 *ICLQ* 545

Murray R. and Evans M. (eds.), *African Charter on Human and Peoples' Rights: The System in Practice, 1986–2000* (Cambridge University Press 2002)

Murray R. and Wheatley S., 'Groups and the African Charter on Human and Peoples' Rights' (2003) 25 *HRQ* 213

Musgrave T. D., *Self Determination and National Minorities* (Oxford University Press 1997)

Mutua M. W., 'Why Redraw a Map of Africa: A Moral and Legal Inquiry' (1994–95) 16 *Mich JIL* 1113

Muyangwa M. and Vogt M. A., *An Assessment of the OAU Mechanism for Conflict Prevention, Management and Resolution, 1993–2000* (International Peace Academy 2000)

Naldi G. J., 'The Aouzou Strip Dispute: A Legal Analysis' (1989) 33 *JAL* 72

   'The Case Concerning the Frontier Dispute (Burkina Faso/Republic of Mali): Uti Possidetis in an African Perspective' (1987) 36 *ICLQ* 893

   'Future Trends in Human Rights in Africa: The Increasing Role of the OAU' in R. Murray and M. Evans (eds.), *African Charter on Human and Peoples' Rights: The System in Practice, 1986–2000* (Cambridge University Press 2002) 1

   *The Organization of African Unity: An Analysis of its Role* (2nd edn, Mansel 1999)

   'Separatism in the Comoros: Some Legal Aspects' (1998) 11 *Leiden JIL* 247

Ngoh V. J., *Constitutional Developments in Southern Cameroons, 1946–1961: From Trusteeship to Independence* (Pioneer 1990)

Niblock T., *Class and Power in the Sudan: The Dynamics of Sudanese Politics, 1898–1985* (State University of New York Press 1987)

Nolte G., 'Secession and External Intervention' in M. G. Kohen (ed.), *Secession: International Law Perspectives* (Cambridge University Press 2006) 65

Nussbaum B., 'African Culture and Ubuntu' (2003) 17 *Perspectives* 1

Nyaba P. A., *Politics of Liberation in South Sudan: An Insider's View* (Fountain Publisher 1997)

Okere B. O., 'The Protection of Human Rights in Africa and the African Charter on Human and Peoples' Rights: A Comparative Analysis with the European and American Systems' (1984) 6 *HRQ* 141

Oppenheim L., *International Law* (Longmans 1905–6)

   *International Law*, vol. I (1st edn, Longmans 1905)

*International Law*, vol. I (8th edn, Longmans, Green & Co. 1955)

*International Law*, ed. by R. Jennings and A. Watts (9th edn, Oxford University Press 1992)

O'Rourke V. A., *The Judicial Status of the Anglo-Egyptian Sudan* (Johns Hopkins 1935)

Pakenham T., *The Scramble for Africa* (Abacus 1991)

Pellet A., 'Article 38' in A. Zimmermann, C. Tomuschat, and K. Oellers-Frahm (eds.), *The Statute of the International Court of Justice: A Commentary* (Oxford University Press 2006) 677

'The Opinions of the Badinter Arbitration Committee: A Second Breath for the Self-Determination of Peoples' (1992) 3 *EJIL* 178

Perkins D., *A History of the Monroe Doctrine* (Brown Little 1955)

Perry M.A., *State Succession, Boundaries and Territorial Regimes* (Cambridge University Press 1995)

Preuss L., 'Article 2, Paragraph 7 of the Charter of the United Nations and Matters of Domestic Jurisdiction' (1949) I *Recueil Des Cours de l'Académie de Droit International* 547

Queneudec J.-P., 'Remarques sur le Reglement des Conflits Frontaliers en Afrique' (1970) 74 *RGDIP* 69

Radan P., 'Post-Succession International Orders: A Critical Analysis of the Workings of the Badinter Commission' (2000) 24 *MULR* 50

Ratner S. R., 'Drawing a Better Line: Uti possidetis and the Border of New States' (1996) 90 *AJIL* 590

Rechner J. D., 'From the OAU to the AU: A Normative Shift with Implications for Peacekeeping and Conflict Management, or Just a Name Change?' 39 *Vanderbil Journal of Transnational Law* 543

Reisman W. M., 'Sovereignty and Human Rights in Contemporary International law' (1990) 84 *AJIL* 866

Rosenstock R., 'The Declaration of Principles of International Law concerning Friendly Relations: A Survey' (1971) 65 *AJIL* 713

Rozakis C. L., *The Concept of Jus Cogens in the Law of Treaties* (North-Holland Publishing Company 1976)

Rushworth D. S., 'Mapping in Support of Frontier Arbitration: Delimitation and Demarcation' (1996 Summer) *IBRU Boundary and Security Bulletin* 60

Sanders A., *International Jurisprudence in African Context* (Butterworths 1979)

Sanger C., 'Toward Unity in Africa' (1963–64) 42 *Foreign Affairs* 269

Schachter O., *International Law in Theory and Practice* (Kluwer 1991)

'State Succession: The Once and Future' (1992–93) 33 *Virginia Journal of International Law* 253

Schwarzenberger G., 'International Jus Cogens' (1964) 43 *Tex L Rev* 455

Schwelb E., 'Some Aspects of International Jus Cogens as Formulated by the International Law Commission' (1967) 61 *AJIL* 946

Scott J. B., 'The Swiss Decision in the Boundary Dispute between Colombia and Venezuela' (1922) 16 *AJIL* 428

Scott J. H., *The Law Affecting Foreigners in Egypt, As the Result of the Capitulations, with an Account of their Origin and Development* (William Green & Sons 1907)

Selassie B., 'Self-determination in Principle and Practice: The Ethiopian-Eritrean Experience' (1997–98) 29 *Columbia HRLR* 91

Seton-Watson C., 'Italy's Imperial Hangovers' (1980) 15 *Journal of Contemporary History* 169

Shaw M., 'Boundary Treaties and their Interpretation' in E. Rieter and H. de Waele (eds.), *Evolving Principles of International Law: Studies in Honour of Karel C Wellens* (Martinus Nijhoff 2012) 239

'The Heritage of States: The Principle of Uti Possidetis Juris Today' (1996) 67 *British YBK Intl L* 75

*International Law* (6th edn, Cambridge University Press 2008)

'Peoples, Territorialism and Boundaries' (1997) 8 *EJIL* 478

'Territory in International Law' (1982) 13 *Netherlands YBK Intl L* 61

'Title, Control, and Closure? The Experience of the Eritrea-Ethiopia Boundary Commission' (2007) 56 *ICLQ* 755

*Title to Territory in Africa: International Legal Issues* (Clarendon 1986)

(ed.) *Title to Territory* (Ashgate 2005)

Sinha S., 'Identifying a Principle of International Law Today' (1973) 11 *Canadian YBK Intl* 106

Slama J. L., 'Opinio Juris in Customary International Law' (1990) 15 *Oklahoma CULR* 603

Smith G., *The Baltic States: The National Self-determination of Estonia, Latvia, and Lithuania* (Palgrave Macmillan 1994)

Sohn L., 'The UN System as Authoritative Interpreter of its Law' in O. Schachter and C. Joyner (eds.), *United Nations Legal Order*, vol. I (Cambridge University Press 1995) 171

Stark F. M., 'Federalism in Cameroon: The Shadow and The Reality' (1976) *Canadian JAS* 423

Stein T. L., 'The Approach of the Different Drummer: The Principle of the Persistent Objector in International Law' (1985) 26 *Harv ILJ* 457

Sticker M., *The Geopolitics of Security in the Americas: Hemispheric Denial from Monroe to Clinton* (Greenwood 2002)

Sudan Government, *Report of the Commission of Inquiry into the Disturbances in the Southern Sudan during August 1955* (McCorquedale 1956)

Sunstein C., 'Constitutionalism and Secession' (1991) 58 *The University of Chicago Law Review* 633

*Designing Democracies: What Constitutions Do* (Oxford University Press 2003)

Svensson E., *The African Union's Operations in the Comoros: MAES and Operation Democracy* (FOI, Swedish Defence Research Agency 2008)

Symons M. T., *Britain and Egypt: The Rise of Egyptian Nationalism* (C. Palmer 1925)

Tanaka Y., 'Reflections on Maritime Delimitation in the Cameroon/Nigeria Case' (2004) 53 *ICLQ* 369

Tancredi A., 'A Normative "Due Process" in the Creation of States through Secession' in M. G. Kohen (ed.), *Secession: International Law Perspectives* (Cambridge University Press 2006)

Teffo J., *The Concept of Ubuntu as a Cohesive Moral Value* (Ubuntu School of Philosophy 1994)

Temperley H. W. V., *A History of the Peace Conference of Paris*, vol. II (Oxford University Press 1920) 227

Tesfagiorgis G., 'Self-determination: Its Evolution and Practice by the United Nations and its Application to the Case of Eritrea' (1987) 6 *Wisconsin ILJ* 75

Thirlway H., *International Customary Law and Codification: An Examination of the Continuing Role of Custom in the Present Period of Codification of International Law* (Martinus Nijhoff 1972)

Tomuschat C., 'Secession and Self-determination' in M. G. Kohen (ed.), *Secession: International Law Perspectives* (Cambridge University Press 2006) 23

Touval S., 'Africa's Frontiers: Reactions to a Colonial Legacy' (1966) 42 *International Affairs* 641

*The Boundary Politics of Independent Africa* (Harvard University Press 1972)

'The Organization of African Unity and African Borders' (1967) 21 *International Organization* 102

'Treaties, Borders and the Partition of Africa' (1966) 7 *JAH* 279

Trédano A., *Intangibilité des Frontières Coloniales et Espace Etatique en Afrique*, vol. 47 (Librairie Générale de Droit et de Jurisprudence 1989)

'Le Principe de l'intangibilité des Frontières Comme Obstacle au Dépassement des Conflits Frontaliers en Afrique' (1985) 9 *Revue Marocaine de Droit et d'Economie de Développement* 117

Trimingham J. S., *Islam in the Sudan* (Oxford University Press 1949)

Umozurike O., 'The African Charter on Human and Peoples' Rights' (1983) 77 *AJIL* 902

*The African Charter on Human and Peoples' Rights* (Martinus Nijhoff 1997)

*Self-determination in International law* (Archon Books 1972)

United States Congress, Senate Committee on Foreign Relations and Dept of State, *A Decade of American Foreign Policy: Basic Documents, 1941–49* (US Govt Print Off 1950)

Vallat F., 'The Competence of the United Nations General Assembly' (1959) 97 II *Recueil Des Cours de l'Académie de Droit International* 203

Verdross A., 'Jus Dispositivum and Jus Cogens in International Law' (1966) 60
    *AJIL* 55
Verzijl J., *International Law in Historical Perspective*, vol. I (A. W. Sijthoff 1968)
Vidmar J., 'Conceptualizing Declarations of Independence in International Law'
    (2012) 32 *Oxford Journal of Legal Studies* 153
    'Confining New International Borders in the Practice of Post-1990 State
    Creations' (2010) 70 *Heidelberg JIL* 319
    'Remedial Secession in International Law: Theory and (Lack of) Practice' (2010)
    6 *St Antony's International Review* 37
Villiger M. E., *Commentary on the 1969 Vienna Convention on the Law of Treaties*
    (Martinus Nijhoff 2009)
    *Customary International Law and Treaties: A Study of their Interactions and
    Interrelations with Special Consideration of the 1969 Vienna Convention on
    the Law of Treaties* (Martinus Nijhoff 1985)
Von-Der-Heydte D. F. A. F., 'Discovery, Symbolic Annexation and Virtual
    Effectiveness in International Law' (1935) 29 *American Journal of
    International Law* 448
Waldock H., 'The Anglo-Norwegian Fisheries Case' (1951) 28 *British YBK Intl L* 114
    'Disputed Sovereignty in the Falkland Islands Dependencies' (1948) 25 *British
    YBK Intl L* 311
    'General Course on Public International Law' (1962) II *Recueil des Cours de
    l'Académie de Droit International* 1
    'Sixth Report on the Law of Treaties' (1966) II *YB Intl LC* 51
Waters R., 'Inter-African Boundary Disputes' in C. G. Widstrand (ed.) *African
    Boundary Problems* (Scandinavian Institute of African Studies 1969) 183
Westlake J., 'England's Duty in Egypt' (1882) 42 *Contemporary Review* 823
    'The Nature and Extent of the Title by Conquest' (1901) 17 *Law Quarterly
    Review* 392
Wet E., 'The Governance of Kosovo: Security Council Resolution 1244 and the
    Establishment and Functioning of Eulex' (2009) 103 *AJIL* 83
Wetter I., 'The Rann of Kutch Arbitration' (1971) 65 *AJIL* 346
Wheaton H., *Elements of International Law*, ed. by C. Phillipson (5th edn, Stevens
    and Sons 1916)
Whelan A., 'Wilsonian Self-determination and the Versailles Settlement' (1994)
    43 *ICLQ* 99
Wright Q., 'Recognition and Self-Determination' (1954) 48 *PASIL* 23
Young J., 'Ethiopia Ethnic Federalism: A Model for South Sudan' (unpublished
    paper, March 2015)
    'Ethnicity and Power in Ethiopia' (1996) 23 *Review APE* 531
    *The Fate of Sudan: The Origins and Consequences of a Flawed Peace Process* (Zed
    Books Ltd 2012)
    'Regionalism and Democracy in Ethiopia' (1998) 19 *Third World Quarterly* 191

'Sudan: A Flawed Peace Process Leading to a Flawed Peace' (2005) 32 *Review APE* 99

'Sudan IGAD Peace Process: An Evaluation' (Sudan Tribune 2007)

Yusuf A. A., 'The Role that Equal Rights and Self-determination of Peoples can Play in the Current World Community' in A. Cassese (ed.), *Realizing Utopia: The Future of International Law* (Oxford University Press 2012) 375

Zartman I. W. and Touval S., 'International Mediation: Conflict Resolution and Power Politics' (1985) 41 *Journal of Social Issues* 27

# INDEX

Organization of African Unity
(OAU) (*cont.*)
reluctance to engage with 106–7
SADR, admission of to 113–14, 124
Somaliland, secession of 112
South Sudan, secession of
110–11, 121–2
state-to-state claims, rejection of
112–15, 124
treaty provisions for territorial
status quo 115
United Nations comparison 92–4
unity, favouring of 123–4

*pacta sunt servanda* 94–5
*Paquete Haban* case 100
parent states
reluctance to engage with OAU/
AU 106–7
support for, against secessionists
100–6, 123–4
passive conduct as state practice
108, 120–3
Pellet, Alain 95
people(s), use and definition of term in
Africa 240–4
Polisario 113
post-colonial *effectivités* 157–61
pre-existing frontiers
and internal legitimacy 56–9
international recognition of
states 59–65
critical date 139–47
respect for in Africa, reasons for 55–65
and self-determination 48–51
state succession 51–5 *see also*
territorial status quo
principles, rules distinguished from 5–6

Radan, P. 15–16
*Rann of Kutch Arbitration* 34, 36–7,
60–1, 148
Ratner, S. R. 40, 45–6
redrawing of boundaries, prohibition
against as *jus cogens* 128–30
*see also* territorial status quo
*Reference re Secession of Quebec* 206–7,
217–22, 242

remedial secession
ACHPR Article 13(1) 202–4
in general international law 205–9
terrorism and secession 208–9
revivalist secession
as correcting historical
mistakes 171–2
Eritrean argument 172–7
Somaliland 183–6
Southern Cameroon 177–82
Rosenstock, R. 221
rules, principles distinguished
from 5–6

Sahrawi Arab Democratic Republic
(SADR) 113–14, 124
Schachter, O. 92
Schwarzenberger, Georg 126, 132
secession
alternative causes adopted 122
Anjouan, attempted secession
of 102–4
Azawad, unilateral declaration of
104–6, 121
Biafra, attempted secession of
100–2, 106–7
black wall of silence 107–12
constitutional right to 201–2
diplomatic isolation 107–12
Eritrea 109–10
Eritrea and South Sudan 2
parent states, support for, against
secessionists 100–6, 123–4
prohibition against 130–2
reluctance to engage with OAU/
AU 106–7
right to egalitarian secession
245–54
Somaliland 111–12
South Sudan 110–11
South Sudan, secession of 121–2
and terrorism 208–9 *see also*
justifications for secession
in Africa
self-determination 35, 44–5
constitutional
advantages of approach 186–7
disadvantages of 202